Law and Politics of the Taiwan Sunflower and Hong Kong Umbrella Movements

Rarely do acts of civil disobedience come in such grand fashion as Taiwan's Sunflower Movement and Hong Kong's Umbrella Movement. The two protests came in regions and jurisdictions that many have underestimated as regards furthering notions of political speech, democratisation, and testing the limits of authority. This book breaks down these two movements and explores their complex legal and political significance. The collection brings together some of Asia's, and especially Taiwan and Hong Kong's, most prolific writers, many of whom are internationally recognised experts in their respective fields, to address the legal and political significance of both movements, including the complex questions they posed as regards democracy, rule of law, authority, and freedom of speech. Given that occupational type protests have become a prominent method for protesters to make their cases to both citizens and governments, exploring the legalities of these significant protests and establishing best practices will be important to future movements, wherever they may transpire. With this in mind, the book does not stop at implications for Taiwan and Hong Kong, but talks about its subject matter from a comparative, international perspective.

Brian Christopher Jones is Lecturer in Law at Liverpool Hope University, UK. He was previously a Postdoctoral Research Fellow at Institutum Iurisprudentiae, Academia Sinica (Taipei, Taiwan). His research interests are in comparative public law, specifically constitutional and administrative law, socio-legal studies, democratic theory, civil disobedience, and IT law and policy. He has published widely on these and related areas.

The Rule of Law in China and Comparative Perspectives

Series Editors:

Yuwen Li, Erasmus University Rotterdam, The Netherlands and Fu Hualing, University of Hong Kong, Hong Kong

There is no doctrine more effective than the rule of law in portraying the complex transformation of Chinese society from the rule of men towards the rule of law - a process inaugurated in post-Mao China which is continuing to advance legal reforms to the present day. In other parts of the world, striving for the rule of law is also evident: countries in transition face a similar mission, while the developed democratic countries are forced to tackle new challenges in retaining the high benchmark of the rule of law that has been established. Research on the legal system in China and in comparison with other countries in the framework of the rule of law covers broad topics of public and private law, substantive law and procedural law, citizens' rights and law enforcement by courts. Based on this broad understanding of the rule of law, the series presents international scholarly work on modern Chinese law including: comparative perspectives, interdisciplinary, and empirical studies.

Other titles in this series:

The Judicial System and Reform in Post-Mao China
Yuwen Li

Administrative Litigation Systems in Greater China and Europe
Edited by Yuwen Li

Conservation and Recreation in Protected Areas
Yun Ma

Legal Reforms and Deprivation of Liberty in Contemporary China
Edited by Elisa Nesossi, Sarah Biddulph, Flora Sapio, and Susan Trevaskes

Law and Politics of the Taiwan Sunflower and Hong Kong Umbrella Movements

Edited by Brian Christopher Jones

Routledge
Taylor & Francis Group
LONDON AND NEW YORK

First published 2017
by Routledge

2 Park Square, Milton Park, Abingdon, Oxfordshire OX14 4RN
52 Vanderbilt Avenue, New York, NY 10017

Routledge is an imprint of the Taylor & Francis Group, an informa business

First issued in paperback 2018

British Library Cataloguing-in-Publication Data
A catalogue record for this book is available from the British Library

Library of Congress Cataloging-in-Publication Data
Names: Jones, Brian Christopher, author.
Title: Law and Politics of the Taiwan Sunflower and Hong Kong Umbrella Movements / Brian Christopher Jones.
Description: Abingdon, Oxon [UK] ; New York : Routledge, 2017. | Series: The rule of law in China and comparative perspectives | Includes index.
Identifiers: LCCN 2016042130| ISBN 9781472486141 (hardback) | ISBN 9781315575063 (e-book)
Subjects: LCSH: Constitutional law--Taiwan. | Law reform--Taiwan. | Rule of law--Taiwan. | Constitutional law--China--Hong Kong. | Law reform--China--Hong Kong. | Rule of law--China--Hong Kong. | Civil disobedience--Taiwan. | Civil disobedience--China--Hong Kong. | Democratization--Taiwan. | Democratization--China--Hong Kong.
Classification: LCC KNP205 .J66 2017 | DDC 320.95125--dc23
LC record available at https://lccn.loc.gov/2016042130

ISBN: 978-1-4724-8614-1 (hbk)
ISBN: 978-0-367-19186-3 (pbk)

Typeset in Galliard
by Cenveo Publisher Services

Contents

Introduction

The Taiwan Sunflower Movement and the Hong Kong Umbrella Movement

Brian Christopher Jones[*]

Hardly do acts of civil disobedience come in such grand fashion as Taiwan's Sunflower Movement and Hong Kong's Umbrella Movement. Both captivated their cities, governments, and citizens for a substantial amount of time; both garnered significant international attention; and both demonstrated that civil disobedience in Asia can be just as democratically based, passionate, and effective as anything found in the West. This book explores the legal and political significance of these vastly important movements. In doing so it provides a contextual juxtaposition of two jurisdictions pivotal to the peace and prosperity of the Asia Pacific region and beyond. The talented collection of writers assembled for this project explore both movements in depth, hoping to illuminate these historical events by thoroughly discussing the controversial issues inherent in protest and civil disobedience. As is evident throughout this book, the Sunflower and Umbrella movements were events whose significance stretched well beyond East Asia. The legal and political issues surrounding both protests are issues that can be found in states and polities around the world. Generally, this book focuses on the role dissent and civil disobedience play in democracies and non-democracies, and how governments can appropriately respond to such action; how social movements can impact politics, public policy, and the law; and how jurisdictions based around the principles of liberty, democracy, and the rule of law can ask difficult questions, in order to better govern themselves.

This book goes beyond anything currently available, certainly in the English-speaking world, as regards the domestic, regional, and international implications of these two movements. Before the individual chapters are presented, however, below I first provide a short synopsis of the two movements, including some general overlapping and diverging issues, followed by introducing and summarising the authors' chapters in this collection.

The Taiwan Sunflower Movement

On 18 March 2014 a contingent of Taiwanese citizens protesting against the unscrupulous passage of a service trade agreement with China managed to peacefully occupy Taiwan's national legislature, the Legislative Yuan. Lawmakers, the House Speaker, and even Taiwan's then-president found themselves on the outside looking in, unable to clear the legislative chamber and also unable to successfully (at least for a while) negotiate with Sunflower Movement members. Undoubtedly, this is a precarious position for a democratic government. The main debating chamber, a place where a significant amount of

* Lecturer in Public Law, Department of Law, Liverpool Hope University.

legislative and governmental business occurs, had been overtaken by disgruntled citizens. But the Movement did not just occupy the Legislative Yuan. There was also a demonstration at Taiwan's main central government building, the Executive Yuan, on 23–24 March, in which a large number of protesters gained access to the building, only to be forcefully evicted by police in the early hours of the 24th. Nevertheless, the Movement's momentum across Taiwan was building. The originally small group of protesters morphed into a significant mobilising force around the Legislative Yuan, culminating in the 30 March 2014 rally in front of the Presidential Palace, where hundreds of thousands of citizens gathered in support of the Sunflowers. On 10 April 2014, after 23 days of occupation, the Movement came to an end, as members peacefully walked out of the legislature and back into society. No police officers in riot gear waited for them as they exited … just cameras, and fellow citizens. At the time, commentators questioned whether this was a transformational moment in Taiwanese politics, a possible change of course in Taiwanese democracy and identity.[1]

Over two years later, there remains little doubt that the Sunflower Movement altered Taiwan's political landscape. January 2015 local elections demonstrated strong support for members of the opposition Democratic Progressive Party (DPP) and other independents (such as Taipei mayor Ko Wen-Je, 柯文哲).[2] Yet the national elections of January 2016 brought about the most sweeping political change Taiwan has ever seen.[3] The first female president was elected, as Democratic Progressive Party (DPP) candidate Tsai Ing-Wen (蔡英文) handily beat Kuomintang (KMT) challenger Eric Chu (朱立倫). But the most surprising result of the national elections was that the DPP, for the first time ever, took control of the legislature. Since its inception the KMT (or a KMT-backed alliance) has controlled the legislature, even when there was a DPP president and the DPP had the largest plurality of members for any single party. Indeed, the political landscape in many areas of Taiwan appears changed, and much of this was the result of Sunflower Movement efforts. Yet such significant repercussions were not always readily apparent.

In the aftermath of the Sunflower Movement, many questioned its success.[4] Although the trade-in-services agreement that the Sunflowers initially protested never went forward, other prominent requests by the group never materialised. One of the major issues for the Sunflowers was the "black-box" decision-making performed by the executive on trade deals – labelled "black-box" because there was little, if any, legislative oversight. While the Sunflowers, in connection with academia and the civic society, campaigned extensively to change the process of scrutiny regarding these deals, no law was ever agreed upon, and as of this writing the DPP legislature has still not passed, or even thoroughly considered, a bill

1 J. Michael Cole, "Sunflowers End Occupation of Taiwan's Legislature" *The Diplomat* (11 April 2014), http://thediplomat.com/2014/04/sunflowers-end-occupation-of-taiwans-legislature/. ("[T]he Sunflower Movement was en [*sic*] entirely new phenomenon in Taiwan, an awakening from a slumber of defeatism that will likely change the face of politics on the island as well as Taipei's relations with Beijing.")

2 Liu Fu-Kuo, "Taiwan's shifting political landscape" *East Asia Forum* (18 January 2015), http://www.eastasiaforum.org/2015/01/18/taiwans-shifting-political-landscape/.

3 "Tsai Ing-wen elected Taiwan's first female president" *BBC News* (17 January 2016), http://www.bbc.com/news/world-asia-35333647.

4 See, e.g. J. Michael Cole, "Was Taiwan's Sunflower Movement Successful?" *The Diplomat* (1 July 2014), http://thediplomat.com/2014/07/was-taiwans-sunflower-movement-successful/; Cindy Sui, "Will the Sunflower Movement change Taiwan?" *BBC News* (9 April 2015), available at: http://www.bbc.com/news/world-asia-32157210.

addressing this issue. Additionally, the Sunflowers desired a national constitutional convention to discuss major legal and political reform issues, but such a gathering has yet to materialise. In particular, a significant amount of discussion focused on Taiwan's governmental structure[5] and the composition of the Legislative Yuan.[6] Many questioned whether the current arrangement of a semi-presidential system, which includes an unelected premier as head of the executive branch, was beneficial for Taiwan. But these issues currently seem just as far away from gaining significant political traction as they did under the previous KMT administration. And whilst it is acknowledged that large-scale constitutional change is no easy task, the lack of a new law for increased legislative scrutiny regarding trade deals could be viewed as a conspicuous failure for the Movement – or at the very least, the new government.

One may even potentially argue that the DPP's recent electoral success had little to do with the Sunflower Movement. Many of the Movement's leaders have refused to align themselves with the DPP, and some have instead begun their own political parties. Huang Kuo-Chang (黃國昌), one of the Movement's academic leaders, is a founding member of the New Power Party (NPP), and was elected to the Legislative Yuan in January 2016. Also elected to the Yuan under the NPP tag were Hung Tzu-yung (洪慈庸) and Freddy Lim (林昶佐). The party was awarded two more seats under the proportional voting system. Shortly after the Movement ended, Lin Fei-Fan (林飛帆), arguably the most prominent Sunflower leader, at one point noted that he did not have "any expectations" of the DPP.[7] Thus some of the prominent Sunflowers have distanced themselves, or explicitly spurned the DPP, in an attempt to initiate even more radical change within Taiwan's political system.

Nevertheless, it would be a considerable mistake to say that the Sunflower Movement did not have a noticeable effect on Taiwanese politics. After all, the first female president was elected, the Legislative Yuan changed hands for the first time ever, and local politics has also been significantly altered; these momentous events would have been unlikely if not for the Sunflower Movement's intervention in the spring of 2014. Further, the government has recently dropped criminal charges for most of those involved in the Executive Yuan protests, noting that "the lawsuits were prompted by political considerations in the first place", and that the situation "should be handled with leniency based on the principle of promoting harmony and defusing conflicts".[8] This is a prominent recognition that, in the face of civil disobedience, governments do not always have to follow the conventional path to punishment; when conditions merit such an approach, they can also advocate democratic compromise for the promotion of civic harmony.

The Sunflower Movement did more than alter Taiwanese politics, however. Protesters brazenly tested the limits of free speech through a unique occupation of the national legislature, which presented many challenges to democratically elected leaders. But Taiwan's political leaders were also vulnerable in the sense that they lacked the legitimacy and popular will to forcefully remove the Sunflowers from the legislative chamber. If the

5 Chris Wang, "Parties at Odds on Reforming the Constitution" *Thinking Taiwan* (1 April 2015), http://thinking-taiwan.com/parties-at-odds-over-constitutional-reform/.

6 Timothy Rich, "Does the Legislative Yuan Need More Legislators?" *Thinking Taiwan* (29 May 2014), http://thinking-taiwan.com/does-legislative-more-legislators/.

7 Bear Lee, "Student protest leader says he has 'no expectations' of DPP" *Focus Taiwan* (31 July 2014), http://focustaiwan.tw/news/aipl/201407310036.aspx.

8 Stacey Hsu and Abraham Gerber, "Cabinet drops charges against students" *Taipei Times* (24 May 2016), p. 1.

legislative occupation lacked public support, there would be little to write about now (and certainly this book would not have been written), as members would probably have been removed from the legislature, similar to how many were forcefully evicted from the Executive Yuan. As it turned out, however, the Sunflowers transformed from a relatively fringe minority into a de facto – albeit unelected – popular majority. Perhaps more importantly, the Sunflowers also challenged the notion that immediate consequential outputs must result from acts of disobedience. Looked at from purely a practical standpoint – besides for holding up the China/Taiwan trade-in-services agreement – nothing immediate resulted from the Sunflower Movement intervention. This led a number of people to question the forcefulness of the Movement's actions and their occupation of the legislature. But unlike our innate human impulse to seek out immediate results, the Sunflowers took a more comprehensive view of politics and political change, and ultimately came out ahead.

While prosecutions have been dropped for a large majority of those involved in the Executive Yuan action, prosecutors still have indictments in place for 21 Sunflowers. A number of them have recently been called to the court to enter pleas, of which they all entered "not guilty".[9] The reality of these prosecutions now moving through the judicial system is a significant mistake. Local and national elections, of which the Sunflower Movement proved to be a weighty issue in each, have now been held. If the populous desired to punish the Sunflowers in any manner, they certainly would have done so in these elections – rather than, say, electing multiple Sunflowers, and the DPP more generally, to prominent positions of power. If there was ever a case where prosecution was not in the public interest, these would certainly provide the clearest of choices: the Taiwanese people have overwhelmingly voted for – and therefore justified – the Sunflowers and their actions. However one views the indictments going forward, the simple facts are that nonviolent acts of political speech could send a number of individuals to jail, have them pay heavy fines, or blemish their records with criminal charges and convictions. This is a dangerous precedent to set in any jurisdiction, let alone in a young democracy. And although the operation of free speech remains one of the most challengingly divisive components to assess – thus requiring continuous monitoring and evaluation – its mere presence as a foundational element of democracy is simply beyond question.

The Hong Kong Umbrella Movement

The Hong Kong Umbrella Movement was a more wide-ranging protest that involved four different locations around the city centre (Admiralty, Causeway Bay, Mong Kok, and Tsim Sha Tsui), the first being the most well-known and longest-lasting location. The idea for such occupations had been in the public consciousness long before the demonstrations, contrary to the Sunflower demonstrations, which were initially impromptu; the Hong Kong protests also received a significantly larger amount of international press coverage. The extensive press coverage was unsurprising given Hong Kong's recent status as a UK colony and its status as an international financial and travel hub. Planning for the civil disobedience demonstrations was long in coming given the Chinese State Council's 10 June 2014 white paper on "One

9 Jason Pan, "Sunflower leaders to face justice system 'head-on,'" *Taipei Times* (15 June 2016), p. 1.

Country, Two Systems",[10] and the decision of the Standing Committee of the National People's Congress (NPCSC) on 31 August 2014.[11] The latter detailed how the Hong Kong Chief Executive (CE) would be elected by "universal suffrage" in 2017, but laid out specific terms in relation to the potential CE's "love of country and love of Hong Kong" that the candidate must possess, in addition to a nominating process by which any candidate must have the endorsement of more than half of all members of the nominating committee. Given the composition of the nominating committee and the de facto control by the central authorities of the majority of the members, this ultimately meant that every candidate for CE would be officially screened by the Chinese Communist Party (CCP), and therefore the promise of "universal suffrage" for Hong Kong was a preposterous sham, a cunning absurdity that may have worked on the Mainland, but not in a place where the citizens believed in the increased rights and freedoms, including those of universal suffrage, promised through their Basic Law.[12]

However, the frustration of Hong Kong citizens and their decision to engage in civil disobedience was not merely because of the NPCSC's 31 August 2014 decision. Since the UK's 1997 handover of Hong Kong to China, citizens have felt increasingly isolated and correspondingly dominated by the political forces in Beijing. This frustration takes place within the wider circumstances of Hong Kong's economic stagnation, and the corresponding rise of China's mainland economy. In 2003, after pressure from CCP leaders, Hong Kong authorities released a draft national security bill that included matters related to treason, secession, sedition, and subversion – among other things – as regards the territory's newfound relationship with the PRC. This prompted widespread protests, and on 1 July 2003 hundreds of thousands of Hong Kongers marched against the measure. Ultimately, after the massive show of disapproval, the bill was shelved and has not been revisited.[13] However, this milestone in China's Hong Kong policy may have been short-lived, as ever since China has taken a hands-on approach to Hong Kong affairs. Significant controversy has also ensued over a new education curriculum – "moral and national education" – that is set to replace Hong Kong's model of "moral and civic education". Wide-ranging debate and protest also occurred in relation to this issue, and some of the leaders and groups that were at the forefront of the Umbrella protests, such as Joshua Wong (黃之鋒) and Scholarism, led these demonstrations. Hong Kong's curriculum programme is now entitled "Moral, Civic and National Education", and includes a section on "national

10 Chinese State Council, "The Practice of the 'One Country, Two Systems' Policy in the Hong Kong Special Administrative Region" *Xinhuanet* (10 June 2014), http://news.xinhuanet.com/english/china/2014-06/10/c_133396891.htm. The paper explicitly states:

> China's central government has comprehensive jurisdiction over all local administrative regions, including the HKSAR. The high degree of autonomy of HKSAR is not an inherent power, but one that comes solely from the authorization by the central leadership.
>
> The high degree of autonomy of the HKSAR is not full autonomy, nor a decentralized power. It is the power to run local affairs as authorized by the central leadership.

11 The Decision of the Standing Committee of the NPC on issues relating to the selection of the Chief Executive of the HKSAR by universal suffrage and on the method for forming the Legislative Council of the HKSAR in the year 2016 (31 August 2014).

12 But as Davis points out, the Basic Law does not explicitly mention "democratic elections", only "universal suffrage" (Michael Davis, "Beijing's Broken Promises" (2015) 26(2) *Journal of Democracy* 101, 104–106).

13 See Fu Hualing, Carole J. Petersen, and Simon N. M. Young, *National Security and Fundamental Freedoms: Hong Kong's Article 23 under Scrutiny* (Hong Kong: Hong Kong University Press, 2005).

identity" as one of the seven "priority values and attitudes".[14] But Hong Kong's troubles and the issues surrounding the Umbrella Movement extend wider than the education system and national security.

The handover to China also brought about other problems: rising prices of commercial rents and residential property; a strain on hospital resources because of an influx of pregnant Chinese mothers; and competition for daily necessities, such as baby milk powder for infants, space on public transportation and in restaurants. There are also complaints that Mainland visitors are not authentic "tourists", but shoppers, evident by the large suitcases many carry around with them.[15] All of these problems led to increasing discontent within the City, and an increasingly wary eye on Beijing's real or perceived influence on the Hong Kong Government. Such policies may have also inspired resentment among local Hong Kongers towards visitors from mainland China.[16] Indeed the steady culmination of these frustrations, what some have referred to as "mainlandisation",[17] directly or indirectly fed into the Umbrella Movement.

The primary intellectual thought behind the Movement initially came from Benny Tai (戴耀廷), a law professor at Hong Kong University, Dr. Chao Kin-Man (陳健民), a sociology professor at Chinese University of Hong Kong, and the Reverend Chu Yiu-ming (朱耀明). Their original title for the protest was "Occupy Central with Love and Peace". However, shortly after the protests were underway, it became obvious that the Occupy Central group no longer had control. Student groups such as Scholarism and the Hong Kong Federation of Students quickly took control of not just the practicalities of the protests, but the intellectual and "democratic" nature of them as well. Student leaders such as Joshua Wong, Agnes Chow (周庭), and Oscar Lai (黎汶洛) rose to prominence. The name of the Movement even changed after the first night of protests brought clashes with the police. Attempting to shield themselves from tear gas being thrown on them, protesters employed umbrellas and gas masks. The moniker "Umbrella Revolution" quickly arose, but it was "Umbrella Movement" that stuck, and which was widely used by those reporting on the protests and by the protesters themselves.

The duration and scale of the protests were impressive. The longest-lasting site in Admiralty persisted for close to two and a half months, almost twice as long as the Sunflower Movement protests. Aesthetically, the movement also captivated its followers. Images displaying numerous yellow umbrellas tantalising, frustrating, and deriding their antagonisers – be they the police, government, or anti-movement citizens – were awash throughout the duration of the movement. The puissant yellow chosen for such symbols aptly mirrored the movement: bold and auspiciously confident in their actions. In fact, the colour echoed the luminescence of the sunflowers used in Taiwan's Movement. A "Lennon Wall" in Admiralty of post-it notes with pro-democracy messages was an inspiring piece of art developed by the Movement. These vibrant symbols transmitted a positive and forward-looking message.

14 Hong Kong Education Bureau, "Moral, Civic and National Education" *Basic Education Curriculum Guide* (2014), http://www.edb.gov.hk/en/curriculum-development/4-key-tasks/moral-civic/.

15 Peter Shadbolt, "Hong Kong protests take aim at 'locust' shoppers from mainland China" CNN (7 March 2014), http://edition.cnn.com/2014/03/07/world/asia/hong-kong-china-visitors-controversy/.

16 Ibid.

17 See Carol A. G. Jones, *Lost in China? Law, Culture and Identity in Post-1997 Hong Kong* (Cambridge: Cambridge University Press, 2015).

The "success" of the Umbrella Movement is difficult to determine, and is an issue that I will primarily leave for the authors to address below, especially Brad Roth's and Jacques deLisle's concluding chapters. Yet there are signs that the Movement has had at least some lasting effect. In Hong Kong's November 2015 local elections, a number of "Umbrella soldiers" (i.e. those that participated in or were inspired by the Umbrella Movement) won district-level elections.[18] Additionally, in recent Legislative Council (LegCo) elections, four "radical" candidates were elected who desire more political autonomy or even independence from China, and who replaced more moderate voices within the legislature.[19] Whether they, or a coalition of pan-democrats, could eventually take control of LegCo remains to be seen. However, it should also be noted that a number of candidates – at least five – were disqualified by Hong Kong authorities in August because of their views on such sensitive issues.[20] Furthermore, in an ominous sign for Hong Kong's future autonomy, Beijing blocked two democratically elected politicians from sitting in LegCo, Yau Wai-ching (游蕙禎) and Sixtus Leung (梁頌恆) because of partially flubbing their oaths of office; the move by Beijing came even though there was a pending case on the issue in the local Hong Kong courts.[21] The Movement may have also potentially affected the amount of visitors from mainland China, which dropped 16% in 2015, and a further 13% in January–April of 2016.[22] While local residents may be feeling some relief on the subway or in shopping centres, local businesses have taken a hit.[23] It is unclear whether this will be a long-term or temporary trend affecting the territory. One thing that we do know, however, is that the PRC will not let Hong Kong fall out of its grasp, nor easily adopt democratic government, for that matter.

Some general overlapping and diverging issues

While the Sunflower Movement and Umbrella Movement events were unique, they also need to be placed within the wider context of citizen unrest throughout the world. Many issues surrounding the events are those in which jurisdictions are struggling with at the moment, as citizen unrest and confrontational protest become increasingly common. Numerous Western democracies recently experienced their own forms of occupation demonstrations based around government fiscal policy and the steady rise of globalisation and neoliberalism, as the Occupy Wall Street movement spread from New York to London

18 Danny Wok and Clare Baldwin, "Hong Kong's 'Umbrella Soldiers' win seats in local elections" *Reuters* (23 November 2015), http://www.reuters.com/article/us-hongkong-politics-election-idUSKCN0TA0WL20151123.

19 Tom Phillips and Eric Cheung, "Hong Kong elections: anti-Beijing activists gain foothold in power" *Guardian* (5 September 2016), https://www.theguardian.com/world/2016/sep/05/hong-kong-poll-pro-independence-activists-poised-to-win-seats-in-record-turnout.

20 Austin Ramzy and Alan Wong, "Hong Kong Restricts Election Candidates, Renewing Fears of Lost Rights" *New York Times* (3 August 2016), http://nyti.ms/2ahB3y8.

21 Michael Forsythe, "Hong Kong Elected 2 Separatists. China Took Drastic Action." New York Times (6 November 2016), http://nyti.ms/2eedyb8. See Jacques deLisle, Chapter 12, for more information on this.

22 Daniela Wei, "Hong Kong Retailers' Chinese Malaise Deepens from Bling to Buns" *Bloomberg* (23 June 2016), http://www.bloomberg.com/news/articles/2016-06-23/hong-kong-retailers-chinese-malaise-deepens-from-bling-to-buns.

23 Frederik Balfour, "Slump in Chinese Tourists Leaves Hong Kong Malls Struggling" *Bloomberg* (20 April 2016), http://www.bloomberg.com/news/articles/2016-04-19/slump-in-chinese-tourists-leaves-hong-kong-malls-struggling.

and elsewhere after the 2008 financial crash. The Arab Spring events of 2010–2011, which arose in a large part because of issues surrounding autonomy and democracy, had a significant impact on many jurisdictions throughout the region. In terms of its civil disobedience methods, such as occupying streets and major highways, over the past couple years the "Black Lives Matter" movement has been involved in demonstrations across the US and abroad. These protests were largely in response to police violence towards African Americans and other minorities. While many of these movements have encountered difficulties and tested the limits of protest and free speech, in the end they demonstrate a type of popular resilience against the status quo, an attempt by citizens to improve upon what they currently have.

Although the Sunflower and Umbrella Movements arose because of different issues and considerations, there remain some distinctive overlapping features of each that demonstrate the value of this collection. First, they were protests about autonomy – and perhaps more importantly, autonomy in the face of China's authoritarian regime. The Sunflower Movement, ever-mindful that Taiwan's economy could potentially be "swallowed" by China, was protesting for an economic (and political) break with China, for greater scrutiny of Taiwan's economic trade deals, for the freedom to make trade deals with other countries, and perhaps most significantly, for decreasing the significance of the "China factor" within Taiwan.[24] For all intents and purposes, Taiwan is an independent, self-governing country. Yet China views Taiwan as a Special Administrative Region (SAR) in a similar mould to Hong Kong; unfortunately this dissuades many states and international organisations – mostly because of direct or indirect pressure from China, but also because of the political or economic fear of doing so – from recognising Taiwan's autonomous nature. Conversely, the Hong Kong Umbrella Movement was seeking to assert its autonomy that the Basic Law and the "One Country, Two Systems" structure (supposedly) provided.[25] The Basic Law provides that, in accordance with the 1984 Sino-British Joint Declaration, Hong Kong enjoys more freedoms and civil liberties than the Mainland. Article 27 of the Basic Law stipulates that these liberties include the freedom of speech and the right of citizens to voice disapproval of their government through assembly and demonstration.[26] Whether the PRC is content with these rights or not, as long as the Basic Law is in effect, they should have little choice but to abide by them, although interpretation through the NPCSC provides Beijing significant leverage on the Basic Law's operation.

Next, and equally important as autonomy, the protests concerned the operation of democracy. In Taiwan's case, the Sunflowers argued that the 30-second incident – where KMT legislators expedited and approved the trade-in-services package through dodgy legislative tactics – threatened Taiwanese democracy, thus necessitating their takeover of the legislative chamber. Although Taiwan is a self-governing entity, talk of "unification" with China, from both the Taiwan side and the Mainland, occurs frequently, and some within

24 On the final point, see Wu Jieh-Min, "The China Factor in Taiwan: Impact and Response" in Gunter Schubert (ed.), *Handbook of Modern Taiwan Politics and Society* (Abingdon: Routledge, 2016), 425–445.

25 Although, as noted above, the 10 June 2014 PRC White Paper does not appear to provide Hong Kong much autonomy. And as Cheng-Yi Huang notes below in Chapter 7, the Basic Law was written by China and never ratified by the Hong Kong citizenry. Thus, there are significant questions as to whether Hong Kongers should be looking to the Basic Law as regards sovereignty issues.

26 Article 27, Hong Kong Basic Law reads: "Hong Kong residents shall have freedom of speech, of the press and of publication; freedom of association, of assembly, of procession and of demonstration; and the right and freedom to form and join trade unions, and to strike."

the KMT openly advocate such a proposition. Should Taiwan's economy weaken to the point of near collapse, opponents believe that China could overtake the country and (officially) declare it as part of their own. Even without such an economic breakdown, fears throughout Taiwan persist that China may forcefully (i.e. militarily) attempt to overtake the country, thus vanquishing Taiwan's hard-fought democracy. While Taiwan's movement hinged on the operation of democracy, Hong Kong's issues centred on democratic attainment. In particular, citizens were expecting to be able to freely elect the Hong Kong Chief Executive in 2017 and the LegCo by 2020, only to have China scuttle this plan through their own interpretation of the Basic Law. Ultimately, the PRC blocked any non-approved candidates for the CE position, which means that a pan-democrat candidate advocating democratic reform – or potentially independence from China – could not even stand for election.

Third, both protests had scholars at their forefronts. As noted above, prominent Hong Kong intellectuals led the beginning of the Occupy Central movement, supplying the intellectual weight behind the idea of mass protests and civil disobedience as a justifiable, and honourable, position among society, and especially for the implementation of democratic principles. On the Sunflower Movement side, the most visible academic presence was Huang Kuo-Chang, at the time a researcher in the law department of the prominent Taiwan research institute Academia Sinica.[27] These of course were not the only academics involved with both movements – a long list of local and international scholars contributed to, supported, and even opposed both movements – but they were the most prominent ones. Besides supplying ideas and strategy to the movements, it is unclear whether or not the academics provided something more, such as potential legal and political cover for them while the governments figured out their next moves. Nevertheless, having academics at the forefront of any social movement, especially one that involves such a plethora of important societal and governmental issues, provided both movements with a legitimacy they may not have otherwise attained.

And finally, while each protest included a broad coalition of citizens,[28] including those from the civic society, student leaders in Hong Kong and Taiwan played a significant part in the organisation, duration, and success of both movements. The willingness of university students to turn out on a large scale for the protests contributed to the sustainability of both movements. Without this segment of the population, the movements would have had little to stand on. Many university students in Taiwan and Hong Kong skipped classes and sacrificed their personal lives – including their relationships with immediate family or partners – and potentially even their academic and professional careers, to participate in the protests. Such passion and commitment in the face of tear gas, police brutality, uncertainty, and distress must be acknowledged. Additionally, in connection with the intellectual leaders of the movements, university students provided a much-needed platform to spread the intellectual foundations attached to their core issues.

27 For full disclosure, for the duration of the Sunflower Movement protests I was also working (as a postdoctoral fellow) at Academia Sinica, within the same department as Huang Kuo-Chang.

28 For the Taiwan perspective, see Hsiao-Wei Kuan, "Connecting Gender and Trade: Gender Framing in the Anti-Cross-Strait Service Trade Agreement Movement" (2015) 45(1) *Hong Kong Law Journal* 249. For the Umbrella Movement perspective, see Victoria Tin-bor Hui, "The Protests and Beyond" (2015) 26(2) *Journal of Democracy* 111.

And yet, it would be a serious mistake to conflate the two movements, which significantly diverged in many ways. One of those differences was the involvement of the courts in diffusing the protests (as Fu Hualing writes about below in Chapter 5). Ultimately, Hong Kong's courts became heavily involved in the Umbrella Movement, issuing injunctions for different protest sites, which divided participants and threw the movement into a tailspin. However, during the Sunflower Movement the courts did not immediately adjudicate anything, at least while the protests were in operation, and thus there were less calls for "rule of law" to be implemented. That is not to say that the courts or the legal process have had no involvement in Sunflower Movement affairs. After protests officially ended, prosecutors charged a large group of Sunflowers, including much of its leadership, with offences ranging from illegal entry to inciting others to commit an offence. Given the political controversy surrounding the Sunflower Movement actions, the cases were slow to reach the courts. As noted above, the Cabinet recently dropped charges for 126 student protesters that entered the Executive Yuan building on the night of 23 March. However, charges against many of the movements leaders, including Huang Kuo-Chang, Lin Fei-Fan, and Chen Wei-ting (陳為廷), are still in place, and the cases are currently travelling through the courts. Thus while there still may be some court involvement in the Sunflower case, the role of the courts was significantly diminished compared to the situation in Hong Kong, where the institution played a vital role not only in fracturing the Umbrella Movement, but ultimately in dismantling it as well.

Also, given that Hong Kong is now officially part of China, in some ways the Umbrella Movement was riskier than the Sunflower Movement. Even though the SAR is supposed to have a degree of independence compared to Mainland China, it has become increasingly apparent that the PRC is unafraid to mettle in Hong Kong affairs. Curtailment of political speech on the Mainland is well-known throughout the world, as is their Internet's "great wall", which prevents citizens from accessing Western websites that may contain news or information contrary to the PRC's narrative (see, e.g. Tiananmen Square, in which search terms involving this incident are still banned around its anniversary every year).[29] While such Mainland speech restrictions are long-standing, the PRC has also recently demonstrated ominous signs that they would like to curtail free speech in Hong Kong. In particular, a number of Hong Kong booksellers that stocked and sold books relating to PRC party gossip recently disappeared, only to reappear on state television and apologise for their "crimes". Yet not all would be silenced. One bookseller stifled his Beijing gag order, attesting that he was blindfolded and kept in a small room after he was kidnapped in the autumn of 2015.[30] Hong Kong citizens have also demonstrated some signs of frustration, which may or may not be related to the Umbrella Movement: in early February 2016, during the Lunar New Year, a government crackdown on street food vendors led to citizen rioting and violent clashes with the police.[31] Thus, as much as the Umbrella Movement stimulates inspiration and hope, these incidents portray a potentially bleak picture as regards Hong Kong's future.

29 Jonathan Kaiman, "Tiananmen Square online searches censored by Chinese authorities" *Guardian* (4 June 2013), https://www.theguardian.com/world/2013/jun/04/tiananmen-square-online-search-censored.

30 Agence France-Presse, "Hong Kong bookseller speaks out about detention in China" *Guardian* (16 June 2016), at https://www.theguardian.com/world/2016/jun/16/hong-kong-bookseller-lam-wing-kee-speaks-out-about-detention-in-china.

31 "Hong Kong's Mong Kok clashes: More than fishballs" *BBC News* (9 February 2016), http://www.bbc.com/news/world-asia-china-35529785.

The chapters in this collection

This book is divided into four parts, the first three of which address the following: the Taiwan Sunflower Movement (Chapters 1–3), the Hong Kong Umbrella Movement (Chapters 4–6), and one that focuses on comparative elements of the Sunflower and Umbrella movements (Chapters 7–10). The final part consists of two closing chapters (11 and 12) that discuss the two movements from more comprehensive perspectives, drawing on many of the chapters throughout the collection.

From the Taiwan part, Yen-Tu Su and I analyse the justifications the Movement provided for their actions, and present a theory of disobedience that we believe the Sunflower Movement gave rise to: "confrontational contestation". We also analyse the virtues of compromise, ultimately concluding that not prosecuting Sunflower protesters would be a significant democratic compromise that would enhance democratic peace and reduce conflict. Wen-Chen Chang explores the Movement from a freedom of speech perspective, analysing both Taiwanese and international jurisprudential developments in regard to where the right to peaceful, but occupational, assembly currently stands. In a novel survey regarding lawsuits that have arisen because of the Sunflower Movement (both those against the protesters and those against the government), she highlights some encouraging signs that judges in Taiwan on the criminal and civil side appear to be strengthening the protection of peaceful assembly. Finally, Jiunn-rong Yeh articulates the transformation to "civic constitutionalism" that has taken place in Taiwan over the past few decades, drawing on its origins from the Wild Strawberry Movement to the ultimate depiction of such change to date: the Sunflower Movement. He further argues that civic constitutionalism may be the answer to many of the problems associated with representative democracy, rigid constitutionalism, and activist constitutional courts.

From the Hong Kong part, Albert H. Y. Chen forensically examines the evolution of constitutional reform and democratisation in Hong Kong from the colonial period to the present. He determines that the Umbrella Movement is a reflection of Hong Kong's increasingly divisive politics, which is present because of the contradictions and tensions in the "One Country, Two Systems" project that China and Hong Kong are currently engaged in. Indeed, the operation of the "One Country, Two Systems" structure is an underlying theme in relation to Hong Kong. Next, Fu Hualing takes into consideration the conundrum of protest in high-income societies, such as Hong Kong's, and whether or not that aspect can be married to the city's new-found sense of the political. He examines the territory's strong traditions of civic constitutionalism and rule of law, and how these interact with the concepts of democracy. Ultimately he finds that the courts, and especially the cherished Hong Kong ideal for the rule of law, drove a fatal wedge into the heart of the Umbrella Movement. Finally, Daniel Matthews attempts to break away from strictly political or legal discussion in his analysis of the *nomos* of the Umbrella Movement. He claims that the Movement was successful for rupturing Hong Kong's spatio-normative distribution, and that this repositioning has brought a form of internal reflection to the territory, including putting forth considerable questions regarding the nature of identity and belonging. Matthews believes that the *nomos* and "right to the city" perspectives provide a better understanding of the Umbrella Movement's wider normative implications.

In the Taiwan and Hong Kong comparative part, Cheng-Yi Huang begins by discussing the failures of both the Basic Law and 1947 R.O.C. Constitution in their respective democratic structures. He stresses that neither of these documents have provided the sovereignty each group of citizens desires, and that ultimately both jurisdictions need authentic constitutions to replace their current constitutional documents in order to become genuine self-governing political communities. Chih-hsing Ho examines the question of whether to punish prominent members of the Umbrella Movement who may have sparked the civil disobedience action. In doing so she incorporates a number of legal and theoretical positions into account, and even examines a prominent court case that recently made it through the Hong Kong legal system. Highly critical of the Hong Kong courts' "restrictive notion of the rule of law", Ho argues that "choosing tolerance rather than punishment" can create room for debate, as opposed to merely the preservation of law and order. Chien-Huei Wu attempts to determine whether Hong Kong and Taiwan governance, rule of law, and press freedom are affected by an increase in trade and (legal and illegal) visitors/immigrants from China. After analysing and interpreting the data, Wu concludes that having an open trade policy is a net positive, but certain types of trade with China (such as trade in services) carry increased risks for both Hong Kong and Taiwan. In a novel and potentially dangerous piece of original research, Han Zhu was able to collect a good amount of data on Mainland Chinese perspectives on the Sunflower and Umbrella Movements. This data provides an inside look into how the Chinese population perceived the events in Hong Kong. Ultimately, she finds that there is a large gap between Hong Kong's *Weiquan* sector and Mainland Chinese views on and support for both movements. She also finds that the media organisations by which people get their news strongly correlated to either positive or negative views of the movements: perhaps unsurprisingly, those getting their news from state-run media were less supportive of both movements, while those obtaining news from Hong Kong media or social networks were much more supportive.

The book closes with two general chapters by Brad Roth and Jacques deLisle, respectively, who discuss the broader significance of the two movements. Roth uses a normative theoretical framework to analyse both, drawing heavily on United Nations and other international perspectives. In focusing on the sovereignty aspects of each movement and the loyalty both demonstrated to their political communities and constitutional premises, Roth fittingly characterises them as a form of "rule of law from below". Meanwhile Jacques deLisle analyses a host of contentious issues that the two movements brought about, including the interaction of politics and law, direct democracy, fundamental principles, and political economy. Yet deLisle buttresses his chapter with a focus on China, first addressing the PRC as the source of challenge or crises in relation to the movements, and then examining the implications for Taiwan–China and Hong Kong–China relationships. Ultimately he contends that the Sunflower and Umbrella Movements represent the "ardent forefront" as regards promoting democracy and constitutional governance in each respective jurisdiction, and that state institutions, political parties, and the civil society may increasingly take their cues from these groups – or those that subsequently develop – in matters dealing with China and beyond.

Part I

The Taiwan Sunflower Movement

1 Confrontational contestation and democratic compromise

The Sunflower Movement and its aftermath

Brian Christopher Jones and Yen-Tu Su+*

Introduction

Clashes over visions of democratic governance can oftentimes be epic and lasting. The Taiwan Sunflower Movement (the Movement) of March and April 2014 ensured these clashes would be epic – whether they will be lasting is yet to be seen. After Kuomintang (KMT) lawmakers pushed a Taiwan–China service trade pact through the legislative process within a matter of seconds, members of the Movement (the Sunflowers) broke through police barricades to occupy the Legislative Chamber, where they would reside for 24 days. In essence the Movement, which even came as a surprise to the opposition Democratic Progressive Party (DPP), decisively challenged the Ma administration and the KMT's version of a "winner-take-all" democracy, providing a competing vision based around deliberation, participation, and Taiwan's sovereignty. It is not unusual to have competing visions of democracy within a given democratic polity. Indeed, democracy is in constant tension with itself, and it often means different things to different people. The Sunflower Movement and its short-term aftermath nonetheless hold promise in becoming an intriguing story for democratic theory – a story about how, after a peaceful yet dramatic confrontation which went one step further than usual protests, people holding very different democratic convictions can still live together in peace and resolve their differences through a democratic political process.

This chapter explores the significance and implications of the Sunflower Movement for democracy in Taiwan and pro-democracy protests elsewhere. Specifically, we are interested not only in whether and how the Movement can be justified in democratic terms but also in which scenario this episode in Taiwan's democratic history will end – either a protracted legal–political confrontation or a regenerative democratic peace. We attempt two major inquiries in this piece: (1) to account for the democratic significance of the Sunflower Movement with a theory of *confrontational contestation* and (2) to make the case for non-prosecution of the Sunflowers on the part of the (KMT) Ma administration as a *democratic compromise* for the sake of fostering democratic peace in Taiwan. While there are apparent inconsistencies or tensions in calling for both contestation and compromise, we hope to demonstrate how they can complement one another as the yin and yang that keep democracy alive and well in Taiwan and elsewhere.

* Lecturer in Public Law, Department of Law, Liverpool Hope University.

+ Assistant Research Fellow, Institutum Iurisprudentiae, Academia Sinica. For disclosure, I have taken my part in the Movement as an intellectual supporting its cause and action. I consider myself one of the Sunflowers.

The Sunflower Movement as confrontational contestation

One central issue of the normative discourse surrounding the Sunflower Movement has to do with its democratic credentials: all things considered, is the Movement a democratic, non-democratic or anti-democratic action? The answer to this question is the key to understanding the causes and consequences of the Sunflower Movement, although the answer appears to depend on whom you ask. For some, especially for the (KMT) Ma administration and their sympathisers, the Sunflowers illegally hijacked the legislative process and thereby put Taiwan's democracy in jeopardy. For others, including many Sunflowers, the Movement constituted a democratic self-revision without which tomorrow's Taiwan could resemble today's Hong Kong. The outcome of the presidential and parliamentary elections held in January 2016 indicated that, for the time being, the people of Taiwan seemed to side with the Sunflowers' side. A disinterested and cautious observer might want to take a middle-of-the-road position by suggesting that the occupation is a non-democratic measure, and only history can tell whether the Movement is positive or negative for Taiwan's democracy. There is much to be said about the virtues of striving for being fair-minded and taking a long-term perspective. But democracy is a history in and of itself,[1] and the very project of democracy compels that we the contemporaries make our own judgement call – right here, right now.

How we conceptualise the Sunflowers' occupation – including the 24-day occupation of the Legislative Chamber (along with the peripheral streets), and the short-lived occupation of the neighbouring Executive Yuan – also affects our thinking about the place of the Movement vis-à-vis democracy in Taiwan and beyond. Viewing the occupation as an exercise of civil disobedience, for instance, might prompt us to argue for or against the Movement as a liberal cause, by which the minorities (as represented by the Sunflowers) seek to counteract what the majority (as represented by the government) has done wrong. However, we think the Sunflowers' occupation comes closer to exemplify what Daniel Markovits terms as democratic disobedience, the goal of which is to ensure that a well-functioning democratic process corrects the perceived democratic deficits in the law and politics of the day.[2] The normative justification for the Movement is better cast in democratic terms, because doing so better captures the mind-set of many Sunflowers – that they were "defending democracy". In addition, in light of the dismal approval ratings of the Ma administration and the KMT-led legislature, it is far from indisputable that they stood for the political majority in Taiwan. The Sunflower Movement often spoke in the name of "we the people" and enjoyed fairly strong public support during their occupation.[3] It appeared to be more of a majoritarian uprising than a counter-majoritarian resistance.

Democratic citizen unrest has been given a number of labels throughout the years: "protest", "civil disobedience", "dissent", "people power",[4] and the relatively newly

1 See Pierre Rosanvallon, "Foreword" in Samuel Moyn (ed.), *Democracy Past and Future* (New York: Columbia University Press, 2006).

2 Daniel Markovits, "Democratic Disobedience" (2005) 114 *Yale Law Journal* 1897.

3 Chris Wang, "Majority Supports Referendum on Trade Agreement: Survey" *Taipei Times* (29 March 2014), p. 1; see also Opinion Poll by TVBS (20–21 March 2014): Do you support the Sunflower's occupation of the Legislative Chamber (Yes: 48%, No: 40%, Undecided: 10%); Opinion Poll by TVBS (24 March 2014): Do you support the continued occupation of the Legislative Chamber (Yes: 51%, No: 38%, Undecided: 11%); Opinion Poll by TVBS (7–8 April 2014): Whether you think this Movement is helpful or not for Taiwan's democracy (Helpful: 65%, Unhelpful: 26%, Undecided: 9%).

4 April Carter, *People Power and Political Change* (London: Routledge, 2012) 7–12.

minted "direct action".[5] Nevertheless, given how the Sunflower events transpired, and especially given the equally dramatic ending of the legislative occupation, labelling the events merely a form of disobedience would be inadequate. In an attempt to alleviate these problems and to designate the unique nature of the events, herein we use the phrase "confrontational contestation". The "contestation" portion is borrowed from Philip Pettit[6] and refers to a citizenry actively contesting the nature of their democracy through political engagement.[7] The "confrontational" part of our phrase is also important and primarily refers to the fact that many contemporary contestatory actions are not necessarily confrontational. Yet the twenty-first century has seen a new wave of protests that are examples of actively confrontational disobedience (i.e. occupying public places, such as streets, parks, and buildings); the Arab Spring protests and the Occupy Wall Street movement are two of the most significant examples. Although, not all these incidents amount to a "confrontational contestation".

Pettit discusses aspects of civil disobedience when confronting the ideas and issues about the legitimacy of a political order. Ultimately he concludes that if the current regime is legitimate, then "attempts to change unjust laws should be restricted to measures that are consistent with the regime's remaining in place".[8] This would seem to encapsulate the Sunflower Movement, which indeed decided to act within the confines of the current regime. However, Pettit also maintains that civil disobedience campaigns should not involve "taking the law into your own hands", and that the recognition of "the state as the appropriate arbiter of legal issues" is essential to challenging the laws.[9] The Movement's actions may have run contrary to this proposition to some extent. After all, by occupying the legislature for 24 days, the Sunflowers arguably took the law into their own hands—at least for the time being. And while the Sunflowers certainly engaged in disobedience, they may have gone one step further than what Pettit would recommend for dissenters within a legitimate political order. Nevertheless, we argue that democratic contestation cannot rule out a priori the use of confrontational yet peaceful disobedience.

The idea of confrontational contestation can also be understood as a revision of the ideas of civil and democratic disobedience. Deficiencies in the liberal view of civil disobedience[10] have been around for years, and recent commentators have become more wary of such a view. Raffaele Laudani notes that from "Rawls's perspective, the whole element of *challenging* the political order is completely absent", and that civil disobedience ultimately becomes a "sui generis 'appeal' to the majority so that they 'reconsider', in the name of a common sense of justice, their decisions made".[11] Laudani further criticises this perspective as

5 April Carter, *Direct Action and Democracy Today* (Cambridge: Polity Press, 2005).

6 Philip Pettit, *On the People's Terms: A Republican Theory and Model of Democracy* (Cambridge: Cambridge University Press, 2012).

7 Of course, we are not the only theorists to be affected by Pettit's ideas. For an interesting and more thorough take on disobedience and democracy, see, e.g. William Smith, *Civil Disobedience and Deliberative Democracy* (London: Routledge, 2013) 128–133.

8 Pettit (n. 6 above), p. 137.

9 Pettit (n. 6 above), p. 137.

10 For prominent examples of the liberal view, see John Rawls, *A Theory of Justice* (Cambridge, MA: Harvard University Press, 1999); Ronald Dworkin, *Sovereign Virtue: The Theory and Practice of Equality* (Cambridge, MA: Harvard University Press, 2000); Bruce Ackerman, *Social Justice in the Liberal State* (New Haven: Yale University Press, 1980).

11 Raffaele Laudani, *Disobedience in Western Political Thought: A Genealogy* (Cambridge: Cambridge University Press, 2013) 113–114. Emphasis in original.

"unable to find a real space of intervention", noting that liberal justification for acts of civil disobedience are possible "only ex post, after its compatibility with the current system has been verified".[12] Tony Milligan also notes that Rawls's account of civil disobedience does not take into consideration issues outwith basic human liberties, such as economic, environmental, or animal rights protests, which make "it ill-suited as a tool for analysing and understanding key instances of twenty-first-century protest and dissent".[13]

Conversely, republican democratic disobedience revolves around the processes of democracy rather than any perceived democratic ideals. Markovits claims that democratic disobedience arose because an important form of political engagement has emerged that "cannot be understood through the prevailing theoretical accounts of legal and political authority".[14] In particular, he notes that "[i]t aims to render plausible the counterintuitive claim that disobeying the laws of the democratic state *can serve democracy*. Indeed, the argument casts democratic disobedience as an unavoidable, integral part of a well-functioning democratic process" (emphasis added).[15] One of the keys to the republican, democracy-enhancing vision is seen in what Markovits labels a "democratic deficit".[16] This occurs when democratic governments open themselves up to deficits of democratic legitimacy. This description of republican disobedience likely categorises the Sunflower Movement as an example of republican democratic disobedience. Indeed, "the republican view opens up the possibility that political disobedience may be democratically justified even when it cannot be cast as protecting basic rights".[17] The Sunflower Movement events are difficult to explain through any basic rights lens; they mostly concerned a lack of governmental/parliamentary accountability and an obvious breach of parliamentary procedures.

The Sunflowers did not merely disobey, however: they also provided a duelling vision of democracy, which is elaborated on below. The unveiling of this vision moved their actions beyond democratic disobedience, and into a "contestation". Pettit states that democratic life must have an "antagonistic" character.[18] Indeed, he argues that a contestatory citizenry

> must be on the watch for proposals or measures that are not suitably supported ... and they must be ready to organize in opposition to such policies. It is only in the presence of concerted, sustained oversight of government activity—only in the presence of civic vigilance, in the old term—that we can have any assurance that government will be forced to remain responsive to popular inputs.[19]

Not everyone in Pettit's democratic ideal must engage in such contestatory activities, which is why watchdog groups and other activists are integral to democracy. As those students and civic groups that formed the Movement were vigilant in the face of government policy which they thought was not suitably supported by the public, the Movement certainly fits

12 Ibid., pp. 115–116.
13 Tony Milligan, *Civil Disobedience: Protest, Justification, and the Law* (London: Bloomsbury, 2013) 14.
14 Markovits (n. 2 above), p. 1902.
15 Ibid., p. 1902.
16 Ibid., pp. 1921–1928.
17 Ibid., p. 1911.
18 Pettit (n. 6 above), p. 226.
19 Ibid.

in Pettit's account for democratic contestation. Ultimately, Pettit's vision "reject[s] the romantic idea of each citizen's exercising a panoramic, altruistic form of oversight; it also rejects the equally romantic idea of a participatory, Rousseauvian engagement",[20] which, according to Pettit, betrayed traditional notions of Republicanism by not acknowledging the contestatory roles of each and every citizen.

In any event, the Sunflowers had taken over the Legislative Chamber for more than three weeks in the spring of 2014.[21] A few critics of the Movement – including, among others, President Ma Ying Jeou – seemed to suggest that, by illegally occupying the chamber and paralysing the legislative process for such long a time, the Movement was by nature anti-democratic. We disagree. As unusual and confrontational as it may be, the Sunflowers' occupation was clearly within the bounds of non-violent disobedience. And if non-violent disobedience is a morally justifiable way of democratic life, there is simply no reason why the legislature (or any other formal institutions of democracy, for that matter) should be insulated from the disruption of otherwise morally justifiable disobedience. The outright rejection of the Sunflower Movement as anti-democratic "mob rule" for no reason other than its disruption of the legislative process makes sense only if we think there is so little room for democracy-compatible disobedience that democracy is little more than what is institutionally practised and legally allowed. The Sunflowers' occupation alone, therefore, did a service to Taiwan by challenging such a deeply reactionary view and thereby enlarging the space as well as our imagination of democratic political engagement beyond the confines of positive law.

Democratic justifications for the Sunflowers' occupation

It remains to be determined whether or not the Sunflowers are justified – from a democratic perspective – to occupy the Legislative Chamber and thereby derail the Ma administration's attempt to finalise the service trade agreement between Taiwan and China. As a matter of democratic political morality, the Sunflowers have to convince not only their own conscience but also their fellow citizens that what they did was morally acceptable (or even morally right) from the perspective of democratic justice. And since the Movement effectively altered the course of the representative democratic process with such forceful intervention, but without express authorisation of the people, the democratic legitimacy of the Movement is dependent, by and large, on whether the democratic justice they sought to achieve, or the democratic injustice they sought to redress, could justify the drastic actions/means they took.

The Sunflowers have put forward a myriad of justifications as to why their (extra-electoral) confrontational contestation with the democratic authorities of the Ma administration and the KMT-led Legislative Yuan should be considered justified from the

20 Ibid., p. 227.

21 It is worth noting that opposition DPP legislators, while surprised by the initial legislative takeover, also played a small but significant role in the events by acting as "security guards" for the Sunflowers. They sat between the police and the protesters, providing the Movement with a buffer zone and a type of protective legitimacy within the Legislative Yuan the Sunflowers probably would not have otherwise received. Indeed, while no DPP representatives participated in the Sunflower Movement leadership, DPP legislators facilitated the entry and exit of Movement participants in terms of gaining access to the Legislative Yuan. On the relationship of the Sunflowers and the DPP, see also Ian Rowen, "Inside Taiwan's Sunflower Movement: Twenty-Four Days in a Student-Occupied Parliament, and the Future of the Region" (2015) 74(1) *The Journal of Asian Studies* 5, 17.

viewpoints of democratic justice. Here, we identify four justifications and analyse them one by one, for, while interrelated to one another, they invoke different principles/ideals of democratic justice, diagnose different pathologies of the institutionalised democratic politics in Taiwan, and encounter different challenges from both within and outside the Movement. These differences serve as a powerful reminder that there exists more than one type of "Sunflower" – that is, the Movement is in fact a political coalition as opposed to a homogeneous or single-issue unity. The democratic case for the Movement, however, is much stronger when these justifications work together rather than separately. Here, the whole is arguably larger than the sum of its parts.

(i) *Defending democracy against China*: Many Sunflowers and their supporters oppose the disputed service trade pact because they deem it a Trojan horse sent by China to suffocate Taiwan's sovereignty and democracy with the force of economy. Specifically, many critics of the agreement have grave misgivings about the threats to free speech and national security posed by the pact's arrangements concerning such industries as printing and telecommunications. The Movement, accordingly, can be understood as a *pre-emptive resistance* to a measure that is alleged to have a democracy-degrading effect of transforming Taiwan into another Hong Kong. In sharp contrast, the Ma administration and their supporters defend the service trade pact as a deal offering more benefits than harms to Taiwan and denounce their opponents as being Sinophobic. The trade policy disagreement aside, much of the ensuing contestation can be explained in terms of identity politics; whereas the patriotic Sunflowers seek to defend democracy – as an integral part of Taiwan's national identity – against China's co-optation, their critics take pride in being more cosmopolitan and/or being Chinese nationalists instead.

The principal location of the protest was no accident; Sunflowers aimed at the legislature primarily because it is the most democratic manifestation of "we the people" sovereignty.[22] The sayings "parliament belongs to the people" and "return the parliament to the people" were commonly chanted throughout the occupation. It seems undisputed that a focus back on democracy, and especially the power of citizens, was an instrumental element of the Movement. Although there may have been similar origins,[23] the Sunflower Movement was quite different from many of the other occupy movements, which manifested in parks, streets, and other public areas. Going to the legislature was a bold, and important, part of the disobedience. Initially, it was easily the Sunflowers' largest bargaining chip. Movements in other places have not had the same access to their legislatures that the Sunflower Movement enjoyed.[24] Therefore, the choice of venue, the Legislative Yuan, was a strategic democratic contestation. In the KMT rush to pass the service trade pact, some saw the authoritarian government of Beijing behind such a move, and not the makings of a democratised Taiwan. A protest focused in and around the legislature, the ultimate democratic symbol of "we the people" popular sovereignty, was a significant reminder that

22 Although, as Post notes, "[d]emocracy is distinct from popular sovereignty". See Robert Post, "Democracy and Equality" (2005) 603 *The Annals of the American Academy* 24, 25.

23 That is, public space belongs to the people.

24 Many citizens simply do not have access to their legislatures, either because of the copious amounts of security surrounding the building or because of the structural layout of the building. As John Parkinson points out, "while the managers of legislatures might celebrate publicness in the abstract, they tend to react to real publics with a great more ambivalence" (John Parkinson, "How Legislatures Work—and Should Work—as Public Space" (2013) 20(3) *Democratization* 438, 439).

Taiwan – unlike the People's Republic of China (PRC), and ultimately, distinct from Hong Kong – is a democracy.

(ii) *Democracy as social economic justice in the age of free trade agreements*: During the Movement's occupation, there was an extensive debate among the Sunflowers about what should be the focus of their campaign—the social economic injustice perpetrated or aggravated by the neoliberalist free trade regime (including not just trade agreements between Taiwan and China, but the overall dearth of socioeconomic justice in twenty-first-century international trade) or the procedural injustice of black box decision-making in the disputed service trade agreement. Although the leadership of the Movement signed onto the latter in the hope of winning more public support, many Sunflowers hold the belief that a truly meaningful democratic process ultimately would lead to the realisation of a socio-economic order that is much more just than it is now. Seen in this light, the Movement has certain genealogical affinities with such protests as Occupy Wall Street, and thereby can be said to be built, at least in part, on the idealism of social democracy.

(iii) *Defending democracy against the imperial executive*: On 17 March 2014, a KMT legislator – acting on his prerogative as Committee Chair and with the backing of the Ma administration and the KMT Caucus – used a hidden microphone to proclaim, in just 30 seconds and without a vote, that the remaining committee sessions for the legislative review of the service trade agreement had lapsed. The infamous move that triggered the Sunflower Movement was defended on the ground that the service trade agreement falls entirely within the purview of the executive branch and thereby should take into effect the moment when the legislative oversight lapsed. The Sunflowers condemned the ludicrous oversight-stopping move as the last straw that broke Taiwan's democracy. Viewing the near absence of checks and balances as the root cause of black box agreement making, they also demanded that such critical agreements between China and Taiwan as the service trade pact at issue be placed under legislative oversight that is much more meaningful and scrupulous than is now. By demanding "legislation (of the oversight act) before review (of the service trade pact)" and later proposing a draft bill on the legislative oversight of cross-strait agreements, the Sunflowers sought to redress the alleged democratic deficits accumulated through the power imbalance between the executive and the legislative branches in the existing regime of the cross-strait law in Taiwan. The Ma administration admitted few mistakes in their handling of cross-strait relations and rejected the Sunflowers' draft bill as a legislative encroachment on the executive prerogative. Under pressure from the Movement, the Ma administration nevertheless introduced a draft oversight bill of their own, which was little more than an attempt to codify the status quo and fell far short of the Sunflowers' expectations. The legislation has since been stalled for more than two years after the Movement, and remains a hot-button issue between the Sunflowers and the subsequent DPP Government.

Attempting to fill a democratic deficit, which was based around an overtly manipulative procedural (mis)calculation, could have been the main action the Sunflowers engaged in. The Movement saw such a procedural manoeuvre as not only dishonest but also as a genuinely significant threat to Taiwan's democracy (in terms of how future bills, economic agreements, and other governmental business may be handled). This is coupled with the reality that at the time of the Movement, the Ma administration and the KMT majority had comparatively low legitimacy/favourability levels. Citizens were largely unhappy with the way Taiwan was being governed, both from an executive and a legislative point of view. This was not just a fraction or segment of discontent; rather, it was widespread. Governments in this situation are vulnerable, even to potentially undemocratic means and ends. Fortunately for the Ma administration, the citizens who contested their authority rooted themselves in democratic principles. In such "democratic deficit" situations, "[a] citizen may reasonably conclude, in such cases, that the policies in question do not reflect the will of any sovereign to which she belongs, in which case her individual sense of authorship of the collective decision will run out".[25] Indeed, this lack of authorship, in addition to the underhanded nature by which the agreement was handled, played an instrumental role in the Movement. Participants considered themselves to have no other option but to forcefully intervene in the democratic process.

(iv) *Defending democracy against "winner-take-all" politics*: The 30-second oversight-stopping showdown may have proven to be a strategic blunder on the part of the Ma administration, but it also epitomises the winner-take-all politics that has so far contaminated democratic governance in Taiwan. Regardless of what legitimate concerns the opposition, the affected interests, and/or the civil society may have over a given policy, those who rule – by winning elections – would implement their policy resolutely, uncompromisingly, and by whatever means they can get away with. This would arguably be the script for the controversy over the service trade agreement if not for the Sunflowers' intervention. After signing the agreement with China in June 2013, the Ma administration first sought a quick up-or-down vote on the whole pact in the Legislative Yuan. Even though the KMT Caucus later on had to make concessions on the holding of public hearings and an item-by-item review under public pressure, there was little doubt that the hearings would have no effect on the final outcome, and it would only be a matter of time before the Legislative Yuan passed the agreement in a party-line vote. The Sunflowers refused to recognise the democratic legitimacy of such winner-take-all governance, for it limits public participation to elections and leaves little room for compromise and deliberation. That the non-deliberative occupation of the Legislative Chamber was soon followed by such deliberative praxis as "deliberation on the street" further strengthens the democratic case for the Movement from a deliberative democratic perspective.[26] Conversely, President Ma and the KMT saw the obstruction of their electoral mandate, by both the opposition and the Sunflowers, as the biggest crisis for Taiwan's democracy.[27]

What happened, then, was an epic confrontation of two competing visions of Taiwan's democracy: one from the Ma administration and their legislative majority, and the other from the Movement. The former is characterised as being more cosmopolitan/pro-China, more receptive to the concentration of powers in the executive's hands, and viewing winner-take-all as the rightful implementation of the electoral mandate. The latter, by sharp contrast, is more patriotic, more critical of China and the neoliberalist economic order, and embraces increased checks and balances, public deliberation, and more consensual politics as to what separates democracy from electoral authoritarianism. While it remains a matter of debate under what circumstances such a confrontational contestation as exemplified by

25 Markovits (n. 2 above), p. 1927.

26 See, e.g. Amy Gutmann and Dennis Thompson, *Why Deliberative Democracy?* (Princeton: Princeton University Press, 2004) 51.

27 Chris Wang, "Crossing the Strait: Ma Slams Service Pact Critics, DPP in Interview" *Taipei Times* (27 June 2014), p. 3.

the Movement is justified in terms of democratic political morality,[28] it seems that the wider the differences between the competing visions of democracy, the more forceful and confrontational the democratic contestation may be.

Mid-game versus endgame

While the Sunflower Movement fiercely contested the democratic legitimacy of the Ma administration, it is important to remember that, in the end, the Sunflowers chose to return to life under the existing order of democracy in Taiwan. The Sunflowers sought democratic enhancement, not revolution.[29] As critical of the Ma administration and the current state of Taiwanese democracy as they were, the Sunflowers were keen to win over general public support by exercising self-restraint and moderation and by establishing themselves as vocal, but reasonable and pragmatic, dissidents. This ultimately led to their peaceful withdrawal from the Legislative Yuan and to the symbolic return of the gavel to its rightful place within the chamber. Similarly, even though the Ma administration vehemently disagreed with the Sunflower Movement, they too were constrained to operating within the bounds of democracy. Opinion polls showed the Movement contained strong support among the Taiwan populace.[30] Therefore, administration officials had to remain sensitive to the limits of their own actions with regard to the Movement, and thus paid homage to the dissenting voices within their democracy. Under these circumstances, the Sunflower Movement played itself out as a mid-game as opposed to an endgame. However fierce the confrontational contestation of the Movement was, democracy remains the only game in town and is arguably the most crucial, enabling as well as limiting rule for confrontational yet peaceful democratic contestation.

In sharp contrast, the Umbrella Movement in Hong Kong faced more significant obstacles, the most obvious being Hong Kong is officially under jurisdiction of the PRC and therefore has no functioning democracy to return to. It was therefore understandable that many pro-democracy activists in Hong Kong considered the Occupy Central/Umbrella Movement the endgame for their cause – democratising the nomination for the long-overdue popular election of the Chief Executive. Given the lack of democratic mid-game options in Hong Kong, the confrontation between Umbrella protesters and the Hong Kong Government (in conjunction with the PRC) was much more intense and more persistent than what occurred in Taiwan. As Victoria Tin-bor Hui observes, the 79-day protest run of the Umbrella Movement was fuelled in part by police brutality and thug violence

28 We did take into consideration whether there should be some kind of *ex ante* limiting principle for confrontational contestation, which goes one step further than contestation by means of typical disobedience. We would draw a bright line between confrontational contestation and armed conflicts (rebellion, insurrection, revolution, civil war, etc.) and would therefore consider confrontational contestation as something like "disobedience plus", the moral justifiability of which, like any form of civil/democratic disobedience, can only be determined on a case-by-case basis. With regard to the Sunflower Movement, and confrontational contestation in general, we believe that the most appropriate justification takes into consideration the totality of the circumstances with regard to the action taken. We leave open the question concerning the allocation of the burden of proof and certainly welcome all comments and inquiries on the matter.

29 Although some Sunflowers might have revolutionary aspirations, it is evident that the most radical and controversial move ever taken by the Sunflowers – that is, the occupation of the Executive Yuan – stayed within the bounds of non-violent disobedience.

30 See Opinion Poll by TVBS (n. 3 above).

which occurred under the watch of a recalcitrant Hong Kong administration, and in part by the insistence of the committed protesters who saw no option other than escalating their street protest.[31] To the extent that the Umbrella Movement in Hong Kong has achieved less than the Sunflower Movement in Taiwan in terms of public policy, it is only because winning an endgame *for* democracy is far more difficult than winning a mid-game *within* democracy.

Democratic compromise (or democratic peace)[32]

> The fundamental problem of human political life is how to address the tension between cooperation and competition: compromise is an essential element in relieving this tension.[33]

By striking the agreement with Legislative Speaker Wang Jin-Pyng to end the occupation of the legislature, the Sunflower Movement ultimately decided to operate within Taiwan's existing democratic order, however imperfect it may be. Although such a short-term agreement with the Speaker was indeed significant, we regard that as distinctly different from a potential democratic compromise not to indict the Sunflower Movement leaders and activists on the part of the Ma administration. Nevertheless, Taipei's district prosecutor indicted more than one hundred Sunflowers on 10 February 2015.[34] But the DPP won the 2016 presidential and parliamentary elections, and the first official decision Premier Lin Chuan (林全) made was for the government to drop charges against 126 Sunflowers involved in the Executive Yuan protests.[35] Citing the rationale of "promoting harmony and diffusing conflicts", this decision was surely a symbolic gesture by the new DPP Government. However, for legal reasons, not all charges were affected by this decision, and many Sunflower leaders still face legal action for incitement of illegal occupation.[36] Originally written before this development, this section has since become a counter-history to the events unfolding in Taiwan. While democratic peace may be achieved through many avenues, we hold that non-prosecution of all Sunflowers would have been the best way forward in this particular situation. Although the time for this option has past, we think the normative case we make here still holds and can serve as a distinct reminder of what the prosecutor has squandered through the far-reaching indictment.

For the first time in the history of Taiwan's democracy, the DPP won the presidency and a clear legislative majority in the January 2016 elections. When the newly elected legislature convened in February 2016, some Sunflowers found themselves returned to the chamber they once occupied, but this time with security credentials as members of the legislature or as legislative staff. When questioned by a DPP legislator in mid-March, however, Premier Simon Chang (張善政) of the outgoing KMT/Ma administration saw no need to

31 Victoria Tin-bor Hui, "The Protest and Beyond" (2015) 26(2) *Journal of Democracy* 111, 116.

32 We wavered between whether to call this a "compromise" or some type of political "reconciliation". In the end, we chose compromise, because we thought that the former is less demanding and therefore more realistic than the latter.

33 Avishai Margalit, *On Compromise: And Rotten Compromises* (Princeton: Princeton University Press, 2010) 38.

34 Jason Pan, "Prosecutors File Charges against 119 Sunflowers" *Taipei Times* (11 February 2015), p. 1. The number of those indicted was later increased to 126.

35 Stacey Hsu and Abraham Gerber, "Cabinet drops charges against students" *Taipei Times* (24 May 2016), p. 1.

36 Jason Pan, "Sunflower leaders to face justice system 'head-on'" *Taipei Times* (15 June 2016), p. 1.

drop the charges against the Sunflowers. As of summer 2016, the case against some leading Sunflowers, as noted above, is still pending in the Taipei District Court. Unlike an explicit democratic compromise as exemplified by the prosecutorial decision not to press charges against the Sunflowers, what Taiwan had experienced in the aftermath of the Sunflower occupation, until the February 2015 indictment, can be viewed as a de facto political ceasefire in which both sides refrained from making major moves that could have reignited conflict. With all deliberate speed, the Taipei District Court appeared to have convened only a few preparatory hearings and as of summer 2016 has yet to decide the case, thereby providing the impression that the court was either trying to stay away from public attention during an election year, or was trying to buy more time for the charges be dropped. Against this backdrop, this section explores the idea and possibility of democratic compromise, and proposes that Taiwan break the cycle of traditional disobedience theory by *not prosecuting* the Sunflower leaders, let alone their fellow participants. We argue that non-prosecution/dropping of charges on the part of the Ma administration could manoeuvre the temporary ceasefire into a democratic compromise, and as such, present the most promising way to achieve the ultimate democratic peace.[37]

Civil disobedience, more often than not, gets punished; this is especially true for prominent examples of civil disobedience, as governments often look to reinforce their authority and rule of law principles in the face of such behaviour. With the hopes of conquering the moral high ground, those participating in the disobedience often accept punishments as marks of credibility and moral integrity. This standard mechanism also swung into motion regarding the Movement: while Sunflowers exited the legislature peacefully and without any state action being administered, several Movement leaders voluntarily turned themselves into authorities shortly after the occupation ended. The leaders were then questioned by prosecutors and released. In a sense, however, the traditional punishment/moral authority cycle had been broken for some time, as what followed in the immediate aftermath of the Movement was a de facto political ceasefire. We argue that the Ma administration should go one step further, implementing a democratic compromise that would fully drop all charges against the Sunflowers. Doing so would allow for a more complete healing of both sides, and permit the democratic process (as opposed to the administrative or judicial branches, the traditional authorities in matters of disobedience) to adjudicate the democratic contestation initiated by the Movement.

Of course, strong cases can be made for and against prosecution of Movement participants. The government may argue, and indeed has publicly advanced the idea, that the Movement was anti-democratic and deserves to be punished for so thoroughly injecting themselves into the democratic process. As we saw above, however, the Sunflowers were widely supported among the citizenry and have even been categorised as a majoritarian uprising in some respects.[38]

Beyond this, however, the administration may be concerned that by accepting such a deal, governmental legitimacy could be undermined, as would long-standing "law and order" principles. From a governmental perspective, the Sunflowers clearly broke the law and should be punished (i.e. they deserve "justice" for their actions). After all, democratic governments are highly dependent on (perceived) legitimacy, and prosecuting those who violate the law is a hallmark of government authority, and ultimately, legitimacy.

37 Margalit (n. 33 above).
38 See n. 3 above.

If governments are unable to enforce their laws, then in some sense they have ceased to govern. Indeed, it may have been the case that the initial prosecution was used as a legitimating device, in order to legitimise the law and also legitimise the government of the day. The charges show, if anything, that the government is still in power and remains willing to uphold the law. However, in the Sunflower Movement context, the "rule of law" argument does not necessarily trump other moral and political considerations and thereby leave no room for compromise. Not prosecuting in this particular situation, we argue, can demonstrate to citizens that the government is responding in a legitimate, democratic manner to significant concerns raised by the populace.

Conversely, the Sunflowers believe that they were far from anti-democratic: in the wake of a highly questionable (if not unconstitutional) legislative manoeuvre, the Movement claims to have filled a democratic deficit by stopping an unruly and unpopular elected government. They halted a far-reaching, non-transparent economic agreement from being imposed on their citizenry and received relatively strong support while doing so. Additionally, while they occupied the Legislative Chamber, the Movement ultimately left the consequences of their actions to be judged within the current political system. Although the Sunflowers sought a radical change, of course, of Taiwan's cross-strait policy, they pressed for such change through democratic processes (including but not limited to the electoral and representative processes). A strong statement on this change and on the Sunflower actions, in general, was potentially made with the 2014 local elections, where the KMT got overwhelmed at the polls.[39] This strength continued into the January 2016 national elections, as the opposition DPP took control over the presidency and the national legislature.[40] The New Power Party (時代力量), which was formed by some leading Sunflowers in the summer of 2015, also won five legislative seats.[41] In this regard the coalition-based Movement has become more of a competitive rival than an anti-democratic opposition – an important distinction with regard to the making of a democratic compromise.

Avishai Margalit writes about sanguine compromise and the importance of recognising the other party's point of view. He stresses acting "for the sake of peace", which is distinct from acting "for the sake of justice", and notes that the Talmud (a Judaic text) contains three types of compromises:

- *compromise to neutralise hostility*
- *compromise to enhance harmony by reducing friction*
- *compromise to indicate to your rival that you recognise the force and the legitimacy of his claim, even if you could win in a trial.*[42]

This third element is distinctly important in the Sunflower Movement context and addresses the strong tension between cooperation and competition noted above. Many Sunflowers could probably be prosecuted and convicted for their actions, and this perspective remains the most obvious and traditional line of thinking under such circumstances.

39 Iok Sin Loa and Hsiu Chuan Shih, "KMT Trounced" *Taipei Times* (30 November 2014), http://www.taipeitimes.com/News/front/archives/2014/11/30/2003605650.

40 Austin Ramzy, "Tsai Ing-wen Elected President of Taiwan, First Woman to Hold Office" *New York Times* (16 January 2016), A6.

41 Abraham Gerber, "ELECTIONS: New Power Party wins five legislative seats" *Taipei Times* (17 January 2016), p. 5.

42 Margalit (n. 33 above), 41.

Conversely, the government could recognise the force and legitimacy of the Movement's claim, distinguishing them not as an anti-democratic opposition but as a competitive and legitimate rival that brought about convincing claims. Making such a distinction would likely move the Sunflowers outside the realm of any judicial retaliation, which would also benefit Taiwan's democracy. Although some may argue to go ahead and prosecute at least the Sunflower leaders and then pardon them upon conviction,[43] this scenario also presents significant problems. For one, there is an implicit revenge element, in that leaders would still be prosecuted and would have to endure the litigation. Additionally, and equally important, it would unnecessarily jeopardise the legitimacy of the judiciary, a branch of government the Taiwanese citizenry already regards as very distrustful. Indeed, the very nature of such a decision would be advocating democratic conflict, albeit within "the bounds of the law", as opposed to promoting democratic peace. To save the courts and Taiwan from being dragged into tortuous legal battles, the subsequent Tsai/DPP administration could still drop the charges after ascending to power (and that was what they did, as noted above, for at least some Sunflowers); but such a move would not be as meaningful as the democratic compromise we expected of the outgoing Ma administration.

A decision by the government *not* to prosecute would have been a grand democratic compromise that is best for Taiwan, and more importantly, is the optimal result for a stable and healthy democracy. Let us be clear: while Premier Lin's decision to drop the Executive Yuan protesters' charges was agreeable,[44] this was not the grand democratic compromise necessary for peace and stability in Taiwan that we envisioned. Standing up for "law and order" principles and governmental legitimacy is perfectly acceptable in certain contexts, but holding an uncompromising position in the face of future democratic unrest only serves to fuel democratic conflict. The latter position is unreasonable, especially for a government that just got badly beaten at the polls based in part on their position regarding the halted service trade agreement. A decision on whether to press/drop charges should not be delayed or dragged out any longer than it must be, considering "[a] process of compromise that involves undue pressure may encourage further polarization over time, weaken a democracy's capacity for cooperation, and make future compromises more difficult".[45] For the sake of democratic peace, the continuing litigation against lawbreaking Sunflowers has been "undue" and should have been dissolved.[46]

Although operating under different circumstances, the same goes for the Umbrella Movement leaders in Hong Kong. A democratic compromise (if it can be called so) in that situation would have been in the best interest of peace, as opposed to conflict, and the government should think hard about further prosecuting any members of the Movement. After all, Hong Kong citizens enjoy more freedoms than citizens of China in regard to

43 The Ma administration may argue, for instance, that "their hands are tied" with regard to the law and that prosecution of Movement leaders must go forward.

44 Hsu and Gerber (n. 35 above).

45 Amy Gutmann and Dennis Thompson, *Why Deliberative Democracy?* (Princeton: Princeton University Press, 2004), 46.

46 Even after the 10 February indictment, the law still provides an out for the prosecution in terms of making a democratic compromise. According to Article 269 of Taiwan's Criminal Procedure Act, the prosecutor may withdraw prosecution before the conclusion of the argument at the trial of the first instance, upon the prosecutorial finding that the indictment should not have been brought or it is appropriate not to prosecute. Although the calculus of whether to drop the prosecution involves further complications, we think our argument for democratic compromise can still factor in the consideration of whether non-prosecution is appropriate.

expression, demonstration, and assembly.[47] No compromise with regard to prosecutions would virtually guarantee further mass protests, disruption of the city's public transit areas, and deeper distrust of the current PRC and Hong Kong governments. In fact there are signs that such tensions may already be developing.[48] Surely the Hong Kong Government knew this. While such a compromise would not necessarily quell a movement that appears determined to one day vote in genuine democratic elections, it would potentially demonstrate that "rule of law" in Hong Kong, or at the very least some form of political compromise, is more than merely disingenuous rhetoric.

Historical lessons should not be ignored. Indeed, past events regarding clashes over differing governmental visions can sometimes help put things in perspective, especially with regard to the consequences of political compromise or the lack thereof. In 1641, the tension between Royalists and Parliamentarians in England was palpable. Royalists believed that the king ruled "by virtue of the divine right of kings", while Parliamentarians believed that sovereign powers were community-based and were "then represented by the King, Lords, and Commons working together".[49] King Charles's ousting of the "Short Parliament", which would not sanction the raising of funds to counter a Scottish rebellion, eventually led to the "Long Parliament" being summoned. One of the leaders of that parliament, John Pym, drafted a "Grand Remonstrance" which boldly outlined over 200 grievances against King Charles and his trusted advisers. From a historical perspective, it is now widely praised as a significantly influential civic protest and is commonly presented as a clash between the "will of the people" versus the hegemony of a monarchy. The Remonstrance passed the House of Commons by 11 votes on 22 November 1641. Yet, Charles did not respond to the petition until 23 December 1641. His response denounced the Remonstrance, but in a more measured and moderate tone than was his usual style. That moderate position did not last, however, and shortly thereafter Charles tried and disastrously failed to arrest and prosecute five Members of Parliament, including Pym. The failed attempt is recognised as one of the key events which led to the decade-long civil war that broke out shortly thereafter.[50]

Of course, the stakes of the Remonstrance compared to the Sunflower Movement actions – actual civil war versus political civil war – are distinctly different. While the Remonstrance is known as one of the most remarkable and significant protests against a monarch, the Sunflower Movement of March–April 2014 (and especially the occupation of the Legislative Yuan) could be categorised as one of the most audacious protests in a contemporary democracy. But while the Sunflower Movement story is still being written, the circumstances surrounding the Grand Remonstrance can potentially be looked to for lessons from its ending. While democratic compromises remain inherently difficult, and in particular circumstances may call into question the legitimacy of a sovereign authority, they are necessary elements to peace, and even more so, to democracy. An unwillingness to

47 Lo Pui-Yin, *The Judicial Construction of Hong Kong's Basic Law* (Hong Kong: Hong Kong University Press, 2014) 79–81, 85, 119–121. Although, such freedoms in Hong Kong are not absolute. The freedom of assembly, for instance, is subject to notification of the Police Commissioner, who has the power to deny the request (120–121).

48 "HK prosecutors charge 37 over Monday night's unrest" *Reuters/Taipei Times* (12 February 2016), p. 1.

49 Elizabeth Wicks, *The Evolution of a Constitution: Eight Key Moments in British Constitutional History* (Oxford: Hart, 2006) 7.

50 Ann Lyon, *Constitutional History of the United Kingdom* (London: Cavendish Publishing, 2003) 217–218.

engage in such agreements, and governments, democratic or not, may eventually crumble.

Conclusion

What the Sunflower Movement initiated, we argue, is an intensified and ongoing contestation for the very heart and soul of Taiwan's democracy. The *confrontational contestation* as signified by the Sunflowers' occupation is merely the beginning of this national soul-searching process, the outcome of which could ultimately decide what kind of democracy Taiwan ends up being. Although the *democratic compromise* we propose breaks with traditional notions of disobedience theory and governmental "responsibility", we believe such a compromise is the best way for Taiwan's democracy to move forward – by putting the ultimate judgement of the democratic contestation into the hands of the people.

2 The right to free assembly and the Sunflower Movement

Wen-Chen Chang[*]

Introduction

One of the major legal issues arising from the Sunflower Movement was the permissibility of "illegal" assemblies within and outside governmental buildings. Such unauthorised sit-ins are quite typical in the context of civil and political protests and have appeared in global citizen movements for causes ranging from political reform to social justice to anti-nuclear movements or to "Occupying Wall Street". Usually these activities – albeit non-violent – were found against the law, and the activists were imposed with administrative or criminal penalties.

Yet, staged for the expression of grave discontent with specific or broad governmental policies, these assemblies are also within the protected scope of free speech and stand at the core of civil and political rights in national constitutions or international human rights instruments. At the same time, however, no right is absolute. National constitutions and international human rights permit a wide range of restrictions to free assembly for the maintenance of public order (including, at times, road traffic). Still, there is no denying the paramount importance of free expression, particularly in the context of political and social movements that engage in non-violent sit-ins in order to express political grievances against the government.

In Taiwan, the past three decades have witnessed a significant transformation, from authoritarian government to a full-fledged constitutional democracy. Prior to lifting the Martial Law Decree in 1987, free associations or free assemblies were all banned. Yet, the fast-growing economic developments in the 1960s and 1970s produced a solid middle class that began to more freely express their political and social complaints against the government.[1] "Illegal" – and at times even violent – protests and demonstrations were staged frequently and often demanded large-scale reforms. Upon lifting the Martial Law Decree, the right to free assembly guaranteed in Art 14 of the Constitution was finally given recognition. The "Assembly and Parade Act Effective during the Period of National Mobilization for Suppression of the Communist Rebellion" was promulgated in January 1988 and was renamed – because of the suspension of national mobilisation for suppression of the communist rebellion in 1991 – as the Assembly and Parade Act in 1992.[2]

* Professor, College of Law, National Taiwan University, wenchenchang@ntu.edu.tw.

1 Wen-Chen Chang, "Public-Interest Litigation in Taiwan: Strategy for Law and Policy Reforms in Course of Democratization" in Po Jen Yap and Holning Lau, *Public Interest Litigation in Asia* (New York: Routledge, 2011) 136–160.

2 The "Temporary Provisions Effective during the Period of National Mobilization for Suppression of the Communist Rebellion" were promulgated in May 1948 in China and not abrogated until May 1991.

The right to assembly was further entrenched by the enactment of the International Covenant on Civil and Political Rights (ICCPR). In 2009, Taiwan's Government ratified the ICCPR and passed an Implementation Act to make the rights and freedoms enshrined in the ICCPR directly applicable to the domestic legal system.[3] Scholarly and judicial attention has since drawn comparisons between the right to assembly (guaranteed by Art 14 of the Taiwan Constitution) and the right to peaceful assembly (ensured in Art 21 of the ICCPR). Debates have arisen on which instrument provides for better protection and whether the Taiwan Constitutional Court should reconstruct its case law on free assembly in light of the ICCPR.

This chapter is thus aimed at discussing the issues surrounding those "illegal assemblies" during the Sunflower Movement on the basis of Taiwan's Constitution, constitutional interpretations, as well as the ICCPR. First it briefly describes the three main "illegal assemblies" that took place during the Sunflower Movement. Then it analyses the interpretations made by Taiwan's Constitutional Court regarding the protection of free assembly, followed by discussions on the right to peaceful assembly ensured in Art 21 of the ICCPR and the comparisons between the two. Then follows a discussion of the lawsuits – against the protesters and against the government – relating to the "illegal assemblies" of the Sunflower Movement and enquires into whether the ongoing processes of these lawsuits have been influenced by both constitutional and international rights of free assembly. The last section provides some concluding thoughts.

"Illegal" assemblies of the Sunflower Movement

The Sunflower Movement began with the occupation of the assembly hall in the Legislative Yuan by hundreds of students and citizens on 18 March 2014, and ended on 10 April, when students and citizens peacefully left the legislature to welcoming crowds of applause.

During this month-long period, three main "illegal" assemblies – the 3/18 occupation of the Legislative Yuan, the 3/23 occupation of the Executive Yuan, and the 4/11 crowd gathering at the police station – defied Taiwan's Assembly and Parade Act, thus characterising the "illegal" nature of the Sunflower Movement. These sit-ins or spontaneous crowd gatherings have led to a series of legal and constitutional challenges to the right of free assembly and revived a discourse on the importance of free assembly in sustaining a healthy democracy.

The 3/18 occupation of the Legislative Yuan

On 17 March, students and several citizen groups gathered at the entrance of the Legislative Yuan, anxiously awaiting the results of the promised clause-by-clause review of the Cross-Strait Trade in Services Agreement (Agreement). To their dismay, the presiding chair of the legislature's Internal Administrative Committee, then ruling party Kuomintang (KMT) legislator Chang Ching-chung (張慶忠), suddenly announced that the review of the Agreement at the committee stage was complete, and that the Agreement could be advanced to the legislative floor.

Such an announcement enraged the students and citizen groups waiting outside and rendered their efforts to halt the Agreement futile. Frustrated, some of the protesters

3 For a discussion on Taiwan's recent efforts in domestic incorporation of international human rights conventions, see Wen-Chen Chang, "An Isolated Nation with Global-Minded Citizens: Bottom-Up Transnational Constitutionalism in Taiwan" (2009) 4(3) *National Taiwan University Law Review* 203.

(a majority of whom were students) broke through the Legislative Yuan's barricades by 9 p.m. that evening and occupied the assembly hall in an attempt at stopping further legislative process of the Agreement. To secure their occupation, the students piled up desks, shelves, and chairs to block all the assembly hall entrances, successfully obstructing dispersal actions by the police. Meanwhile, to show support for those who were occupying the assembly hall, hundreds – at times even thousands – of students and citizens quickly flooded the surrounding areas and adjacent streets of the Legislative Yuan to stage peaceful sit-ins. The occupation inside and the sit-ins outside eventually lasted for twenty-four days, ending on 10 April, owing in part to the tolerance of KMT Speaker Wang Jin-pyng (王金平) and to the strong support of the then opposition, Democratic Progressive Party (DPP).

Although it ended peacefully, the actions of those involved in the occupation and sit-ins were deemed criminal. Such actions included: breaking the barricade; occupying the assembly hall; piling up desks, shelves, and chairs to block entrances and stop the police from dispersing involved criminal trespassing; damaging government property; and obstructing officers in charge of their duties. Sit-ins and public assemblies in the surrounding areas and adjacent streets, without obtaining prior authorisation, violated the Assembly and Parade Act, the leaders of which could be sentenced for up to two years.

The 3/23 occupation of the Executive Yuan

Having occupied the legislature for about a week, the students did not hear any government response to their demands. On 23 March, then President Ma Ying-jeou (馬英九) reiterated in a press conference the government's resolve to pass the Agreement. Later that night, a group of frustrated student protesters decided to occupy the Executive Yuan. Crowds flooded into the surrounding areas of the Executive Yuan and staged peaceful sit-ins to show support for those inside.

Fearing that these sit-ins might develop to a similar scale as those happening at the Legislative Yuan and in surrounding areas, the government ordered the police to forcefully disperse protesters both inside and outside the Executive Yuan. At dawn on 24 March, police officers armed with batons and shields were dispatched to evict protesters. Water cannons and baton strikes were used against non-violent protesters, many of whom were seriously wounded during the forceful evacuation. Journalists were also evicted and banned from any on-site reporting.

This incident has led to a number of subsequent legal actions. The protesters who entered the Executive Yuan were accused of trespassing, damaging government property, and obstructing officers in charge of duties. A few student protesters who demonstrated with loud speakers outside the Executive Yuan building were also accused of inciting unlawful activities. In addition, those individuals who suffered serious injuries from the forced dispersals by the police also decided to sue the government. With the assistance of volunteer attorneys, they filed lawsuits against the government officials that made the dispersal orders, including then President Ma Ying-jeou and the President of the Executive Yuan, Premier Jiang Yi-huah (江宜樺) along with a few police chiefs, on charges of attempted murder and personal injury.

The 4/11 crowd gathering at the police station

Although the occupation of the Legislative Yuan ended on 10 April, a few citizen groups refused to leave, including the Alliance of Referendum for Taiwan, which continued to rally outside the legislature. In fact, even before the Sunflower Movement's formation, the Alliance of Referendum for Taiwan had already staged sit-ins outside the Legislative Yuan with a permit they obtained for their outdoor assemblies pursuant to the Assembly and Parade Act.

However, due to their joining the legislative occupation, the Alliance of Referendum for Taiwan was accused of staging illegal assemblies and obstructing officers in charge of their duties. Their assembly permit was thus suspended, and the police in charge of issuing their permit, the Chongcheng First Precinct police office, even publicly announced that the office would not issue any future permits to the Alliance for public assemblies. This announcement was quickly spread over the Internet, infuriating not only the Alliance but also many citizens and social groups. On 11 April, huge crowds – without any organising efforts or leadership – quickly gathered around the Chongcheng First Precinct police office building to protest against such a permanent ban on the Alliance's outdoor assemblies. Among the protesters, a few individuals stood out to help keep the crowd in order. One graduate student of National Taiwan University who shouted slogans with a loudspeaker was quickly accused of being the chief leader for the "illegal" assembly, and of obstructing public officers in charge of their duties.

In all of these incidents surrounding the Sunflower Movement, the role of public assemblies and the right to free assembly and free speech were pivotal. Whether citizens gathering around government buildings without obtaining permits were obstructing public order or merely exercising their right to free assembly was heatedly debated. The former view unsurprisingly deemed the Sunflower Movement and the surrounding activities illegal, while the latter saw it as civic engagement in public and constitutional discourse.[4]

Constitutional right to free assembly

In Taiwan, Art 14 of the Constitution guarantees that "the people shall have the freedom of assembly and association".[5] According to Art 23 of the Constitution, this freedom of assembly and association "shall not be restricted by law, except by such as may be necessary to prevent infringement upon the freedoms of other persons, to avert an imminent crisis, to maintain social order or to advance public welfare".[6] As mentioned above, the Assembly and Parade Act was promulgated in 1988 and was renamed in 1992. Even though enacted in the wake of political liberalisation and democratisation, the Act nevertheless imposed quite extensive restrictions to the free exercise of outdoor assembly and parade.

A permit system was created under the Assembly and Parade Act. Those who sought to hold an outdoor assembly or parade must first apply for a permit issued by the police, who were given a wide range of discretion regarding issuance or denial. A flat ban was imposed on assemblies or parades advocating communism or secession of territory.[7] Once an unauthorised outdoor assembly or parade was held, the police had the discretion to warn, stop,

4 See Jiunn-rong Yeh, "Marching Towards Civic Constitutionalism with Sunflowers", Chapter 3.

5 Constitution of the Republic of China (1947), Art 14.

6 Ibid., Art 23.

7 The previous Art 11, s 1 of Assembly and Parade Act provides: "Applications for outdoor assemblies or parades shall be approved except for one of the following conditions: 1. Violating the provision of Article 4, Article 6 or Article 10." Assembly and Parade Act (1988), Art 11, s 1. Art 4, Assembly and Parade Act provides: "Communism or secession shall not be asserted in any assembly or parade." Ibid., Art 4.

or disperse any unauthorised activity.[8] When an unauthorised outdoor assembly or parade failed to disperse after three dispersal order warnings from the police, the chief leader/s of such outdoor assemblies or parades could be criminally punished for up to two years in jail.[9] This harsh and restrictive nature of the Assembly and Parade Act has been strongly criticised. In the late 1980s and early 1990s, many social activists and political dissidents were penalised merely for holding unauthorised outdoor assemblies or parades of a social or political nature.

JY Interpretation No. 445

In 1993 a group of environmental activists, including university professors and students, sought to block a road to prevent solid waste dumping across Taipei city and county lines. However, their application for an outdoor assembly permit was denied. Nevertheless, the group blocked the road in protest, and three chief leaders were convicted, with criminal punishments imposed on all three.[10] Arguing that the permit system was unconstitutionally violating their right to free assembly, these environmental activists petitioned the Constitutional Court. In January 1998, the Constitutional Court rendered Judicial Yuan (JY) Interpretation No. 445, thus invalidating a few provisions in the Assembly and Parade Act, but maintaining the permit system and criminal sanctions.

i. The distinction between content-based and content-neutral control

In JY Interpretation No. 445, the Constitutional Court stresses the importance of a constitutional right to free assembly. In view of the Constitutional Court, "the freedom of assembly is mainly a form of freedom of speech exercised by the people through action", and "for the general public who do not have easy access to the media, the freedom of assembly is an important means to express their opinions openly".[11] Having defined the freedom of assembly as "a collective expression of opinions" and "a means of communication between the people and the government", the Constitutional Court derives the guarantee of free assembly from the principle of popular sovereignty, in that "the people may take the initiative in offering their opinions to the government, thus participating in the formation of the State's will or influencing the policy-making process".[12] Hence the government should not "only passively protect freedom of assembly and not interfere with it, but also actively provide appropriate places for assembly and protect the safety of assemblies and parades so as to facilitate their smooth proceeding".[13] In other words, there is a constitutional duty for the government to ensure that those participating in an assembly or parade can proceed without fear.[14]

8 Ibid., Art 15.
9 Ibid., Art 29.
10 83 Shang Yi Decision No. 5278 (Taiwan High Court). The three chief leaders, Cheng Yen Kao, Zhen Xiu Chang, and Mao Nan Cheng staged the protest primarily against the illegal soil disposal conducted by the Taipei City Government.
11 JY Interpretation No. 445 (1998), Reasoning, para 8.
12 Ibid.
13 Ibid.
14 Ibid.

Based upon the paramount nature of the right to free assembly, the Constitutional Court decided to invalidate the flat ban on assemblies or parades that advocate communism or secession of territory.[15] It is interesting to note that the petitioners in this case were engaged in an environmental – but not political – protest, but the Constitutional Court nevertheless felt the need to review all relevant provisions in the Assembly and Parade Act, arguing that the function of constitutional review is "not only to protect the fundamental rights of the parties concerned, but also to elaborate on the genuine intent of the Constitution so as to safeguard the constitutional order", and thus "the scope of interpretation may, of course, so extend as to review the constitutionality of the provisions of law relevant and necessary to a specific case".[16]

In the Court's view, a flat ban on assemblies or parades advocating communism or secession of territory "is tantamount to prohibiting the assembly or parade merely for its advocacy" and empowers the police to "conduct a substantive review of the contents of the speech prior to the assembly or parade".[17] Here, a distinction between content-based and content-neutral controls over outdoor assembly and parade was made. While no reference to American free speech jurisprudence was noted, it is widely believed that such influence was evident.[18]

ii. Constitutionality of the permit system

Considering the content-based and content-neutral distinctions, the Constitutional Court came to justify the permit system on content-neutral grounds. In their view, it is entirely within the scope of legislative discretion to adopt a permit system so long as the issuance – or denial – of a permit is made solely on content-neutral grounds, such as time, space, or the manner of outdoor assemblies or parades, that are clearly prescribed by law and are necessary for the maintenance of social order and the advancement of public welfare.[19] If content-neutral conditions under which a permit is issued or denied are clearly stipulated by law and are met with the principle of proportionality, as well as with the principle of clarity and certainty of law, a permit system is constitutionally justified.

Having justified the permit system, the Constitutional Court reviewed one-by-one those content-neutral grounds stipulated in the Assembly and Parade Act, finding only Art 11(2) and 11(3) in violation of the principle of legal clarity and certainty. The impugned provisions providing that a permit should be denied if "there are facts showing the likelihood that national security, social order or public welfare will be jeopardized", or "there is the likelihood that public safety or freedom will be jeopardized, or there will be serious damage to property", were neither specific nor clear enough.[20] The Court decided that the future possibility of occurrence in any public danger cannot serve as a sufficient basis to deny a permit. Instead, there must be "a factual showing of clear and present danger" for the right to free assembly to be restricted.[21]

15 Ibid., Holding, para 2.
16 Ibid., Reasoning, para 8.
17 Ibid., Reasoning, para 11.
18 Wen-Chen Chang and Jiunn-rong Yeh, "Judges as Discursive Agent: The Use of Foreign Precedents by the Constitutional Court of Taiwan" in Tania Groppi and Marie C. Ponthoreau (eds), *The Use of Foreign Precedents by Constitutional Judges* (Oxford: Hart Publishing, 2013) 373–392.
19 JY Interpretation No. 445 (1998), Reasoning, para 9.
20 Ibid., Holding, para 3.
21 Ibid., Holding, para 3.

Under the permit system, those who intend to hold an outdoor assembly or parade must apply for a permit six days prior to the event. The period of six days was shortened to two days in case of urgent events due to natural disasters or any other unforeseeable incidents. However, the Court ruled that such an expedited review was still not enough. Because "denying an application for an incidental assembly or parade that is not filed two days prior to such assembly or parade is in violation of the constitutional intention of protecting the people's freedom of assembly", the Court decided to request a prompt and speedy review and revision by the legislature on the said provision.[22]

iii. Constitutionality of criminal sanction

The harshest aspects of the Assembly and Parade Act are the criminal sanctions imposed on the chief leaders holding an unauthorised outdoor assembly or parade that fails to disperse upon the police's third dispersal order.[23] The Constitutional Court, however, stresses that similar to the adoption of a permit system, the imposition of criminal responsibility on those leaders who disobey dispersal orders falls squarely within the scope of legislative discretion.[24]

To justify criminal sanctions, the Constitutional Court argues that such measures are necessary to the maintenance of public order[25] and that they are not disproportionate, because the police may exercise discretion as to whether to warn or to issue dispersal orders.[26] Only when a dispersal order is issued three times may the chief leaders in an unauthorised event be criminally sanctioned. In other words, not all unauthorised outdoor assemblies or parades are issued with dispersal orders, and neither are dispersal orders always issued three times. Consequently, not all chief leaders engaging in such unauthorised events may be criminally convicted. The Court also reminds criminal courts that "in weighing the offense and imposing a penalty", they "should make a precise determination as to whether the requisite elements of the criminal act are met" and "attention should also be paid to the existence of intent, especially, as a requisite element for the punishment of the act at issue".[27] Thus, the justices have ruled that criminal sanctions are not unduly harsh when all relevant considerations are taken and if discretion is appropriately exercised.

iv. Legal uncertainties facing illegal assemblies

Discretionary powers accorded to the police when issuing warnings or dispersal orders against unauthorised assemblies are quite paradoxical. From one perspective, including that of the Constitutional Court, police discretion is used to mitigate the harshness of criminal sanctions, so that not all chief leaders engaging in unauthorised outdoor assemblies or

22 Ibid., Holding, para 3.

23 Assembly and Parade Act, Art 29.

24 JY Interpretation No. 445 (1998), Holding, para 4.

25 "The reason to subject the chief violator to a punishment of imprisonment … is to punish his or her repeated refusal to obey the disbursal and restraining order. If the competent authority does not enforce it, not only will it pose unforeseeable danger to other people or public order, but the competent authority will not be in a position to take necessary action pursuant to the applicable provisions of the Code of Criminal Procedure." Ibid., Reasoning, para 17.

26 Ibid., para 17.

27 Ibid.

parades may face criminal prosecution.[28] Additionally, Art 26 of the Assembly and Parade Act also expressly requires that the denial of a permit or the issuance of a dispersal order must be made in accordance with the principle of proportionality (which must not be overly excessive), and based around due consideration for balance between the right of free assembly and other public interests. From another perspective, discretionary powers may be exercised in arbitral, unfair, or even manipulative fashion to favour one specific group over another and to substantially interfere with freedom of expression or even with contentious politics.

As scholars have demonstrated, selective prosecutions continue to exist.[29] The most well-known examples of selective ***non-prosecution*** are the two unauthorised protests against former President Chen Shui-Bian (陳水扁): one was held in 2004 challenging the result of the presidential election and the gunshot incident that took place prior to the election; and the other was held in 2006 by the Red-Shirt protesters demanding Chen's resignation upon corruption charges. At both events, Taipei Mayor Ma Ying-Jeou, then a presidential hopeful, decided to tolerate the two-month-long assemblies in front of the presidential office. Rather than issuing dispersal orders, the Taipei city police merely gave warnings against these two unauthorised assemblies. As a result, in both cases, no chief leaders faced any criminal prosecution. Leaders of other unauthorised outdoor assemblies or parades, however, were not as lucky. The students protesting against the increase in tuition fees in front of the Ministry of Education were convicted,[30] as have been labour union members, evicted residents, environmental activists, and many others.[31]

JY Interpretation No. 718

JY Interpretation No. 445 in 1998 was praised for unequivocally recognising the paramount function of free assemblies in a democratic society, and invalidating content-based controls over the holding of any outdoor assemblies or parades. At the same time, however, it was also heavily criticised, because it maintained the permit system and possible criminal sanctions, which provide extensive discretionary powers to the police.

Almost two decades have passed since JY Interpretation No. 445 was decided in 1998, and Taiwan has continued to witness various social and political protests as a vibrant civil society has evolved.[32] Also noteworthy were the changes in the government leadership in 2000 (from KMT to DPP) and 2008 (from DPP to KMT). The KMT's policy to develop closer ties with China has stirred confrontation not only in the parliament but also on the streets. In November 2008, because of a visit by Chen Yun-Lin (陳雲林), the top Chinese negotiator, various protests took place (including one staged by students and university professors). These developed into what was called the Wild Strawberry Movement. Regrettably, the lead university professor engaged in peaceful sits-ins before the executive

28 Ibid.

29 See Ching Yi Liu, "The Unfulfilled Promise of Human Rights Protection: An Analysis of Freedom of Speech and Freedom of Assembly and Parade in Taiwan's Democratic Transition" (2009) 6(3) *Taiwan Democracy Quarterly* 1, 5, 27–28 (in Chinese).

30 95 Shang Yi Decision No. 1336 (Taiwan High Court).

31 Ibid.

32 See Yeh (n. 4 above).

office was once again criminally charged through the Assembly and Parade Act.[33] The judge presiding over the case decided to petition the Constitutional Court, requesting reconsideration of the constitutionality of the Assembly and Parade Act. Additionally, a student who was criminally convicted because of an unauthorised (peaceful) protest against tuition increases in front of the Ministry of Education also filed a petition. Amidst the events surrounding the Sunflower Movement, the Constitutional Court rendered JY Interpretation No. 718 on 21 March 2014.[34]

i. Maintenance of the permit system with criminal sanctions

Although there was strong criticism of the permit system, a majority of the Constitutional Court maintained that the adoption of such a system was squarely within the legislature's discretion.[35] In its view, a permit system provides the police timely and sufficient information so that they can be better prepared to protect those engaging in outdoor assemblies or parades, while also maintaining public order.[36] Moreover, the concurring opinion by Grand Justice Su Yeong-Chin (蘇永欽) stressed that there was no need for reconsideration on the constitutionality of the Assembly and Parade Act, since there was no significant change in the social or political fabric, and all relevant considerations had been made in JY Interpretation No. 445.

The dissenting opinion by Grand Justice Li Chen-Shan (李震山), together with three other justices, expressed a very different view. Having understood the right to free assembly as a core fundamental right, the dissenting justices insisted that a permit system is in its nature overly restrictive to the exercise of free assembly. Only a system of notification or reporting can survive scrutiny under the principle of proportionality. A few international and comparative references were made to support this position. In the dissent's view, the contrast between a permit system and a reporting system is stark: approvals are exceptions in a permit system whereas denials are exceptions in a reporting system. Because the exercise of free assembly should be approved rather than denied, a permit system should be rejected. The dissenting opinion also notes serious problems in the discretionary powers accorded to the police. Such discretion often leads to questionable law enforcement decisions, and even worse, may induce chilling effects on certain kinds of speech and overly interfere with freedom of expression. Nevertheless, the imposition of criminal sanctions was sustained without reconsideration. Strong dissents, however, expressed significant concerns. For example, in the concurring-in-part opinion, Grand Justice Tsai Ching-Yu (蔡清遊) referred to German jurisprudence, arguing that such criminal sanctions would be held as contradictory to proportionality.

ii. Permit exceptions for urgent or spontaneous assemblies

The only issues dealt with in JY Interpretation No. 718 surround the constitutionality of Arts 8(1), 9(2), and 12(2) of the Assembly and Parade Act regarding the application for permits in urgent and spontaneous outdoor assemblies and parades. As mentioned above,

33 98 Yi Decision No. 1707 (Taipei District Court).

34 JY Interpretation No. 718 (2014). English translation is available at http://www.judicial.gov.tw/constitutionalcourt/EN/p03_01.asp?expno=718.

35 JY Interpretation No. 718 (2014), Reasoning, para 2.

36 Ibid., Reasoning, para 2.

JY Interpretation No. 445 concerns with the requirement of obtaining a permit two days prior to an urgent assembly or parade due to natural disasters or other similar incidents.[37] This time, in JY Interpretation No. 718, the majority opinion decided to exempt permits from such urgent and spontaneous events.

In the Constitutional Court's view,

> it is unlikely that urgent assemblies and demonstrations which result from an urgent need and which cannot achieve their purpose unless they are held immediately, can be held only after obtaining approval. In addition, for incidental assemblies and demonstrations where a crowd gathers without prior convention due to special causes, and where there is in fact no convener or responsible person, it is not possible to apply for approval or make a report in advance.[38]

Consequently, the Court found such requirements contradictory to the proportionality principle and therefore overly restrictive, ultimately deciding the provision should lose effect from 1 January 2015.[39]

Remaining challenges

Although there have been two significant constitutional interpretations regarding it, strong criticisms against the Assembly and Parade Act remain. Most problematic is the broad discretionary power given to the police in issuing warnings or dispersal orders when confronted with unauthorised outdoor assemblies or parades. Because the imposition of criminal sanctions is conditioned upon the failure of compliance with dispersal orders, it is the police that may wield unparalleled powers to determine the legal consequences of any unauthorised outdoor assemblies or parades. Any unfair, arbitrary, or selective exercise of such discretionary power is a grave interference with the freedom of expression, not to mention its potential chilling effects.

There are additional concerns with criminal sanctions. In exercising the right to free assembly, individuals should not be intimidated by legal uncertainty or criminal sanctions. Some have long advocated for the imposition of administrative fines instead of criminal sanctions. Even the imposition of administrative fines must be cautiously considered, so as not to imply that the wealthy may speak "louder" than others. After all, as is well understood by Taiwan's Constitutional Court, the right to assembly is especially important for ordinary individuals who do not have easy access to the media or the government.

Another highly debated issue is whether the constitutional right to assembly should be construed in conjunction with the ICCPR. This issue was brought up in separate opinions regarding JY Interpretation No. 718 by Grand Justices Li Chen-Shan and Dennis Tang (湯德宗). The right to peaceful assembly as enshrined in Art 21 of the ICCPR is believed to provide better protections than the right to assembly thus construed by the Constitutional Court. As long as outdoor assemblies or parades remain peaceful, any restrictions should be placed under strict scrutiny and only for very substantial government interests.

37 JY Interpretation No. 445 (1998), Holding, para 3.
38 JY Interpretation No. 718 (2014), Reasoning, para 2.
39 JY Interpretation No. 718 (2014), Holding.

The ICCPR's right to peaceful assembly

The right to assembly facilitates the expression of opinions and encourages dialogue among the civil society, political representatives, and the government.[40] Given its indispensable democratic functions in the course of producing and developing political opinions,[41] the right to assembly is recognised as a core human right enshrined in Art 21 of the ICCPR. The following discusses the protected scope and limitations of the right to assembly as provided in the ICCPR and the obligations of states to guarantee such a right.

Protection of peaceful assembly

Art 21 of the ICCPR recognises the right of peaceful assembly, which is closely linked to the right of free speech and can be understood as one of its institutional forms.[42] The guarantee of the right of peaceful assembly includes both intentional and temporary assemblies staged for various purposes.[43] The protection covers both the preparation and conduct of a peaceful assembly by organisers and participants.[44] While the right to peaceful assembly is essential and fundamental, it is not considered absolute. Art 21 of the ICCPR guarantees only the right to *peaceful* assembly.[45] Here, "peaceful" is determined through the actions of participants in the assembly, not by the opinions expressed.[46] "Civil disobedience", which involves non-violent action or peaceful demonstration, is usually protected by Art 21.[47]

If participants in the assembly are armed, such an assembly immediately loses its peaceful nature, even if weapons are not used.[48] Thus, an assembly containing violence in any form loses its legal protection under Art 21 of the ICCPR. Notably, state parties have discretionary powers to prohibit or dissolve violent assemblies; however, this does not mean that state parties may waive human rights obligations in dealing with violent assemblies. For example, the Human Rights Committee, in its concluding observations with regard to Denmark, expressed concern with the use of dogs by police in dealing with a violent assembly.[49]

Public assemblies are usually held against the government or the interests of other power holders. Given their very nature, it is even more important to demand that the government fully guarantees a right of peaceful assembly so that citizens may publicly express their opinions without fear, and thus the development of democracy may be sustained. It is therefore not surprising that the ICCPR requires state parties to fully and effectively implement the right to peaceful assembly.[50]

40 OSCE Office for Democratic Institutions and Human Rights (ODIHR), "Guidelines on Freedom of Peaceful Assembly" (2nd, OSCE Office for Democratic Institutions and Human Rights, 2010) 23–24.
41 Manfred Nowak, "UN Covenant on Civil and Political Rights: CCPR Commentary" (2nd, N.P. Engel, 2005) 481.
42 Ibid., p. 485.
43 Ibid., p. 484.
44 Ibid., p. 483.
45 Ibid., p. 486.
46 Ibid.
47 Ibid., p. 487.
48 Ibid.
49 Sarah Joseph and Melissa Castan, *The International Covenant on Civil and Political Rights: Cases, Materials, and Commentary* (Oxford: Oxford University Press, 2013) 646.
50 Nowak (n. 41 above), p. 482.

State obligations to freedom of assembly

Art 2 of the ICCPR acknowledges the duty of state parties to protect all rights. This means the state parties should ensure that all individuals can enjoy the rights enshrined in the ICCPR without any discrimination, and further requires state parties to take measures to provide effective remedies to any person whose rights or freedoms are infringed.[51] According to General Comment No. 31 of the Human Rights Committee, the obligations under Art 2 of the ICCPR are binding on all branches and at all levels of government.[52] Additionally, the Human Rights Committee requires that state parties have a duty to establish appropriate and effective judicial and administrative mechanisms for addressing human rights violations within the domestic legal system. It also obligates state parties to investigate allegations of human rights violations and provide an effective remedy to victims whose rights are violated. Since the overarching purpose of Art 2 is to provide the most effective realisation of all recognised rights in national systems,[53] there is no doubt that such state obligations also apply to the right to peaceful assembly, recognised as a core human right in the ICCPR.

Similar to Art 2, Art 21 also obligates state parties to "recognize" the right to peaceful assemblies with positive measures.[54] The phrase "must recognize" in Art 21 conveys a positive duty to protect peaceful assemblies and regulate violent ones. It also suggests that the states take positive measures to guarantee peaceful assemblies, free from interference by state authorities or by private individuals.[55] Such positive measures may vary in form and are subject to further stipulation by domestic statutes. These measures may include route or traffic control, appropriate police protection through the ban on counter-assembly to avoid conflict, a requirement not to discriminate against certain assemblies by denying them access to public buildings, and other measures aimed at facilitating the peaceful and orderly gathering of individuals.[56]

Permissible restrictions to peaceful assembly

Although it is recognised as a core human right, the right to peaceful assembly is not absolute and may be restricted under conditions set by the ICCPR. First, Art 4 of the ICCPR permits state parties to derogate from their obligations of guaranteeing the right to peaceful assembly in times of war or a public emergency threatening the life of the nation. Nevertheless, restrictive measures taken by state parties are not allowed to be inconsistent with their other obligations under international law.[57] Additionally, Art 21 of the ICCPR permits restrictions to the right of peaceful assembly as long as they are: 1) in conformity with the law, and 2) necessary in a democratic society to accomplish one of the following purposes: national security, public safety, public order (*ordre public*), the protection of public health or morals, or the protection of rights and freedoms of others. These limits

51 ICCPR, Art 2.

52 General Comment No. 31, para 4.

53 Anja Seibert-Fohr, "Domestic Implementation of the International Covenant on Civil and Political Rights Pursuant to Its Article 2 Para. 2" (2001) 5 *Max Planck Yearbook of United Nations Law* 399425.

54 Nowak (n. 41 above), pp. 383–384.

55 Ibid., p 487.

56 Ibid., p. 488.

57 General Comment No. 28, para 9.

must not be used to undermine the right to peaceful assembly as a fundamental civil and political right that facilitates democratic governance.[58] The limitations must be restrictively interpreted and given all due consideration regarding the realisation of such a right.[59]

The first limitation in Art 21 of the ICCPR is "conformity with the law". This term allows the state parties, through statutory authorisation, to regulate assemblies (e.g. such as the requirement of prior notification).[60] The police or other competent authorities may disperse public assemblies that produce a threat to public order or public safety on the ground of statutory authorisation.[61]

The second restriction to peaceful assembly is "necessary in a democratic society in the interests of national security or public safety, public order (*ordre public*), the protection of public health or morals or the protection of the rights and freedoms of others". Many jurisdictions have relied upon the principle of proportionality in deciding whether restrictions made to the right of peaceful assembly are within the definition of necessity in a democratic society. The dispersal of a peaceful assembly by armed force is the final means to be undertaken when all others fail.[62] In addition to the principle of proportionality, restrictions to the right of assembly should also be consistent with a minimum democratic standard.[63] The European Court of Human Rights in *Handyside v. The United Kingdom* developed the elements of a "democratic society" to include pluralism, tolerance, and broadmindedness.[64] These elements are essential to democracy and are closely associated with the principle of popular sovereignty, upon which the guarantee of right to assembly is premised.[65]

Additionally, the national security limitation is only allowed in situations of political or military danger against the protection of territorial integrity or political independence against foreign forces or threats of force. This limitation may deprive the right of members in a peaceful assembly to overthrow the government, and under such circumstances the imposition of criminal sanctions to those participants is permitted.[66] Public safety allows states to disrupt or dissolve assemblies that threaten the safety of either those assembling or other citizens.[67] The protection of public safety is usually linked to the protection of public order. In a very broad sense, public order (*ordre public*) includes the maintenance of the order in the street and the functioning of the state organisations,[68] which not only allows state parties to maintain order within its territory but also ensures the common welfare by satisfying the collective needs of citizens. Public health and public morals may also serve as grounds for restrictions to peaceful assembly. For example, assemblies may be prohibited on grounds of public morals or protections to the natural environment.[69]

58 Nowak (n. 41 above), p. 488.
59 Ibid.
60 Joseph and Castan (n. 48 above), p. 647.
61 Nowak (n. 41 above), p. 490.
62 Ibid., p. 491.
63 Ibid.
64 *Handyside v. The United Kingdom*, European Court of Human Rights, Application no. 5493/72 [49] (1976).
65 Nowak (n. 41 above), p. 491.
66 Alexandre Charles Kiss, "Permissible Limitations on Rights" in Louis Henkin (ed.), *International Bill of Rights: International Covenant on Civil and Political Rights* (Columbia: Columbia University Press, 1981) 297.
67 Nowak (n. 41 above), p. 492.
68 Ibid., p. 493.
69 Ibid.

The right to peaceful assembly is also subject to the protection of the rights and freedoms of others, particularly the protection of private rights. Hence, the opening up of privately owned buildings served for public purposes – such as shopping malls or privately owned parks – usually requires sensitive consideration.[70] Yet, given the state's positive obligation to realise the right of peaceful assembly, the state parties must – without discrimination – make public spaces available specifically for assemblies and facilitate the reasonable use of parks and other open spaces.[71]

Comparisons and critiques

Compared to the constitutional jurisprudence on the right to assembly developed by Taiwan's Constitutional Court, the ICCPR jurisprudence on the right of peaceful assembly presents some similarities, but also marked differences. In terms of similarities, both require that restrictive measures undertaken against the right of assembly to be stipulated by statute, and also be proportional to a set of stipulated purposes. There are, however, a number of marked differences between the two.

Comparisons: Restrictive purpose, permit system, and criminal sanction

First, on the restrictions placed against the right of assembly, Art 21 of the ICCPR expressly requires a further consideration: restrictions must be necessary in a democratic society. Given the paramount function of the right to assembly in the expression of public opinion and the facilitation of democracy, ICCPR jurisprudence demands that restrictions to the right of assembly must be as strictly and narrowly construed as possible. In contrast, having relied on the content-based and content-neutral distinction, Taiwan's Constitutional Court has not exercised judicial scrutiny as stringently as other ICCPR jurisprudence. Although content-based controls are not permitted, content-neutral restrictions are left entirely for legislative discretion. It is due to this far less stringent scrutiny that Taiwan's Constitutional Court has easily come to justify the adoption of a permit system,[72] and recognised the imposition of criminal sanctions for merely holding an unauthorised assembly.

The second marked difference is on the adoption of a permit system. Art 21 of the ICCPR does allow the state parties through statutory authorisation to adopt various forms of regulation on public assemblies, which does not pre-empt the use of a permit system. This has been made to accommodate various political and social contexts of the state parties. At the same time, however, the United Nations Special Rapporteur Report on Peaceful Assemblies and Associations – along with international human rights jurisprudence on peaceful assembly – does urge states to adopt a reporting, but not permit, system, and demands that restrictive measures be crafted as narrowly as possible.[73] The problem with a permit system is the discretionary power accorded to the police. As is evident in Taiwan, the exercise of such discretionary power – which is nevertheless required by law to be proportional and not arbitrary – has been selective, politically manipulative, and prone

70 Ibid., p. 494.

71 Ibid.

72 For similar criticism, see the concurring opinion, Grand Justice Denis Tang, JY Interpretation No. 718.

73 OSCE Office for Democratic Institutions and Human Rights (ODIHR) (n. 39 above). See also the dissenting opinions, Grand Justice Li Chen-Shan, JY Interpretation No. 718.

to contentious politics. In March 2013, a group of international experts invited to independently review Taiwan's initial state report on the ICCPR expressed the same concern over the selective enforcement of the Assembly and Parade Act, advising the government to adopt a reporting system and to substantially reduce the discretionary powers exercised by the police.[74]

The last key aspect of comparison is on the imposition of criminal sanctions. As analysed above, the ICCPR ensures the right of *peaceful* assembly, and thus no criminal sanctions are to be imposed on the leaders or participants of peaceful assemblies, unless they are attempting to overthrow the government or engage in violent activities.[75] Evidently, the imposition of criminal sanctions is excessive and disproportional to an act of merely holding a peaceful – albeit unauthorised – public assembly or parade. The Taiwanese Constitutional Court clearly erred in JY Interpretation Nos. 445 and 718, leaving the imposition of criminal sanctions entirely to legislative discretion. The key point lies in the right of *peaceful* assembly. So long as the assemblies are of a *peaceful* nature, the right to hold such assemblies should be accorded with paramount importance in order to guarantee core democratic human rights. Art 14 of Taiwan's Constitution guarantees the freedom of assembly without distinction as to the nature of assemblies. What should be distinguished here is not between "authorised or unauthorised" assemblies but between "peaceful or violent" assemblies. Restrictions to any peaceful assembly, without authorisation, should still face the most stringent judicial scrutiny.

Critiques

Overall, the comparisons above show that ICCPR jurisprudence on the right of peaceful assembly does entail stronger guarantees and better protections. As urged by the concurring and dissenting opinions in JY Interpretation No. 718,[76] Taiwan's Constitutional Court should incorporate the ICCPR jurisprudence into its constitutional interpretations, in order to provide for more exacting judicial scrutiny on the restrictions to the right of assembly in the Assembly and Parade Act.

The ICCPR jurisprudence on the right of peaceful assembly, however, is not entirely without criticism. First, as the right of peaceful assembly is a derogable right, it may be restricted in times of war or public emergencies that threaten the life of a nation. Yet, derogation is easily manipulated, as governments usually prohibit the holding of assemblies or parades because of public emergencies or national security concerns. These grounds must be narrowly construed, and if public assemblies are of purely a peaceful nature, such assemblies – especially those directly expressing dissent against government measures undertaken for emergencies or national security – should still be permitted.

The most problematic aspect of the ICCPR jurisprudence on the right of peaceful assembly is the use of broad, vague, and uncertain concepts – such as public morals or public order (*ordre public*) – as permissible grounds for restriction. If purely peaceful in nature, public assemblies may still be restricted for the maintenance of road traffic or the order of business or government districts, even though such restrictions may run counter

74 See also the dissenting opinions, Grand Justice Li Chen-Shan, JY Interpretation No. 718.

75 Kiss (n. 66 above).

76 See individual opinions by Grand Justice Denis Tang and Grand Justice Li Chen-Shan, JY Interpretation No. 718.

to the paramount functions concerning the right of peaceful assembly. Although the principle of proportionality is required to strike a balance between the right of peaceful assembly and other public interests, these balances are not always struck in a proper, fair, and consistent manner.[77] Discretionary abuse or manipulation does exist, especially when governments confront wide-scale dissent or deep opposition.

Lawsuits relating to "illegal" assemblies after the Sunflower Movement

Lawsuits after the Sunflower Movement are divided into two categories: lawsuits brought by the government against the protesters, and lawsuits brought by protesters against the government. It is particularly important to examine if – and in what way and to what extent – these lawsuits have reflected the above-mentioned constitutional or international protections of free or peaceful assembly.

Lawsuits against the protesters

After the Sunflower Movement, public prosecutors launched a series of lawsuits against 118 protesters on criminal offences of trespassing, damaging government property, and obstructing officers in charge of duties.[78] So far, these lawsuits are still pending in the courts. Hence, the influences of JY Interpretation No. 708 as well as the ICCPR's jurisprudence on these lawsuits are yet to be seen.

Noteworthy, however, is a recent decision on the criminal charges of the chief leaders of an unauthorised assembly that took place after the Sunflower Movement.[79] The assembly in question was held at the end of April after the Sunflower Movement ended. The cause of the demonstration was to call for the government to suspend a nuclear power plant construction. Partly inspired by the Sunflower Movement, the anti-nuclear demonstration again employed the strategy of occupation. The group used a permit for an anti-nuclear power plant parade during the day, but refused to end their activities in the night. They eventually occupied a main road around the central station in Taipei City over night. Before dawn, they were expelled by the police with water cannons and baton strikes. Consequently, two protesters who used a loud speaker to help keep the crowd in order were charged by public prosecutors as the chief leaders for this unauthorised demonstration.[80]

Nevertheless, these two protesters were eventually acquitted by the Taipei District Court and the High Court. According to both, there was no evidence to prove that these two

77 Aharon Barak, "Proportionality (2)" in Michel Rosenfeld and András Sajó (eds), *The Oxford Handbook of Comparative Constitutional Law* (Oxford: Oxford University Press, 2012) 747–749 (noting that a criticism regarding the principle of proportionality is that the balance between the individual rights of freedom and the collective interests of people is usually ambiguous); Matthias Klatt and Moritz Meister, "The Constitutional Structure of Proportionality" (Oxford: Oxford University Press, 2012) 66–72 (indicating that the broad definition of public interest and the rule of balancing sometimes produces uncertain outcomes that infringe fundamental human rights).

78 Prosecution Indictment of Taipei District Court, 103 Chen Tzu No. 6678; 103 Chen Tzu No. 7121; 103 Chen Tzu No. 7242; 103 Chen Tzu No. 9428; 103 Chen Tzu No. 10305; 103 Chen Tzu No. 10388; 103 Chen Tzu No. 10979; 103 Chen Tzu No. 12454 (Taiwan).

79 Taipei District Court, 104 Shen Yi Tzu No. 130, 17 August 2015 (Taiwan); High Court, Shang Yi Tzu No. 1889, 31 December 2015 (Taiwan).

80 Prosecution Indictment of Taipei District Court, 103 Chen Tzu No. 10651; 103 Chen Tzu No. 11721(Taiwan).

protesters were the chief leaders of the demonstration.[81] More importantly, the courts reasoned that the dispersal orders by the police violated the principle of proportionality in terms of balancing with the right of free assembly, in addition to reasoning that the order was not issued by a competent authority.[82] This decision was certainly a promising sign for the ongoing lawsuits of the Sunflower Movement and reflected well on the above-mentioned constitutional and international rights discourse of the right to free – and peaceful – assembly.

Another promising sign was provided by the newly established DPP Government, which handily beat the KMT in 2016 executive and legislative elections.[83] Immediately upon the inauguration of new President Tsai Ing-wen on 20 May, the government decided to withdraw the lawsuits against the protesters on 23 May.[84] Yet, according to the Criminal Code, the government could only withdraw the charges on trespassing and damaging government property.[85] Other more serious charges, such as obstructing officers in charge of duties or being a chief leader for an unauthorised assembly, would remain solely in the hands of public prosecutors to exercise their powers independently.

Lawsuits against the government

Recent constitutional and international discourse on the right of free assembly has made Taiwanese citizens and social groups more aware of the government's duty in ensuring the right of free assembly and not using excessive force in dispersing unauthorised peaceful assemblies. Aided by volunteer attorneys, a number of lawsuits against the government have been brought by citizens, including: 1) criminal suits against the government for personal injuries; and 2) civil suits for claiming state compensation.

i. Criminal suits

After the Sunflower Movement, the government pledged to punish and issue disciplinary measures against police officers who used excessive force for dispersal. Yet, few believed these promises, which have yet to materialise. A few injured protesters decided to take the matter into their own hands, undertaking private prosecution[86] by suing the government for their personal injuries based on the Criminal Code.[87]

The first person to launch such a criminal lawsuit against the government was Mr Chou Jung-tsung (周榮宗). He accused the former President Ma Ying-jeou along with the former Premier Jiang Yi-huah and other high-ranking police officers of attempted murder.[88] The second person to follow suit was the former legislator Chou Ni-an (周倪安), who also

81 Note 77 above.

82 Ibid.

83 Austin Ramzy, "Tsai Ing-wen Elected President of Taiwan, First Woman to Hold Office" *New York Times*, 17 January 2016, http://nyti.ms/1Rru2sV.

84 Austin Ramzy, "Taiwan Drops Charges against Protesters in Government Sit-In" *New York Times*, 23 May 2016, http://nyti.ms/27QjqKt.

85 Articles 308 and 357 of the Criminal Code.

86 In Taiwan, private prosecution – different from public prosecution in which only public prosecutors can prosecute crimes – is still permitted for certain types of crimes on personal injuries.

87 Articles 271 and 277 of the Criminal Code.

88 Taipei District Court, 103 Tzu Tzu No. 18, 23 January 2015 (Taiwan); High Court, 104 Kang Tzu No. 158 Tsai Ting, 26 February 2015 (Taiwan).

accused the former Premier Jiang Yi-huah and other high-ranking police officers of attempted murder. In addition, a few others who had suffered personal injuries in the course of dispersals accused the former Premier Jiang Yi-huah and other high-ranking police officers of the crime of wilful and malicious injury.

There were, however, unexpected procedural hurdles. First was concerned with the issue of double jeopardy. The district courts, with which these lawsuits were filed, decided to admit only the first lawsuit and dismissed all of the others. In the view of the courts, as these lawsuits were based on the same criminal facts, the accused would bear the same criminal responsibility, and thus according to the principle of double jeopardy, all of the lawsuits other than the first should be dismissed.[89] It was also noted that in other jurisdictions, a possible solution might be the combination of cases, but such a possibility is not made available under the current criminal procedure, and therefore, the only option for the courts was the dismissals. Not surprisingly, these dismissals were appealed,[90] but eventually sustained by the Supreme Court.[91] Petitions for the Constitutional Court were filed and, as of this writing, are still pending.

Perhaps even more dramatic was the death of the plaintiff who filed the first lawsuit against the government during the trial proceeding because of severe illness. Although his daughter applied for succeeding his litigation with the assistance of public interest lawyers, the Taipei District Court and the High Court have both dismissed her case.[92]

Another procedural hurdle was how to identify defendants. As mentioned above, these lawsuits were filed primarily against the former Premier Jiang Yi-huah and other high-ranking police officers who ordered forcible dispersals resulting in attempted murder or personal injuries. Yet, how to identify the police officers who followed the order and used excessive force to cause those injuries was a considerable challenge. It was extremely difficult to have any recorded evidence showing the use of excessive force by the police in the course of the dispersals. Even if there were camera images that caught evidence of excessive force, the police routinely hide their official identification patch, which would render difficulty in identifying defendants or co-defendants in trial proceedings.[93] At present, most courts still hold that the obligation to identify defendants must be borne by those plaintiffs rather than requesting the government to investigate police officers who used excessive force.[94]

89 Taipei District Court, 103 Tzu Tzu No. 21, 13 September 2014. (Taiwan).

90 High Court, 104 Sang Su Tzu No. 406 Pan Chueh, 14 May 2015 (Taiwan); High Court, 104 Sang Su Tzu No. 1135 Pan Chueh, 9 June 2015 (Taiwan); High Court, 104 Sang Su Tzu No. 1139 Pan Chueh, 29 July 2015; High Court, 104 Sang Su Tzu No. 2630 Pan Chueh, 22 February 2016 (Taiwan).

91 Supreme Court, 104 Sang Tai Tzu No. 239 Pan Chueh, 22 January 2015 (Taiwan); Supreme Court, 104 Tai Sang No. 2453 Pan Chueh, 12 August 2015 (Taiwan); Supreme Court, 104 Tai Sang Tzu No. 2674 Pan Chueh, 9 September 2015 (Taiwan); High Court, 104 Sang Yi Tzu No. 714 Pan Chueh, 15 April 2015 (Taiwan).

92 Taipei District Court, 104 Sheng Tzu No. 1130, 22 April 2015 (Taiwan); High Court, 104 Kang Tzu No. 488, 17 June 2015 (Taiwan).

93 Taipei District Court, 103 Chien Tzu No. 107, 7 August 2015 (Taiwan).

94 Taipei District Court, 103 Tzu Tzu No. 35 Tsai Ting, 31 July 2015 (Taiwan); Taipei District Court, 103 Tzu Tzu No. 48 Tsai Ting, 11 June 2015 (Taiwan); Taipei District Court, 103 Tzu Tzu No. 56 Tsai Ting, 3 March 2015 (Taiwan); Taipei District Court, 103 Tzu Tzu No. 56 Pan Chueh, 13 April 2015 (Taiwan); Taipei District Court, 103 Tzu Tzu No. 61 Pan Chueh, 7 January 2015 (Taiwan); Taipei District Court, 103 Tzu Tzu No. 61 Tsai Ting, 23 January 2015 (Taiwan); Taipei District Court, 103 Tzu Tzu No. 90 Tsai Ting, 21 October 2014 (Taiwan); Taipei District Court, 103 Tzu Tzu No, 90 Pan Chueh, 10 December 2015; High Court, 104 Shang Su Tzu No. 406, 14 May 2015 (Taiwan), Supreme Court, 105 Shang Tai Tzu No. 433, 18 February 2016 (Taiwan).

Finally, there was the issue concerning superior responsibility. It would certainly be an unprecedented challenge for the courts to examine whether former President Ma Ying-jeou and the former Premier Jiang Yi-huah, along with other high-ranking police officers, should bear – or not – the superior responsibility for the crowd dispersal order and the ensuing use of excessive force.

ii. State compensation suits

Another encouraging development in the guarantee of free assembly after the Sunflower Movement was the success of state compensation suits brought by citizens against the government. One of the injured persons who was expelled at the Executive Yuan occupation on 24 March filed a state compensation lawsuit and was awarded NTD $300,000 from the district court.[95]

This case, however, was not the first in which an injured individual in the dispersal of unauthorised assembly was awarded state compensation. The first of such cases occurred after the Wild Strawberry Movement in 2008, discussed above. During that movement, one journalist was injured due to an inadequate use of force by the police. Although it was difficult to identify the policeman who used the force, there was an image proving that the injury of the journalist resulted from police enforcement, and the court eventually decided in favour of the plaintiff and awarded state compensation. Encouraged by these developments, quite a few injured protesters during the Sunflower Movement have launched state compensation lawsuits with the assistance of public interest lawyers.

Conclusion

Throughout all democracies, citizens should enjoy the right to peaceful assembly in order to publicly express their disagreements with the government and with their fellow citizens. Such a right is especially important when the system of representative democracy fails to function, and citizens are left only with votes, but with their voices unheard. Citizens' right to peaceful assembly, therefore, should be accorded with the highest degree of protection, and courts must exercise caution when restricting it. As long as public assemblies remain peaceful in nature, the actions of citizens should not be restricted, even in the face of other – broadly defined – public interests.

In Taiwan, the successful transition to democracy has brought for its citizens stronger protection of fundamental rights and freedoms, including that regarding freedom of assembly. Through the interpretations by the Constitutional Court and the vibrant discourse in embracing international human rights, particularly in the ICCPR, the right to free – and peaceful – assembly has gradually materialised and been significantly strengthened throughout the years. The Sunflower Movement in 2014 – along with many other citizens' movements before it – was a genuine test as to the promise for the right to assembly, as well as to the strength of Taiwan's democracy. Although it is difficult to state with certainty, the aftermath of the Sunflower Movement – in both political and legal respects – has provided a promising sign for this young constitutional democracy.

95 Taipei District Court, 103 Chien Tzu No. 107, 7 August 2015 (Taiwan).

3 Marching towards civic constitutionalism with Sunflowers

Jiunn-rong Yeh[*]

Introduction

Constitutional change in Taiwan has occurred in tandem with a fascinating process of democratic transformation. Incremental and fragmented as it may seem, Taiwan's constitutional change since democratisation in the late 1980s could be summarised as a process of representation-reinforcing, as reflected in the seven rounds of constitutional revisions, in the more representative legislature, in the general and direct presidential elections, and also in the larger participatory state apparatus.[1] This level of progress in building representative democracy, albeit miraculously successful, did not stop the civil society from increased engagement with the constitutional order. In fact, following democratic transition and constitutional reform, the civil society stayed vigilant and active with the realisation of full suffrage and better representation in the government, including for the legislature and also the president. More than two decades since this democratic transformation, the Sunflower Movement that occurred in 2014 consolidated an ongoing move from representative democratic constitutionalism to a more civic-centric constitutional order, which can be considered "civic constitutionalism".

Often, constitutionalism is viewed from the perspective of the constitution and the adjudications of a supreme court or constitutional court, and how they construct or understand the constitution in a rights-based or power-centric disposition. Often, the president, the legislature, and the state apparatus are the foci of the constitutional order, and this thinking has driven a general concern for the diminishing of civic democratic engagement and the stifling of social society.[2]

Some new democracies in East and Central Europe have begun to reflect the so-called crisis of the new democracies, which operates under the shadow of rigid constitutionalism and activist constitutional courts.[3] Conversely, Taiwan has demonstrated a continuous civil engagement in the process of democratic constitutional reform, all amidst an evolving constitutional rule of law and judicial review. The civil society "punished" their representatives in the 2005 constitutional revisions by halving the number of Legislative Yuan seats. In that same effort, the distrusted National Assembly that exercised monopolistic

* National Taiwan University Chair Professor, JSD: Yale, 1988.

1 Jiunn-rong Yeh, "Democracy-Driven Transformation to Regulatory State: The Case of Taiwan" (2008) 3(2) *National Taiwan University Law Review* 31–60.

2 See, e.g. David C Williams, "Civic Constitutionalism, the Second Amendment, and the Right of Revolution" (2004) 79 *Indiana Law Journal* 379, 380–381.

3 Paul Blokker, *New Democracies in Crisis? A Comparative Constitutional Study of the Czech Republic, Hungary, Poland, Romania and Slovakia* (Oxford: Routledge, 2014).

power to amend the constitution was abolished altogether, mainly driven by strong public outcry against it. In 2014, students physically occupied the Legislative Yuan building for more than a month because of irresponsible legislative deliberation on the Cross-Strait policy, which became known as the Sunflower Movement. This civic uprising not only posed a threat to the then ruling Kuomintang (KMT) regime but also humiliated the then opposition Democratic Progressive Party (DPP). It was believed that the Sunflower Movement, that brought a wave of distrust towards the KMT, had a major impact on the landslide 2014 nine-in-one local elections and the 2016 presidential and legislative elections. The DPP garnered 13 of 22 cities – including four of the six largest cities – in the 2014 local election for village chiefs, councillors, and mayors. The DPP further won the presidency, as well as a first-time majority in the legislature, in the 2016 general election.

This chapter argues that the Sunflower Movement is not the downfall of Taiwan's maturing democracy nor is it a threat to the embraced values of liberal constitutionalism. Rather, it is a strong confirmation of the march towards civic constitutionalism – a march of discontent with representative democracy and the judicial constitutional dispositions enshrined in the flux of democratic and constitutional reform. This transformation has been driven and will be further fuelled by the ambiguous Cross-Strait policies that put Taiwan's political institutions and civic structure through serious tests. Although the primary underlying issue of the Sunflower Movement was increased Cross-Strait engagement, the transformation to civic constitutionalism, with challenges to the younger generation in an increasingly digital world and a globally competitive job market, bears tremendous significance far beyond the Taiwan Strait.

The legacy of transition: Representative democracy, courts, and civil society

In the flux of democratic transitions (such as in East and Central Europe, South Africa, or East Asia), a system of periodical elections and levels of representative bodies were established with full suffrage, so that the public could build up a legitimate representative democracy. Often courts, and constitutional courts in particular, are entrusted with mandates for protection of rights and the resolution of political disputes in the course of transition.[4] The legislature and the courts gradually take charge of the constitutional issues, as increasing institutionalised capacity-building ensues. On the surface, this may seem to be a perfect result as regards democratic transition and corresponding constitutional reform for the new democracies. Along this line of constitutional institutionalisation, however, the role of the populace has ironically become an intriguing area for many scholars: after the installation of representative democracy, should the populace stay active and watchful or be more passive? This, thus, creates post-transitional concerns on many levels.

The post-transitional concern: The ambivalent role of the civil movement

Democratic transition often coincides with constitutional reform, focusing on building democratic institutions and competitive electoral mechanisms. This institutional reform, if

4 Jiunn-rong Yeh and Wen-Chen Chang, "Introduction: Asian Courts in Context: Tradition, Transition, and Globalization" in Jiunn-rong Yeh and Wen-Chen Chang (eds), *Asian Courts in Context* (Cambridge: Cambridge University Press, 2014) 14–15.

successful at all, may stifle the civil society and reduce civic engagement, posing a crisis to even vibrant democracies.

After the collapse of the Iron Curtain, post-Soviet states formed new constitutional democracies in Central and East Europe. Czech Republic, Hungary, Poland, Romania, and Slovakia drew up their own constitutions and established political systems of democracy. Two decades later, however, these new democracies are considered in crisis in terms of constitutional democracy.[5] Overemphasised formal institutions for the rule of law have resulted in the neglect of civic participation within these constitutional systems. The lack of dynamic political participation from the society, and even some legal resentment, can be seen in these years. For example, independent constitutional courts and judicial review by constitutional experts hold absolute power regarding constitutional interpretation. Such "juristocracy" – one-sided institutional legal formalism – discourages wider public debates over constitutional issues.[6] Also, it damages the core value of democracy, leading to questions about the legitimacy of the democratic system. If the crisis of democracy observation is correct, then a change to a more robust public engagement in terms of civil constitutionalism should result. An institutional design to increase the possibility of constitutional dialogue among the civil society, political, and legal departments should be introduced, even without a strong tradition of civic constitutionalism.

Conversely, in a similar context of democratic transition, Taiwan presents an example of heightened civic engagement that is, allegedly, non-existent in the East and central European states after democratic constitutional reform. The Sunflower Movement exemplifies this scenario, as autonomous students occupied the legislative building and altogether paralysed the legislature, thus resulting in a plethora of constitutional ramifications, as discussed below. Therefore, even after the institutional establishment of representative bodies, one may see disobedient social movements in defiance of representative democracy.

Indeed, in the outbreak of the event, commentators spared no time to lament this happening as a setback to the maturing democracy. Was this the beginning of democratic failure? It turned out that the student groups exercised a high degree of discipline and, not long after their occupation, won social support through impressive dialogue with both the general public and government authorities. The students and social groups argued in constitutional terms about rights infringement, due process, and the boundaries of congressional oversight and public monitoring in concluding the trade pact with China.[7] Passionate lectures about contemporary constitutional law topics were offered in the occupied legislature and even in the surrounding streets. With general concern regarding the accountability of the president and the legislature, the student/civic groups continued to discuss and propose issues for constitutional reform.

Not long after the occupation, the group had morphed into a large social movement with increasing social support. Again, is this a threat to democracy? The answer by the general public in Taiwan was an unequivocal "no". In fact, it is indeed the practice of civic

5 Paul Blokker (n. 3 above).

6 Ran Hirschl, *Towards Juristocracy: The Origins and Consequences of the New Constitutionalism* (Cambridge, MA: Harvard University Press, 2007).

7 See Hsiaowei Kuan, "Connecting Gender and Trade: Gender Framing in the Anti-Cross-Strait Service Trade Agreement Movement" (2015) 45(1) *Hong Kong Law Journal* 249 (demonstrating the women's anti-CSSTA movement that was made up of more than student groups).

constitutionalism, after a democratic constitutional transition, that is missing from the eastern and central European context.[8]

Towards civil constitutionalism

The lack of recognition of the role of civic engagement in constitutional order could be attributed to two possible supremacies: judicial and legislative. Judicial supremacy of constitutional interpretation has been advanced through a court-centric reading of the constitution. Many believe that judges have the last word when it comes to constitutional interpretation and court decisions that determine the meaning of the constitution, leaving the general public little role in the evolving constitutional order.[9] Under general notions of representative democracy, citizens are supposed to be more passive regarding public affairs after electing their representatives. Aside from the courts, people's representatives exercise a public mandate, which includes embracing the constitutional order. In a presidential system, the directly elected president is also entrusted with a mandate to protect the constitution for the general public. Yet, in the Westminster tradition, the embedded notion of parliamentary supremacy could further exemplify this tension.

The idea of finding a civic role in constitutional founding, interpretation, or dialectic engagement is not innovative and, in fact, has been argued in different social contexts and in different terms. The constitutional moment's higher lawmaking, as articulated by Bruce Ackerman, has given recognition to the normative significance of popular mobilisation through the lens of direct voting for the president or Congress during transformative moments.[10] However, popular constitutionalism advocates asserting a significant role for public interpretation of the constitution, against judicial supremacy (which places opinions of judges as final and absolute in the shaping of constitutional order and rights recognition).[11] A more sophisticated civic constitutional argument places civic engagement within the dialectic shaping of the constitution during founding and other crucial junctures of constitutional transformation, such as the adoption of a bill of rights, the abolition of slavery, women's suffrage, and the passage of national civic rights legislation.[12]

During a time of profound change, who actually shapes the contours of the reform agenda and constitutional order? Aside from the key figures usually noted, such as founding fathers, renowned politicians or intellectuals, often ignored are the constitutional views, debates, and activities of civic groups and engaged citizens in interpreting the constitution, refashioning democratic citizenship, and constructing civic scaffoldings for new constitutional rights and commitments.[13] Thus, it is not unusual to see the engaged citizen take an active and ongoing role in the interpretation and enforcement of constitutional law. Even in a world of judicial dominance, judges interpret the constitution according to their best

8 Paul Blokker (n. 3 above).

9 Robert Post and Reva Siegel, "Popular Constitutionalism, Departmentalism, and Judicial Supremacy" (2004) 92(4) *California Law Review* 1027.

10 Bruce Ackerman, *We the People: Foundations* (Cambridge, MA: Harvard University Press, 1991).

11 Larry Kramer, "Popular Constitutionalism, circa 2004" (2004) 92 *California Law Review* 959 (2004); Larry Kramer, *The People Themselves: Popular Constitutionalism and Judicial Review* (Oxford: Oxford University Press, 2005).

12 Elizabeth Beaumont, *The Civic Constitution: Civic Visions and Struggles in the Path toward Constitutional Democracy* (Oxford: Oxford University Press, 2014).

13 Ibid., p. xv.

judgment, but with the awareness that citizens are the higher authority, with the power to overturn their decisions.[14] By the same token, even legislatures have a public mandate with regard to constitutional underpinnings, as they constantly face the reality that the public, their higher authority, may overturn them.

Civic constitutionalism as exemplified in Taiwan's case could thus be articulated through the following accounts. First, civil society stayed critical and engaged Congress by enhancing representative democracy through a series of constitutional reforms. Civil society thus engaged in the understanding, interpretation, and shaping of the constitution through the direct or indirect impact on their representatives. Second, after democratisation, civil society remains vigilant and active, even with an increasingly trusted constitutional court. On the one hand, civil society remains a motivation for judicial review with regard to rights protection and government integrity, as they often bring issues to the courts for resolution, thus pushing forward the consolidation of constitutional principles and values. On the other hand, while weaving the fabric of the constitution, the court remains watchful of public views on matters concerning constitutional adjudication. Third, engaged citizens and civic groups play a pivotal role in launching, deliberating, and steering the agenda of constitutional reform in spite of the institutionalised form of constitutional amendments. These features have enriched the way we see constitutions, and how they operate in post-democratised societies.

Civic perspectives of constitutionalism: Discovering civil constitutionalism through and beyond the Sunflower Movement

The journey of Taiwan's constitutional development has been characterised by the historical legacies of foreign occupations and colonisation, externally imposed constitutions, constitutional manipulation and authoritarian governance, and, finally, the incremental constitutional indigenisation and democratic reforms. We see constitutional change through institutional betterment or enhanced government performance, such as government integrity, congressional oversight, or judicial review. Civic roles in the making of a constitutional order, however, are often overlooked in the modern constitutional landscape.

In fact, engaged citizen and civic groups have played a crucial role at many critical junctures of constitutional transformation in Taiwan, thus presenting a strong mode of civic constitutionalism. Even with the increasingly creditable periodical elections, representative institutions, and courts, the civil society has stayed vigilant and engaged in shaping a democratic constitution that they fought over for decades during the transition era. In the path of Taiwan's constitutional change, the Sunflower Movement is the pinnacle of development.

The Sunflower Movement and civic constitutional discourse

On 18 March 2014, Taiwan was shocked when a group of university students broke into the Legislative Yuan to protest against the way their representatives handled the Cross-Strait Service Trade Agreement (CSSTA). Thousands of citizens soon followed, rallying on the streets outside the building in support of the occupation. At that time, no one was able to predict that the Movement could last for almost a month, only to come to an "end" on 10 April 2014.

14 Post and Siegel (n. 9 above), p. 1028.

The major cause of the Movement was the hasty signing of the CSSTA. Before, during, and after the signing of the agreement, the public was not properly informed. While the legislature should be the organ to give a comprehensive review, some partisan legislators of the ruling KMT managed to smuggle the agreement through the process, in order to avoid such a review.

Students and civil groups argued that the pact was negotiated secretly, without proper public oversight, and were worried that some sections included in the CSSTA might allow for China to gain more political control over Taiwan.[15] In their campaigns, students and activists demanded for a piece of legislation to guarantee legislative oversight and to enhance greater public supervision of such trade agreements with China, including that the CSSTA should not pass before the enactment of such legislation.

Opposing such demands, the KMT Government argued that the legislative oversight of the Cross-Strait negotiations proposed would be a legislative encroachment on executive power,[16] and thus preferred to pass the CSSTA in its original form. Given their deep disappointment with the government, on 23 March, protesters broke into the Executive Yuan and were later forcibly evicted by riot police, an episode that caused serious human rights concerns. This "incident" brought public resentment to an even higher level, leading to a demonstration on 30 March, which was joined by half a million citizens.

The deadlock between the government and the protesters was slightly resolved when on 6 April, the Parliamentary Speaker, Wang Jin-Pyng (王金平), pledged to halt the review of CSSTA until the "supervising" legislation was enacted. Thus, the protesters finally left the parliament on 10 April 2014, with a general recognition that the CSSTA review would be contingent on the successful passage of a legislative framework regulating the oversight of Cross-Strait agreements.

Regardless of the viewpoint one may take in observing the Movement, it is undeniable that the Sunflowers turned the CSSTA and the failing government oversight mechanisms into a national issue. Also, the Movement has rejuvenated civil society in Taiwan.[17] From the lens of civic constitutionalism, these facts bear significant meaning.

There is little doubt that the current constitution serves as the normative basis for the exercise of powers, and the checks and balances among them. However, when it comes to constitutional interpretation, there is always a civic deference to government authority, be it the executive, the legislature, or the court. The constitutional process of concluding the CSSTA exemplified this, as the executive often exerts its power of interpreting the constitution so as to legitimise its monopoly over the negotiations (even at the sacrifice of the necessary legislative oversight). Bearing this in mind, we can see the Sunflower Movement as more than just a protest against government, but as the exercise of civic views on the constitutional requirements of Cross-Strait negotiations. Because of this Movement, the general populace no longer sees the constitution as out-of-touch. Indeed, the Movement reminded society of their duty not only to establish the constitution, but also to maintain the constitution by strengthening or reshaping it.

15 "Sunflower Sutra" *The Economist* (8 April 2014), http://www.economist.com/blogs/banyan/2014/04/politics-taiwan.

16 Yen Tu Su, "Translating Protest into Law Test for Sunflowers" *Taipei Times* (4 May 2014), http://www.taipeitimes.com/News/editorials/archives/2014/05/04/2003589509.

17 J. Michael Cole, "Was Taiwan's Sunflower Movement Successful?" *The Diplomat* (1 July 2014), http://thediplomat.com/2014/07/was-taiwans-sunflower-movement-successful/.

There were at least four instances that can be drawn from the Movement to demonstrate the trend towards civic constitutionalism. First, the Movement allowed civic groups to present their definition on the concept of "separation of powers". The legislative oversight debate on the CSSTA indeed shows very different understandings between the government and the people regarding what the legislature should and should not do. After the Movement, the CSSTA was postponed as a response to the demand that a Cross-Strait Agreement Supervisory Act (CSASA), with a clear stance as regards legislation and referendum, be passed prior to any further substantial deliberation on the CSSTA. Second, the Sunflower Movement empowered the public through knowledge on both policy and the constitution, a significant tool in the practice of civic constitutionalism. During the Movement, scholars voluntarily went on the streets and gave public lectures on "constitutional law", "analysis of the CSSTA", and other topics. The knowledge transferred on the street spurred further discourse, enabling the public to strengthen their arguments and to compete with their representatives in the legislature as regards redefining the constitution. These efforts of civic groups and scholars have since continued and have been further strengthened.

Third, the Movement established a level of transparency long-forgotten by the current government. Because the Taiwanese Government did not inform the public about the CSSTA's details, throughout the Sunflower Movement a number of citizen-initiated websites were created to explain the agreement and its potential impact on various sectors and vulnerable groups. These explanations were often strengthened with statistics and sound analysis.[18] After the Movement, many CSASA drafts proposed by either the government or the civic groups contained provisions demanding earlier release of Cross-Strait negotiation information as well as the holding of public consultations or hearings. The primary issue of the ongoing enactment of CSASA was to implement the consensus reached by the Movement that the process of Cross-Strait agreements must be made transparent and more publicly accountable.

Last but not least, the "Executive Yuan incident" following the occupation of the Legislative Yuan reminded the public of the significance of human rights protection against police power. This time, the protesters' rights were argued on a constitutional level. Also, the legality and legitimacy of such state violence was seriously questioned by the public. Although there have been other incidents and court decisions defining the boundaries between law and public order when it comes to citizen demonstrations,[19] the high-profile and complex questions brought about by the Sunflower Movement with regard to rule of law and civil disobedience demand further constitutional reflection. In May 2016, soon after the new president's inauguration, the DPP Government decided to drop criminal charges against 126 students and other individuals involved in the Movement.

Post–Sunflower Movement developments show that the journey of civic constitutionalism did not essentially end on 10 April. Civic groups, scholars, and students managed to form a forum group called "Civil Constitutional Conference". This "conference" established a forum for public discussion regarding the deficits in the constitution as well as possible amendments. To date, the group has been providing valuable input for the civil

18 "How Technology and Citizen Media Shaped Taiwan's Sunflower Movement" *Global Voices* (20 April 2014), http://globalvoicesonline.org/2014/04/20/how-technology-and-citizen-media-shaped-taiwans-sunflower-movement/.

19 JY Interpretation No. 718 (2014).

society when lobbying their representatives, especially after the 2016 presidential and legislative election.[20]

Civic struggle for better representation: The people and their representatives

Some have argued that the Sunflower Movement resembles a new "moment" for Taiwan's constitutional order. Yet, it should be noted that civic constitutionalism did not begin with the Sunflowers and nor will it end with them. For instance, not long ago, a few major media deals spurred the anti-media monopoly movement in Taiwan. If we trace this a bit earlier, to the beginning of Taiwan's democratic transition, we also find civic groups exerting their influence over the reform agenda, when the legislature was filled with representatives they had never voted for. In fact, along the lines of civic engagement with their representatives in the legislature, the Sunflower Movement was in fact the sequel to the Wild Lily Movement, which coincided with the beginning of Taiwan's democratisation.

The pinnacle of Taiwan's democratisation has been the autonomous citizen uprisings – the student movements, in particular – in contrast to the partisan debates within and outside the legislature. The most celebrated of these has been the Wild Lily Student Movement. On 16 March 1990, students started to gather in front of the Chiang Kai-Shek monument, chanting for political reform. Eventually, this contingent formed the largest student movement in Taiwan's history. The students requested a reform agenda with four foci: 1) dissolving the National Assembly, 2) abolishing the Temporary Provisions, 3) calling for a national affairs conference, and 4) providing a timeline for political and economic reforms. At about the same time, proposals to reform the Legislative Yuan were debated within the KMT and with other opinion leaders.

Confronting an increasing outcry for reform, President Lee Teng-hui (李登輝) decided to hold out an olive branch to the students. He invited student leaders into the presidential office and vowed for reform. Many requests from the students were met with positive feedback from the president. A National Affairs Conference convened by the president and attended by 141 representatives, chosen from all corners of society, was held three months later and entrusted with deliberation over a political and constitutional reform agenda. A major consensus was reached during the National Affairs Conference that paved the way for a series of incremental constitutional reforms. This consensus included the total demolition of the Temporary Provisions, which also put an end to the mobilisation period. As for the legislature's reorganisation, the Constitutional Court issued interpretations that requested total re-election before any resolution reached the National Affairs Conference.[21] Together, these measures provided legitimacy for a series of constitutional reforms in the following decade. Thus, it is fair to say that landmark constitutional interpretation no. 261 was fuelled by and through this mass social movement.

Following the Wild Lily Movement, a series of constitutional revisions were undertaken to develop a legislature fully seated by elected representatives. Engaged citizens continue to monitor the representatives they have voted for in constitutional terms. Before the

20 The arrangement of the forum began from September 2014. First, it sought the opinions about constitutional reform from citizens. Second, they had conversations with non-governmental organisations and scholars to further organise the opinions. Finally, the forum influenced both political parties and the government before and after the 2016 presidential election.

21 JY Interpretation No. 261 (1990).

Sunflower Movement, the general public mobilised to push forward a constitutional amendment that downsized the number of legislature seats from 225 to 113 as a way to "punish" their representatives for poor governance.

All things considered, the 1990 Wild Lily Movement and the 2014 Sunflower Movement are iconic moments of civic engagement in their respective eras. While the Wild Lily Movement pushed for constitutional reform towards full suffrage and representation, the engaged Sunflower Movement students exercised their constitutional rights by holding their chosen representatives in the legislature accountable in constitutional terms.

Civic engagement in rights discourse: The people and their courts

Civic constitutionalism presents a place where citizens and civic groups can engage in rights discourse in their words and deeds, both inside and outside the courts. The rights discourse in Taiwan has primarily been championed by civic groups, which has burgeoned since the 1980s. As economic growth reached an apex, a more vibrant civil society was made possible with the rise of a middle class. Also, free association that had been prohibited by the Martial Law Decree in 1949 was now legal, with the ban lifted in 1987.

There have been two major waves regarding the establishment of non-governmental organisations: one in the early 1980s, and the other in the late 1980s.[22] For instance, a rice oil incident in 1979 led to the creation of the first consumer group one year later. Thereafter, the Awakening Foundation, a group of female lawyers, was established in 1982. The Taiwan Association for Human Rights, composed primarily of human rights lawyers, was founded in 1984 (even before the first opposition political party, the DPP, was established in 1986).[23] The second wave of founding for non-governmental groups came upon the lifting of the Martial Law Decree in July 1987. The Taiwan Environmental Protection Union and the Humanistic Education Foundation were both formed in 1987, followed by the Homemaker's Union and Foundation, a female environmental group. In the 1990s, further democratisation saw the establishment of social groups for the advocacy of rights, social justice, and political reform. Particularly impactful groups include the Judicial Reform Foundation (created by a group of human rights lawyers), the Gender/Sexuality Rights Association (advocating for gay rights), and the Wild at Heart Legal Defense Association (the first environmental lawyers group).[24]

These human rights organisations and social groups vigorously participated in political and constitutional reforms throughout the 1990s and 2000s. They advanced a wide array of rights agendas, including discussion about constitution-making or constitutional revision. When attempts at pushing through the incorporation of additional rights and freedoms in the course of constitutional reform failed, these groups have turned their attention to the enactments of quasi-constitutional statutes or to the accession of international human rights conventions.

To illustrate, the quasi-constitutional Referendum Act of 2003 was a great leap forward in terms of the right to referendum that was never realised under the authoritarian rule of

22 Wen-Chen Chang, "Public-Interest Litigation in Taiwan: Strategy for Law and Policy Reforms in Course of Democratization" in Po Jen Yap and Holning Lau (eds), *Public Interest Litigation in Asia* (New York: Routledge, 2011) 138–139.

23 Ibid.

24 Ibid., p. 139.

martial law. In the 1980s, as the calls for democratic reform intensified, the people's right to referendum emerged at the centre of the debate. It was not until the 1990s that it became possible for a civil movement to advocate people's right to referendum. In 2003, after more than a decade of advocacy, the Referendum Act was passed and people's right to referendum – on both the national and local levels, regarding matters of constitutional amendments, laws, policies – was finally realised.[25]

Taiwan has made more significant progress in the accession of international human rights conventions under the strong initiative of civic groups. In 2007, accession to the Convention on Elimination of All Forms of Discrimination against Women (CEDAW) was passed by an overwhelming parliamentary majority and formally announced by the president. In 2009, the Legislative Yuan ratified the International Covenant on Civil and Political Rights (ICCPR) and the International Covenant on Economic, Social and Cultural Rights (ICESCR); and an act to implement the ICCPR and the ICESCR was also passed to ensure the applicability of all rights protected by the two covenants in the domestic legal system.[26] In 2014, two acts to implement the Convention on the Rights of the Child (CRC) and the Convention on the Rights of Persons with Disabilities (CRPD) were passed and soon became effective. State reports of the CEDAW, ICCPR, and ICESCR have been released and reviewed by international experts.

Finally, the other way for these non-governmental organisations to advance rights is to seek constitutional interpretations by the Constitutional Court.[27] Adjudication sought in the courts by human rights groups and social organisations has been namely undertaken with the Constitutional Court in two particular types of litigation. First, the undertaking of constitutional petitions by these groups often challenges statutes that encroach upon fundamental rights and freedoms already written into the constitution. This line of litigation burgeoned at the beginning of democratisation in the late 1980s and early 1990s. Second, constitutional petitions are made to request the Constitutional Court to construe new rights not already written in the constitution. This happens especially through Art 22, which accords constitutional protection to "all other freedoms and rights that are not detrimental to social order or public welfare".[28] On occasion, such judicial construction of new rights and freedoms has been channelled through the reference to international human rights and comparative constitutional law.[29]

The petitions brought before the Constitutional Court in the beginning of the democratic transition entailed a wide array of rights. One of the first petitions challenged the constitutionality of the mandatory death penalty imposed on three young men involved in

25 Jiunn-rong Yeh and Wen-Chen Chang, "A Decade of Changing Constitutionalism in Taiwan: Transitional and Transnational Perspectives" in Albert H. Y. Chen (ed.), *Constitutionalism in Asia in the Early Twenty-First Century* (Cambridge: Cambridge University Press, 2014) 150–152; Jiunn-rong Yeh and Wen-Chen Chang, "The Changing Landscape of Modern Constitutionalism: Transitional Perspective" (2009) 4(1) *National Taiwan University Law Review* 145, 156–157 (for instance, in Taiwan, individual claims for compensation for past rights infringements or property takings were allowed by special laws).

26 Jiunn-rong Yeh and Wen-Chen Chang, "A Decade of Changing Constitutionalism in Taiwan" (n. 25 above), pp. 152–155; Wen-Chen Chang, "An Isolated Nation with Global-Minded Citizens: Bottom-Up Transnational Constitutionalism in Taiwan" (2009) 4(3) *National Taiwan University Law Review* 203.

27 Wen-Chen Chang (n. 22 above), pp. 138–139.

28 Constitution of the Republic of China (1947), Art 22.

29 Wen-Chen Chang and Jiunn-rong Yeh, "Judges as Discursive Agent: The Use of Foreign Precedents by the Constitutional Court of Taiwan" in Tania Groppi and Marie-Claire Ponthoreau (eds), *The Use of Foreign Precedents by Constitutional Judges* (Oxford: Hart Publishing, 2013) 373–392.

a widely known kidnapping case. The Taiwan Association for Human Rights – formed in 1984 – was the first human rights organisation to publicly criticise the mandatory death penalty. Although the Constitutional Court in Judicial Yuan (JY) Interpretation No. 263 upheld the constitutionality of the mandatory death penalty, it nevertheless urged judicial caution in such impositions.[30] This petition – albeit a failed one – helped at least to generate public awareness on the numerous problems with the mandatory death penalty.

The next successful line of constitutional petitions was made by women lawyers and women's organisations such as the Awakening Foundation – established in 1982 – to challenge statutes violating sex and gender equality. In 1990, several women's groups were working on a three-year project to propose a revision of the Civil Code respecting the equal rights of women with families. They not only tried a test case in the court but also lobbied the newly elected Legislative Yuan to overhaul the Civil Code. Joined by a number of legislators, women's groups made petitions to the Constitutional Court challenging the constitutionality of a provision in the Civil Code which privileged the fathers in cases of parental disagreements over child custody. In JY Interpretation No. 365, the Constitutional Court found such a violation and demanded that the impugned provision be amended two years before being made null and void.[31] This victory was followed by even more successful petitions, such as JY Interpretation No. 410 and JY Interpretation No. 452, in which provisions of the Civil Code disadvantageous to women were found unconstitutional.[32]

The success of constitutional litigation by women's groups triggered even more litigation by other human rights organisations and social groups. These groups began to see constitutional litigation as an effective way to advance their rights agendas. To illustrate, scholarly associations asserted their freedom of association in JY Interpretation No. 479, which held certain restrictions on the naming of associations as unconstitutional.[33] The right of free speech for gay and lesbians was further expanded with JY Interpretation No. 617.[34]

The variety of rights agendas pushed forward by social groups or concerned individuals have substantially enriched the docket of the Constitutional Court. Judicial construction of fundamental rights and freedoms has not been merely a reflection of judicial preference, but rather, a response to ongoing social and political demands in a society that has been undergoing profound transformations.[35]

Towards civic constitutionalism after the Sunflower Movement

Taiwan has demonstrated a mode of civic constitutionalism beyond representative democracy that has been built upon during democratic transition, exemplified by the

30 JY Interpretation No. 263 (1990).

31 JY Interpretation No. 365 (1994).

32 JY Interpretation No. 410 (1996); JY Interpretation No. 452 (1998). In a recent case, JY Interpretation No. 728 (2015), the Court was challenged with the internal regulations of guilds that follow the traditional perception of clans in restricting succession to male offspring only. Although the Court did not find relevant provisions unconstitutional in terms of gender equality, the Court urged the government to conduct a timely review and modification of the related law in this regard.

33 JY Interpretation No. 479 (1999).

34 JY Interpretation No. 617 (2006).

35 Jiunn-rong Yeh and Wen-Chen Chang, "The Emergence of East Asian Constitutionalism: Features in Comparison" (2011) 59(3) *American Journal of Comparative Law* 805–840.

Sunflower Movement, the follow-up landslide changes in the 2014 nine-in-one local elections, and the 2016 presidential and legislative elections. Civic constitutionalism honours the existing constitutional institutional framework but puts engaged citizens and civic groups in a more visible place in the constitutional order in relation to the state apparatus, namely the representative bodies and the courts that exert constitutional power and political mandates.

The increased recognition of civic constitutionalism in Taiwan indicates first the failing of parliamentary supremacy, in which the parliament is no longer regarded as an absolute and must be constantly checked by other coequal branches as well as by citizens. This changing understanding of the parliament and its relationship with citizens departs from the traditional understanding of parliamentary sovereignty that has stood as the backbone to parliamentary democracies in the Westminster tradition. In this changing context, while courts have continued to exert judicial review as a check on the legislature, the legitimacy and level of judicial scrutiny might have scaled up. Constitutional adjudication, in political conflict resolution or rights protection, will continue to be pro-dialogue and leave much room and time for resolution by the political branches.[36] But the tendency of judicial rulings will be even more receptive to social consensus and keen to be in dialogue with the civic society.[37] With this civic orientation, courts must respond to citizens and become more inclined to deal with inter-generational justice concerns in terms of financial stability, welfare distribution, and environmental justice.

In the scope of civic constitutionalism, engaged citizens and civic groups exert much influence in public matters under the constitutional order but also engage with the constitution through dialectic interpretation and formation. The general public still values each election by going to the ballot box and honouring the electoral results, thus creating representative bodies and formal state apparatus. These functions still operate in constitutional terms but are keen to involve citizen participation and face continuous civic oversight. More institutional measures facilitating transparency and deliberation in lawmaking functions such as legislation, budgeting, and policy resolution are in even greater demand. Civic groups engage not only in all facets of constitutional transformation but also in constitutional maintenance and interpretation. Accordingly, the recent landslide losses by the ruling KMT in both the 2014 local elections and the 2016 presidential and legislative elections have aroused very strong civic views of constitutional matters relating to transparency, the monitoring of Cross-Strait deals, and the legitimacy of the presidency in handling such negotiations.

Despite the rigid constitutional amendment process as the result of the 2005 constitutional amendments, citizens and civic groups have been vigilant and engaged about the issues and mechanisms of constitutional revision. The proposal to lower the voting age from 20 to 18 years, for example, has been pushed forward with more general consensus in light of the Sunflower Movement events, and especially after the 2016 general election.

36 Jiunn-rong Yeh, "Presidential Politics and Judicial Facilitation of Dialogue between Political Actors in New Asian Democracies: Comparing the South Korean and Taiwanese Experiences" (2011) 8(4) *International Journal of Constitutional Law* 911–949.

37 For instance, the Constitutional Court, at around the same time the Sunflower Movement took place, declared to exempt permits for urgent and spontaneous events in an Assembly and Parade Act case. JY Interpretation No. 718 (2014).

The primary underlying issue of the Sunflower Movement was the increased engagement across the Taiwan Strait, in addition to the challenges to the younger generation in an increasingly digital world and a globally competitive job market. Thus the transformation to civic constitutionalism in light of Taiwan's Sunflower Movement bears tremendous significance not only to China and Hong Kong but also far beyond.

Part II

The Hong Kong Umbrella Movement

4 The law and politics of constitutional reform and democratization in Hong Kong

Albert H. Y. Chen[*]

Introduction

A few weeks after China's National People's Congress Standing Committee (NPCSC) promulgated its Decision of 31 August 2014 on the model for the election by universal suffrage of Hong Kong's Chief Executive in 2017, the "Occupy Central" Movement – also known as the "Umbrella Movement" – engulfed several key government and business districts in Hong Kong. As in the case of the Sunflower Movement in Taipei earlier in the same year, students played a very important role in the Hong Kong movement. Whereas the movement in Taipei was in protest against the ruling regime's policy of economic cooperation with Beijing, the movement in Hong Kong was a popular protest against Beijing's policy towards, or restrictions on, democratization in Hong Kong.

Beijing's policy on Hong Kong's democratization was purportedly based on the provisions of the Basic Law of the Hong Kong Special Administrative Region (HKSAR), which was enacted by the National People's Congress (NPC) in 1990 and came into force when Hong Kong's status changed from that of a British colony to a Special Administrative Region (SAR) of the People's Republic of China (PRC) on 1 July 1997. Ironically, so were the demands of the protesters, who alleged that the NPCSC Decision of 31 August 2014 constituted a breach of Beijing's promise to the people of Hong Kong that the democratic election of the Chief Executive (CE) of the HKSAR by universal suffrage would be introduced – a promise enshrined in the text of the Basic Law itself.[1] In this sense, the "Occupy" Movement in Hong Kong can be considered a social movement that drew on legal norms as an important component of its strategy of mass mobilization. How then could both the legitimacy of the NPCSC Decision of 31 August 2014 and the claims of the protesters be simultaneously based on the Basic Law – the constitutional instrument of the HKSAR? This chapter seeks to answer this question by reviewing the evolution of Hong Kong's political system and investigating into the different understandings and interpretations of the Basic Law on the part of the Chinese regime and on the part of democracy activists in Hong Kong.

This chapter consists of the following parts, apart from this introduction. First it examines the development of Hong Kong's political system since colonial times, and the provisions of the Basic Law governing the political order of the HKSAR. It then briefly reviews the movements towards democratization that took place since the establishment of the HKSAR in 1997. Next it considers developments since early 2013, when the "Occupy

* Cheng Chan Lan Yue Professor in Constitutional Law, Faculty of Law, University of Hong Kong.

1 See Article 45 of the Basic Law.

Central" campaign was launched to struggle for the realization of "genuine universal suffrage" in the election of the CE of the HKSAR. Finally, it concludes by reflecting on the contradictions and tensions inherent in the project of "One Country, Two Systems" that were revealed by the failure of the "Occupy" Movement in realizing its democratic aspirations, particularly the conflict between the Communist Party-led socialist political system in mainland China and the aspirations towards Western-style liberal democracy on the part of democracy activists in Hong Kong.

The development of Hong Kong's political system since colonial times

The British Empire acquired the colony of Hong Kong – the geographical territory of which is now the Hong Kong Special Administrative Region (HKSAR) of the People's Republic of China (PRC) – from China in three stages: the cession of Hong Kong Island by the Qing emperor in China to Britain in 1842 after the "Opium War"; the cession of Kowloon Peninsula (to the north of Hong Kong Island) by the Qing to Britain in 1860 after the Anglo-French forces invaded Peking; and the 99-year lease by the Qing to Britain of the "New Territories" (north of Kowloon) in the midst of the foreign powers' "scramble for concessions in China" in 1898.[2]

Although the British transplanted to colonial Hong Kong its common law and its tradition of the rule of law, it did not introduce in Hong Kong the British style of parliamentary democracy or the "Westminster-style" of government. Instead the colonial government ruled Hong Kong by means of a kind of "soft authoritarianism".[3] Power was concentrated in the hands of the Governor (appointed directly by the British Crown) and senior expatriate officials of the colonial government of Hong Kong appointed by the Governor, who formed the top tier of a civil service bureaucracy which at its lower levels was recruited largely from the local Chinese populace. The legislature – known as the Legislative Council (LegCo) – consisted of senior government officials and "unofficial members" chosen by the Governor from the local British and Hong Kong business and professional elite and appointed to sit in the Legislative Council.[4] The system was described as "administrative absorption of politics".[5] Since the 1950s, Hong Kong enjoyed rapid economic growth as one of the "Four Little Dragons" of East Asia (together with Taiwan, Singapore, and South Korea). Hong Kong's population consisted largely of migrants from the Chinese mainland and their descendants, particularly migrants who fled to Hong Kong during the communist revolution in the mainland in the late 1940s.[6] They were willing to accept colonial rule in Hong Kong, and did not engage in struggles for democratization and decolonization that

2 See generally Peter Wesley-Smith, *Constitutional and Administrative Law* (Hong Kong: China & Hong Kong Law Studies, 2nd edn, 1994) 23–30.

3 For a thorough description of the political system of colonial Hong Kong, see generally N. J. Miners, *The Government and Politics of Hong Kong* (Hong Kong: Oxford UP, 3rd edn, second impression 1982).

4 See generally Kathleen Cheek-Milby, *A Legislature Comes of Age: Hong Kong's Search for Influence and Identity* (Hong Kong: Oxford University Press, 1995).

5 Ambrose Y. C. King, "Administrative Absorption of Politics in Hong Kong: Emphasis on the Grassroots Level" in A. Y. C. King and R. P. L. Lee (eds), *Social Life and Development in Hong Kong* (Hong Kong: Chinese University Press, 1981), chap. 7.

6 See generally Albert H. Y. Chen, "The Development of Immigration Law and Policy: The Hong Kong Experience" (1988) 33 *McGill LJ* 631.

might provoke the PRC (established in 1949 after the defeat of the Nationalist Party government by the Chinese communists) government to claim Hong Kong from the British.

As the British "lease" over Hong Kong's New Territories would expire in 1997, British Prime Minister Margaret Thatcher visited Beijing in 1982 and initiated negotiations with the PRC government on Hong Kong's constitutional future. The result was the Sino-British Joint Declaration signed at the end of 1984.[7] The Joint Declaration provided for Hong Kong's return to China in 1997. The PRC undertook to allow Hong Kong to practice a high degree of autonomy as a "Special Administrative Region" (SAR) of the PRC after 1997. There would be "Hong Kong people ruling Hong Kong" instead of the PRC government sending its Communist Party cadres to rule Hong Kong.[8] Hong Kong would be permitted to retain its existing economic, social, and legal systems (including capitalism, private property, the English common law, and existing provisions for the protection of human rights and civil liberties) in accordance with Deng Xiaoping's (鄧小平) concept of "One Country, Two Systems": Hong Kong would become an integral part of the "One Country" of China, but the Chinese mainland and Hong Kong would practise different "systems" – "socialism" and "capitalism" respectively.[9]

The Joint Declaration contains detailed provisions on the systems and policies to be practised by the HKSAR. The Joint Declaration is a treaty that is binding on the Chinese and British governments in international law, but the PRC would need to translate its provisions into domestic law so as to provide a legal basis for the operation of the HKSAR. The drafting of such a domestic law began in 1985 and was completed in 1990, when the National People's Congress (NPC) of the PRC enacted the Basic Law of the HKSAR of the PRC – the product of nearly five years of work, including two public consultation exercises on its drafts in 1988 and 1989. This Basic Law would serve as a "mini-constitution" for Hong Kong after 1997. It provides for the constitutional relationship between the HKSAR Government and the Central Government in Beijing; it defines the structure, mode of formation, and powers of the HKSAR Government; it guarantees the rights and liberties of the Hong Kong people; and it also sets out the social and economic policies and systems to be practiced in the HKSAR.

As regards Hong Kong's political system, the Joint Declaration had only provided for it briefly, while the Basic Law provides for the details. One of the main areas of controversy during the drafting of the Basic Law[10] was the extent to which the political system of the HKSAR should be democratic, given that the colonial political system at the time the Joint Declaration was signed in 1984 was hardly democratic in that neither the executive nor the legislature was elected by the people of Hong Kong. The Joint Declaration did contemplate

7 See generally Yash Ghai, *Hong Kong's New Constitutional Order* (Hong Kong: Hong Kong UP, 2nd edn, 1999), chap. 2.

8 Paragraph 3(4) of the Joint Declaration provides that "[t]he Government of the Hong Kong Special Administrative Region will be composed of local inhabitants". See also the third paragraph of Section 1 of Annex I to the Joint Declaration.

9 Section 1 of Annex I to the Joint Declaration provides that "after the establishment of the Hong Kong Special Administrative Region the socialist system and socialist policies shall not be practised in the Hong Kong Special Administrative Region", and "Hong Kong's previous capitalist system and life-style shall remain unchanged for 50 years".

10 See generally Peter Wesley-Smith and Albert Chen (eds), *The Basic Law and Hong Kong's Future* (Hong Kong: Butterworths, 1988).

some degree of democratization of this colonial political system. On the mode of selection of the Chief Executive of the HKSAR – who would replace the colonial governor as the head of the Hong Kong Government – the Joint Declaration provided that the Chief Executive "shall be selected by election or through consultations held locally and be appointed by the Central People's Government".[11] As regards the legislature, which was an entirely appointed body at the time of the Joint Declaration, the Joint Declaration provided that the HKSAR legislature "shall be constituted by elections", but did not elaborate further on the precise mode of election.[12] As regards the relationship between the executive and the legislature, the Joint Declaration provided that the executive "shall be accountable to the legislature".[13]

The provisions of the Basic Law on the political system of the HKSAR may be summarized as follows. The Basic Law declares that the "ultimate aim"[14] of the political evolution of the HKSAR is the election of both the Chief Executive and all members of the Legislative Council by universal suffrage. However, it is also provided that such political evolution depends on "the actual situation in the HKSAR" and "the principle of gradual and orderly progress".[15] The Basic Law provides for a progressive increase in the number of directly elected members (i.e. members elected by universal suffrage in geographical constituencies in different parts of Hong Kong, as distinguished from members elected by the "functional constituencies" discussed below) of LegCo from 20 (out of a total membership of 60) in the first-term LegCo of the HKSAR, to 24 in the second LegCo, and then to 30 in the third LegCo.[16] As regards the selection of the CE, it is provided that the first CE would be chosen by a Selection Committee of 400 members, and the second and third CEs elected by an Election Committee of 800 members largely elected from four sectors of Hong Kong society. Given that the Joint Declaration provided that the Chief Executive may be chosen either by election or consultation, and did not make it clear that the elections to LegCo must be by direct election rather indirect election or election by "functional constituencies", the gains for democracy in the making of the Basic Law may be recognized.[17]

A noteworthy feature of the political system prescribed by the Basic Law is that it is not a static one but an evolving one, and the logic and mechanism of its evolution are provided for in the Basic Law itself. The ultimate aim of universal suffrage, the principle of gradual and orderly progress, and the phased increase in the number of directly elected legislators have been mentioned above. Another important characteristic of the political system established by the Basic Law is its openness to change after 2007. Annexes I and II to the Basic

11 This is provided for in the third paragraph of Section 1 of Annex I to the Joint Declaration, and in paragraph 3(4) of the Joint Declaration itself.

12 This is provided for in the third paragraph of Section 1 of Annex I to the Joint Declaration.

13 Ibid.

14 Basic Law, arts. 45 and 68.

15 Ibid.

16 See Annex II to the Basic Law, and the Decision of the NPC on the Method for the Formation of the First Government and the First Legislative Council of the HKSAR. In the first and second LegCos, ten and six members respectively were to be elected by an Election Committee. In the first, second, and third LegCos, 30 members were to be elected by functional constituencies.

17 It is noteworthy in this regard that in the Basic Law of the Macao Special Administrative Region, which is in most respects almost identical to the Hong Kong Basic Law, there is no mention whatsoever of the direction of political evolution or any eventual destination of universal suffrage for the election of the Chief Executive and all members of the legislature. This testifies to the relative strength of the democracy movement in Hong Kong in the 1980s.

Law expressly provide that the methods for electing the CE and LegCo may change after 2007. They also expressly provide for the procedure for such constitutional change, which involves the support of a two-thirds majority in LegCo, the CE's consent, and the approval of (in the case of a change in the electoral method for the CE) or "reporting for the record" to (in the case of a change in the electoral method for LegCo) the NPCSC.

The Basic Law, though already enacted in 1990, would only fully come into effect in 1997 upon the establishment of the HKSAR. In the "transition period" between 1984 (the year the Joint Declaration was signed) and 1997, the British colonial government continued to govern Hong Kong. It introduced a series of measures for Hong Kong's democratization in preparation for the handover of Hong Kong to China in 1997. Some of these measures were contested by the PRC government, which argued that constitutional reforms in Hong Kong during the transition period must "converge" with the model of the HKSAR political system prescribed by the Basic Law.[18] However, not all of the political reforms introduced by the colonial government were objected to by Beijing. Actually, some of the political institutions created by the colonial government in the transition period were recognized by and incorporated into the Basic Law itself. The most important of such institutions was that of "functional constituencies", the origins of which will now be elaborated.

In 1985, the colonial government introduced its first major measure towards Hong Kong's democratization.[19] This was the creation of 24 elected seats in the LegCo. Twelve of these seats were elected by electoral colleges comprising the District Boards, the Urban Council, and the Regional Council, which were largely consultative bodies at local levels. The other 12 were elected by "functional constituencies" consisting of business and professional groupings, such as chambers of commerce, industrialists' federations, trade unions, and members of professions such as lawyers, doctors, engineers, and teachers. The original logic of functional constituencies,[20] as explained by the colonial government, was that they represented sectors of society from which appointed unofficial members of LegCo were formerly drawn, and in the course of democratization, it was appropriate that the corporate bodies or individual members of these sectors would elect their own representatives into LegCo. These two modes of election of LegCo members were incorporated into the Basic Law when it was enacted in 1990. Thus the first LegCo of the HKSAR would consist of 20 members elected by universal suffrage, 30 members elected by functional constituencies, and ten elected by an electoral college. The number of members elected by universal suffrage would increase to 30 in the third LegCo.

Functional constituencies also have a role to play in the election of the Election Committee for the Chief Executive of the HKSAR. As prescribed in Annex I to the Basic Law, the Election Committee would consist of persons from four sectors, with equal numbers of members from each sector. The sectors are: (a) business (comprising mainly of corporate voters in various commercial, financial, and industrial fields), (b) professional bodies, (c) labour and other social sectors, and (d) the political sector (including legislators,

18 See generally Albert H. Y. Chen, "From Colony to Special Administrative Region: Hong Kong's Constitutional Journey" in Raymond Wacks (ed.), *The Future of the Law in Hong Kong* (Hong Kong: Oxford University Press, 1989) 76–126.

19 White Paper, *The Further Development of Representative Government in Hong Kong* (Government Printer, November 1984).

20 See generally Christine Loh and Civic Exchange (eds), *Functional Constituencies: A Unique Feature of the Hong Kong Legislative Council* (Hong Kong: Hong Kong University Press, 2006).

Hong Kong deputies to the NPC, and Hong Kong members of the Chinese People's Political Consultative Conference, etc.). Thus in the Election Committee of 800 members, there were 200 members from each of the four sectors. (Annex I to the Basic Law was subsequently amended in 2010, increasing the size of the Election Committee to 1,200 members, including 300 members from each of the four sectors.[21])

Post-1997 movements towards democratization[22]

In the first few years of the history of the HKSAR, elections by the Election Committee to the office of the Chief Executive and elections of the LegCo partly by universal suffrage and partly by functional constituencies took place in accordance with the relevant provisions of the Basic Law. A major turning point in the post-1997 history of Hong Kong was the Hong Kong Government's attempt to enact a national security law for the purpose of implementing Article 23 of the Basic Law, which requires the HKSAR to enact laws on treason, secession, sedition, subversion, and protection of state secrets. This legislative exercise was aborted after a march of an estimated half a million people on 1 July 2003 in opposition to the bill for the proposed law.[23] The bill was supported by the "pro-China" camp (also known as the "pro-establishment" camp) in Hong Kong politics, but opposed by the "pro-democracy" camp (also known as the "pan-democrats")[24] which led the social movement against the bill. With their prestige bolstered by their success in opposing the national security bill, the pro-democracy camp launched a movement to demand the speedy democratization of the HKSAR.[25] In late 2003 and early 2004, a number of pro-democracy assemblies and demonstrations were held and were attended by tens of thousands of people. Pro-democracy politicians found in the Basic Law a powerful source of legitimacy for their demands. As mentioned above, the provisions of the Basic Law itself allows change to the existing "undemocractic" system for the election of the third-term CE in 2007 and the fourth-term LegCo in 2008. Thus the pan-democrats' slogan was "double universal suffrage": the introduction of universal suffrage for the election of the CE in 2007, and universal suffrage for the election of all legislators in 2008.

In early 2004, Beijing decided to respond to the democracy movement in Hong Kong. Departing from its normal practice of holding one session of meetings once every two months, the NPCSC held two successive sessions in April 2004. At the end of the first

21 The political reform of 2010 is discussed below.

22 This section and the following section draw on my chapter, "Development of Representative Government" in Johannes Chan and C. L. Lim (eds), *Law of the Hong Kong Constitution* (Hong Kong: Sweet & Maxwell, 2nd edn, 2015), chap. 8.

23 See generally Fu Hualing *et al.* (eds), *National Security and Fundamental Freedoms: Hong Kong's Article 23 Under Scrutiny* (Hong Kong University Press, 2005); Ngok Ma, "Civil Society in Self-Defense: The Struggle Against National Security Legislation in Hong Kong" (2005) 14 *Journal of Contemporary China* 465.

24 The basic cleavage in the politics of the HKSAR has been the division between the "pro-China" camp and the "pro-democracy" camp or "pan-democrats". The pro-China camp supports the policies of the PRC government towards Hong Kong, including its cautious and gradualist approach to its democratization. The camp also supports one-party rule in mainland China and does not criticize its human rights record. The pan-democrats advocate Western-style liberal democracy for Hong Kong, and are critical of authoritarian one-party rule in China and its human rights record.

25 See generally Ming Sing, "Public Support for Democracy in Hong Kong" (2005) 12(2) *Democratization* 244 (explaining the upsurge in public support for democracy in Hong Kong since the rally of 1 July 2003).

session, the NPCSC on 6 April issued an Interpretation of the Basic Law.[26] It elaborates upon Annexes I and II to the Basic Law by stipulating a procedure for initiating changes to the relevant electoral methods: the CE should first submit a report to the NPCSC on whether there is a need to introduce electoral reform, whereupon the NPCSC will decide the matter in accordance with Articles 45 and 68 of the Basic Law. After this interpretation was promulgated, Chief Executive Tung Chee Hwa (董建華) submitted a relevant report to the NPCSC on 15 April 2004.[27] Another session of the NPCSC was immediately convened to consider the report, and on 26 April the NPCSC promulgated its Decision on the matter. The Decision rules out the introduction of universal suffrage for the CE and all legislators in 2007 and 2008 respectively, but permits political reforms in 2007 and 2008 within certain parameters (e.g. the proportion of directly elected legislators to those elected by functional constituencies shall remain unchanged).[28]

After the NPCSC Decision, the Constitutional Development Task Force of the Hong Kong Government conducted public consultations on political reform for 2007–2008, leading to the publication of its Fifth Report in October 2005.[29] This was a major initiative on the part of Mr Donald Tsang (曾蔭權), who had succeeded Mr Tung Chee Hwa following the latter's resignation from the office of CE in spring 2005. The Fifth Report proposed the election of the CE in 2007 by an Election Committee of 1,600 persons (which would include, inter alia, all members of the District Councils, formerly known as District Boards), and the expansion of LegCo in 2008 from 60 members to 70 members (including five new seats to be directly elected by universal suffrage and five new seats elected by District Councillors). Under Annexes I and II to the Basic Law, the adoption of the proposed reform would require the support of a two-thirds majority in LegCo. On 21 December 2005, the proposal was defeated by 24 "pan-democrats" in LegCo voting against it, mainly on the grounds that it was not democratic enough (e.g. the District Councillors entitled to vote under the proposed system included not only elected Councillors but also appointed Councillors, who comprised approximately one-fifth of all District Councillors), and that the government had failed to provide a timetable for the introduction of universal suffrage.[30]

After the defeat of the political reform proposal in December 2005, discussion on political development continued to be carried out in the Committee on Governance and Political Development of the Commission on Strategic Development of the Hong Kong Government.

26 This was the second interpretation of the Basic Law issued by the NPCSC. For the first interpretation, see Johannes M. M. Chan *et al.* (eds), *Hong Kong's Constitutional Debate: Conflict Over Interpretation* (Hong Kong: Hong Kong University Press, 2000).

27 *Report by the Chief Executive of the Hong Kong Special Administrative Region to the Standing Committee of the National People's Congress on whether there is a need to amend the methods for selecting the Chief Executive of the Hong Kong Special Administrative Region in 2007 and for forming the Legislative Council of the Hong Kong Special Administrative Region in 2008* (Hong Kong Government, 2004); the *Second Report of the Constitutional Development Task Force: Issues of Principle in the Basic Law Relating to Constitutional Development* (Hong Kong Government, 2004).

28 See generally Albert H. Y. Chen, "The Constitutional Controversy of Spring 2004" (2004) 34 *HKLJ* 215; Johannes Chan and Lison Harris (eds), *Hong Kong's Constitutional Debates* (Hong Kong Law Journal Limited, 2005).

29 *The Fifth Report of the Constitutional Development Task Force: Package of Proposals for the Methods for Selecting the Chief Executive in 2007 and for Forming the Legislative Council in 2008* (Hong Kong Government, 2005).

30 See generally Albert H. Y. Chen, "The Fate of the Constitutional Reform Proposal of October 2005" (2005) 35 *HKLJ* 537.

The Committee was established by Tsang in late 2005 partly in response to criticisms that the government was not able to provide any timetable for the introduction of universal suffrage. It was on the basis of the deliberations in this Committee that the Green Paper on Constitutional Development[31] was published on 11 July 2007, initiating a three-month consultation on the subject.

On 12 December 2007, the government published its Report on Public Consultation on the Green Paper on Constitutional Development.[32] At the same time, Chief Executive Donald Tsang submitted his report to the NPCSC on "the Public Consultation on Constitutional Development and on whether there is a need to amend the methods for selecting the Chief Executive of the HKSAR and for forming the Legislative Council of the HKSAR in 2012".[33] On 29 December 2007, the NPCSC enacted its Decision on Issues Relating to the Methods for Selecting the Chief Executive of the HKSAR and for Forming the Legislative Council of the HKSAR in the Year 2012 and on Issues Relating to Universal Suffrage (the NPCSC Decision).[34] The most significant provisions may be set out as follows:

(a) In 2012, neither the Chief Executive (CE) nor all legislators may be elected by universal suffrage. In 2012, the ratio (50:50) of legislators elected by universal suffrage to those elected by functional constituencies will remain unchanged. Subject to these parameters, the electoral arrangements for the CE and LegCo in 2012 may be amended in accordance with the "principle of gradual and orderly progress" as provided for in the Basic Law.
(b) At its meeting, the NPCSC was "of the view" that "the election of the fifth CE of the HKSAR in the year 2017 may be implemented by the method of universal suffrage; that after the CE is selected by universal suffrage, the election of the LegCo of the HKSAR may be implemented by the method of electing all the members by universal suffrage".
(c) "At an appropriate time prior to" the election of the CE or of all legislators by universal suffrage, the five-step procedure prescribed in Annexes I and II to the Basic Law and the NPCSC Interpretation of 6 April 2004 should be followed: (1) the CE making a report to the NPCSC, (2) the NPCSC rendering a decision thereon, (3) a Government bill for electoral reform being passed by a two-thirds majority in LegCo, (4) the CE consenting to the bill, and (5) the bill being reported to the NPCSC for approval or for the record.
(d) At its meeting, the NPCSC was "of the view that" the nominating committee (referred to in the Basic Law) for candidates for election of the CE by universal suffrage "may be formed with reference to the current provisions regarding the Election Committee in Annex I to the Hong Kong Basic Law". The nominating committee shall in

31 Hong Kong: Government Logistics Department, 2007.
32 Hong Kong: Government Logistics Department, 2007. The Green Paper on Constitutional Development was published on 11 July 2007, and the consultation period for the Green Paper ended on 10 October 2007.
33 Hong Kong: Government Logistics Department, 2007.
34 *Gazette of the HKSAR Government*, Special Supplement No. 5 to Gazette Extraordinary No. 48/2007 (31 December 2007) pp. E48 (Chinese version), E49 (English version). For a commentary on the decision, see Albert H. Y. Chen, "A New Era in Hong Kong's Constitutional History" (2008) 38 *HKLJ* 1.

accordance with democratic procedures[35] "nominate a certain number of candidates for the office of the CE, who is to be elected through universal suffrage by all registered electors of the HKSAR, and to be appointed by the Central People's Government".

On the basis of the 2007 Decision of the NPCSC, Mr Donald Tsang introduced the political reform exercise of 2009–2010, which was designed to revise the models for the election of the Chief Executive and the Legislative Council in 2012. This exercise began with the publication in November 2009 of the Government's Consultation Document on *Methods for Selecting the Chief Executive and for Forming the Legislative Council in 2012* ("the Consultation Document"),[36] which put forward proposals (the 2009 Proposal) for electoral reforms in 2012 largely similar to, but designed to be an improved version of, the reform proposals (the 2005 Proposal) contained in the Fifth Report of the Constitutional Development Task Force that were vetoed by the pan-democrats in LegCo in December 2005.

The 2009 Proposal was similar to the 2005 Proposal in at least three ways: (1) the proposed expansion of the size of the Election Committee for the CE; (2) the proposed increase of the total number of seats in LegCo from 60 to 70; and (3) the prominent role proposed for District Councillors in the election of LegCo and in the Election Committee. There were, however, two main differences between the two proposals. First, the expanded Election Committee under the 2009 Proposal would have 1,200 members instead of 1,600 members. Second, under this proposal, the District Councillors who would participate in the election of the five additional seats in LegCo and of relevant additional seats in the Election Committee would only include elected members of District Councils and exclude the appointed members.

More precisely, the expanded Election Committee in the 2009 Proposal would be elected by four sectors of society, each of which originally elected 200 members of the Election Committee under the existing system. Each of these sectors would elect 300 members under the 2009 Proposal. As regards the additional 100 seats allocated to the fourth sector (the "political sector"), the 2009 Proposal suggested that most of them may be elected by the elected members of the District Councils. On the issue of the "nomination threshold" for candidates for CE, it was proposed that it would remain at one-eighth of the total number of members of the Election Committee (i.e. 150 among the 1,200-member committee, as compared to the existing rule of 100 among the 800-member committee).

35 The reference to "democratic procedures" is not new but exists in Article 45 of the Basic Law (which provides for "the selection of the Chief Executive by universal suffrage upon nomination by a broadly representative nominating committee in accordance with democratic procedures"). The meaning of this phrase has been a major source of controversy in the context of the debate on universal suffrage for the election of the CE in Hong Kong. According to one school of thought, the phrase means that all members of the nominating committee should vote for the purpose of selecting a number of candidates who may then participate in the election of the CE by universal suffrage. Under Annex I, Article 4 of the Basic Law and the Chief Executive Election Ordinance (as it stood at the time of the 2007 NPCSC Decision), nomination by not less than 100 members of the 800-member Election Committee was sufficient to enable a person to become a candidate in the election of the CE.

36 The document was published on 18 November 2009 and was available in both hard copy and electronically.

After considering the views of members of the public collected during the three-month consultation period for the Consultation Document, the government on 14 April 2010 formally announced its *Package of Proposals for the Methods for Selecting the Chief Executive and for Forming the Legislative Council in 2012* – a constitutional reform proposal ("the Reform Package") that was basically the same as that proposed in the Consultation Document. The motions for the relevant amendments to Annexes I and II of the Basic Law for the purpose of implementing the Reform Package were formally submitted to LegCo on 7 June 2010 for debate and voting before the end of June 2010.

After the publication of the Consultation Document, the pan-democrats publicly stated their opposition to the Reform Package on the ground that it was not democratic enough. The scenario as of 7 June 2010 was that the motion for the Reform Package would be vetoed by the pan-democrats – a repetition of what had happened in December 2005. To the surprise of most observers, the situation suddenly changed on 14 June 2010, when Mr Henry Tang (唐英年), Chief Secretary of the HKSAR Government, met with Mr Albert Ho (何俊仁), Chairman of the Democratic Party (DP) and one of the pan-democratic political parties, and asked him whether the DP would support the government's LegCo motion for constitutional reform if the government were to modify the Reform Package and accept the DP's counter-proposal regarding the five additional District Council functional constituency seats being elected (after each of the candidates from the District Councils has been jointly nominated by several elected District Councillors) by all voters in Hong Kong who did not already have the right to vote in any existing functional constituency.[37] In the light of the affirmative answer given by Mr Ho, Chief Executive Donald Tsang announced on 21 June the government's acceptance of the DP's counter-proposal as a modification to its original Reform Package. Although not all the pan-democrats in LegCo supported the modified Reform Package, the government with the support of the DP secured the necessary two-thirds majority in LegCo for the modified Reform Package to be passed by LegCo on 24–25 June 2010.[38]

The Struggle for "genuine" universal suffrage in 2013–2015

To the pan-democrats, the political reform of 2010 was only of limited significance, since Hong Kong's political system was still far away from achieving the goals of what they called "double universal suffrage" – the election of the CE and of all members of LegCo by universal suffrage. As the NPCSC in its 2007 Decision had set the target date for the implementation of universal suffrage for the election of the CE at the year 2017, a third exercise in political reform (following the first two exercises in 2005 and 2010 respectively) would need to be conducted in 2013–2015 to work out the precise model for such election. Pro-democracy political activists in Hong Kong started in early 2013 to prepare for this exercise.

On 16 January 2013, Associate Professor Benny Tai (戴耀廷) of the law school of the University of Hong Kong published a newspaper article[39] in which he put forward the idea

37 Approximately 200,000 persons had the right to vote in existing functional constituencies. According to the DP's proposal, more than three million registered voters would be enfranchised with regard to the five newly created LegCo functional constituency seats, and all voters in Hong Kong would have two votes – one in a geographical constituency, and one in a functional constituency.

38 See generally Albert H. Y. Chen, "An Unexpected Breakthrough in Hong Kong's Constitutional Reform" (2010) 40 *HKLJ* 259.

39 The article was in Chinese and entitled "公民抗命的最大殺傷力武器" ("The most powerful weapon of civil disobedience"), and was published in the newspaper《信報》(Hong Kong Economic Journal).

of an "Occupy Central" campaign to pressurize the Central Government and the Hong Kong Government to introduce a model for universal suffrage that is consistent with international standards of democratic elections. The idea was widely circulated on the Internet and received much media attention, snowballing into a real "Occupy Central" campaign,[40] supported by many civil society groups in addition to the pro-democracy politicians in Hong Kong. "Occupy Central" in this context referred to demonstrators practising civil disobedience and occupying the Central District – the central business district of Hong Kong – to paralyse it in case the government fails to come up with a model for universal suffrage that complies with international standards on free and fair elections.[41] After months of deliberation, the Occupy Central Movement proposed on 6 May 2014 three models for election of the CE by universal suffrage for public consideration, all including the element of civic nomination (also known as "public nominations" or "citizens' nominations", which are translations of the original Chinese term *gongmin timing*), that is, nomination of candidates by prescribed numbers of citizens. In the week of 22 June 2014, the Occupy Central Movement held a "referendum" at which people could vote by mobile phone, on the Internet, or at voting booths to indicate whether they supported any of the three proposed models, and whether they believed that LegCo should reject any model introduced by the government which was inconsistent with international standards of universal suffrage. More than 700,000 people in Hong Kong participated in the "referendum" and indicated their support for the demands put forward by the Occupy Central Movement.

Another major development in the struggle for democracy was the formation on 21 March 2013 of the Alliance for True Democracy,[42] consisting of all the pan-democrats in LegCo, all the "pro-democracy" political parties, and some civil society organizations. The objective of the Alliance was to promote the realization of "genuine" universal suffrage in Hong Kong. After months of deliberation, the Alliance proposed on 8 January 2014 a "three-track" model for the election of the CE by universal suffrage – the three tracks being nominations by citizens ("civic nominations"), by political parties, and by the nominating committee, respectively.

Earlier, on 17 October 2013, Mr C. Y. Leung (梁振英), the CE of the HKSAR, had announced the establishment of a three-person "Task Force on Constitutional Development", led by Chief Secretary Mrs Carrie Lam, which would launch a public consultation exercise on the electoral reforms for the LegCo and the Chief Executive to be elected in 2016 and 2017, respectively. The exercise formally commenced on 4 December 2013 with the publication of the Consultation Document entitled "Let's talk and achieve universal suffrage", initiating a five-month consultation period which ended on 3 May 2014.[43] During the consultation period, many political parties and civil society groups,

40 See the website of this movement (the full English name of which is "Occupy Central with Love and Peace"), http://www.oclp.hk/.

41 For such international standards, see generally Michael C. Davis, "The Basic Law, Universal Suffrage and the Rule of Law in Hong Kong" (2015) 38 *Hastings International and Comparative Law Review* 275; Alvin Y. H. Cheung, "Road to Nowhere: Hong Kong's Democratization and China's Obligations under Public International Law" (2015) 40 *Brooklyn Journal of International Law* 465.

42 See its website http://www.atd.hk/.

43 For official documents relating to this consultation exercise and subsequent developments relating to the introduction of universal suffrage for the CE election in 2017, see the government's websites http://www.2017.gov.hk/en/home/index.html (English version); http://www.2017.gov.hk/tc/home/index.html (Chinese version).

including those that are "pro-China" and those that are "pro-democracy", put forward their proposed electoral models.[44] On 15 July 2014, the government released its report on the outcomes of the consultation exercise. On the same day, the Chief Executive, Mr C. Y. Leung, submitted to the NPCSC his "Report on whether there is a need to amend the methods for selecting the Chief Executive of the HKSAR in 2017 and for forming the Legislative Council of the HKSAR on 2016",[45] recommending the introduction of universal suffrage for the election of the CE in 2017, and recommending no constitutional change regarding the electoral arrangements for LegCo in 2016.

On 31 August 2014, the NPCSC rendered its Decision on political reform in the HKSAR.[46] It accepted the Chief Executive's recommendation that no constitutional change regarding the election of the Legislative Council was called for in 2016. On the question of the election of the CE by universal suffrage, the following points in the Decision are particularly noteworthy:

(1) "Since the long-term prosperity and stability of Hong Kong and the sovereignty, security and development interests of the country are at stake, there is a need to proceed in a prudent and steady manner."
(2) "The formulation of the method for selecting the Chief Executive by universal suffrage must strictly comply with the relevant provisions of the Hong Kong Basic Law, accord with the principle of 'one country, two systems', and befit the legal status of the HKSAR. It must meet the interests of different sectors of the society, achieve balanced participation, be conducive to the development of the capitalist economy, and make gradual and orderly progress in developing a democratic system that suits the actual situation in Hong Kong."
(3) "Since the Chief Executive of the HKSAR shall be accountable to both the HKSAR and the Central People's Government in accordance with the provisions of the Hong Kong Basic Law, the principle that *the Chief Executive has to be a person who loves the country and loves Hong Kong* must be upheld. This is a basic requirement of the policy of 'one country, two systems'. It is determined by the legal status as well as important functions and duties of the Chief Executive, and is called for by the actual need to maintain long-term prosperity and stability of Hong Kong and uphold the sovereignty, security and development interests of the country. *The method for selecting the Chief Executive by universal suffrage must provide corresponding institutional safeguards for this purpose.*" (Emphasis added.)
(4) The CE of the HKSAR may be elected by universal suffrage "starting from 2017".
(5) As regards the "number of members, composition and formation method" of the "broadly representative nominating committee" that nominates candidates for the CE, provisions "shall be made *in accordance with* the number of members, composition and formation method of the Election Committee for the Fourth Chief Executive." (Emphasis added.)

44 For information on various models that were proposed, see the government's report on the consultation exercise published on 15 July 2014, entitled the *Report on the Public Consultation on the Methods for Selecting the Chief Executive in 2017 and for Forming the Legislative Council in 2016* (see n. 43 above).

45 See the websites mentioned in n. 43 above.

46 The Decision of the Standing Committee of the NPC on issues relating to the selection of the Chief Executive of the HKSAR by universal suffrage and on the method for forming the Legislative Council of the HKSAR in the year 2016 (31 August 2014): see n. 43 above.

(6) "The nominating committee shall nominate *two to three candidates* for the office of the Chief Executive in accordance with democratic procedures. Each candidate must have *the endorsement of more than half of all the members of the nominating committee.*" (Emphasis added.)

On 1 September 2014 – the day following the NPCSC Decision – several senior Chinese officials visited Hong Kong and made important speeches to explain the Decision to members of the public and to Hong Kong Government officials.[47] They pointed out that the model for universal suffrage prescribed by the Decision provides the institutional guarantee that the CE elected by universal suffrage in the future would be someone who is both trusted by the Central Government and supported by the people of Hong Kong, and that non-patriots or those confrontational towards the Central Government could not become the CE. It was also said that the question of the model for universal suffrage in Hong Kong involves "a struggle for the power to govern the HKSAR". It further notes that some people in Hong Kong are:

> unwilling to accept the fact that the PRC has resumed the exercise of sovereignty over Hong Kong, and are unwilling to accept the governing power of the central authority over Hong Kong; they adopt an 'alternative interpretation' of 'One Country, Two Systems' and the provisions of the Basic Law; they make use of foreign forces, continuously stir up political disputes, pointing their fingers at the central government, and attempt to turn Hong Kong into an independent political entity. On the issue of universal suffrage, their views and demands may be summarized in one sentence: let their representative become the Chief Executive. This, of course, cannot be permitted. If they are allowed to become the Chief Executive, this would necessarily prejudice the central government's governing power over the HKSAR, prejudice our country's sovereignty, security and developmental interests, and damage the stability and prosperity of Hong Kong … If we understand the political nature of the question of universal suffrage, we can see that the question involves matters of fundamental principles on which there can be no compromise. … Those who insist in being confrontational towards the central government cannot be the Chief Executive, whether in the past, present or future.[48]

The Decision of the NPCSC was met by strong protest from pro-democracy forces in Hong Kong, which condemned the electoral model as "fake universal suffrage", and accused Beijing of acting in breach of its promise of universal suffrage in the Basic Law. They launched the "Umbrella Movement" or "Occupy Central Movement" that started in late September and continued until mid-December 2014, resulting in the occupation by demonstrators of central business and government districts in Admiralty, Causeway Bay, and Mong Kok. After the occupation came to a peaceful end, the government on 7 January 2015 launched the "second round consultation" on political reform by publishing the consultation document entitled "2017 Seize the Opportunity: Method for Selecting

47 See various Hong Kong newspapers of 2 September 2014, e.g. Ta Kung Pao, Wen Wei Pao.

48 Extract from Li Fei's speech, http://news.takungpao.com.hk/paper/q/2014/0902/2707720.html, my own translation from the Chinese original. See also his other speech in Chinese on the same day, http://www.fmcoprc.gov.hk/chn/xwdt/zt/rdjd/t1187495.htm.

the Chief Executive by Universal Suffrage Consultation Document",[49] for the purpose of consulting the public on the concrete model for electing the CE in 2017, which was to be formulated on the basis of the parameters set by the NPCSC Decision. The pan-democrats boycotted the consultation exercise, stating that they would reject any electoral model that conformed to the parameters set by the NPCSC Decision.

On 22 April 2015, the Government published a policy document entitled "2017 Make It Happen! Method for Selecting the Chief Executive by Universal Suffrage: Consultation Report and Proposals",[50] proposing a concrete model for nominating candidates for and electing the CE in 2017. The proposed model was subsequently introduced in the Legislative Council and put to a vote on 18 June 2015. With 28 (including 27 pan-democrats) of the 70 members of the Council voting against the proposal, it failed to secure the requisite two-thirds majority for amendment of Annex I to the Basic Law.[51] The veto meant that the existing system of the election of the Chief Executive by a 1,200-member Election Committee would continue in force in the foreseeable future.

Contradictions and tensions inherent in the project of "One Country, Two Systems"

In the struggle over the model of universal suffrage to be introduced in Hong Kong in 2017, the key players were the Central Government on the one hand and the pan-democrats and their supporters (including the Occupy Central Movement) on the other hand. The HKSAR Government and the pro-China/pro-Establishment political forces in Hong Kong largely followed the line taken by the Central Government. The most crucial issues in the debate on the model of universal suffrage for the election of the CE concerned the "nomination threshold" or "screening of candidates" in the operation of the nominating committee and the "civic nomination" proposed by the pro-democracy forces. Beijing's position and that of the pan-democrats may be analysed as follows.

The Central Government in Beijing would like to ensure that the candidates for election by universal suffrage to the office of the Chief Executive are all acceptable, trustworthy, and appointable from Beijing's point of view, in the sense that they are not "confrontational" towards the Central Government or ideologically opposed to the "socialist political system" in mainland China. The system of nominations of candidates by a nominating committee as provided for in Article 45 of the Basic Law enables this objective to be achieved if the majority of the members of the nominating committee are "pro-China" or "patriots", and if the nominations the committee makes are "institutional

49 See n. 38 above.

50 Ibid.

51 Actually the Government's motion was rejected by a vote of 8 (for the motion) to 28 (against). Less than one minute before the voting took place, 31 pro-government legislators walked out of the chamber en masse, intending to precipitate an insufficient quorum so that the voting could be delayed until one absent pro-Government legislator (Lau Wong-fat) could come back to vote with the others. Due to failure in coordination and communication, nine pro-government legislators did not join the walk-out, hence the quorum (half of the membership of LegCo) was still satisfied and the voting in the chamber was completed a few seconds after the walk-out. In the state of confusion, one of the nine pro-government legislators who stayed in the chamber failed to press the voting button in time, hence only eight votes in support of the government's motion were recorded. Jasper Tsang, President of LegCo, followed the convention of the president not voting. See the reports in Hong Kong newspapers of 19 June 2015, e.g. "Reform Package Fails, as Does Walkout" *South China Morning Post* (19 June 2015).

nominations", expressing the majority will of members of the committee.[52] Thus the 2014 Decision of the NPCSC requires the size and composition of the nominating committee to follow closely that of the pre-existing Election Committee for the Chief Executive. The political reality since the handover in 1997 has been that with the four-sector composition of the Election Committee and its members being largely elected by functional constituencies in these sectors, the majority of the committee's members were indeed "pro-China", "pro-Establishment", or "patriots", and those who were pan-democrats or sympathetic to them only constituted a minority (slightly more than one-eighth) in the Election Committee.[53]

On the other hand, the pan-democrats were firmly opposed to any "screening" to be performed by the nominating committee for the purpose of preventing persons (such as leading members of the pan-democrats) who have considerable public support among Hong Kong voters, but are not "patriots" in Beijing's eyes, from becoming candidates for election by universal suffrage to the office of the Chief Executive. In their view, this would be "fake" universal suffrage and inconsistent with international standards of democracy and elections, which prohibit unreasonable restrictions on the right to be a candidate in an election (such as restrictions or discrimination based on a person's political opinion).[54] "Genuine" universal suffrage, in their view, requires a truly competitive election in which candidates with different platforms and political opinions (including opinions critical of Beijing and its policies towards Hong Kong or the mainland itself) may freely and fairly compete for votes. Ever since direct election by universal suffrage was introduced for a portion of LegCo seats in 1991, the pan-democrats had in every election obtained a majority of the popular votes for those LegCo seats that were elected by universal suffrage (as distinguished from seats elected by functional constituencies).[55] Thus they felt justified in believing that any nomination system for the election of the Chief Executive by universal suffrage which makes it impossible for their leaders to be nominated as candidates would not be genuine universal suffrage. Hence the pan-democrats and their supporters condemned the model for universal suffrage stipulated in the NPCSC Decision, and boycotted the government's "second round" of consultation regarding more detailed arrangements for universal suffrage. They eventually vetoed in LegCo the government's electoral proposal which was based on the model stipulated by the NPCSC.

During the debate in 2013–2014 on the nomination system for election of the CE by universal suffrage in 2017, the principal demand of the pan-democrats and the Occupy Central Movement was civic nomination, although there were proposals from

52 The concept of "institutional nomination" (*jigou timing*) was first mentioned by Qiao Xiaoyang, Chairman of the Law Committee of the NPC, in his speech in Shenzhen to "pro-Establishment" Hong Kong legislators on 24 March 2013. See various Hong Kong newspapers of 25 March 2013, e.g. Ta Kung Pao, Wen Wei Pao.

53 In the existing system for election of the CE by the Election Committee under Annex I to the Basic Law, a candidate may be nominated jointly by at least one-eighth of the members of the Election Committee, followed by election by members of the Election Committee. In the CE elections of 2007 and 2012, persons supporting or sympathetic to the pan-democrats won more than one-eighth of the seats in the elections to the Election Committee, and thus Alan Leong (of the Civic Party) and Albert Ho (of the Democratic Party) were nominated respectively as one of the two candidates in the 2007 election and one of the three candidates in the 2012 election.

54 See n. 41 above.

55 The pan-democrats have consistently won approximately 55–60% of the popular votes in each election, and the pro-China camp approximately 40–45% of the popular votes. Such distribution has hardly changed in 20 years.

pro-democracy scholars considered to be "moderate", and also a proposal from Mr Ronny Tong,[56] a legislator who was also a member of the Civic Party, that did not insist on civic nomination but advocated a relatively low threshold for nomination by a nomination committee (such as one-eighth of its members being able to nominate a candidate)[57] which, according to these proposals, should be more democratically constituted than the existing Election Committee. The pan-democrats and other democracy activists in Hong Kong considered civic nomination to be more consistent with democracy and free election than nominations by a nominating committee that is not elected by universal suffrage, as civic nomination would allow everyone who has the requisite degree of popular support (say tens of thousands of eligible voters) to participate as a candidate in the election. They argued that civic nomination is not necessarily inconsistent with Article 45 of the Basic Law, as in their view Article 45 leaves open the possibility of allowing the nominating committee to endorse the candidates nominated by the requisite number of citizens, in addition to members of the nominating committee making their own nominations of candidates. However, in the eyes of Beijing, civic nomination was totally out of the question as it was plainly inconsistent with Article 45 of the Basic Law.

The Decision of the NPCSC in August 2014 might be understood as the outcome of a cost-and-benefit analysis conducted by Beijing regarding the introduction of elections of the Chief Executive by universal suffrage in Hong Kong. The benefit would be to be seen to honour the promise of universal suffrage made in the 2007 Decision of the NPCSC and in the Basic Law, and to win the support of Hong Kong people who aspire towards democracy. Furthermore, some believed that the Hong Kong Government would become more effective if its CE is elected by universal suffrage and thus has a popular mandate and greater legitimacy to govern Hong Kong. On the other hand, an electoral model that was acceptable to the pan-democrats would be one in which the pan-democrats would have a reasonable chance of getting their leader(s) nominated by the nominating committee as candidate(s) in the CE election by universal suffrage. For Beijing, agreeing to such an electoral model means to accept that there is a chance that a pan-democrat would be the winner in the CE election by universal suffrage. Beijing would have assessed the likelihood of this scenario materializing, and considered how to deal with this scenario should it materialize. Would it appoint the pan-democrat as Chief Executive? Or would it decline to make an appointment, a power which it has under the Basic Law,[58] so that another election should be held? What would be the nature and magnitude of the political crisis in Hong Kong should this happen? How would such a crisis (taking into account its likelihood and its magnitude) compare with the crisis (including, for example, "Occupy Central" materializing) that would be precipitated by the electoral model favoured by Beijing being unacceptable to the pro-democracy forces in Hong Kong? These, then, were likely to have been

56 Tong's proposal was first publicized at a press conference on 15 October 2013. See http://designdemocracy.hk/ronny-tong-proposal/?lang=tw and http://specials.mingpao.com/cfm/Category.cfm?SpecialsID=137&Page=1&CategoryID=4660.

57 This was the existing threshold for nomination of candidates for election of the CE by the Election Committee as prescribed in Annex I to the Basic Law.

58 Article 15 of the Basic Law provides that "The Central People's Government shall appoint the Chief Executive and the principal officials of the executive authorities of the Hong Kong Special Administrative Region in accordance with the provisions of Chapter IV of this Law." Chapter IV, Article 45(1) provides that "The Chief Executive of the Hong Kong Special Administrative Region shall be selected by election or through consultations held locally and be appointed by the Central People's Government."

the considerations which Beijing had taken into account in reaching the Decision in August 2014 on the model for universal suffrage for the Hong Kong Chief Executive in 2017. The Decision implies that according to Beijing's analysis, the risk and negative consequences of a non-patriot winning an election by universal suffrage and of a crisis precipitated by Beijing refusing to appoint him or her as CE are more serious than the risk and negative consequences of "Occupy Central" materializing or of any discontent or unrest flowing from Beijing's model for universal suffrage being rejected by the pro-democracy forces in Hong Kong.

Interestingly, a cost-and-benefit analysis may also be used to explain why the pan-democrats in LegCo vetoed the model of universal suffrage for the election of the CE proposed by the HKSAR Government on the basis of the NPCSC Decision of August 2014. As the composition of the Nominating Committee and the high nomination threshold specified by the Decision effectively rules out the possibility of at least one leader of the pan-democrats being nominated as a candidate to compete in the CE election by universal suffrage, the adoption by LegCo of the electoral model proposed by the government would effectively mean that the CE election by universal suffrage in 2017 would be a competition among two or three "pro-China" candidates considered to be "patriots" by a majority of the members of the Nominating Committee. The candidate eventually elected can then claim a popular mandate and political legitimacy greater than that of any leader of the pan-democrats. This would work against the interests of the pan-democrats, because their claim would then be weakened that they represent the majority of Hong Kong voters – a claim which they have been able to make continuously so far because the majority of Hong Kong voters who voted in LegCo elections from 1991 to 2012 actually voted for the pan-democrats rather than "pro-China" or "pro-Establishment" candidates. For the pan-democrats, therefore, there was little to be gained, but much to lose, from the introduction of universal suffrage for the election of the CE in 2017 in accordance with the nomination model prescribed by the NPCSC Decision of August 2014. This, then, can explain why they vetoed the electoral package in LegCo, despite the fact that opinion polls showed that members of the public who supported electoral reform outnumbered those opposed to it.[59]

Neither the considerations which Beijing probably took into account in conducting the cost-and-benefit analysis discussed above, nor those which probably led to the pan-democrats vetoing the electoral reform as discussed in the preceding paragraph, were the publicly stated reasons for the NPCSC Decision of August 2014 and the pan-democrats' rejection of the electoral package, respectively. Beijing insisted that the NPCSC Decision was made in accordance with, and was consistent with, the text of Article 45 of the Basic Law. Pan-democrats condemned the Decision and accused Beijing of breaching its promise of universal suffrage – which for the pan-democrats meant "genuine universal suffrage" – for Hong Kong people under the Basic Law and the timetable for democratization stipulated in the NPCSC Decision of 2007. Yet what the Basic Law and the NPCSC Decision

59 The LegCo vote on the electoral reform proposal took place on 18 June 2015. The following opinion polls conducted in June 2015 are thus particularly relevant. According to the "Survey on 2017 CE Election Proposal" conducted by the University of Hong Kong's Public Opinion Programme, among those polled on 5–14 June 2015, 51% supported LegCo adopting the proposal, while 37% were opposed to it. See www.hkupop.hku.hk/english/report/superSurvey2015/index.html. According to the "Joint-University Rolling Survey on 2017 CE Election Proposal", among those polled on 12–16 June 2015, 47% supported the government's electoral reform proposal, while 38% were opposed to it. See https://www.hkupop.hku.hk/english/features/jointUrollingSurvey/.

of 2007 promised was no more than a system of appointment of the Chief Executive by the Central People's Government after an election by "universal suffrage upon nomination by a broadly representative nominating committee in accordance with democratic procedures".[60] Control or pre-selection – or what the pan-democrats objected to as the "screening" – of candidates by a nominating committee had thus been written into the Basic Law as enacted in 1990.

In inaugurating the grand experiment of "One Country, Two Systems", the Hong Kong Basic Law has not only provided for the co-existence of two economic systems – one socialist and the other capitalist – within the PRC, but also envisioned a process of democratization in Hong Kong towards eventual election of the CE by universal suffrage and election of all legislators by universal suffrage, thus moving the political systems of Hong Kong and of mainland China further apart in the course of time (unless the latter also democratizes). The Basic Law has thus nourished the aspirations of many people in Hong Kong towards a full liberal democracy. But are these aspirations consistent with, and realizable within, the concept and structure of "One Country, Two Systems", under which the "One Country" adheres to the supremacy of the Chinese Communist Party, which must resist Western-style liberal democracy in order to survive? The story of the debate on and struggle for universal suffrage in Hong Kong thus reveals such underlying tensions behind, and the contradictions inherent in, the very concept and practice of "One Country, Two Systems".

It is unlikely that these tensions and contradictions can be resolved in the foreseeable future. The most likely scenario is that the existing "semi-democratic" political system in Hong Kong[61] will be maintained without further democratization or a move towards election of the CE by universal suffrage, and the confrontation and stalemate between the "pro-China" camp and "pan-democratic" camp in the politics of the HKSAR will continue to plague it and make it difficult to govern.[62] There thus seems to be an inexorable logic that the political costs, and ultimately also the economic and social costs, of "One Country, Two Systems" are rising as a result of the clash between Hong Kong people's aspirations towards Western-style democracy and the Chinese Party-State's insistence that the government of the HKSAR must be led by "patriots" loyal to the Party-State. Whether such costs can be contained, and whether social stability and economic prosperity can continue to be maintained in Hong Kong, amount to a severe challenge for the people of Hong Kong and the government of the PRC in the years to come.

60 Article 45 of the Basic Law.

61 The existing political system of the HKSAR has been described as a semi-democracy: see e.g. William H. Overholt, "Hong Kong: The Perils of Semidemocracy" (2001) 12(4) *Journal of Democracy* 5; Ming Sing, "Origins of Anti-Partyism in Hong Kong" (2004) 21(3) *East Asia* 37; Ma Ngok, *Political Development in Hong Kong* (Hong Kong: Hong Kong UP, 2007) 226. See also Sonny Shiu-hing Lo, *Hong Kong's Indigenous Democracy* (New York: Palgrave Macmillan, 2015).

62 The difficulties of Hong Kong's governance have been exacerbated by the filibuster in LegCo by radical pan-democrats which has steadily increased in scale since 2012 and resulted in partial paralysis of the LegCo's functions of lawmaking and financial approval.

5 Political protest in high-income societies

The case of the Occupy Central Movement in Hong Kong

Fu Hualing[*]

Introduction

Hong Kong is a metropolitan city that enjoys prosperity, freedom, and the rule of law. It is also a city that recently (1997) came under China's authoritarian rule. The tension in Hong Kong's political system is manifested in the continued struggle to reconcile with its new political master and the corresponding demand for democratic advancement. As a "semi-democracy", Hong Kong is constitutionally committed to universal suffrage, and there is a deeply felt passion and aspiration among residents in the city for liberal constitutional democracy. But the commitment to democracy is ironically made by a Communist Party authoritarian state that is fearful of, if not hostile to, the very concept.[1] The fight for democracy in the sub-national unit within an authoritarian regime has defined and continues to define Hong Kong's political landscape.

Hong Kong has been a difficult place for China to govern. Its political freedom and openness, independent and powerful legal system, and vibrant and challenging civil society are alien to the Central Authorities in Beijing. For them, Hong Kong remains uncharted water in many fundamental aspects. Yet as difficult and costly as it has been, China has grown confident in its ability to govern Hong Kong with a degree of effectiveness, and increasingly has resorted to constitutional rules and legal process in shaping Hong Kong's political future.[2] The Decision of the National People's Congress Standing Committee on 31 August 2014,[3] as discussed below, is the most recent example of how China suffocates Hong Kong's democratic impulses through legal interpretation. But China's rule of law concept is an authoritarian one. Will it prove effective in deflecting and silencing resistance from political and legal institutions in Hong Kong and in limiting Hong Kong's constitutional options?

* The author would like to thank Brian Christopher Jones and Richard Cullen for their valuable comments on this chapter, and Rachel Li and Caleb Li for their research assistance.

1 Albert H. Y. Chen, "The Law and Politics of the Struggle for Universal Suffrage in Hong Kong, 2013–15" (2016) 3 *Asian Journal of Law and Society* 189–207; and Michael C. Davis, "Beijing's Broken Promises" (2015) 26 *Journal of Democracy* 101–110.

2 Eric C. Ip, "Constitutional Competition between the Hong Kong Court of Final Appeal and the Chinese National People's Congress Standing Committee: A Game Theory Perspective" (2014) *Law & Social Inquiry* 824; and Benny Y. T. Tai, "The Constitutional Game of Article 158(3) of the Basic Law" (2011) 41 *Hong Kong Law Journal* 377.

3 Decision of the Standing Committee of the National People's Congress on Issues Relating to the Selection of the Chief Executive of the Hong Kong Special Administrative Region by Universal Suffrage and on the Method for Forming the Legislative Council of the Hong Kong Special Administrative Region in the Year 2016 (31 August 2014).

Deeply concerned with a real decline in Hong Kong's way of life, frustrated by the authoritarian rule of law that the Central Authorities impose on Hong Kong, and desperate for the lack of democratic mandate that may entrench Hong Kong's value and institutions, various groups in the city decided to make their political demands outside the established political and legal routes, launching the largest civil disobedience movement to date by occupying main streets at the heart of the city to protest against the 31 August Decision (the movement was referred to as the Occupying Central Movement, hereafter OCM). In doing so, Hong Kong residents took the constitution into their hands, insisting on their own alternative constitutional interpretation.

While the pursuit of democratic value through civic participation and the rule of law are both close to the heart of the Hong Kong people, the OCM, as the largest civil disobedience movement to date, reveals a rare moment of a clear tension between the ideals of democracy and the rule of law. The OCM clearly demonstrated Hong Kong's democratic passion and resilience. For a brief period, the movement gathered so much momentum that the students appeared to be unstoppable. However, with the prolonged nature of the OCM, the movement started to show its adverse social and economic impact, leading to a split in the community which initially showed a high degree of support and solidarity. The democratic potential of civil disobedience for the OCM began to decline and diminish, and its potential instability started to come to the forefront. As time progressed, the OCM was associated more with frustration, fatigue, and disorder,[4] and even became linked with political conspiracy and a continued threat to Hong Kong's rule of law.[5] When pro-OCM activists struggled to cope with internal conflicts, anti-OCM forces were mobilized and brought the occupiers to courts to account. Ironically, it was a court order that drove a fatal wedge into the OCM, dividing the supporter community and undermining the morale of the occupiers.[6] It was the authority of the court and the willingness of the people in the city to obey the rule of law that effectively suppressed citizens' democratic impulses.

With the peaceful ending of the OCM, Hong Kong's struggle for democracy has turned a new page. The two-and-a-half-month display of mass civil disobedience was unprecedented in its scale, epic in its manifestation, and potentially lasting in its impact on Hong Kong's constitutional development; but it was also highly controversial and divisive. There was the expectation that when all the dust settles, Hong Kong will have to do some serious soul-searching to rediscover its core values, redefine its identity, and locate itself within China. Unfortunately, the OCM has not brought political antagonism to an end. The OCM is as much a reflection of divisive society as a catalyzer of a more radical movement, one that may spin Hong Kong out of control.

The burden of "One Country, Two Systems"

Notwithstanding China's political and economic power, Hong Kong proves that it is extremely costly and difficult, if possible at all, for Beijing to censor its media, clamp down on its civil society, and control its judiciary. The Communist Party of China

4 Victoria Tin-bor Hui, "The Protects and Beyond" (2015) *Journal of Democracy* 111–121.

5 HKSAR Government, LCQ7: Impact of "Occupy Central" (HKSAR Government Press Releases, 2014), http://www.info.gov.hk/gia/general/201411/05/P201411050729.htm.

6 See notes 48 to 53 below.

(hereafter CCP) has yet to master the art of governing a free society such as Hong Kong. From a governance perspective, "one country, two systems" (hereafter OCTS) presents an unprecedented challenge to the Chinese government. To maintain Hong Kong's unique capitalist, social, economic, and political system requires extraordinary efforts from both sides of the border. Absent those efforts, there is a natural tendency for Beijing to create political assimilation and fusion that would result in the eventual diminution of Hong Kong's alternative system.

Maintaining Hong Kong's economic prosperity, rule of law, and political stability has been a thorny issue for Beijing. Seen from Beijing, Hong Kong has, since 1997, become not only an economic burden but also a political liability. The prevailing perception on the mainland is that Hong Kong's continuous economic stagnation necessitates policy support from the Central Government and restriction of competition from other Chinese cities, in order to pump up the Hong Kong economy.[7] Politically, Hong Kong's persistent demand for democratization, at a pace that the CCP feels uncomfortable with, and its direct and indirect influence on the mainland, may be posing a challenge to the mainland political system, triggering a colour revolution that has swept other parts of the world. Hong Kong's resilient struggle for autonomy is seen as presenting similar challenges already apparent in China's peripheries: terror attacks in Xinjiang, self-immolations in Tibet, and political agitation in Taiwan.[8] The worry in Beijing is that Hong Kong may slip away from Beijing's grip and create opportunities for foreign intervention, and that a democratized Hong Kong may cause a chain reaction in other parts of the mainland. Indeed, the more conservative wing of the CCP may prefer to roll back China's commitment to gradual democratization in Hong Kong, if at all possible, and would be happy to see Hong Kong settle with a limited reform package. It is within this context that we understand the difficult relations between Hong Kong and the central government authorities.

While China tries to limit Hong Kong's political ambition and control Hong Kong's democratic impulses, it has increasingly resorted to constitutional and legal instruments to achieve those objectives. Hong Kong has become a pilot for China to practise its authoritarian legality. The rule of law is often said to be a double-edged sword limiting and empowering the government at the same time, and the empowerment dimension is at full play in managing Beijing–Hong Kong relations.

Although the Basic Law works well in separating Hong Kong from the rest of China, hence the creation of OCTS, it does not create an independent and effective body for dispute resolution between the two separate jurisdictions. There is no channel for effective dialogue between the Central and SAR governments and between the socialist mainland and capitalist Hong Kong. The existing mechanisms, such as the Basic Law Committee, have failed miserably in providing a bridging and conflict resolution function, which is

7 For a full list of China's economic assistance to Hong Kong, see Information Office of the State Council of the People's Republic of China, *The Practice of the "One Country, Two Systems" Policy in the Hong Kong Special Administrative Region*, http://www.scmp.com/news/hong-kong/article/1529167/full-text-practice-one-country-two-systems-policy-hong-kong-special.

8 Bill Chou, "New Bottle, Old Wine: China's Governance of Hong Kong in View of Its Politics in the Restive Borderlands" (2015) 44(4) *Journal of Current Chinese Affairs* 177. Historically, the mainland authorities have always had the concerns that Hong Kong may become a "subversive basis". See Fu Hualing, "Past and Future Offences of Sedition in Hong Kong" in Fu Hualing, Carole Peterson, and Simon Young (eds) *National Security and Fundamental Freedoms: Hong Kong's Article 23 under Scrutiny* (Hong Kong: Hong Kong University Press, 2005).

sorely needed. The Basic Law only succeeds in building a wall between Hong Kong and the rest of China and offers little beyond that.[9]

While there is a great need to engage in constructive dialogue, no serious dialogue appears to have taken place at a structural level, given the inherent political conflict and the flaws in constitutional design. First of all, there is a mismatch in terms of the parties involved in the dialogue. For the most part, constitutional dialogue only takes place between the Standing Committee of the National People's Congress (hereafter NPCSC) for the Central Government, and the Court of Final Appeal (hereafter CFA) for Hong Kong. NPCSC is a political body making political decisions according to the political interest. Second, the parties to the dialogue follow their distinct logic. Political decision-making is informal and opaque, and often not rule-bound. On the contrary, judicial decisions are characterized by rigid legal formality, transparency, and often glamorous adversarial proceedings. Finally, there is a significant deficit of political trust between the two parties. There is misunderstanding of each other's position; such misunderstandings breed suspicion, and suspicion generates intolerance and hostility towards each other.[10]

Frustrated with what has been perceived as the country's political burden, China has learned to rein in political power through means that are often wrapped in the form of constitutional legality. As the regime has quickly learned, the rule of law in China's authoritarian system is more empowering than restraining for political authorities. While the Basic Law allows a constitutional dialogue between the court and the NPCSC on the interpretation of the Basic Law, little meaningful dialogue has taken place to date due to the lack of common ground and political trust on both sides. Naturally, each side seizes opportunities to maximize its respective interests. There may be escalation on each side, but ultimately little meaningful dialogue in enhancing mutual understanding and trust. In *Ng Ka Ling and Another v. The Director of Immigration*,[11] the CFA seized the opportunity to widen its constitutional jurisdiction and grant itself the power to scrutinize and invalidate national law, a move that is constitutionally impossible and politically offensive under the mainland system. In retaliation, the NPCSC exercised its ultimate veto power to invalidate the ruling in *Ng Ka Ling* and reclaim its authority as the final decision-maker of the Basic Law's meaning.[12]

Law has empowering and enabling functions, and this has clearly been seen throughout constitutional debates in Hong Kong. China exercises sovereign power over Hong Kong and employs theories of a unitary state (one constitution with one source of power), delegation (Hong Kong derived its authority from authorization), and residual power (unspecific power belonging to the Central Government) which derives from the Constitution, and shift the gravitas of power decisively to Beijing. On the contrary,

9 Yash Ghai, *Hong Kong's New Constitutional Order: The Resumption of Chinese Sovereignty and the Basic Law*, 2nd edn (Hong Kong: Hong Kong University Press, 1999); and Daniel Gittings, *Introduction to the Hong Kong Basic Law* (Hong Kong: Hong Kong University Press, 2013).

10 Yash Ghai, "The Political Economy of Interpretation" in Fu Hualing, Lison Harris, and Simon N. M. Yong (eds), *Interpreting Hong Kong's Basic Law: The Struggle for Coherence* (New York: Palgrave Macmillan, 2007).

11 *Ng Ka Ling and Another v. The Director of Immigration* [1999] HKCFA 72; [1999] 1 HKLRD 315; (1999) 2 HKCFAR 4; [1999] 1 HKC 291; FACV 14/1998 (29 January 1999).

12 Ibid. The Interpretation by the Standing Committee of the National People's Congress of Articles 22(4) and 24(2)(3) of the Basic Law of the Hong Kong Special Administrative Region of the People's Republic of China (26 June 1999). For a critical analysis, see, Albert H. Y. Chen, "Ng Ka-ling and Article 158(3) of the Basic Law" (2001–2002) 5 *Journal of Chinese and Comparative Law* 221.

Hong Kong has limited political authority; it is a special region with high autonomy, playing a marginal role in the Chinese political process. As entrenched in the Constitution, the Chinese Communist Party, the leading party in China, does not constitutionally operate in Hong Kong. Only 36 members from Hong Kong participate in the almost 3,000-membered National People's Congress, the "highest organ of state power", and there the Hong Kong delegates' influence is negligible.[13]

With all the political and constitutional power in the hands of the Central Authorities, Hong Kong is governed through legislative interpretations and decisions, on which Hong Kong has little control. Over the years the Central Authorities have become more sophisticated and legalistic in governing Hong Kong, and this has also been displayed in their dealings with the international community. For example, the NPCSC has developed a Chinese theory of legislative interpretation, which privileges original legislative intent, takes into account a broader view of history and politics, and also allows political and social consequences to be taken into consideration. The NPCSC makes, interprets, and implements the Basic Law according to its own legal theories and political interests, and in the process often forces Hong Kong into constitutional confrontations that it is bound to lose.[14]

Under the OCTS design, the NPCSC occupies the highest constitutional place as regards constitutional interpretation. Through a series of creative interpretations, noted below, regarding various articles in the Basic Law, the NPCSC created a different set of constitutional rules for Hong Kong's democratic reform, under which the Central Authorities monopolize both the power to initiate Hong Kong's constitutional reforms and also to determine the meaning of democracy in Hong Kong.[15]

There are a number of milestones which signify the decisive shift of power from Hong Kong to Beijing. In April 2004, the NPCSC, through a creative interpretation of Annexes I and II of the Basic Law, decided that it has the exclusive power to determine whether there is a need to amend the electoral rules for the Chief Executive (hereafter CE) and members of the Legislative Council.[16] In the same month, the NPCSC released another decision ruling out universal suffrage for elections to the CE in 2007 and for the Legislative Council in 2008.[17] In December 2007, the NPCSC again ruled out universal suffrage for selecting the CE and the Legislative Council in 2012, but provided a roadmap for elections of the CE in 2017 and for the Legislative Council in 2020.[18]

The 2007 Decision does not provide any specifics for how universal suffrage would be implemented regarding the 2017 election of the CE. There have been strong demands to interpret Article 46 of the Basic Law in light of prevailing international human rights

13 Ghai (n. 9 above).

14 Ibid.

15 Ibid.

16 The Interpretation by the Standing Committee of the National People's Congress of Article 7 of Annex I and Article 3 of Annex II to the Basic Law of the Hong Kong Special Administrative Region of People's Republic of China (6 April 2004).

17 Decision of the Standing Committee of the National People's Congress on Issues Relating to the Methods of Selecting the Chief Executive of the Hong Kong Special Administrative Region in the Year 2007 and for Forming the Legislative Council of the Hong Kong Special Administrative Region in the Year 2008 (26 April 2004).

18 Decision of the Standing Committee of the National People's Congress on Issues Relating to the Methods for Selecting the Chief Executive of the Hong Kong Special Administrative Region and for Forming the Legislative Council of the Hong Kong Special Administrative Region in the Year 2012 and on Issues Relating to Universal Suffrage (29 December 2007).

standards, which would allow candidates of different political persuasions a fair chance to be nominated as formal candidates. Failure to accomplish that standard would trigger a prolonged public protest on an unprecedented scale. At the same time, the Central Authorities insisted on a literal interpretation of the Basic Law, which requires the vetting of candidates by a Selection Committee, and remained firm on the political requirement that a candidate must be someone who is politically acceptable to the Central Government.

Finally, on 31 August 2014, the NPCSC made a Decision on the meaning of universal suffrage within the meaning of Article 46 of the Basic Law.[19] As expected, the Decision requires all candidates for the CE to be vetted by a 1,200-member Nomination Committee (effectively controlled by the Central Government). What shocked and offended the Hong Kong community was the requirement that a formal candidate for CE must receive the consent of more than half of the Nomination Committee members, making it impossible for any pan-democratic members from becoming a formal candidate.[20]

Hong Kong's frustration

How does one account for the unprecedented scale and support[21] for the Occupying Central Movement (OCM), including the subsequent political repercussions and implications? Are people in Hong Kong, the younger generations in particular, exercising a massive movement of civil disobedience largely out of the concerns for maintaining Hong Kong's prosperity, freedom, and rule of law? Now, nearly 20 years after Hong Kong's return to China, the city's high degree of autonomy is under assault, and Hong Kong's way of life may be vanishing right in front of the Hong Kong people's eyes. Can Hong Kong's democratic impulses, as amplified in the OCM, be best explained by the desire to maintain Hong Kong's way of life, rather than be indicative of an ambitious pursuit of a distant political goal?

By many measures, Hong Kong's achievements in recent decades have been exemplary. It is a high-income society, with a GDP per capita of $38,364.2 USD in 2013.[22] Hong Kong shares many characteristics with other high-income societies: it is open and cosmopolitan, has a solid economic foundation, and also fosters a vibrant civil society. Hong Kong has also been known in the past for its responsible and accountable government and for tackling perceptions of corruption. Transparency International ranked Hong Kong 15 out of 177 countries in its 2013 Corruption Perceptions Index.[23] With a score of 75 (out of 100), Hong Kong was comfortably the second best in Asia, after Singapore.[24] By any measure Hong Kong has a solid rule of law in place. The judiciary is independent, competent, and effective; and the legal profession remains professional, independent, and well-awarded financially, socially, and politically. Hong Kong's freedoms and civil liberties have also been

19 Decision of the NPCSC, 31 August 2014.

20 Ibid.

21 Davis (n. 1 above); Hui (n. 4 above); and (forthcoming) Edmund W. Cheng and Wai-yin Chan, "Explaining Spontaneous Occupation: Antecedents and Contingencies in the Making of the Umbrella Movement" 2016 *Social Movement Studies.*

22 World Bank, *National Accounts Data* (World Bank, 2016), http://data.worldbank.org/indicator/NY.GDP.PCAP.CD?end=2013&start=1997.

23 Transparency International, Corruption Perceptions Index 2013 (Germany: Transparency International, 2013), http://www.transparency.org/cpi2013/results#myAnchor2.

24 Transparency International, Corruption Perceptions Index 2013.

recognized throughout the world. The Fraser Institute, a Canadian think tank, ranked Hong Kong third in the world for "human freedom" in 2013, just below New Zealand and the Netherlands.[25] In the same year Freedom House, a US non-profit focused on democracy and human rights, assigned Hong Kong a rating of 2 (on 1 to 7 scale, 1 being the best) for its respect for civil liberties.[26]

So, how does one explain the passion and determination of young people who have taken to the streets to make their voices heard in the unprecedented participation and support for the OCM? What are their worries?

The primary concern in Hong Kong is not whether there will be universal suffrage for the election of the Chief Executive in 2017, but rather whether Hong Kong can maintain its prosperity, freedom, and way of life, summed up in the "high degree of autonomy" promised to Hong Kong's people by Beijing as part of the conditions for the handover of sovereignty by Britain. All of these, according to common perceptions, are vanishing right in front of the eyes of the Hong Kong people. Hong Kong's protests highlight bigger questions about the future of a city that risks losing hard-won political and economic gains. Indeed, while Hong Kong is still performing reasonably well according to some key indicators, there are certainly valid reasons for concern.

Since its handover from Britain to China in 1997, Hong Kong has experienced slower economic growth than South Korea, Singapore, and many other nations – not to mention China, from which Hong Kong's economy was expected to benefit. Hong Kong's economic status vis-à-vis Singapore, a major rival in the region, illustrates the point. In 1997, Hong Kong's GDP per capita (27,330 USD) was higher than that of Singapore (26,386.5). But by 2013, the positions were reversed in a significant way.[27]

Politically, as a Special Administrative Region (SAR) of China, Hong Kong has a political destiny constrained by China's authoritarian system, and that constraint has recently started showing a cascade-like impact within many spheres in Hong Kong. The judiciary has had a difficult time interacting with the National People's Congress, China's legislature and ultimately Hong Kong's sovereign authority. There has also been a sharp decline in Hong Kong's press freedom, with allegations of increased censorship and self-censorship. In the first World Press Freedom Index prepared by Reporters without Borders in 2002, Hong Kong ranked 18 out of 134 countries. However, in recent years Hong Kong's ranking sunk to 61 of 180 countries in 2014 and to 69 of 179 in 2016.[28]

Despite the well-known success of Hong Kong's anti-corruption of endeavour,[29] corruption and improper business dealings among elites are also a serious concern. Again, the comparison with Singapore is enlightening. Singapore has been among the top five in Transparency International's list since 2001, while also enjoying impressive economic growth.

25 Fred McMahon (ed.), *Towards a Worldwide Index of Human Freedom* (Canada: The Fraser Institute, 2012), 63, http://www.freetheworld.com/2012/freedomIndex/Towards-Worldwide-Index.pdf.

26 Freedom House, *Freedom in the World: Democratic Breakthrough in the Balance* (USA: Freedom House, 2013), p. 19, https://www.freedomhouse.org/sites/default/files/FIW%202013%20Booklet.pdf.

27 It was 38,364.2 in Hong Kong and 55,617.6 in Singapore. World Bank, *National Accounts Data* (World Bank, 2016), http://data.worldbank.org/indicator/NY.GDP.PCAP.CD?end=2013&start=1997.

28 "End of 'One Country, Two Systems?'" Reporters without Borders, https://rsf.org/en/hong-kong.

29 Melanie Manion, *Corruption by Design: Building Clean Government in Mainland China and Hong Kong* (Cambridge: Harvard University Press, 2004).

Hong Kong's global ranking, in contrast, was knocked down to 17 in 2014 and 18 in 2015, one of its lowest rankings since 2000.[30]

Surveys of Hong Kong residents reveal growing concerns about quality of life, including issues ranging from housing affordability to pollution, inequality, stress, and press freedom. According to a survey by the Chinese University of Hong Kong, quality of life in Hong Kong has generally declined in the past ten years.[31] A 2012 Quality of Living report by global consulting firm Mercer ranked Singapore (25 out of 221 countries) well ahead of Hong Kong (70 out of 221 countries), a factor that could impact Hong Kong's ability to attract top-flight talent as a global financial centre.[32]

With the perception that Hong Kong's hard-won advantages are slipping away and promised democratic reforms have stalled, Hong Kong's politics have become more polarized and static than ever before.[33] Can Hong Kong move forward economically, socially, and politically without the reforms some people – such as the OCM – are demanding? Unfortunately, in recent years, Hong Kong's political parties have largely been reduced to single-issue political machines. Protesters argue that without first achieving genuine universal suffrage to produce a legitimate political leader who can transcend the political divide, the many advances Hong Kong has made, including its well-established rule of law and reasonably ethical and accountable government, will disappear.

The OCM and popular constitutionalism

In a rule of law society like Hong Kong's, citizens invariably demand and exercise their rights and freedoms through available institutions in accordance with legal procedures. As stated above, Hong Kong is proud of its rule of law tradition and has listed rule of law as one of its core values. Peace, order, and obedience of law define Hong Kong society. But when the democratic aspirations of the people have been effectively blocked, citizens can legitimately resort to non-institutional forums for political remedies. It is understandable that citizens would not use a court if such a court is weak and irrelevant; and would not participate in the political process if the participation is significantly constrained or merely democratic window-dressing. People may nevertheless continue to make their constitutional claims through other forums such as online mobilization, peaceful vigils, street demonstrations, and ultimately civil disobedience.

We may refer to those non-institutional mobilizations as "civic" or "popular" constitutionalism, which can be defined as a type of civic political participation – an informal constitutional practice. Civic constitutionalism takes place when citizens move beyond elite discourse, judicial judgment, or other official constitutional decisions and opt to assert their

30 Transparency International, Corruption Perceptions Index 2014 (Germany: Transparency International, 2014), http://www.transparency.org/cpi2014/results#myAnchor2.

31 Sai Leung Ng *et al.*, "CUHK Quality of Life Index 2012" (Hong Kong: The Centre for Quality of Life, 2013), http://www.cuhk.edu.hk/ssc/qol/eventdoc/QoL%20report/eng%20QoL%20index%20report%202012.pdf.

32 "2012 Quality of Living worldwide city rankings – Mercer survey" (Press Release), Mercer, http://www.mercer.com/press-releases/quality-of-living-report-2012.

33 Tony Cheung and Gary Cheung, "Top HKU professor says Hong Kong is too polarised under 'one country, two systems'" *South China Morning Post* (31 July 2015), http://www.scmp.com/news/hong-kong/politics/article/1845493/hong-kong-failing-solve-conflicts-under-one-country-two.

constitutional voices, independent of institutions, in alternative forums with a clear intention to interact with, and influence, official decisions.[34]

But how are regular citizens inspired by constitutional possibilities? Most people regard constitutional interpretation and practice as highly formalized procedures within legal and governmental institutions. They are generally apathetic toward constitutional matters and are happy to leave those matters to the government and other professionals. People are either ignorant of their constitutional rights, satisfied to defer to the official interpretation, or are complacent with the constitutional status quo.[35] As it happens the state, with rare exceptions, speaks on behalf of the people (often through elected representatives), and courts interpret constitutions at the exclusion of the people.[36]

Civic constitutionalism represents a break from conventional constitutional practices, where citizens create an alternative forum to insist on their own constitutional interpretations. According to Finn, "the Civic Constitution is a statement of our collective identity – it defines who we are, first by calling into being the collective 'We' and second by articulating what 'We' believe and that to which we aspire".[37] Civic constitutionalism is possible because constitutional engagement is only partly about law; it is also about normative commitments. For many in Hong Kong, that normative commitment has manifested itself in clear, direct, and measurable ways through self-organized referendum and other public actions.[38] During the days of the OCM, the streets were the courtrooms, and occupiers and their supporters become lawyers, judges, and lawmakers. For a brief moment ordinary citizens appeared to be in charge of their constitutional destiny. For the younger generation in Hong Kong, who have grown up in the shadow of the Basic Law controversies, the bargains that were struck by generations before them, including the OCTS as enshrined in the Basic Law, were simply not acceptable. The younger generation demanded to exercise the power to decide what constitutional law meant to them.

Following civic constitutionalist practices elsewhere,[39] people in Hong Kong relied on constitutional provisions, especially constitutional rights, but insisted on giving them their own interpretation. When that happens, the people shift from passive observers to active participants in constitutional matters. In exercising civic constitutionalism, constitutional discourse is no longer about procedures, rule-based articulation, or political mobilization within the contour of normal politics; it is all about making substantive demands. In occupying the streets, students and others usurped the role of lawmakers and judges and exercised their rights by asserting to the powers in Beijing that the August 31 Decision was wrong. But in the end, civic constitutionalism, by definition, operates within the current constitutional framework, with the clear intention to cause changes within the existing political structure. It necessitates a dialogue between non-institutional popular mobilization and established political and legal institutions in order to cause meaningful changes in

34 John E. Finn, "The Civic Constitution: Some Preliminaries" in Sotirios A. Barber and Robert P. George (eds), *Constitutional Politics: Essays on Constitution Making, Maintenance, and Change* (Princeton: Princeton University Press, 2001); Bruce Ackerman, *We the People, Volume 1: Foundations* (USA: Belknap Press, 1993).

35 Ibid.

36 Ibid.

37 Ibid., 44.

38 Cheng and Chan (n. 21 above).

39 Paul Harris, *Raising Freedom's Banner: How Peaceful Demonstrations Have Changed the World* (Oxford: Aristotle Lane, 2015). See Jiunn-rong Yeh's chapter in this volume.

constitutional practices. Civic constitutionalism in that sense is not revolutionary, but the challenges are to absorb the powerful energy it has released within a society.

Hong Kong's fragility

The tension between the democratic pursuit of civil disobedience and Hong Kong's rule of law tradition generates powerfully divisive and politicized forces that pose significant challenges to three foundational institutions: the police, the judiciary, and the civil society.

One neglected aspect in Hong Kong's rule of law discourse, especially by the police, during the OCM was the important role that an accountable and effective law enforcement can play in creating a sustainable rule of law tradition. Political scientists since Thomas Hobbes have identified the maintenance of peace and order as the core function of a legitimate state. In a society with a deficit of democracy, social stability and effective control of crime provide adequate governmental legitimacy.[40] In that regard, police effectiveness and accountability are indispensable in legitimizing a political order.

It may not be much of an exaggeration to say that Hong Kong is one of the safest cities on earth, and that Hong Kong has one of the best police forces in the world.[41] But Hong Kong has come a long way in building and maintaining a well-disciplined, highly-regarded, and effective police force. It has taken the collective effort of generations of people to create this reality. The Hong Kong Police Force excels in two fundamental ways. The first is through its political neutrality, in the sense that the police enforce the law fairly, equally and, above all, effectively, without political considerations entering into the process. This important, relative distance from politics has allowed the police to develop a high level of professionalism, effectiveness, and accountability in Hong Kong. Second, an accountable and effective police force in turn nurtures well-established police-and-community relations. The degree of mutual trust between the police and citizens is high.[42]

An unfortunate aspect of the OCM was that it placed tremendous pressure on the police and posed challenges to both political neutrality and community relations. Without doubt, it is extremely difficult, if not impossible, to insist on neutrality in all circumstances given the inevitable closeness between policing and politics. Given the sensitivity of all parties involved in the OCM and the political attention that the movement has received, it is not possible to completely avoid political pressure, either from Beijing or from a worried Hong Kong Government. The use of force on the first evening of the OCM was plainly excessive and unnecessary.[43] It is hard to believe, as the government has argued, that it was merely an operational decision. The Hong Kong police force, given its experience in public order policing and its level of professionalism, should have known how to better manage such matters. It is highly likely that the OCM has rattled either Beijing or the Hong Kong government into dictating some operational policing matters. Police professionalism may have been sacrificed to political expediency.

40 Bruce Gilley, *The Right to Rules: How States Win and Lose Legitimacy* (New York: Columbia University Press, 2009).

41 Kevin Sinclair and Nelson Ng Kwok-cheung, *Asia's Finest Marches on: Policing Hong Kong from 1841 into the 21st Century* (Hong Kong: Kevin Sinclair Associates Ltd, 1997).

42 Carol A. G. Jones (with Jon Vagg), *Criminal Justice in Hong Kong* (London: Routledge-Cavendish, 2007); Kam C. Wong, *Policing in Hong Kong* (Farnham: Ashgate, 2012).

43 Cheng and Chan (n. 21 above), p. 6.

There is also a second, and more significant, concern – the high level of tension between the police and a large sector of the public. Effective police work relies on public support and trust between the police and the public as keys to any successful maintenance of public order. Unfortunately the OCM – which started with a demand for Beijing to withdraw its most recent decisions on the 2017 election of the Chief Executive – painfully mutated into a direct confrontation between the police and the public. The frustration arising from this process hijacked the Movement's original objectives, and there is a real possibility that the police become the scapegoat.[44]

As the OCM continued, it became crystal-clear that Hong Kong's political system, and the policing system in particular, are more fragile than previously thought, and have been taken for granted. Hong Kong has a decent police force that the people in the territory are proud of, but the city may lose it more quickly than people can imagine. As a law enforcement agency, the police are ill-equipped to face competing political demands. The force is bound to be hard-pressed to maintain order in an increasingly polarized society. Significant changes in the external environment could swiftly cause a chain reaction within the police force, leading to a qualitative change in the internal dynamics. Yet any police force may find an authoritarian DNA that manifests itself in certain circumstances. As events have shown, the OCM generated such massive international and domestic pressure that our policing system had difficulty bearing it at times. Even if, as almost everyone hoped, the OCM were wound back greatly, and some more discussions had taken place, we have learned a most important lesson: the foundations of our high-quality police force can easily (and rapidly) be placed in jeopardy.

While Hong Kong has long enjoyed judicial independence, an active legal profession, and a free press, it did not always have such a well-established rule of law. It was the changes in policing in Hong Kong, especially since the 1970s, which played a key part in this vital change. A police force that is ethical, effective, and accountable is what makes Hong Kong's rule of law possible.

The double-edged sword of rule of law

While the pursuit of democratic values and the rule of law are both close to the heart of Hong Kong citizens, the OCM revealed a rare moment of possible tension between the ideals of democracy and the rule of law. The OCM, its lack of planning and organization notwithstanding, has clearly demonstrated Hong Kong's democratic passion and resilience. For a brief period of time, the movement gathered so much momentum that the students appeared to be unstoppable. Tear gas, pepper spray, police batons, and water cannons did not intimidate them; triad societies did not terrorize them; political smear and character assassination did not shake them; and well-intentioned counsel did not move them.

As the OCM persisted, its adverse impact on people's daily life and public order started to affect perceptions towards the movement. Frustrated by the movement's lack of direction and the burden that ordinary people had to shoulder due to city blockage, people's perception of the OCM started to shift from: the OCM as a democratic impulse to strengthen Hong Kong's rule of law, to one associated with disorder, chaos, and from a wider perspective, a disoriented movement that was undermining the very idea of the rule of law, a value that OCM's organizers originally intended to promote. Rule of law became

44 Ibid., Hui (n. 4 above).

a rallying cry for the anti-OCM groups and, with apparent political support from the pro-government DAB, those groups brought a series of cases to the courts, predominantly applying for orders of injunctions against the occupiers.

The DAB-orchestrated legal mobilization put a strain on the courts. In post-transition Hong Kong, the courts have always been perceived as a friend of the liberals and democrats who use the judicial forum as the battle ground to challenge the governmental authorities. In a political system with broad executive power, a weak legislature and limited citizen political input into the political process, aggrieved individuals and groups tended to resort to the courts for remedies through judicial and constitutional review of executive and legislative action. The use or abuse of the judiciary has been a contentious issue in Hong Kong's political and legal communities, and conservative politicians and pro-government groups often criticize pan-democrats in Hong Kong for judicialising politics and for bringing increased pressure on the judiciary by bringing overly political matters to courts. The perception that democrats over-use the court process is reinforced by the fact that lawyers play a pivotal role among the opposition in the Legislature,[45] and a key political party supportive of the OCM, the Civic Party, is often called the "Party of the Barristers" to showcase the fact that the party is led by senior barristers. Given the democratic deficit in Hong Kong and the hands-on control on the executive government by the Central Authorities, it is only natural that problems that may be solved through the political process elsewhere have been fought in the judicial process.[46]

But access to courts is not a liberal monopoly, and conservative sections are well known for legal mobilization in order to satisfy their right-wing agendas.[47] The DAB, which has lamented the use or abuse of judicial review in Hong Kong by the pan-democrats, have also used impact cases strategically, and ultimately its legal mobilization proved effective and instrumental in ending the OCM. How does a rights-friendly or democracy-supporting court tackle challenges from pro-establishment forces? And how do Hong Kong courts strike a balance between order and the pursuit of democracy?

Ironically, it was the court order that provided a fatal wedge in the OCM, dividing the supporter community and undermining the morale of the occupiers. The court has been straightforward in declaring its political neutrality through adjudication. First, the court laid out its foundational principle: that law is the only thing that matters for courts. In rejecting the argument that the OCM was essentially a political problem which should be left to the political process, Justice Au stated:

45 Former Court of Final Appeal judge Henry Litton criticized some of the judicial review application as "simply grandstanding, inappropriate posturing and should be roundly condemned" (John Chan, "Hong Kong's courts' judicial review screening system is working well, despite a few high-profile abuses" *South China Morning Post* (8 December 2015), http://www.scmp.com/comment/insight-opinion/article/1888331/hong-kong-courts-judicial-review-screening-system-working).

46 For a review of some of the controversial cases, see Anthony B. L. Cheung and Max W. L. Wong, "Judicial review and policy making in Hong Kong: Changing interface between the legal and the political" (2006) 28 *The Asia Pacific Journal of Public Administration* 117–141; see also Johannes Chan, "Administrative Law, Politics and Governance: The Hong Kong Experience" in Tom Ginsburg and Albert H. Y. Chen (eds) *Administrative Law and Governance in Asia: Comparative Perspective* (London: Routledge, 2009) 143; Karen Kong, "Public Interest Litigation in Hong Kong: A New Hope for Social Transformation" (2009) 28 Civil Justice Quarterly 327–343; and Waikeung Tam, *Legal Mobilization under Authoritarianism: The Case of Post-Colonial Hong Kong* (Cambridge: Cambridge University Press, 2013).

47 Ann Southworth, *Lawyers of the Right: Professionalizing the Conservative Coalition* (Chicago: University of Chicago Press, 2008).

> in deciding cases ... the court would determine them *only* by applying the law and would not take into account any political considerations ... this is precisely what this court is doing: adjudicating and resolving disputes concerning the parties' legal rights in accordance to the law, and the law alone. The fact that it also happens that there is political [considerations] underlying these disputes does not and should not affect the court's role in adjudicating those *legal* rights. Nor should the court refrain from adjudicating those *legal* rights in the dispute.[48]

The court is aware of and accepts the fact that the OCM "is avowedly a form of civil disobedience".[49] But the OCM, as it happened on Hong Kong's streets, adversely affected others' rights and had to be stopped. According to Justice Poon:

> on the materials before me when the demonstration in question based on civil disobedience have taken place for so long, in such a scale which has affected so many people and which had the real risk of turning into civil disorder, I do not think the fact that the demonstration is civil disobedience, no matter how noble the underlying cause that participants may consider it to be, can constitute a factor which militates against the granting of an injunction.[50]

In renewing the injunction later on 10 November 2014, the court makes it clear that:

> Hong Kong has always adhered to the concept of rule of law. This concept is treasured and has always been jealously guarded by the general public. It is universally regarded that the rule of law is one of Hong Kong's most important foundations that has led to her being a civilised, safe and orderly society.[51]

The court continues:

> Under the rule of law, even if the defendants are of the view that a court order (including an *ex parte* order) is wrongly granted, instead of simply disobeying it, they should first comply with it but seek to challenge and argue against that order in court under due process and in accordance with the law. As said by Hoffmann LJ (as Lord Hoffmann then was) in *Department of Transport v. Lush* (unreported, 29 July 1993)[1]: "*... the law cannot allow obedience of its orders to be a matter of individual choice even on grounds of conscience*".[52]

When the "noble cause" of fighting for democracy places the rule of law in Hong Kong at risk, the courts are not, and have not been, hesitant to uphold the rule of law to maintain peace and order. As the court concludes:

48 *Kwoon Chung Motors Co Ltd v. Kwok Cheuk Kin and Others* [2014] HKCFI 2161; HCA 2222 & 2223/2014 (1 December 2014), para. 51.

49 *Chiu Luen Public Light Bus Co Ltd v. Persons Unlawfully Occupying or Remaining on the Public Highway* HCA 2086 & 2104/2014 (20 October 2014), para. 30.

50 Ibid., para. 31.

51 *Chiu Luen Public Light Bus Co Ltd v. Persons unlawfully occupying or remaining on the public highway* HCMP 2086/2014 (10 November 2014), para 138.

52 Ibid., para. 140.

> It is therefore wrong for any suggestions that the rule of law is not undermined or under challenged if people can freely or intentionally disobey the law *first* and then accept the consequences of breaking the law. The rule of law cannot realistically and effectively operate in a civilised and orderly society on this basis.[53]

After a few rounds of clarification and appeals, it became abundantly clear that judges had ordered the end of the OCM, and the remaining issue was how to exit. It was the authority of the court that effectively suppressed such democratic impulses. An independent court is a first-order institution in Hong Kong's constitutional system, and judicial independence is a core value of Hong Kong, of which the people are immensely proud.[54] Many occupiers and their supporters were willing to accept the fate that once the judges have spoken, their decision should be respected. After all, the OCM was a rights based resistance. Although it was an exercise of civil disobedience by gathering in a public place without permission, the movement largely violated procedural legal rules to pursue a greater constitutional right that is, according to the interpretation of the occupiers, enshrined in the Basic Law. Their claims were largely made within the framework of the Basic Law. After all, lawyers, lawyer-politicians, law professors, and law students played a significant role in the designing, organizing, maintaining and otherwise shaping of the movement, and thus there were various degrees of fidelity to the law instilled within the consciousness of the actors.

An excessive promotion of political neutrality and judicial professionalism without politics may produce what Hilbink refers to as the "agents of anti-politics",[55] where an apolitical judicial identity reproduces a compliant judiciary. Facing political demands, judges hide behind their professional identity, arguing that they are legal technicians and not politicians. They shy away from controversies, especially controversial cases that may require them to confront significant moral and political issues, such as the issues faced by the courts in the OCM-related cases.[56]

It must be said that the Hong Kong courts have acted no differently from those elsewhere in similar situations, democracies or otherwise. Their non-partisan nature and political neutrality provide courts institutional integrity and political capacity. There is certainly a danger that judges can take an apolitical identity and play a technical legal role. When courts shy away from political sensitivity, they face a degree of marginalization in significant social, economic, and political issues. As important cases are shifted to extra-judicial forums and solved at a political level, courts are increasingly marginalized and become irrelevant.

53 Ibid., para. 141.

54 Carol A. G. Jones, *Lost in China? Law, Culture and Identity in Post-1997 Hong Kong* (Cambridge: Cambridge University Press, 2015).

55 Lisa Hilbink, "Agents of Anti-Politics: Courts in Pinochet's Chile" in Tom Ginsburg and Tamir Moustafa (eds) *Rule by Law: The Politics of Courts in Authoritarian Regimes*, (Cambridge: Cambridge University Press, 2008); Lisa Hilbink, *Judges beyond Politics in Democracy and Dictatorship: Lessons from Chile* (Cambridge: Cambridge University Press, 2007).

56 In the subsequent criminal trials of OCM organizers and active participants, judges in Hong Kong recognized the relevance of the political cause of civil disobedience and showed lenience in imposing sentencing, with community service orders being the predominant penalty imposed. See, for examples, Raymond Yeung, "Convicted Occupy activist says UK visa decision will indicate how Hong Kong protesters are viewed abroad" *South China Morning Post* (16 August 2016), http://www.scmp.com/news/hong-kong/politics/article/2004511/uk-visa-decision-after-conviction-good-indicator-how-hong.

However, a court that is politically active risks significant pushback from other institutions.[57]

In dealing with applications for injunctions against the OCM, the courts first declared their political neutrality, stating that political aspirations of the occupiers were irrelevant to the courts' deliberation. Once a case entered the court, a passionate political campaign was effectively reduced to a legal issue, subject to sophisticated legal analysis. Lawyers on behalf of the OCM were mobilized to challenge the order, but were straightjacketed into making technical arguments that were relevant to the legal case, as if the entire OCM was about the interpretation of legal rules, and therefore to a large extent the entire political motivations and political pursuits were effectively reduced to irrelevance.

The Hong Kong courts remain an effective and powerful institution in making the OCM accountable to the law. Indeed, the courts were the only institution powerful enough to disarm the passionate participants. In an authoritarian system, judicial neutrality is the aspiration of generations of law reformers, and independent courts are often called upon to empower citizens and to bring arbitrary power under judicial control. However, in Hong Kong's mature rule of law system, where the courts are most treasured, the institution has ultimately worked to contain democratic aspirations and frustrate democratic pursuits.

A polarized society continues to radicalize

Hong Kong has a mature and vibrant civil society. Hong Kong's civil society started to grow in the 1970s after the economic take-off; it gained some momentum during the Sino-British negotiation on the return of Hong Kong to China, entered an age of maturity after 1997, and may have peaked in 2003 during the protest against the national security legislation.[58] By and large, civil society in Hong Kong is not politically divisive and does not have entrenched political confrontation at its foundational level. The society tolerates and respects diverse political opinions and organizations. As a thriving metropolitan city, people of different political persuasions live largely in harmony and there is not a fault line in Hong Kong that divides its people. Without a sharp identity politics that may tear a society apart, Hong Kong is hostile to party politics and until recently has shown little taste for political agitation beyond a tiny fraction of the society.[59] British rule of law and good governance principles delivered prosperity and freedom to Hong Kong, which served as an effective alternative to democracy; and the legacy survived the 1997 transition. A large population of Hong Kong were political or economic refugees from the mainland who, given what they had experienced in the mainland, treasure what they currently have.[60] For them, political agitation is morally questionable and politically risky. While a limited amount of political contention existed before and after the transition, it has been effectively absorbed by the legislative and judicial process and, where street action has occurred, it has been primarily symbolic, and inconsequential in the sense that it did not polarize society at some fundamental level. Resistance, if it existed at all, was largely civil, liberal, and legal.

57 For a general study of the limit of constitutional law in authoritarian states, see Tom Ginsburg and Alberto Simpser (eds) *Constitutions in Authoritarian Regimes* (Cambridge: Cambridge University Press, 2014).

58 Brian C. H. Fong, "State-Society Conflict under Hong Kong's Hybrid Regime" (2013) 53 *Asian Survey* 860.

59 Ibid.

60 Siu-kai Lau, *Society and Politics in Hong Kong* (Hong Kong: The Chinese University Press, 1982) 71–72.

The prolonged constitutional debate since the early 1980s, and especially since 2003, has no doubt had an impact on Hong Kong's society, and on the young generations in particular who have grown up in the shadow of such political contention. Without the historical baggage but with deep concerns about their future in Hong Kong, the younger generation has become the driving force in terms of social mobilization. As China tightens its control over Hong Kong, institutional channels to advocate for constitutional changes begin to narrow. In response, constitutional debate gradually shifted from the legislature, the courts, and classrooms to offices, families, and streets. Non-institutional protest tends to be more scattered and de-centralized. At the same time, it has been commonly observed that Hong Kong does not have the political leaders effective enough to coordinate the highly divided political parties and civil society organizations.[61] Thus, where a new social movement in Hong Kong may be lively, spontaneous, and resilient, it ultimately is scattered and lacks coordination and organization.

The forceful mobilization of the OCM invited counter-mobilization, which, supported by established political forces, was equally powerful and effective, leading to the politicization and polarization of society. As Poon observes:

> Political polarization is the biggest domestic challenge facing Hong Kong today. The stark difference in political views among family members, friends, colleagues and neighbors is altering the social and professional fabric of Hong Kong society.[62]

In a polarized society, members often abandon the middle ground and compete for extreme positions at the respective ends of the political spectrum. Those who are pro-establishment may be prepared to embrace the most offensive intrusion into Hong Kong's autonomy, such as apologizing and legitimizing the forced disappearance of booksellers from Hong Kong and advocating for the persecution of political dissidents. On the other hand, radical democrats could start violent confrontations with the police, as witnessed in the Mong Kok riot, and may eventually organize advocacy for independence through violence or other means. Beijing has expressed its grave concerns that there may have been a paradigmatic shift in protest from peace, love, and non-violence that characterized the OCM to intolerance, radicalism, and violence. According to this interpretation, the frustrated civil disobedience of the OCM may have encouraged that shift.[63] The OCM, which was meant to restore Hong Kong's rule of law and freedom, may have worked to exacerbate the further narrowing of civic space, and enhance radicalization and polarization within Hong Kong's society.

The OCM, the strength and the vulnerability of Hong Kong

The OCM has shown the outside world, and especially China, that there is a *political* Hong Kong in addition to the commercial and cultural Hong Kong. It has demonstrated the

61 Cheng and Chan (n. 21 above).

62 Jonathan Poon, "Umbrellas in Hong Kong: Youth and Reform in a Polarized City" (2015) *The Asia Pacific Affairs Council Journal* 15.

63 Daniel Lee, "A Paradigm Shift in Civil Society: From the Umbrella to the Fishball Revolution" *Hong Kong Free Press* (18 March 2016), https://www.hongkongfp.com/2016/03/18/a-paradigm-shift-in-civil-society-from-the-umbrella-to-the-fishball-revolution/.

determination and agency of the younger generation in the territory to take their future into their own hands and to control their own destiny. Hong Kong should not be taken for granted. More importantly, the OCM has showcased the strength of Hong Kong's legal system, the power of the rule of law, and the willingness of the residents to ultimately work through the existing institutions, no matter how difficult that may be. In many ways Hong Kong is the envy of the world, and, at the end of the day, people realize they have a lot to lose if the delicate constitutional reform is not handled with great care.

The OCM has made it clear that there is a democratic deficit in Hong Kong's governance structure, the deficit is fatal to Hong Kong's future development, and there is a deep urgency to fix it. The OCM also confirms the democratic determination of the people and the centrality of democracy as a practice in Hong Kong politics. Whether in support of the OCM or not, people from different political stances claimed their commitment to future democracy in Hong Kong. The movement saw the birth of a new generation of potential political leaders who, with proper nurturing, are better prepared and positioned than their mentors to lead Hong Kong forward.

But there is no doubt that the OCM placed Hong Kong's core values and institutions under tremendous stress, and the society was torn apart between the competing ideals for peace and order and the democratic impulse. While the society at large is seeking a proper balance to strike, it has become self-aware of its vulnerability that may eventually erode Hong Kong's institutional strength. Political neutrality and community support are two pillars of police legitimacy and effectiveness in Hong Kong. They both remain solid, but the OCM and the radicalization of protest in its aftermath have posed challenges to both pillars by eroding their support. Hong Kong courts are independent and forceful, and continue to serve as the moral compass for Hong Kong's citizens. But the continuing invitations of the court to solve highly politically charged matters, such as those involving the OCM, the Mong Kok riots, and potentially the advocacy for secession, will certainly test the courts' wisdom and eventually their authority. While Hong Kong's civil society remains resilient, vibrant, and influential,[64] the increasing polarization and radicalism may take the essential component of civility out of the equation, thus fundamentally altering the nature of the society.

But Hong Kong is not a typical transition society. Compared with societies that have undergone colour revolutions in the past decades, Hong Kong remains a unique place. For the protesters and people in Hong Kong generally, the battle has been fought mainly to keep what they already have. The icing of democracy has been sought after not to achieve new freedoms but to entrench the freedoms, prosperity, and rule of law currently in existence, and which is potentially at risk. Here are the dilemmas that Hong Kong faces: can it preserve its existing freedoms and prosperity without achieving genuine universal suffrage? Can the mass protests through civil disobedience persuade Beijing to allow Hong Kong genuine universal suffrage? And finally, will civil disobedience, as it continues to escalate, ultimately endanger Hong Kong's freedom and rule of law?

64 Ho-Fung Hung and Iam-Chong Ip, "Hong Kong's Democratic Movement and the Making of China's Offshore Civil Society" (2012) 52 *Asian Survey* 504.

6 The *nomos* of Hong Kong's Umbrella Movement

Daniel Matthews[*]

> [The] error consists in … [the] belief that there is only one type of law, whereas there are at least two: state law, and a law that precedes the state and gives it an absolute value.
>
> (Maurice Hauriou)[1]

Introduction

Written in the early 1980s, Xi Xi's *Marvels of a Floating City* is an allegorical interpretation of Hong Kong's imminent transition from British to Chinese rule. The English language edition of this multi-media short story, comprising thirteen vignettes that obliquely respond to paintings by the French surrealist René Magritte, was published in 1997 to coincide with the formal handover of sovereignty. The text begins with an image of Hong Kong's foundation as a "floating city" and conjures a sense of a nebulous Hong Kong identity, forged in the midst of competing interests: "many, many years ago, on a fine day, the floating city appeared in the air in full public gaze, hanging like a hydrogen balloon. Above it were the fluctuating layers of clouds, below it the turbulent sea. The floating city hung there, neither sinking nor rising."[2] Caught between a colonial past and a Chinese future, Xi Xi captures the shifting sands on which Hong Kong cultural and political identity are founded. The sense of this complexity is brought to the fore in the text through multifarious references to both Chinese and Western cultural traditions. This assemblage of Eastern and Western references conjures a vivid impression of Hong Kong's variegated culture that, like the city itself, "floats" between shores.[3] Unlike Eva Hung who suggests that Xi Xi's approach is "based on an assumption that … readers will take such diverse cultural references in their stride",[4] I would argue that this broad range of references – from Song dynasty artists to Italian postmodern novelists – works precisely to *trouble* rather than *assert* any sense of stable identity. The cultural heterogeneity that Xi Xi brings out underscores a sense of unassuredness rather than confidence about questions of identity in Hong Kong. This was clearly a sign of the times. As the Sino-British negotiations got under way in 1982,

* Assistant Professor, Faculty of Law, University of Hong Kong.

1 Maurice Hauriou, *Précis de droit constitutionnel* (Paris: Recueil Sirey, 1923) 284; quoted in Carl Schmitt, *The* Nomos *of the Earth in the International Law of the* Jus Publicum Europaeum (New York: Telos Press Ltd, 2003) 83, n. 7.

2 Xi Xi, *Marvels of a Floating City and Other Stories* (Hong Kong: University of Hong Kong Press, 1997) 3.

3 On Hong Kong's "floating" identity, see Ackbar Abbas, *Hong Kong: The Culture and Politics of Disappearance* (Minneapolis, University of Minnesota Press, 1997).

4 Eva Hung, "Editor's Introduction" to *Marvels of a Floating City and Other Stories* (Hong Kong: University of Hong Kong Press, 1997), xii.

many in Hong Kong felt that a return to Chinese sovereignty was the beginning of the end for this "floating city". Hong Kong's indeterminate status between East and West, offering a cultural and economic bridge between worlds, felt decidedly under threat in the 1980s as the future became unclear; as Xi Xi herself notes, this was "a dim and uncertain age".[5]

Marvels of a Floating City, though written for another time, has a particular resonance in the wake of Hong Kong's Umbrella Movement. The questions of space, place, and identity that Xi Xi poses in the context of transition once again dominated the city's politics during the occupations in 2014. The nature of Hong Kong's distinct cultural heritage and its uncertain future as it grapples with the increasing influence of Beijing and the Chinese Communist Party (CCP) animated the Umbrella Movement. In what follows I aim to unpack some of these issues, focusing on how the movement engaged questions of space, belonging and identity by challenging the normative assumptions that structure everyday life in the territory. The movement posed, as Xi Xi's story does, the question of what it means to *belong* in Hong Kong and who has the right to shape the city's destiny. Whilst these questions are perhaps broader than the traditional cut and thrust of legal or constitutional analysis, without attention to the normative force of the spatial and cultural orderings that framed the movement, our analysis of these events remains limited.[6] My claim is that the great success of the movement was to temporarily rupture the background ordering of the city that we – as legal scholars – so often take for granted. This interruption of the existing normative order or *nomos* of the city re-posed the questions of belonging, and by paying due attention to the interruption that the movement enacted allows us to see its enduring significance for Hong Kong's legal and political settlement. The argument proceeds by first setting out the shift that I propose to take: away from "law" and towards the "nomos", a term that, as will become clear, opens our thinking to a broader and more dynamic sense of normative ordering than that afforded by a strictly legalistic lens. I then turn to two distinct senses of the "nomos" that I will discuss in relation to the Umbrella Movement. The first, inspired by the German jurist Carl Schmitt, foregrounds the normative force of *spatial* ordering and the second, inspired by sociologist Peter Berger and the legal theorist and historian Robert Cover, assesses the *discursive* dimension to normativity, stressing how shared normative commitments are central to the formation of community and a common identity. My claim is that, beyond raising technical, constitutional issues concerning voting rights, the Umbrella Movement's interruption of the city's existing spatio-normative distribution posed fundamental questions about the nature of identity and belonging in the territory that goes to the heart of its political significance.

From law to *nomos*

The proposed shift away from the "law" may appear odd. Undeniably, the Umbrella Movement had a perspicuously legalistic tone and orientation. The subject of its concerns,

5 Xi Xi, (note 2 above), p. 68.

6 As I have argued elsewhere, the purely legalistic analysis of events fails to address some of its key achievements and, in particular, privileges a statist perspective that disavows attention to the lived and felt reality of the occupations themselves. See (forthcoming) Daniel Matthews, "Narrative, Space, Atmosphere: A Nomospheric Inquiry into Hong Kong's Pro-Democracy Umbrella Movement" (2016) *Social and Legal Studies* doi:10.1177/0964663916649257. The present analysis seeks to explore these issues further with a particular focus on the intersection between the spatial (re)ordering the movement achieved and questions of cultural identity.

the terrain on which opposition was mounted, and the key actors involved all attest to the movement's juridical inflection. From interpretative battles over the meaning of "the rule of law" and "civil disobedience" to detailed proposals for constitutional change and debates about the legality of police tactics used to control the occupations, the law was on everyone's lips in late 2014. The unique constitutional settlement in the SAR plays an important role in explaining this fact. The rule of law – guaranteed by the Basic Law and the "one country, two systems" model – has played a decisive role in developing a sense of Hong Kong's exceptionalism with respect to the rest of China.[7] In this sense, legal concepts, values, and institutions have an uncommon cultural and political piquancy within the territory. This "legalistic" orientation is striking and worthy of careful reflection; indeed much of the existing literature on the events of 2014, including chapters within this very volume, focuses on these very issues.[8] As intimated above, I want to take a different approach. I argue that attention to the juridical effects engendered by the movement obscures and de-politicises some of the movement's key achievements. The occupation sites expressed not only a desire to change the procedures governing the election of the CE but temporally reordered the city's normative distribution in a way that has an enduring political significance.

As I set out below, this intervention within Hong Kong's spatial ordering is not simply a *quaestio facti* but engages the most fundamental of *legal* questions and concerns. The appropriation and distribution of space shapes the normative world of a given community, establishing the conditions of possibility for positive law. I refer to this spatial distribution as the *nomos,* a Greek term that is often rendered simply as "law" – but "order" or "ordering" perhaps comes closer to the sense of *nomos* that I deploy here. *Nomos* refers to an originary ordering of the world, prior to and distinct from formal legality. With the risk of a somewhat Kafkaesque formulation, it is a *law before the law*, or as our epigraph from Hauriou has it, a "law" that precedes the state.[9] This sense of *nomos* has been largely forgotten or misconstrued within the jurisprudential literature, particularly since the rise of positivism in Europe in the early nineteenth century. Even a thinking of *nomos* in antiquity offers mixed perspectives, Plato's *Nomoi* (*Laws*) suggests a certain synonymity between *nomos* and *thesmos* (legislation), and the famous distinction made by the Sophists between *nomos* and *physis* understands *nomos* as a matter of the formal dictates of political and juridical institutions in contradistinction to the "order" of the natural world. Carl Schmitt and Robert Cover have both sought, though in different ways, to reconnect legal thinking to the *nomos,* to a force that orders the world, quite distinct from a particular body of rules made and maintained by a set of juridical institutions. Schmitt and Cover's approaches to

7 The increasing focus on the rule of law in China – the rule of law, *with Chinese characteristics* – might be seen to counter this claim. However, it is precisely the qualificatory supplement (*with Chinese characteristics*) that is revealing here. The rule of law in Hong Kong is indebted to the rendering promoted through the common law and is framed by reference to international instruments like the ICCPR. For an assessment of comparative approaches to the rule of law with a particular focus on Hong Kong, see Benny Y. T. Tai, "Developing an Index of the Rule of Law: Sharing the Experience of Hong Kong" (2007) 2(1) *Asian Journal of Comparative Law*, art. 4.

8 See, in particular, Sebastian Veg, "Legalistic and Utopian: Hong Kong's Umbrella Movement" (March–April 2015) 92 *New Left Review* 55–73; Samson Yuen, "Hong Kong After the Umbrella Movement: An Uncertain Future for 'One Country, Two Systems,'" (2015)1 *China Perspectives* 49–53; Michael Davis, "Occupy protests breaking law, but not undermining Hong Kong's rule of law" *South China Morning Post* (7 November 2014).

9 See Franz Kafka, "Before the Law" in *The Complete Short Stories* (London: Vintage, 1999), pp. 3–4 and Hauriou (n. 1 above), p. 284.

the term are divergent in many important respects, with Schmitt developing a purely *spatial* and Cover an exclusively *discursive* reading of the *nomos*. Whilst I follow Schmitt in grounding *nomos* in the concrete order of the material world, Cover's account of *nomos* as a discursive "force field"[10] in which the normative life of a community is immersed offers a useful supplement to this account. In particular, Cover's examination of the role that narrative plays in shaping and giving direction to the normative life of a community provides a helpful heuristic by which we can assess the senses of cultural identity and belonging that animated the movement.

By relying on certain aspects of Schmitt and Cover's thinking, I argue that we can attend to aspects of Hong Kong's Umbrella Movement that remain inaccessible through a purely "legalistic" or "constitutional" lens. A detailed account of Schmitt and Cover's accounts of *nomos* is beyond the scope of the present argument. Whilst I rely on their work in some respects, I am not claiming any fidelity to their broader projects; in fact I depart quite radically from Schmitt's thinking by reading the *nomos* at a local rather than global scale. As will become clear, assessing the movement through the language of *nomos* allows us to approach the movement's key strategies and understand the political aspirations that underpinned them.

Nomos denotes a background ordering of social life, made possible by the appropriation and division of material space and the mobilisation of conceptual and ideational demarcations and divisions. For Schmitt, *nomos* describes the means by which the social and political order becomes immediately visible, achieved through the appropriation of space.[11] But the operative power of the *nomos* is largely invisible in our daily lives, describing the *assumed* order of things in a given situation. In the main, lawyers are particularly guilty of overlooking the normative force of a given spatial distribution.[12] A focus on posited rules and conventions is the natural attitude for the jurist, who too often takes for granted the spatial (and discursive) *nomos* on which such rules ultimately rest. The near-total dissimulation of the *nomos* remains effective until that order is interrupted, challenged, or mis-performed, when a normally busy highway is converted into a space for public deliberation or a nondescript concrete wall or pavement is transformed into a canvas for the expression of dissent. This chapter inquires into how the Umbrella Movement's intervention in the city's *nomos* (re)attunes our senses to the normative force of the city's extant normative order. In tracing the nomic effects of the Umbrella Movement, I ape the phenomenological strategy of *epoché* (or "bracketing") whereby the "natural attitude" is suspended in an effort to reveal a more radical appreciation of "things themselves". My argument temporally "brackets" the jurists' usual concerns with ordinance, statutes, and case law in order to trace the implications of the movement in the distinct, prior register of the *nomos*. I will start by focusing on the ordering of space, exploring the spatial and material intervention that the movement made.

10 Robert Cover, "The Supreme Court, 1982 Term – Foreword: *Nomos* and Narrative" (1983) 97(4) *Harvard Law Review* 10.

11 Schmitt (n. 1 above), p. 70.

12 The burgeoning scholarship in law and geography is an obvious exception to this. For an overview of this literature, see Nicholas Blomley, David Delaney, and Richard T. Ford (eds), *The Legal Geographies Reader* (Oxford: Blackwell, 2001). Indicative recent publications include: Andreas Philippopoulos-Mihalopoulos, *Spatial Justice: Body, Lawscape, Atmosphere* (Abingdon Routledge, 2015); Chris Butler, *Henri Lefebvre: Spatial Politics, Everyday Life and the Right to the City* (Abingdon: Routledge, 2012); and David Delaney, *Nomospheric Investigations: The Spatial, the Legal and the Pragmatics of World-Making* (Abingdon: Routledge, 2010).

Nomos I – Lawscape and rupture

Etymologically, *nomos* is tied to *neimen* the Greek verb generally taken to mean "take", "assign", or "manage". In his account of *nomos* Schmitt identifies three specific meanings of *neimen*, each describing an aspect of his tripartite understanding of *nomos*: (i) to take or appropriate, (ii) to divide or distribute, (iii) to pasture or set to productive use.[13] A decisive stage in the more than three-thousand-year history of the term is the connection made between *nomos* and *oikos* noted by both Plato and Aristotle. As Plato describes it, the nomad-shepherd was engaged in a particular form of *neimen* that involved nourishing his flock, achieving an order and just distribution through the quotidian search for pasture. The *nomos* of a household – an *oiko-nomia* or "economy" – is quite distinct from the nomad's *nomos* because it presupposes the appropriation and settlement of land. For Schmitt, the binding of *oikos* and *nomos* reveals the term's most originary sense: that of land appropriation. For Schmitt, it is this that is the basis of all social and legal systems: "prior to every legal, economic, and social order, prior to every legal, economic, or social theory are these elementary questions: *Where and how was it appropriated? Where and how was it divided? Where and how was it produced?*"[14] It is the processes of land appropriation – conquest, expropriation, or discovery – that provides the basis for all forms of division and distribution, every subsequent form of social or legal order. Schmitt uses *nomos* to explain the changing fortunes of land appropriation and the distribution of space on an international scale, arguing that a global – but unashamedly Eurocentric – "*nomos* of the earth" emerged in the age of discovery. Relative stability and mutual recognition amongst European states was predicated on a radical spatial division between European and non-European land. Those tracts of land beyond the reach of the *jus publicum europaeum* were considered free for occupation, exploitation, and appropriation. This fundamental division purported to order the entire globe and remained dominant until the end of the nineteenth century. The rise of American power and the emerging political settlement in Europe in the wake of World War I saw this "*nomos* of the earth" come to an end.

Schmitt moves very quickly from a concrete and local *nomos* – the *nomos* made possible through the settlement of land and the establishment of an *oikos* – to global questions concerning the movement of peoples and the conquest of land over the *longue durée* of European history. Nonetheless, Schmitt's thinking provides us with a key insight that will help in our analysis of the Umbrella Movement. What is stressed here is the normative force of spatial distribution and appropriation. Following Locke, Rousseau, and Kant, Schmitt stresses the fundamental importance of land appropriation and distribution. Before formal law – written or otherwise – there is first a law of *mine* and *thine*, of circumscription, and of a radical claim to possessive control of land. Through the language of the *nomos*, we can inquire into this register of spatial ordering, the immediately present and affective distribution of space that is constitutive of a community's normative order. As Schmitt suggests, *nomos* describes a "legal power, not mediated by laws … it is an act of *legitimacy* whereby the legality of a mere law is first made meaningful".[15] It is this prior register that is of interest to me. However, it is worth noting here that I depart from Schmitt in two respects. First, I want to explore the *nomos* at a different scale to Schmitt. It is the local and quotidian

13 Schmitt (n. 1 above), pp. 324–355 (emphasis in the original). See also pp. 67–80.

14 Ibid., p. 328.

15 Ibid., p. 73.

rather than the global and epochal that is my concern here. Second, I want to stress how the *nomos* – at this more local level – is routinely dissimulated or obscured; we remain largely oblivious to the normative force of our spatial surroundings, taking for granted effects of spatial distribution. The Umbrella Movement, through its intervention within the existing *nomos* of the city, suddenly made visible this normative distribution, and its reordering of the cityscape was central to understanding the political ambitions by which it was animated.

Let us begin, then, by attuning ourselves to the *nomos* of the city. Given Hong Kong's geographic restrictions and the predominance of corporate power, meaningful public space is extraordinarily limited within the city. Indeed, such space is often included within the footprint of buildings designed for commercial use. This means that "public space" is not uncommonly found *within* shopping malls or other retail sites, achieving the near-complete capture of public space by corporate power.[16] The private ownership of networks of pedestrian walkways within the city centre attests to this; even "the street" – that much vaunted site of public encounter and refractory assembly – is often not "public" in Hong Kong. Large corporations have the power to police these walkways, ensuring the steady flow of consumers through the city's spaces. These factors are key aspects of the city's *nomos*, shaping the comportment of citizens, prohibiting stasis, and enforcing a continual movement in search of the next bargain. This imbrication of legal and spatial ordering is made possible through the everyday engagements and interactions of citizens, producing what Andreas Philippopoulos-Mihalopoulos calls a city's "lawscape", referring to the enfolding of space and law that constructs a distinct normative fabric within the urban environment.[17] The lawscape encompasses a range of spatial demarcations and signs that control the normative ordering of space. Philippopoulos-Mihalopoulos argues that the "lawscape" is animated by a play of in/visibility where its normativity becomes more or less visible at any moment. On our daily commute, for example, the normative ordering of space retreats and we become barely conscious of the various materialities that shape our behaviour and express a particular normative imposition: from the front door or gate that determines the public/private division to the ticket barriers in the subway that police your contractual obligations to your carrier, from the panoply of signs and instructions that order your travel, to the shifting rules of etiquette that emerge in the different spaces you inhabit on your journey. What the notion of the lawscape stresses, then, is that a city's *normative architecture* is not reducible to the sum total of its legal texts and executive orders but must include the spatial and material, *architectural* even, ordering of the city.

One of Philippopoulos-Mihalopoulos's key insights, relevant for the present argument, is that the lawscape is reproduced through the habituated *performance* of our spatial surroundings. As Schmitt reminds us, once land appropriation has occurred and a community is able to distribute, divide, and produce within a given space, the underlying spatial matrix recedes into the background.[18] However, we should not approach this underlying *nomos* of a city as being static or somehow abstracted from the lives of citizens. The everyday engagement with the city, through the repetitive retracing and reaffirmation of its

16 Alexander Cuthbert and Keith McKinnell, "Ambiguous Space, Ambiguous Rights—Corporate Power and Social Control in Hong Kong" (1997) 14(5) *Cities* 295–311.

17 See Andreas Philippopoulos-Mihalopoulos, *Spatial Justice: Body, Lawscape, Atmosphere* (Abingdon: Routledge, 2015) and Andreas Philippopoulos-Mihalopoulos (ed.) *Law and the City* (Abingdon: Routledge, 2012).

18 Schmitt (n. 1 above), p. 341.

spatial divisions, is key to the maintenance of its *nomos.* Like any normative coding, the division and production of space requires constant engagement; indeed, what is the *nomos* of the city apart from these repetitive inscriptions in its fabric, the reproduction of private/public divisions, the reaffirmation of the boundaries of personal space, and the reiteration of normative codes of behaviour that attach to the city's locales? It is precisely this repetitive reproduction of the city's *nomos* that reenforces, amongst other things, the expropriation of public space by private actors in Hong Kong, mentioned above. And it is this that the Umbrella Movement challenged and in so doing made suddenly visible the spatial ordering that is so often simply assumed.

The movement ruptured the city's lawscape through the strategy of occupation: an act, to give it a Schmittian gloss, of land appropriation. In political terms, the strategy of occupation is about making immediately visible dissent and discontent within a polity through the seizure of physical space. Within an established normative order, the occupation of a library, a public square, or a street corner is also an act of normative creativity. The existing spatial order is temporarily suspended and the contingency of these existing divisions revealed. As we saw throughout the uprisings in the "Arab Spring" and in the occupations of the squares in southern Europe in 2011, public space became sites of normative experimentation with the dominance of state law being directly challenged and new forms of decision-making and modes of representation taking hold. It is the public square or park – Tahrir, Syntagma, Taksim, or Puerta de Sol – that provides a space for such dissent. A city's square is a small fissure within the *nomos* of the city that can be reappropriated and reimagined in times of political contestation or unrest.

Nowhere do we find such a public space in Hong Kong. As Lisa Law has argued, one possible candidate, "Statue Square" in Central, is more closely aligned with either exclusionary colonial power or to the might of the city's financial institutions than it does with "the people" of Hong Kong.[19] This was what was so striking about the creation of "Umbrella Square" in the city's Admiralty district. Echoing the occupations of Tahrir, Syntagma, and beyond, the Umbrella Movement fashioned its very own public space. The "square" was a space for public discourse and debate: a temporary *polis* within the streets of the city, it was a space dedicated to political creativity through shared speech and action. As Hannah Arendt argues, the *polis* is a space in which "I appear to others and others appear to me, where men [*sic*] ... make their appearance" as explicitly political actors.[20] For the ancients, the *polis* necessitated a spatial division. The political space it names is made possible through an act of circumscription, produced by the division of the land and the establishment of walls that divide within from without. If, for Arendt, a key political task involves rediscovering the classical political divisions between the public and private realms, the Umbrella Movement's rupture of the city's *nomos* worked precisely to undo them. The daily rituals of private life – breakfast, afternoon naps, homework, and late-night gossiping – took on a new significance when performed in the street, distorting easy delineations between private and public spaces. Umbrella Square was only roughly delimited, marked by porous borders that, rather like Antonin Artaud's "theatre of cruelty", troubled any easy distinctions between actor and audience, participant and passer-by. The square became a messy assemblage of actors, observers, critics, and commentators. This invention

19 Lisa Law, "Defying Disappearance: Cosmopolitan Public Spaces in Hong Kong" (2002) 39(9) *Urban Studies* 1630–1635.

20 Hannah Arendt, *The Human Condition* (Chicago: Chicago University Press, 1998) 198–199.

of a new *polis* where political contestation and debate were rife was engendered by the opening in the city's *nomos* made possible by the occupation. This revealed the possibilities of new spatio-normative orderings within the city. The creation of a "public square" in the heart of the political and business district of the city reappropriated space that had been consigned to very different uses. The "square" interrupted the existing spatial distribution of the city, reordering the city's *nomos*. The Lennon Wall, covered in fluorescent notes of solidarity and political aspiration, used the street as a canvas for creative artistic expression,[21] gestures made possible by the fundamental act of land appropriation. The division of the "square" into study areas; kitchens; first aid tents; sites for public meetings, prayer, and relaxation is central to the spatial ordering at the register of the *nomos*. The occupation site asserted the public's role at the heart of city, allowing for the expression of an alternative form of life to emerge which reordered the relation citizens had with their spatial surroundings.

In this sense, the movement disavowed the typically modern attitude that understands space as empty and abstract, a neutral backdrop against which social life is played out. Through the reappropriation of space within the city, the Umbrella Movement underscored the lived reality of (social) space, reminding us – and following Henri Lefebvre – that space itself is always being *produced*.[22] The interruption of the city's *nomos* posed the spatial ordering of the city *as a question* and refused to reduce the spatial to a background issue. The force of Umbrella Square came in part through its interruption of the normal routes of transit through the city: bus routes changed, commutes were suspended, shopping trips stymied. This rupture of the quotidian production of space was one of the movement's key effects. Beyond the disputes over the constitutional settlement and the "legalistic" terrain on which much of existing debates have been conducted, the Umbrella Movement asserted a more radical questioning of the *nomos* of the city. The occupations of space in the heart of the city performed – through a creative "acting out" – a key claim: *the normative ordering of space matters*. In a city with exceptionally small apartment spaces and in which almost all young people live in the family home well into their twenties, the opportunity to occupy, divide, and produce space on one's own terms was seized by young Hongkongers. The existing order that has erased public space, isolated individuals, and alienated living space from the communal environment largely prohibits political expression and abstracts citizens from a sense of the *polis*, a public realm fashioned through a shared creative endeavour. It was an effort to reinvent an immanent and temporary sense of this very *polis* that animated the movement.

To draw on another Lefebvrian motif, we can perhaps associate the invention of Umbrella Square with a specific normative claim: the "right to the city".[23] This right reasserts the fact that cities are shared creative endeavours in which all residents participate. The city, Lefebvre claims, is "more or less the *oeuvre* of its citizens"[24] to which all members of the community have a right of participation. Emphasising the way in which certain groups or classes within the city are excluded from its central spaces though ghettoization and other forms of urban exclusion, Lefebvre asserts the right to the city as "refusal to allow oneself to be removed from the urban reality".[25] In its most fundamental expression, this

21 See Janny Leung, "Umbrella Movement" (2014) 18(12) *Law Text Culture* 134–137.

22 Henri Lefebvre, *The Production of Space* (Oxford: Blackwell, 1991).

23 Henri Lefebvre, *Le Droit à la Ville* (Paris: Economia, 2009).

24 Henri Lefebvre, *Writing on Cities*, (Oxford: Blackwell, 1996) 117.

25 Ibid., p. 195.

right is expressed through the physical presence of citizens within the city's spaces; it is a right performed through the appropriation of space in which space is *used*, *created*, and *managed* by citizens themselves.[26] This is a "right" – and therefore a matter of law – but a right that is more at home in the street than in the courtroom, a material and practical right that is claimed through the assembly of bodies in urban space. As Judith Butler suggests in the context of the emergent politics of protest in post-2008 America, we should understand the right to the city as a right that "comes into existence *when exercised*, and exercised by those who act in concert, in alliance".[27]

It was this communal reordering of the city's spaces that was perhaps the most powerful effect of the movement. The collective expression of a right to belong in the city's space, to have an active role in shaping the city and its future, posed the question of belonging in Hong Kong: whose space is this and who has the power to control the city's *nomos*? Viewing the Umbrella Movement through the spatial lens in which the *nomos* and the spatio-normative take precedence over formal law, we can reveal some of the deeper problematics that the movement revealed. Beneath the technical and legalistic disputes over the election of the CE was a political and normative claim by a generation that feels an increasing detachment from Hong Kong's institutional politics and the material ordering of the city's spaces. To ignore this spatio-normative dimension in the Umbrella Movement de-politicises its strategies and practices, transforming the movement into a technocratic debate about election procedures and constitutional interpretation rather than being closer to the more radical "right to the city" that seeks to reclaim the city's spaces. I have sought in this section to offer an unorthodox perspective on the Umbrella Movement by stressing the normative effects of its spatial intervention. Notwithstanding the importance of this move, an exclusive attention to the spatial represents, in itself, an incomplete account of the pro-democracy campaign. The Schmittian approach to the *nomos* as a purely spatial and material ordering of things ignores the discursive constructions that affect our normative worlds. In the following section I turn to these issues through a very different thinking of the *nomos* developed by Robert Cover. Through Cover – along with Peter Berger's work, the sociologist of religion who inspired Cover's thinking – we can develop a richer account of the motivations that animated the Umbrella Movement from within. Still the language of *nomos* will dominate our thinking, but in the next section we move from the material to the cognitive, from the spatial to the discursive, in an effort to expand the analysis.

Nomos II—Narrative trajectories and shifting identities

Our normative worlds are concretely constructed. The panoply of material techniques used to impose a set of norms over human activity – whether international borders, picket fences, or speed bumps – is key to the ordering of social life by attaching norms to a concrete locale. But what of our discursive normative constructions? The socially contingent empire of "dos and don'ts", "oughts and ought nots" is as effective – sometimes more so – than the outward, material manifestations of a given normative order. Our socially constructed

26 Central to Lefebvre's understanding of the right to the city is the claim that the *use value* of space be privileged over its *exchange value*. Lefebvre sees the commodification of space as a key aspect of it becoming increasingly abstracted from the lives of citizens in late modernity.

27 Judith Butler, *Notes Towards a Performative Theory of Assembly* (Cambridge, MA: Harvard University Press, 2015) 80 (my emphasis).

and immediately *invisible* normative worlds are "made real" – as Elaine Scarry puts it[28] – through the feelings of guilt, shame, and instincts of obedience without which normative orders could not function. These purely discursive "inventions" are not without their operative effects. The purely spatial account of the *nomos* outlined above approaches these issues at a different register of analysis, suggesting that discursive normative formations are superstructures built on the purely material notion of land appropriation and spatial division. This stark distinction between the material and the discursive, however, cannot hold. The acts of land appropriation that make immediately visible a given social order can only be efficacious in the context of a shared discursive milieu in which such divisions and demarcations are themselves associated with particular categories like "ownership" or "property", and national borders can only be effective if "imagined communities" with a shared sense of identity have been formed to bind actors in a common endeavour. Let's turn then to an alternative account of the *nomos* that will offer a supplement to the materialist sense on which we have focused until now.

The sociologist Peter Berger uses the *nomos* to describe the everyday, background discursive ordering of social life.[29] The *nomos*, for Berger, is something that is constantly being produced by actors within a community; to this end he speaks of *nomizing acts* more often than the *nomos* itself, emphasising the creative activities that produce a given order. The original "nomizing act" is to distinguish between *this* and *not that*, to make clear delineations in discursive space. Indeed, Berger's reliance on spatial metaphors is striking, as he comments: "seen from the perspective of society, every *nomos* is an area of meaning carved out of a vast mass of meaninglessness, a small clearing of lucidity in a formless, dark, always ominous jungle".[30] Berger mobilises the very same notions of appropriation, division, and demarcation, but where Schmitt emphasises the material, Berger focuses on the discursive. Berger's *nomos* is a shared world that, whilst socially constructed, is precisely what allows community members access to "reality", a shared body of meaning and knowledge through which social interaction is possible. As with the spatial *nomos*, this discursive register very quickly recedes into the background and passes-by largely unquestioned; until, that is, it is interrupted, disputes arise, or one is dislocated from one's indigenous discursive order. In fact, Berger argues that the *nomos* very often becomes completely dissimulated, with communities assuming that their particular and contingent *nomos* is co-extensive with the *cosmos* or natural world. Drawing on this account, Robert Cover ties the *nomos* to an explicitly *normative* ordering, describing the *nomos* as a normative universe in which we constantly create distinctions between valid and void, the interdicted and the permissible. The *nomos* is an expansive normative register that infiltrates our everyday lives. This allows Cover to position the particular claims and proscriptions made by formal legal regimes against a grander set of concerns. As he suggests, the administrative functions of state law are a part of our normative universe but only "a small part … [of what] ought to claim our attention".[31] In this way, Cover argues directly against jurisprudential orthodoxy that understands normative authority as being tied to a commonly recognised, sovereign authority. For Cover, the *nomos* offers a different perspective. Normativity is generalised and radicalised in Cover's hands, akin to the physical forces of "gravity or momentum", or

28 Elaine Scarry, "The Made-up and the Made-real" (1992) 5(2) *The Yale Journal of Criticism* 239.
29 Peter Berger, *The Sacred Canopy: Elements of a Sociological Theory of Religion* (New York: Anchor Books, 1969).
30 Ibid., p. 23.
31 Cover (n. 1 above), p. 4.

a "force field" through which we are constantly moving.[32] Julen Etxabe suggests that we understand the *nomos* as a "language" by which particular claims or statements are charged with a normative force.[33]

Cover's crucial intervention, and one that will assist in the context of our account of the Umbrella Movement, is the function of *narrative* in relation to the *nomos*. For Cover, the linguistic divisions and distinctions that Berger sees as founding the *nomos* only tell part of the story. More significant than the distinctions between *this* and *not that* is the narratological context in which such divisions are made. All normative systems are mobilised by narratives that give a normative proposition or a linguistic designation sense and direction: "for every constitution there is an epic and each decalogue a scripture".[34] Cover describes the function of narrative in his theory of the *nomos* in the following terms:

> To live in a legal world requires that one know not only the precepts, but also their connections to possible and plausible states of affairs. It requires that one integrate not only the "is" and the "ought" but the "is", the "ought", and the "might be". Narrative so integrates these domains.[35]

For our present concerns, Cover's insistence on the connection between *nomos* and narrative allows us to approach the deep political divergences within Hong Kong and shed light on some of the defining features of the Umbrella Movement. The emerging narratives within the pro-democracy caucus, in particular, deserve a little unpacking.

Since the return of Hong Kong sovereignty to China in 1997, the pro-democracy movement has become dominated by an increasingly radical student movement. Two recent actions stand out. First, the movement to stop the passing of national security legislation – due to be implemented according to Article 23 of the Basic Law that provoked widespread popular protests on Hong Kong's streets, politicising a new generation of Hongkongers. And second, the civil action led by high school students in 2012 to resist the introduction of the "Moral and National Education" programme. The latter campaign gave birth to the "Scholarism" association that played a decisive role in the Umbrella Movement and ended with the occupation of government offices and a student-led hunger strike. These recent mobilisations evidence a growing sense that the pro-democracy organisations and parties formed in the 1980s and 1990s are no longer able to effectively manage the desired transition to a more democratic settlement in the SAR.[36] The intransigence of pro-establishment parties and the conservative tactics of LegCo's pan-democrats have led to increasing frustrations, particularly amongst young Hongkongers who have shown that more radical and confrontational methods can be effective in bringing about change.

32 Ibid., p. 10.

33 Julen Etxabe, "The legal universe after Robert Cover" (2010) 4(1) *Law and Humanities* 115–147.

34 Cover (n. 1 above), p. 4.

35 Ibid., p. 10

36 For a fuller account of the background to the pro-democracy movement in HK, see: Joseph Cheng, "The Democracy Movement in Hong Kong" (1989) 65(3) *International Affairs (Royal Institute of International Affairs 1944–)* 443–462; Benjamin Leung, "The Student Movement in Hong Kong: Transition to a Democratizing Society" in Chiu and Lui (eds) *The Dynamics of Social Movements in Hong Kong* (Hong Kong: Hong Kong University Press, 2000); and Ming Sing, "Mobilization for Political Change – the Pro-Democracy Movement in Hong Kong (1980s–1994)" in Chiu and Lui (eds) *The Dynamics of Social Movements in Hong Kong* (Hong Kong: Hong Kong University Press, 2000).

These insurgent political tactics should be understood in the context of shifts in political and cultural identity in recent years. As Veg points out, recent campaigns to save iconic Hong Kong landmarks from destruction, like the old Star Ferry pier and the Choi Yuen Tsuen village, evidence a growing civic and cultural attachment to a local, rather than national, heritage.[37] These local attachments are part of a changing dynamic concerning ethnic and cultural identity in the SAR. Polling conducted in 2015 suggests that only 18 % of the population identifies as "Chinese" with over 40 % identifying as "Hongkongers", an identification that has risen dramatically since its 18 % low in 2008.[38]

The shifting foci of social and cultural identification in Hong Kong have been the subject of intense scrutiny and debate since the transfer of sovereignty in 1997 when "a distinctive social identity associated with being both Hong Kong and Chinese" was established.[39] This identification that pushed against Western or expressly British influence spiked in 1997[40] in the wake of the handover. But the superordinate identity in the complex imbrication between "Hongkonger", "Hong Kong–Chinese", and "Chinese" associations has shifted back and forth along with the changing social and political winds. These complexities were born out in the occupations themselves that displayed a wide range of local, national, and international influences. In his analysis of artworks created during the movement – whether large-scale installations or *ad hoc* street art – Marco Wan argues that a *bricolage* of identities was present in the occupation sites.[41] Strikingly, colonial nostalgia, with the former colonial flag of Hong Kong and British establishment slogans like "Keep Calm and Carry On", was appropriated for new localist ends by some.[42] Perhaps more significant is Wan's attention to the cultural specificity of many of the artworks that used puns, word play, and specifically *local* references that necessitated an intimate knowledge of both the Cantonese language and Hong Kong pop culture; as Wan suggests, "one needs to be a Hong Konger" to understand the subtleties of much of the aesthetic output of the occupations.[43]

Any effort to offer definitive statements on the complex nature of the shifting modes of identification in the territory is a fool's game that I will not enter into here. What is perhaps clearer are the prominent and divergent narratives concerning Hong Kong's political and social trajectory to which the Umbrella Movement points. As the pro-establishment forces in Hong Kong mount a firm footing for ever-closer bonds with the CCP in the build-up to the expiration of the Basic Law in 2047, young Hongkongers are becoming increasingly reticent about these ties. The tactics in the fight for a democratic future and the increasing tendency to foreground a unique Hong Kong identity rather than a broader "Chinese" categorisation evidence a marked division between those who want to stick to the narrative of "orderly and gradual" democratic progress that leads inexorably towards ever-closer ties with Beijing and those who imagine another story to be told. Perhaps most dramatically, this is a narrative that rejects any easy connection between the Basic Law and the quest for democracy. Cover's evocation of the "might be" which any normative order must marshal is no longer, for many,

37 Veg (n. 8 above), p. 70.

38 HKUPOP survey, https://www.hkupop.hku.hk/english/popexpress/ethnic/eidentity/poll/datatables.html.

39 Marilyn B. Brewer, "Multiple Identities and Identity in Transition: Implications for Hong Kong" (1999) 23(2) *International Journal of Intercultural Relations* 191.

40 Anthony Fung, "What Makes the Local? A Brief Consideration of the Rejuvenation of Hong Kong Identity" (2001) 15(3/4) *Cultural Studies* 591–601.

41 Marco Wan, "The Artwork of Hong Kong's Occupy Central" (2016) (forthcoming).

42 Ibid., 11.

43 Ibid., 18.

tied to the possibilities mapped out by the Basic Law. As I have argued elsewhere, the emerging localist narrative can also be sensed in the key shift that took place in September 2014 when the limited civil disobedience action proposed under the banner of "Occupy Central with Love and Peace" (OCLP) gave way to the more radical tactic of prolonged occupation, giving birth to the "Umbrella Movement" proper.[44] Here a shift took place that took the movement away from arguing for change within the existing constitutional framework of Hong Kong towards a more radical, performative *living out* of a democratic alternative in the occupation camps themselves.

It was these changes in narrative orientation that allowed for the articulation of a deeper political claim to the spaces and modes of belonging in the city that we discussed above. The performative claim of a "right to the city", enacted through the presence of bodies in the city centre, demonstrated a new generation's desire to have a stake in their city's future. It was a claim that was longer possible through existing channels and modes of representation. By tracing this more radical gesture within the movement, we can appreciate how the seeds were sown for the now growing localist politics that has dominated the post-Occupy landscape in Hong Kong.[45] My suggestion here is that by understanding the movement at the register of the *nomos*, which stresses the importance of situating its claims in the context of sociocultural narratives about the identity and trajectory of Hongkongers, and the material orderings that the movement interrupted, we can reveal some of the underlying, and perhaps tacit, political commitments that have an enduring significance in Hong Kong's current political climate.

Conclusion

By shifting to the register of the *nomos*, I have sought to offer an alternative perspective on the Umbrella Movement. In particular, I have resisted the temptation to view events through a purely "legalistic" interpretative frame by inquiring into how the movement affected a deeper sense of the "ordering" of the city. Drawing on Schmitt's account of the *nomos* as an originary spatial ordering of the world and Lefebvre's understanding of the "right to the city", I underscored the normative significance of the movement's intervention within Hong Kong's spatial matrix. By interrupting the everyday production of (social) space in the city, the movement brought to the fore the spatio-normative constructions that shape urban life and, in temporarily suspending them, reimagined the city's *nomos*. Beyond the technicalities of constitutional interpretation and voting reform, the movement made a more fundamental assertion of a right to belong in the city's spaces and

44 Matthews (n. 6 above), pp. 10–12.

45 The localist movement has taken hold in the territory in the wake of the Umbrella Movement. The "Hong Kong Indigenous" group – whose political leanings are pithily captured in their motto, "Local Values, Valiant Resistance" – put up a very strong fight against the mainstream pan-democratic Civic Party's candidate in a recent by-election. Student bodies at both HKU and CUHK have recently voted to support localist groups and leaders indicating strong sympathy for the movement amongst young Hongkongers. As Suzanne Pepper suggests, the localist movement is orientated around a robust identity politics that seeks to support all aspects of Hong Kong's local culture, economy, and politics, including the "disruptions" caused by cross-border traders operating in the New Territories. The movement is associated with a more radical set of tactics than the mainstream pan-democrats and was directly involved in the violent unrest in Mong Kok in support of local street food hawkers. See Suzanne Pepper, "Holding the line ... But only just" (2 March 2016), http://chinaelectionsblog.net/hkfocus/.

have a stake in its future. Through Cover and Berger's account of the *nomos* as a discursive normative world through which communities are always shaping their future commitments, we were able to trace the shifting dynamics of identity within Hong Kong and examine some of the key tactical choices the movement made. The imagined future for the territory is precisely what was at stake in the movement. For those involved in the messy process of post-Occupy institutionalisation and electioneering, this remains an open question: the "might be" of Hong Kong's future.

The expansive and rather nebulous register of the *nomos* in no way provides all the answers for unpacking this complex social movement, but I hope that shifting our attention away from legalistic technicalities to an "other law" that precedes and prefigures these matters has revealed another dimension to the normative significance of the Umbrella Movement. I stressed above that the *nomos* of the city – understood as a spatio-normative ordering – is produced through the quotidian practices of citizens, reiterating its demarcations and networks. In this sense, the real test for any campaign for political change is to alter these everyday practices, to intervene within these deep structures and habits that shape the lives of actors in a community. By any measure the situation for the pro-democratic movement in Hong Kong is worse today than it was before the Umbrella Movement took hold of the streets in September 2014. There is no realistic prospect of LegCo passing democratic reform of any sort in the near future, a situation that cannot be said for the pre-Occupy context. The question of the legacy of these encampments remains open to debate: was the Umbrella Movement an ultimately failed act of self-indulgence, a training ground for future political action, or simply a signal of the deep political and generational divisions that mark the city? Plato used the term *nomos* to refer to those customs and conventions that were of educational significance, describing as *nomoi* those rules which instilled values within the young. The hope must remain that the *nomos* of the Umbrella Movement will fulfil precisely this *paideic* function, inculcating democratic values within a new generation of activists. However, the results of these "lessons in dissent" remain to be seen.

Part III

Comparative elements involving Taiwan and Hong Kong

7 Unpopular sovereignty

Constitutional identity through the lens of the Sunflower and Umbrella Movements

*Cheng-Yi Huang**

The relevant question is not only whether we govern ourselves in our politics, but also whether we govern ourselves in our constitutionalism.

(Kathleen M. Sullivan[1])

Sovereignty on the battlefield

The idea of sovereignty, though fictional, has always been coupled with nations or people. The term underlies the expressive function of a self-ruling polity, which exercises monopolized power over its subjects on an exclusive territory.[2] Ever since the proclamation of the US Constitution, "We the People" has become a magic wand, turning the constitution into the reification of sovereign power. Meanwhile, as the conceptual invention of Abbé Sieyes indicates, "we the people" represents constituent power (*pouvoir constitué*) at the founding moment, which is quite different from constituted power (*pouvoir constituant*) in ordinary constitutional politics.[3] The notion of constituent power enshrines the general will of the founding moment and becomes the origin of political authority in the post-founding era. Therefore, much constitutional theory stipulates that there is nothing more sacred than the constitution, which embodies the constituent moment as well as the general will. It is "we the people" who constitute the political community and enjoy sovereignty over itself after the founding moment.

However, in contemporary times the primacy of constitutions as the reification of sovereignty has been thoroughly challenged throughout the world.[4] A wave of constitutional

* Associate Research Professor, Institutum Iurisprudentiae, Academia Sinica.

1 Kathleen M. Sullivan, "Epistemic Democracy and Minority Rights" (1998) 86 *California Law Review* 445.

2 As Rosanvallon cogently argues, "[T]he primary character of a democratic regime is the anointment by the people of those who govern. [...] It is assumed that the general will coincides with the will of the majority. [...] Out of this developed a certain ideal of unanimity, which has been one of the underpinnings of the democratic idea from the beginnings: 'democratic,' in the broadest possible sense, means 'expressive of social generality.'" Peirre Rosanvallon, *Democratic Legitimacy: Impartiality, Reflexivity, Proximity*, trans. by Arthur Goldhammer (Princeton: Princeton University Press, 2011) 1–2.

3 Sieyes combines the notion of nation with constituent power. He emphasizes, "The nation is prior to everything. It is the source of everything. Its will is always legal; indeed, it is the law itself." This political romanticism has great influence upon later German philosophers like Carl Schmitt and Hermann Heller. For Sieyes' idea of constituent power, please see Emmanuel Joseph Sieyes, *What is the Third Estate?* [1789], M. Blondel trans. (London: Pall Mall Press, 1963) 126.

4 See, e.g. Mila Versteeg, "Unpopular Constitutionalism" (2014) 89 *Indiana Law Journal* 1133; Denis J. Galligan, "The Sovereignty Deficit of Modern Constitutions" (2013) 33(4) *Oxford Journal of Legal Studies* 703; Brian Christopher Jones, "Preliminary Warnings on Constitutional Idolatry" (2016) *Public Law* 74.

showdowns have emerged from severe political cleavages, mostly through social movements, which have witnessed the fragmentation, transformation, and reconfiguration of this nineteenth-century brainchild of popular sovereignty and constitutional legitimacy.[5] This chapter explores the disentanglement of sovereignty and people through the cases of the Hong Kong Umbrella Movement and the Taiwan Sunflower Movement.

In 2014 Taiwan and Hong Kong both witnessed gigantic political protests, first initiated by young people but which immediately inflamed their respective societies. The movements were largely based around issues regarding controversial legislation and political disagreement and there were overlapping features. Both the Sunflower Movement and the Umbrella Movement fought against their respective governments' increasing dependence on China, though the former was mainly concerned with economic integration and the latter with political integration. As other authors in this collection have noted, participants in the Sunflower Movement occupied the national legislature and also broke into and briefly occupied the Executive Yuan, the country's top executive branch. Many have criticized their action as illegal and unjustifiable, though the participants claimed their right to defend the polity against the government's abuse of power in passing the Service Trade Agreement with China without due process of legislation. Accordingly, their actions were a type of civil disobedience that pursued a higher value of democracy and self-government.[6] On the other hand, the Umbrella participants kept urging crowds to obey the law, since the rule of law has been the most significant hallmark of Hong Kong's legal development.[7] However, the police in Hong Kong were reported to exercise unprincipled discretion when enforcing the law both during and after the movement,[8] which has prompted many youngsters to reconsider alternatives, including forceful struggle.[9] While Taiwanese protesters appealed to civil disobedience to justify their commitment to democracy, Hong Kong citizens upheld the rule of law as their jurisdiction's supreme value, which could not be trumped by aspirations for democracy. However, participants in both movements gradually realized the "elephant in the room" was not about the rule of law or democratic values, but the uneasy and unspoken tension between sovereignty and the people.

Disentangling popular sovereignty

Hong Kong provides a prominent case of the disentanglement of sovereignty and the people. Since 1997, Hong Kong has officially been a part of China, though its Basic Law follows the institutional design of "One Country, Two Systems", guaranteeing that the Mainland's socialist system would not be applied to Hong Kong. Meanwhile, according to

5 For debates over sovereignty in regard to emergence of the European Union, please refer to Hent Kalmo and Quentin Skinner (eds), *Sovereignty in Fragments: The Past, Present and Future of a Contested Concept*, (Cambridge: Cambridge University Press, 2010). In addition to Hong Kong and Taiwan, Japan has also witnessed mass protests about constitutional controversy, please refer to Chaihark Hahm and Sung Ho Kim, *Making We the People: Democratic Constitutional Founding in Postwar Japan and South Korea* (Cambridge: Cambridge University Press, 2015) 66–96.

6 Jones and Su characterize it as a case of "confrontational contestation". Jones and Su, Chapter 1.

7 See Fu Hualing, Chapter 5, and Chih-hsing Ho, Chapter 8.

8 See Chih-hsing Ho, Chapter 8, pp. 136–145.

9 Victoria Tin-bor Hui, "Fishball Violent Protest and the Call for Independence –Why Not 'Forceful Nonviolence'?" Hong Kong's Umbrella Movement and Beyond, https://victoriatbhui.wordpress.com/2016/02/13/fishball-protests-the-fateful-turn-to-violence/.

Sec. 2 of Article 45, the selection of the Chief Executive should be gradually transformed into a Hong Kong general election.[10] But even before this, the 800 members of the nominating committee still control who are allowed to be put forward for selection. Moreover, disputes over the meaning of the Basic Law are decided by the Standing Committee of the National People's Congress in Beijing. Although the Court of Final Appeal in Hong Kong enjoys the power of final adjudication, it is the Standing Committee that authorizes the courts in Hong Kong to interpret the Basic Law within the limits of autonomy granted in the Basic Law. Revision of the Basic Law also exclusively belongs to the National People's Congress rather than any representative institutions in Hong Kong. In brief, the authority of the Basic Law originates from and is dependent upon the political power of the Chinese government, not the people of Hong Kong.

As the premier showcase of "One Country, Two Systems", it is heatedly debated to what extent the Basic Law is the embodiment of "We the People of Hong Kong".[11] Since Hong Kong's political transition from a colony of the United Kingdom to a Special Administrative Region (SAR) of China, people in Hong Kong have had little chance to express their own political preference or cast a vote over their Basic Law, though some legal and political scholars from Hong Kong were invited to participate in the drafting process. The issue of sovereignty was never on the negotiating table between China and the United Kingdom, since the Hong Kong people have not been regarded as a "people" having a right to self-determination. Meanwhile, to most Hong Kongers in the 1990s, the Basic Law was a realization of Hong Kong autonomy, at least on paper, which could function as the bedrock of self-government.

Nevertheless, it would be far too optimistic to regard the autonomy provided in the Basic Law as the equivalence of self-government. Since 1997, the Basic Law has increasingly functioned like a provincial statute regarding the division of labour in the view of the National People's Congress Standing Committee (NPCSC), and at most provides a limited amount of rights protection to the Hong Kong people.[12] In this regard, the Basic Law is not Hong Kong's constitution. In fact, it is the PRC's constitution that has final authority over Hong Kong's political structure. "One Country, Two Systems" means there shall be only one constitutional authority. It did not say "One Country, Two Sovereignties". He who rules is the sovereign. Under the current arrangements, no matter how severe the grudge they bear against the Beijing government, the people in Hong Kong are subject to the constitutional authority of the People's Republic of China. The failure of the Umbrella Movement can be understood as the failure of the Hong Kong people to demarcate the boundaries of their political community so as to promote their own political constitution.

Two years after the Umbrella Movement, in 2016, six candidates in local elections that lent their support to the independence movement of Hong Kong were disqualified from

10 In fact, the language of Article 45, Section 2 does not directly mention a general election among Hong Kong citizens. It still gives the nomination power to the nominating committee: "[T]he ultimate aim is the selection of the Chief Executive by universal suffrage upon nomination by a broadly representative nominating committee in accordance with democratic procedures." See Michael Davis, "Hong Kong's Umbrella Movement: Beijing's Broken Promises" (2015) 26(2) *Journal of Democracy* 101, 104–06.

11 See Johannes Chan, "Hong Kong's Constitutional Journey, 1997–2011" in Albert H. Y. Chen (ed.), *Constitutionalism in Asia in the Early Twenty-First Century* (Cambridge: Cambridge University Press, 2014) 169–193, especially pp. 190–193.

12 Ibid., especially the four interpretations by NPCSC, pp. 172–179.

the election,[13] and yet the first rally for the Hong Kong independence movement attracted more than 2,500 people, according to Hong Kong police.[14] But whether or not Hong Kong independence is a politically viable strategy is not the issue this chapter aims to address. Its emergence and increasing popularity should provide serious concerns for Beijing. From the perspective of constitutional authority, the origins of the Hong Kong independence movement lie at the heart of sovereignty. China claims its sovereignty over Hong Kong, while Hong Kong asserts that self-government is provided by its Basic Law. The conflict remains unresolved, and the arrangement of "One Country, Two Systems" will only perpetuate this conflict.

Unpopular sovereignty: Dislocation of the ROC Constitution

If Hong Kong presents a pessimistic story about sovereignty and self-government, Taiwan provides the other side of the coin. As mentioned above, the unspoken issue behind Hong Kong's Umbrella Movement was "people without sovereign power". Taiwan's Sunflower Movement in turn revealed the uncomfortable truth of "sovereignty without people", which can be described as "unpopular sovereignty". The government in Taiwan, namely the Republic of China, still claims its sovereignty over mainland China, given the People's Republic of China has taken over power since 1949. In reality, Taiwan hardly enjoys any type of sovereignty over China, but according to the Constitution of the Republic of China, it does.

The Constitution of the Republic of China – which is now valid only in Taiwan – was adopted in 1946 by representatives from each province of China, including Taiwan, and went into effect on 25 December 1947. However, during the civil war the KMT (Chinese Nationalist Party) was defeated by the Chinese Communist Party (CCP) and retreated from mainland China to Taiwan in 1949. The KMT ruled Taiwan with martial law for about 40 years. Martial law was lifted in 1987, and general elections for the National Assembly and the Legislative Yuan resumed in 1991 and 1992, respectively. The reason elections were suspended for over 40 years was because the KMT government continued to claim their sovereignty over China during this period. Thus as political symbolism, the representative institutions, including the Legislative Yuan, National Assembly, and the Control Yuan, had to be composed of members elected before 1949, representing the whole constituency of China.[15] However, as a Greek philosopher once pointed out, "change presides over all things mortal".[16] In 1969 President Chiang Kai-shek announced in an administrative rule that the three representative institutions should hold elections for the vacancy left by the deceased members. Even so, the majority in the three branches were still composed of representatives from mainland China.

13 Joyce Lim, "More than 1,000 protest in Hong Kong over pro-independence activists' disqualification from LegCo polls" *Straits Times* (21 August 2016), http://www.straitstimes.com/asia/east-asia/more-than-1000-protest-in-hong-kong-over-pro-independence-activists-disqualification.

14 Liam Fitzpatrick, "Hong Kong Makes History With First Pro-Independence Rally" *Time* (5 August 2016), http://time.com/4440708/hong-kong-independence-china-localist/.

15 Taiwan's Constitutional Court, the Council of Grand Justices, regarded these three branches all together as the parliament provided in the original text of the ROC Constitution. Please see Judicial Yuan Interpretation No. 76 of 3 May 1957. For the description of this constitutional history of "legitimacy-maintenance", please refer to Jiunn-rong Yeh, *The Constitution of Taiwan: A Contextual Analysis* (Oxford: Hart Publishing, 2016) 32–34.

16 Quoted from Hannah Arendt, *On Revolution* (New York: Viking Press, 1963) 27.

This arrangement was held in place until 1991, when the Temporary Provisions Effective During the Communist Rebellion ("Temporary Provisions") were abolished and the government held national elections for the representative institutions, voted on by the Taiwanese people. The "old delegates" from China had all retired. From the perspective of political constituency, the Legislative Yuan (Taiwan's parliament) now represents constituencies from Taiwan, and does not include any from China. However, the 1947 constitution remains intact. Although the Temporary Provisions are no longer in effect, the original texts of the constitution regarding constituency are still suspended. Before the "old delegates" had left, Taiwan passed an Additional Article, which acknowledges the current situation as pre-unification, so the country as a whole consists of two parts: the free area, i.e. Taiwan, and the mainland area, i.e. the PRC and Mongolia. Without a doubt, the ROC Constitution has turned into the most important symbol of political legitimacy in the KMT's claim of sovereignty over China.

What does this history matter to the Sunflower Movement? Article 11 of the Additional Article provides that "Rights and obligations between the people of the Chinese mainland area and those of the free area, and the disposition of other related affairs may be specified by law." This is the delegating clause that enabled the Legislative Yuan to pass the Act Governing Relations between the People of the Taiwan Area and the Mainland Area ("Cross-Strait Act"). The negotiation, execution, and approval of the Economic Cooperation Framework Agreement (ECFA) and the Service Trade Pact were – and still are, for that matter[17] – regulated by the Cross-Strait Act (Article 4, 4-2, 4-3, 4-4, Article 5, 5-1, 5-2). According to Article 5 of the Cross-Strait Act, the agreement shall be sent to the Legislative Yuan for "consideration" (ex post review), if the content of the agreement requires "any amendment to laws or any new legislation". The process of legislative review is not specified in the law regarding the authority of the Legislative Yuan. Therefore, the KMT caucus decided to approve the Service Trade Pact swiftly, literally within 30 seconds. This episode enraged thousands of youngsters concerned with the relationship and ongoing negotiations between China and Taiwan. They went all out to occupy the Legislative Yuan.

The root of this political outrage is not primarily about the free trade issue nor the legislative process. The overwhelming anxiety comes from worries about derogation of Taiwan's sovereignty. On the one hand, the Additional Article created a dilemma between the post-1991 political constituency and the 1947 constitution. The constitution still claims its validity throughout China on the basis of its constituent power derived from "We the People" of 1947. However, since 1949 the document no longer enjoys any political power over China. The political constituency has changed, and the Additional Article of 1994 provided a constitutional basis for popular election of the president. In 1996, Lee Teng-hui (李登輝) was elected to the presidency through universal suffrage in Taiwan. Thereafter, the president has possessed two identities: from a constitutional perspective, she or he represents the Republic of China, which still covers all of China; but from the level of democratic election, she or he represents the population of Taiwan. Her political power comes from Taiwanese citizens, but her constitutional authority emanates from the ROC Constitution. This schizophrenic constitutional identity is the root of the Sunflower Movement.

17 The Legislative Yuan has still failed to pass any replacement for the Cross-Strait Act, which was one of the Sunflower Movement's main demands.

As president, Ma Ying-jeou (馬英九) oversaw his executive members to negotiate with the Beijing Government on the ECFA and the Service Trade Agreement; as the chairman of the KMT, he demanded its caucus in the Legislative Yuan approve the Service Trade Agreement as soon as possible. President Ma believed his actions strictly followed the requirements of the ROC Constitution, which mandates him to be the president of China, both of the free area and the Mainland area. In actuality this is more like a delusion. The Republic of China has lost its "people" for over 60 years. The sovereignty it claims over China is "sovereignty without people" (or "unpopular sovereignty"). However, the expressive function of the KMT's "unpopular sovereignty" is not to ask China to return the territory or its people to the ROC Government. On the contrary, it restrains people in Taiwan from establishing a different country, or leaving "China", both politically and constitutionally. And yet the KMT also understands that their ideology of "one China means the Republic of China" (or "reclaiming Mainland China") is widely unpopular, if not a fantasy nowadays, given the increasing political, economic power of China and the intricacies of international politics. The only way to carry out their agenda of unification is to work with the Chinese Communist Party to push economic – and then political – integration. From the perspective of Sunflower participants, this means that Taiwan would eventually be integrated into China, rather than continue to have a mutually agreeable political structure with China. In the Sunflowers' view, Taiwan's citizens elect the president, and the citizenry in a democratic society determines the boundaries of the political community. Therefore, the president should represent his or her constituency rather than assume a hypothetical role of "Chinese president". The movement believed that the president should uphold the interest of the Taiwanese people beyond any unification agenda located in the ROC Constitution.

Ironically, the Chinese government also claims sovereignty over Taiwan. The PRC passed an Anti-Secession Law in 2005 and it keeps reiterating that "Taiwan is a part of China", even though the Chinese Communist Party has never controlled this region before or after 1949. Therefore, there is an overlapped claim of sovereignty: the ROC Government claims to rule China on the ground of its constitution, regardless of the constituency change, while the PRC Government also claims to rule Taiwan since it succeeded the political status of the ROC after 1949. Therefore, both governments are making claims of sovereignty without the consent of people in either China or Taiwan. In this convoluted penumbra of overlapped sovereignty, the citizens of Taiwan lose their own political identity, as both the PRC and the ROC regard them as "part of China". Therefore, to the disappointment of hundreds of thousands of Taiwanese citizens, their country, Taiwan, is not a sovereign state. … They are, like the people of Hong Kong, a people without sovereignty, though they do have their own constitution, democratic institutions, and periodic elections. But their democracy does not bring them any sovereign power over themselves. They are ruled by an "unpopular sovereignty" enshrined in the ROC Constitution.

Owning sovereignty: Democratic deepening versus the rule of law in practice

The situations in Hong Kong and Taiwan lead us to ponder where the notion of sovereignty comes from. All political theories regarding sovereignty would confirm that sovereignty is a mythical construction, not only formulated by domestic public law but also reflecting the Westphalia order of international law.[18] Popular sovereignty implicates that "We the People" have the supreme power to govern the political community under the foundations of the constitution, either written or unwritten. However, as Taiwan's constitutional history shows, sovereignty is not necessarily derived from the will of the people. Neither can the constitution reflect the exact scope of sovereignty. As Joseph de Maistre insightfully observed two centuries ago, "the people are the sovereign which cannot exercise their sovereignty".[19] This oft-cited quote precisely describes the dilemma faced by contemporary Taiwan and, more or less, post-1997 Hong Kong.

The ROC Constitution has gradually become a symbolic representation of a national narrative, which has been separated from the people it claims to rule as well as from the people it rules. Although scholars often argue that after more than two hundred years, the United States Constitution has become a political symbol rather than a living document ratified by each generation of American citizens, the US government has never claimed to legitimately rule Canada or the United Kingdom through its constitution. However, every president elected after 1996 in Taiwan has vowed to obey the ROC Constitution, which commands them to be president for all of China. Thus, the ROC Constitution preserves an outdated sovereignty "rejuvenated" by popular elections every four years in Taiwan. Taiwanese people attempt to broaden the practice of democracy so that they can assert their popular sovereignty. However, the democratic approach to generating sovereignty suffers vicious "defects" when the president assumes her or his constitutional role. This perennial self-contradiction entails a fundamental inquiry for the legitimacy of reunification, mainly located in the Preamble and Article 11 of the Additional Articles. The Sunflower Movement urged the government to initiate a Citizens Assembly for Constitutional Reform, an extra-constitutional mechanism focused on resolving the legitimacy issue. Given that it would be extra-constitutional, it would not be confined to the current constitutional framework of Chinese representativeness. In this regard, the Sunflower Movement actually crystallizes the constituent moment defined by Abbé Sieyes. The constituent power, coming before constitution-making, engenders the political genesis of order in a constitutional democracy. The predecessor of the Sunflower Movement, the Wild Lily Movement of 1990, successfully pushed the government to abolish the Temporary Provisions and to get rid of the "old delegates". In fact, the democratic approach to sovereignty in Taiwan owes its debts to the Wild Lily Movement. However, ever since President Lee Teng-hui compromised with KMT's intraparty leaders and military juntas, the symbolic representation of the ROC Constitution has been preserved by way of the Additional Articles. The Sunflower Movement brought this undemocratic compromise into the fold again. However, the elections after 2014 have once again diminished the necessity for reshaping Taiwan's constitutional identity. Most of the post-Sunflower proposals for constitutional reform focused on issues of separation of powers or institutional choices like semi-presidentialism, parliamentarism, or presidentialism. These institutional designs were responses to the expansion of presidential power

18 Loughlin argued that sovereignty is "the foundational concept of modern public law". See Martin Loughlin, *The Idea of Public Law* (Oxford: Oxford University Press, 2003) 73. Also see Dieter Grimm, *Sovereignty: The Origin and Future of a Political and Legal Concept* (New York: Columbia University Press, 2015) 4; Richard Tuck, *The Sleeping Sovereign: The Invention of Modern Democracy* (Cambridge: Cambridge University Press, 2015) 249–251.

19 Joseph de Maistre, "Study on Sovereignty" in *The Works of Joseph de Maistre*, trans. Jack Lively (London: George Allen & Unwin, 1965 [1794]), pp. 93–129.

under the Ma administration. However, once the focal point was redirected to constitutional powers, the constituent moment faded away.

On the other hand, the appeal to the Basic Law has allowed a very distinctive way of Hong Kong's political activism after the handover. Although it was not passed by Hong Kong citizens, the Basic Law has applied to Hong Kong citizens since 1997. Meanwhile, it is not like the ROC Constitution, which unrealistically claims to be applied to China. The debates surrounding the application of the Basic Law have entrenched it as Hong Kong's constitution, which is quite a phenomenon given that it has been in force for less than two decades.[20] Before 1997, the Basic Law was regarded only as a political document that demonstrated "One Country, Two Systems". It had nothing to do with the political identity of Hong Kong. However, much social activism emerged in the first decade of the twenty-first century (such as the high-speed rail controversy, the public school textbook debates, or the social benefits issues), and the Hong Kong people gradually realized their loss of political autonomy. At the same time, lawyers, pro-democracy legislators, and public intellectuals in Hong Kong started to build their argument for self-government on the autonomy promised in the Basic Law. Even in the post-Umbrella election in 2016, most candidates for the Legislative Council asserted to uphold the Basic Law as the fundamental political document in Hong Kong.[21] However, when the SAR Government proposed to enact legislation regarding Article 23 of the Basic Law, the argument of the Basic Law as the constitution of Hong Kong appeared to be moot.[22] When the State Council in Beijing issued the White Paper in June 2014 on the practice of "One Country, Two Systems" policy in Hong Kong, it became clear that final authority for interpreting the Basic Law lies in the hands of the PRC Central Government. Finally, when the National People's Congress Standing Committee (NPCSC) announced that the design of the nominating committee for the 2017 election of the Chief Executive would be similar to the current election committee, the decision aroused the Hong Kong people's consciousness regarding their self-determination. To the extent that the Basic Law could bring about autonomy for Hong Kong now appears to be a contradictory thesis.

"Democratic deepening" and "the rule of law tradition" have been the two different routes taken by Taiwan and Hong Kong in the past 20 years, with both aiming towards self-government.[23] Outcomes of the Sunflower Movement and the Umbrella Movement reflect the divergence and convergence of political reform in these two polities.

20 See Cora Chan, "Reconceptualising the Relationship between the Mainland Chinese Legal System and the Hong Kong Legal System" (2011) 6(1) *Asian Journal of Comparative Law* 1–28; Karen Kong, "Adjudicating Social Welfare Rights in Hong Kong" (2012) 10 *International Journal of Constitutional Law* 588–599.

21 This could be interpreted as the chilling effect of ousting the pro-independence candidates. The SAR Government declared that all the candidates should "love Hong Kong, love China". Stuart Lau, "Legco election candidates to face 'follow-up action' if they back Hong Kong independence, government warns" *South China Morning Post* (30 August 2016), http://www.scmp.com/news/hong-kong/politics/article/2011174/legco-election-candidates-face-follow-action-if-they-back.

22 Article 23 of the Basic Law provides, "The Hong Kong Special Administrative Region shall enact laws on its own to prohibit any act of treason, secession, sedition, subversion against the Central People's Government, or theft of state secrets, to prohibit foreign political organizations or bodies from conducting political activities in the Region, and to prohibit political organizations or bodies of the Region from establishing ties with foreign political organizations or bodies."

23 For a recent observation on Taiwan's democratic deepening approach, please see Cass R. Sunstein, "Taiwan's Fragile Success Story" *Bloomberg View* (15 December 2015), http://origin-www.bloombergview.com/articles/2015-12-15/taiwan-s-fragile-success-story.

Concluding remarks: One sovereignty, two tales

Two years after the Sunflower Movement, Taiwan witnessed landslide victories of the opposition Democratic Progressive Party (DPP) against the KMT in local and national (legislature and presidential) elections in 2015 and 2016. Critics have commented that this is a strong rejection to the pro-China policy advanced by the presidency of Ma Ying-jeou. Periodic election allows "political revolution" without any further turbulence or mass protest. Political optimists believe this is the great power of democracy, which creates peaceful turnovers of political power: "If you don't like this president, wait for the next one." On the other hand, after the Umbrella Movement, the people of Hong Kong are trying to reclaim their political autonomy through a democratic game, i.e. election. The surprise victory of pro-democracy candidates in the 2016 Legislative Council (LegCo) elections breathed some fresh air into the desperate politics of Hong Kong. Among them, Eddie Chu Hoi-dick, a long time social activist, got more than 70,000 votes, becoming the largest winner; and Nathan Law Kwun-chung, an Umbrella Movement student leader, become the LegCo's youngest legislator. The LegCo election is the first of its kind post-Umbrella Movement, so many feel very optimistic about the outcome.[24] However, it also shows that after the movement, Hong Kong is trying a more democratic approach and setting aside their more traditional rule of law approach. Since the majority in the Legislative Council still consists of legislators from the so-called functional constituencies, the victory is more symbolic than practical. Moreover, once Hong Kong steps onto the journey of democratic election, it will be very hard to keep the Basic Law as the constitutional document of Hong Kong. Citizens will realize a political document like the Basic Law, without any democratic participation from local citizens, does not equate to self-government at all. Nevertheless, if the end of political autonomy means singular sovereignty, the Hong Kong people should look to Taiwan as an unpromising lesson: periodic election that includes true universal suffrage still has not generated any seeds of Taiwanese sovereignty.

The two movements tell a similar tale about sovereignty. While Taiwan is still confined to the ROC Constitution's political symbolism, Hong Kong strives to maintain its autonomy from the grounds of the Basic Law. While political movements in Taiwan have washed away the party state and democratic election has become a fixture of everyday life, Hong Kong is pursuing universal suffrage and direct election for the Chief Executive and members of the Legislative Council. Democracy does give people in Taiwan the opportunity to change the government every four years. It makes politicians and parties more responsive to popular votes and to some extent more accountable. And yet responsiveness and accountability promise good governance, but not sovereignty. In realpolitik, Taiwan is still not a member of the United Nations, and its sovereignty is still highly contestable in the international realm. On the other hand, everything written in the Basic Law is subject to the final control of the People's Congress in Beijing. The endeavour to uphold the rule of law seems simply to reaffirm the legal order ordained by the PRC Central Government. Constitutional legitimacy, if that is an argument for defending the Basic Law, has to derive

24 Please see the post-election report here: Stuart Lau, Jeffie Lam, Joyce Ng, and Tony Cheung, "Veteran lawmakers cast aside as Legco's new generation appeals for greater say in Hong Kong's political future" *South China Morning Post* (5 September 2016), http://www.scmp.com/news/hong-kong/politics/article/2014824/veteran-lawmakers-cast-aside-legcos-new-generation-appeals.

from civic engagement and mutual consent in the process of constitutional life, rather than a decree from outside the community. The situation is the same in Taiwan. The cycle of national elections for the ROC president or legislators simply reaffirms the existence of the ROC constitutional order, but the question of Chinese representativeness remains. Unless Taiwan can demarcate a clear line of its citizenship and therefore establish a boundary for its political community, the ROC Constitution refers to an unsettled constitutional identity.

Sovereignty is a two-way street. It certainly shapes the constitutional identity of the people. However, it also depends on how people rule themselves, with fundamental documents agreed upon by the citizenry. As Kathleen Sullivan argues, "The relevant question is not only whether we govern ourselves in our politics, but also whether we govern ourselves in our constitutionalism."[25] Constitutionalism does not merely mean the formality of separation of powers and the establishment of rule of law. It is deeply intertwined with how a political community defines itself and rules itself. A constitution is the product of identity formation growing out of political self-consciousness. Therefore, it should not be something imposed by an authority other than the people itself, as the Beijing Government has done to Hong Kongers or the 1947 ROC Constitution has done to contemporary Taiwanese. Democratic processes may entail the formation of political identity, but it will not necessarily bring a constituent moment that creates an authentic constitution. An authentic constitution will encourage its citizens to engage in constant democratic participation and vindicate the rule of law within the self-governing political community. The boundaries of the political community may wax or wane over time, but sovereignty is a Hamletian question of existence. The outburst from the Sunflower and Umbrella Movements came close to the tipping point of a constituent moment, although the regularity of constitutional politics gradually tamed this vital moment. The dialectic of democracy and the rule of law has very little to do with the dilemma of unpopular sovereignty. Only when democratic practice (be it electoral or deliberative) is attached to an authentic constitution of the people will popular sovereignty come into being. Until then, unpopular sovereignty will remain an unending spell on these two political communities. Further disenchantment is certainly on its way.

25 Kathleen M. Sullivan, "Epistemic Democracy and Minority Rights" (1998) 86 California Law Review 445.

8 To punish or not to punish

The question of civil disobedience and the Umbrella Movement

Chih-hsing Ho[*]

Introduction

This chapter examines the punishment side of civil disobedience. Whether and how to punish a conscience-based deliberative action of breaching the law remains a challenging prospect in modern legal and political philosophy. The fundamental concerns of these difficulties invite re-thinking not only of the relations between civil disobedience and punishment, but also the justification of civil disobedience when the punishment turns out to have a legitimate basis and firm moral grounding. This chapter tries to analyse these intriguing issues by first discussing traditional theories of punishment. It evaluates deterrent and retributive grounds and their proposed defence to the punishment of civil disobedience. Further, this chapter investigates whether engagement in civil disobedience might be deemed to be a right of conduct, and whether this moral right to civil disobedience could provide a normative protection against state punishment. Apart from these theoretical considerations, this chapter uses Hong Kong's Umbrella Movement as a practical example in order to engage in dialogue with the theoretical discussions presented here. By analysing Hong Kong court injunctions and adjudication related to the Occupy Central Movement, the chapter further delineates the role of the Hong Kong courts and the image of the rule of law constituted by Hong Kong's judiciary.

The punishment of civil disobedience

The term "civil disobedience" can be traced back to the American writer, humanitarian, and poet Henry David Thoreau's essay *Resistance to Civil Government*, published in 1848.[1] In it, Thoreau argued that conscientious citizens have an obligation not to commit injustice produced by the government or give it practical support to collaborate an injustice. By refusing to pay the poll tax, Thoreau demonstrated his disobedience to fund the US government, which in his eyes had already abused state power by enforcing the Fugitive Slave Act and invading Mexico in the Mexican–American War (1846–1848).[2] For Thoreau, a dutiful response to an unjust law is not to act passively, such as using the political process to change the law by voting and then accepting the outcome of the democratic process.

* Assistant Research Fellow, Institute of European and American Studies, Academia Sinica, Taipei, Taiwan; LLM (Columbia), JSM (Stanford), PhD in Law (London School of Economics).

1 Henry David Thoreau, *Resistance to Civil Government* (1848). The essay was later reprinted in 1866 after Thoreau's death as a part of a collection of Thoreau's work that is given a title *Civil Disobedience*. Henry David Thoreau, *Civil Disobedience* (Chicago: Great Books Foundation, 1966).

2 Brian Walker, "Thoreau on Democratic Cultivation" (2001), 29(2) *Political Theory* 155.

Rather, he asserted that majorities often do not gain the virtues of justice, and therefore individuals need to rely on the judgement of their own conscience in order to act justly. In addition, Thoreau claimed that even though a minority cannot confront the majority by voting, it is irresistible to constitute a peaceable revolution "when it clogs by its whole weight"[3] in the words of the poet. The theorist's skeptical perceptions of government and his deliberative actions of refusing allegiance to the state influenced many after him to engage in civil disobedience.

Thoreau's writings and actions reveal certain features about the conception of civil disobedience that have been long debated by legal and political philosophers. John Rawls, for example, has given a relatively narrow and restrictive explanation of civil disobedience, defining it as: a public, conscientious, non-violent, and politically motivated breach of law that is undertaken with the aim of communicating issues with society with the goal of instigating a change in law or government policy.[4] In addition, Rawls suggests that what makes an act of civil disobedience be distinguished from "militant action" is that the civil disobedient expresses his willingness to accept the legal consequences of his violation of law.[5] Based on the willingness not to evade punishment, Rawls claims that civil disobedience may be justified within liberal democracies, whilst ordinary offences may not.

However, under Rawls's notion of civil disobedience, moral justification does not necessarily lead to legal justification. For Rawls, moral conviction is an imperative element of civil disobedience, and represents not only a moral consistency within the disobedient but also his perception of the society's higher interests; this element makes conscientious acts of disobedience selfless. By the same token, Rawls asserts publicity as another feature that demonstrates civil disobedience is never secretive, as it is crucial to engage in dialogue with both society and the authorities by committing the act publicly. A willingness to accept punishment is regarded by Rawls as a crucial feature of civil disobedience as it demonstrates the disobedient's fidelity to the law and the legal system. It is such "disobedience to law within fidelity to law"[6] that constitutes a logical connection between civil disobedience and punishment. Nevertheless, is this logical association a necessary one? Should a civil disobedient who deliberately breaks the law always be punished for the offence he commits? Or are there times when it would be appropriate for a civil disobedient to be exempted from the standard legal sanctions, due to the strong moral presumptions which make his or her disobedient action justifiable?

A further analysis of these questions would be beneficial for a deeper understanding of the role that punishment plays in response to civil disobedience. First, however, there are some theoretical considerations: determining how the law should respond to an act of civil disobedience needs to be distinguished from the conception of civil disobedience itself. (Dis)embedding punishment in the justifiable constitution of civil disobedience can help avoid the tendency to follow predetermined conclusions. Rawls's definition of civil disobedience accepts that the legal consequences of the violation are a necessary component of the very notion of disobedience. It is also an element that distinguishes civil disobedience from other types of protest. Nevertheless, it remains a question as to whether such willingness has constituted a moral obligation or commitment which can only be fully satisfied by

3 Ibid., p. 774.

4 John Rawls, *A Theory of Justice* (Oxford: Clarendon Press, 1973), 366–367.

5 Ibid.

6 Ibid., p. 366.

the disobedient's acceptance of punishment. In other words, should the acceptance of the legal consequences of an action be regarded as a moral duty by disobedients as a means of expressing fidelity to the law? Can disobedients seek to avoid punishment or find an alternative means of expressing fidelity to the legal system?

Analysing Rawls's argument further, it seems that acknowledgement of the legitimacy of the existing legal system distinguishes civil disobedience from other ordinary offences, and *by means of this*, it also places disobedients under an obligation to accept punishment for their actions. In other words, what constitutes disobedients' obligation to accept punishment is defended by reference to the political obligation of the citizen towards the state. However, this may not always be a valid defence. In some circumstances one can still make public statements by acknowledging the obligation to an existing legal system, yet refuse to accept punishment for conduct that breaches the law out of conscientiousness.[7] While the obligation to accept punishment may not necessarily be established based on such firm logical grounds, Sidney Hook has tried to establish such an obligation through an ethical stance. For Hook, since one of the purposes of civil disobedience is to accentuate fellow citizens' awareness of the issues involved and motivate them to undertake the necessary actions to address the problems, evasion of punishment would therefore seriously challenge the sincerity (and legitimacy) of the protesters' actions.[8]

Though Hook's assertions may sound convincing, it mistakenly commingles the conception of civil disobedience, which includes the moral weight of the notion that involves a conscientious and communicative breach of law, with a deliberative aim to contribute to a change in that law or policy. In other words, the acceptance of the punishment functions more like a tacitly strategic aim rather than a moral obligation that is inclusive to the notion of civil disobedience.[9] Refusing to accept punishment may weaken disobedients' moral weight, as it demonstrates an inconsistency in their heroic images of defiance. Such deficiencies would also lead to less effective communication between the demonstrators and their fellow citizens for whom they would like to mobilise.[10] That said, such ethical reasoning would still fail to lead to a *moral obligation* for demonstrators to accept punishment (merely) in order to consolidate moral height. The failures of establishing an obligation to accept punishment for civil disobedience on either ethical or logical grounds greatly challenge whether such moral obligations exist as regards accepting punishment. Conversely, it is worth noting that breaking such connections between civil disobedience and punishment does not necessarily lead to a conclusion that, for law enforcement agents, the moral obligation to punish civil disobedience is not justified.

Theories of punishment

Now we turn to a different aspect regarding the relationship between punishment and civil disobedience. The question asked here is no longer if there is any moral obligation for disobedients to accept punishment (as Rawls argues). Rather, it is to ask if punishment is

7 Nicholas Buttle, "Civil Disobedience and Punishment" (1985) 33(4) *Political Studies*, 649, 651.

8 Sidney Hook, "Social Protest and Civil Disobedience" in J. G. Murphy (ed.), *Civil Disobedience and Violence* (Belmont: Wadsworth Publishing, 1971), p. 59.

9 Buttle (n. 7 above), p. 652.

10 In reality, however, this argument has been frequently challenged in the courts. A recent example can be found at Taiwan's Sunflower Movement. See also Brian Christopher Jones and Yen-Tu Su, Chapter 1.

an appropriate response at all, or if it is morally right for civil disobedients to be punished.[11] To understand these questions better, we need to revisit theories of punishment. The first is the theory of deterrence, which can be identified as a consequentialist or utilitarian approach. When considering the nature and justification of punishment, for those who support this utilitarian view, such as Jeremy Bentham, it would take a forward-looking perspective to claim that punishment is justified on deterrence grounds, if its use prevents greater harms than would arise from not punishing.[12] Such theory is nevertheless criticized in that it justifies only a prudential reason, rather than offer a valid *moral ground*, for one to refrain from breaching the law. Besides, it is doubtful that the expectations for future deterrence will truly be effective. Yet if we take into account the moral commitment of civil disobedients, whose motivation for violating the law derives mainly from their conscientious decisions, it is highly doubtful they would be easily deterred merely based on the fear of punishment.[13] Additionally, the utilitarian grounds for punishment will only be established by demonstrating that such punishment is useful, as there would be beneficial consequences in punishing disobedients. Nevertheless, in terms of evaluating if some beneficial consequences exist, it remains arguable as to whether punishment would prevent greater harms than would the decision not to punish. This is especially true considering that such harms may be outweighed by beneficial consequences, such as the restraint on the abuse of the state power.

Another theory of punishment focuses on retribution. According to the retributive ground, those who engage in civil disobedience deserve to be punished as they have breached the law and are thus guilty of a legal offence. In essence, retribution is about proportionality, or balance, within the justice system. In Mabbott's famous defence of the retributive stance, he argues that it is irrelevant to consider if disobedience is morally justifiable or not, and as a result, civil disobedience needs to be treated in exactly the same way as we treat other types of unjustifiable disobedience as regards its breach of the law.[14] For Mabbott, a law enforcement agent has no right to exempt a disobedient from legal sanction if the latter has deliberately breached the law, even if that breach could be morally justified.

From Mabbott's perspective, what justifies punishment without discretion lies neither on utility grounds nor on treating punishment as a morally appropriate way of responding to the violation of the law.[15] Rather, he argues that such justification lies upon the promise that we have agreed to adopt a system of rules and are thus bound to stick to this system, as collectively society's interests are better served by the legal system than without it.[16] Under this rationale, a law enforcement agent has no power of discretion not to punish when it is faced with the scenario of civil disobedience, even if the conduct of the disobedients may be morally justified. By drawing an analogy to the execution of a contract, Mabbott asserts that law enforcement agents must administer the punishment prescribed by law just as persons are bound by the terms of the contract they agreed upon, and

11 Ibid.

12 Jeremy Bentham, *An Introduction to the Principles of Morals and Legislation*, J. H. Burns and H. L. A. Hart (eds) (Oxford: Oxford University Press, 1996 158.

13 Buttle (n. 7 above), p. 653.

14 J. D. Mabbott, "Punishment"(1939) 48 *Mind* 152, 160–161.

15 Daniel M Farrell, "Paying the Penalty: Justifiable Civil Disobedience and the Problem of Punishment" (1977) 6(2) *Philosophy and Public Affairs* 168.

16 Mabbott (n. 14 above), pp. 162–163.

therefore law enforcement agents have no freedom to look at facts and then to decide the cases based on standards of moral appropriateness.[17]

Nevertheless, many scholars have criticized Mabbott's simplistic justification of punishment. Daniel Farrell has argued that such justification ignores that discretion may have been specified and readily acknowledged within legal systems, so execution of such discretion is not necessarily exercised through the free will of the law enforcement agent; it is inclusive in the enforcement of the law.[18] The traditional *necessity* defence implies that within a legal system, it is acceptable for one to evaluate a situation and judge that he or she could not avoid serious harm or injury unless by disobeying a certain law. Thus if the harm sought to be avoided outweighs the evil sought to be prevented by the law, one can then defend unlawful action through the reason of forced choice. If such defence is successful, a person is unlikely to be considered culpable, as the legal breach has been justified.[19] Taking *moral necessity* as an example, one may choose to disobey certain laws (e.g. property laws) by breaking a water barrier and inundating a farm in order to save lives in an emergency situation. In this circumstance, the offensive conduct is morally obligatory, as by doing so it would lead to a lesser evil. Such necessity has been recognized as a valid defence in the legal system for this particular scenario.[20]

If we allowed civil disobedients to make a similar defence under necessity, such a defence may enable a legal right for them to be exculpated from punishment. But what constitutes this proposed defence? Could it be regarded as an extended application of the traditional necessity defence that already exists? In fact, the traditional necessity defence imposes rather narrow limits on the sorts of means, harms, and scenarios under which one's offensive conduct may be deemed to be necessary. The Model Penal Code in the American legal system, for instance, provides an illustration of certain cases under which the application of the traditional necessity defence would be regarded as appropriate.[21] Under these circumstances, unlawful conduct tends to be emergency measures to avoid imminent public or private injuries,[22] and according to ordinary standards of morality, the urgency of avoiding such injury outweighs the injuries sought to be prevented by the law.

Further argued by Farrell, the proposed defence applying to civil disobedience could be analogous to the traditional necessity defence. To make such a defence valid, Farrell suggests that the harm the disobedients seek to avoid shall not be limited to physical harm. Rather, it could be extended to the serious injustice that may include the violation of basic rights of citizens in a reasonably just society.[23] By the same token, for the requirement of urgency associated with the traditional defence, it shall also be attenuated to include an *urgent need* for preventing the operation of unjust laws.[24] In this sense, urgency is not necessarily restricted to an emergency situation in its spatial and temporal meaning, as prescribed by the traditional necessity defence. Rather, it may refer to a

17 Ibid., pp. 155–157.

18 Farrell (n. 15 above), p. 172.

19 Ibid.

20 Ibid.

21 American Model Penal Code, Section 3.02; those may include but are not limited to the following: e.g. to destroy a property in order to prevent the spread of a fire, or to pass a traffic light to pursue a suspected criminal.

22 It usually needs to be urgent and straightforward danger or physical harm; see American Model Penal Code, Section 35.05(2).

23 Farrell (n. 15 above), p. 175.

24 Ibid.

serious injustice – for example, the violation of principles and standards against which basic rights are defined in a just society. In Rawls's theory, when deciding what the conditions are for conduct to be regarded as morally justified in resorting to civil disobedience, he proposes that the disobedients must have exhausted ordinary modes of legal redress and have no prospects for improvement in this respect for the foreseeable future. Under this condition, the civil disobedients encounter no alternative situation, which is similar to the one associated with the traditional necessity defence in which disobedients have no choice but to disobey the law in order to avoid the greater harm prescribed by the law.

Although one may criticize this line of thinking, such an analogy has overly extended the sorts of cases to which the necessity defence can be adopted. In Farrell's view, the purpose of this analogy is to help illustrate the point of the proposed defence, not to use it as a way of arguing for its acceptance. Whether this proposed defence would be allowed to be used as a valid legal defence to exempt civil disobedients from punishment still depends on the evaluation of current judicial practices. Final judgement should be based on whether or not allowing such a defence, as opposed to completely excluding it from judges' discretion, would better serve the course of justice.

A right to civil disobedience

Apart from discussions on the proposed defence that focus mainly on the power of discretion as regards law enforcement agencies, there is another issue associated with civil disobedience justifications, though distinct from the defence, which is: whether engagement in civil disobedience is a right of conduct. If so, it provides an even more solid normative protection against state punishment. As Joseph Raz argues, rights of conduct protect a certain sphere of liberty from interferences by others.[25] Even though he suggests that people do not require a right to do what they think is the right thing, the legal philosopher imposes certain restrictions on applying this right of conduct account. In particular, the conduct needs to be in an illiberal regime in which those individuals whose rights are violated are entitled to exercise their moral right to political participation, which is not recognized in law.[26] By contrast, Raz claims that those living in liberal states lack grounds for civil disobedience to be regarded as a right of conduct, as one's political participation is already protected by law.[27] Contrary to Raz's argument, David Lefkowitz proposed another view on the right to public disobedience. For Lefkowitz, even in a liberal state where democratic discussions have been protected, voices from minority members within the system may not easily to be heard. In this sense, the right to political participation shall include the right to civil disobedience, even though that right needs to be suitably constrained as the best compromise between the existing voting system and the need to accommodate continued debate.[28] In Lefkowitz's view, treating public disobedience as a moral right of conduct allows citizens a means to contribute to other possible resolutions over collective decisions.

Even though Lefkowitz takes a different perspective from Raz regarding if a liberal state is a precondition for justifying the moral right to civil disobedience, they both share a

25 Joseph Raz, *The Authority of Law: Essays on Law and Morality* (Oxford: Clarendon Press, 1979 272.
26 Ibid., p. 272.
27 Ibid., p. 273.
28 David Lefkowitz, "On a Moral Right to Civil Disobedience" (2007) 117 *Ethics* 202.

common view that the right to public disobedience derives from rights to political participation. Given this reasoning, Lefkowitz maintains that this moral right gives citizens no claim against state punishment, as accepting penalisation allows disobedients to symbolically show that they are willing to act within the boundaries of political discourse.[29] An alternative response to Lefkowitz and Raz questions whether the right to civil disobedience could be grounded on something other than the right to political participation. Ronald Dworkin, for instance, argues that a person has a moral right to breach the law that does not need to be grounded on the right to political participation, but on the recognition that such a right is important to a person's dignity if the government violates his or her fundamental rights.[30] In his famous essay – *On Not Prosecuting Civil Disobedience* – Dworkin argues that a society would eventually suffer a loss if it chooses to punish a group that includes some of its "most thoughtful and loyal citizens".[31] Prosecuting and jailing such people would only solidify their alienation from society and would also alienate like-minded citizens who are deterred by such a threat.

For Dworkin, if a law is doubtful, one may properly follow his or her own judgement, even after a contrary institutional decision has been made by the highest competent court. By considering what society would lose or gain if people are able to be encouraged to pursue their own understanding of a doubtful law, Dworkin proposes his testing theories. In this scenario, whether and to what degree the principles of liberty, justice, or fairness would be offended by a particular solution remains to be discussed, and it is useful to experiment by testing societal responses.[32] The society would therefore lose the advantages from these tests, particularly if constitutional issues are involved, and if we only expect that citizens should act on the assumption that the law is not doubtful, even though they believe otherwise. By doing so, the law would eventually suffer and become less fair and just, and we would lose an important vehicle to examine the law based on moral grounds.

The pressure of dissent, according to Dworkin, allows an opportunity to reflect as to whether the law is in line with the fundamental principles guaranteed by the constitution. Following his argument, a person's social duty in the community should be his or her allegiance to the law, and not to any particular person's interpretation of what the law is, including the decisions made by courts. So long as the person proceeds on his own reasonable view of what the law requires, what the person does is within his social rights, as even the decisions made by courts may later be changed along with the development of the society. Even though Dworkin claims that the government has a special responsibility to try to soften disobedients' predicaments, at the same time, he also claims that such lenience does not necessarily follow that the government must grant them immunity, namely to restrain from adopting a rule to prosecute or convict those who breach the law out of conscience. In so doing, by Dworkin's reasoning, it would not only paralyse the government's ability when implementing rules, but more importantly, it would prevent the court from an opportunity to examine the law and act on the arguments generated from the dissent. Nevertheless, in some circumstances under which the practical reasons for

29 Ibid., p. 222.

30 Ronald Dworkin, "On Not Prosecuting Civil Disobedience" *The New York Review of Books* (6 June 1968), http://www.nybooks.com/articles/1968/06/06/on-not-prosecuting-civil-disobedience/.

31 Ibid.

32 Ibid.

prosecuting are relatively weak, Dworkin suggests that out of the responsibility of the government, the true path of fairness may lie in tolerance for particular cases.[33]

Here Dworkin draws a distinction between ordinary offences and breaking the law by those who act on their own dutiful judgment of a doubtful law, and claims that a path of fairness does not merely lie in the enforcement of the law according to the rules. Rather, by considering what the society would eventually lose or gain, a legal system should pursue its goals by inviting citizens to decide for themselves the strengths and weaknesses of their reasonable judgements and to act on these judgements, even though such an invitation is subject to a restriction that they may suffer if the courts think otherwise. Following this, the government ought to make room as much as possible for those who act on a reasonable judgement that the law is invalid, so long as it is consistent with other policies; and in Dworkin's view, it is the special responsibility of the government to do so. For instance, a prosecutor's decision on whether to prosecute is an exercise of balance in the prosecutor's evaluations. When considering if tolerance is justified, a prosecutor needs to calculate and balance leniency against the possible damage of the law, by taking into account not only what the harm could be and its extent, but also how law evaluates such harm. A situation where disobedients encouraged violence or trespassed on the rights of others would be a strong case for prosecution, although the balance of fairness and utility functions as a benchmark against which a law enforcement agent must decide whether to press charges.[34]

On the other hand, Dworkin further argues that when a consensus has not yet been reached regarding the validity of a law, it is acceptable for the state to delay any prosecution until the effect of that law or policy becomes clearer. In Dworkin's view, postponing adjudication is expected to create room for debate to be continued, until it is clear that the issues are ripe for adjudication and can be settled in an acceptable manner that would decrease further dissent. Choosing tolerance rather than prosecuting conscientious offenders creates an invitation where the society is willing to open a dialogue to reflect together on the scope of the moral issues and the strength of the invalidity involved in the law, which may not (for the time being) be settled well through adjudication. By the same token, a court can choose not to convict in some circumstances or exercise sentencing discretion to impose minimal or even suspended sentences to demonstrate its respect to different voices in a pluralist society, which in the long run may bring beneficial effects and consolidate the rule of law.

The Hong Kong Umbrella Movement

In June 2014 the PRC State Council in Beijing issued a White Paper outlining the main principles governing the political reform process and how the practice of the "One Country, Two Systems" policy applied in Hong Kong. In the White Paper, Beijing claims that it has "comprehensive jurisdiction"[35] over the territory of Hong Kong. It emphasizes

33 Ibid.

34 Ibid.

35 It claims that "The high degree of autonomy of the HKSAR is not full autonomy, nor a decentralized power." In Beijing's interpretation, it is the power to run local affairs as authorized by the central leadership. See "The Practice of the "One Country, Two Systems" Policy in the Hong Kong Special Administrative Region" (referred to as Beijing White Paper), published by the Information Office of the State Council on 10 June 2014, http://ssc.undp.org/content/dam/ssc/dgspaces/China/files/China%202nd%20White%20Paper%20on%20Foreign%20Aid%202014.pdf/.

Beijing's sovereign authority to interpret the Hong Kong Basic Law (hereinafter Basic Law), which is often deemed to be Hong Kong's mini-constitution, and lists "patriotism to the country" as a political requirement for Hong Kong's administrators that, according to the interpretation, applies not only to government officials and the Chief Executive but also to members of the Legislative Council and judges. About two months later in August 2014, the Standing Committee of the National People's Congress (NPC) released a decision on issues relating to the selection of the Chief Executive and the method for forming the Legislative Council in Hong Kong.[36] The decision imposes a vetting system for candidates presented to voters and sets up a 50% threshold nomination process by stipulating that candidates for the 2017 Chief Executive election must receive support from at least half of the members of the Nominating Committee. This was criticized as a breach of the universal suffrage agreed upon by Beijing according to Article 45 of the Basic Law.[37]

These two documents have raised public concerns over the infringement of Hong Kong's high degree of autonomy and the rule of law that have been enshrined by the 1984 Sino-British Joint Declaration and the Basic Law.[38] Before the release of the White Paper, heated debates took place throughout Hong Kong society about electoral reform and the method for selecting the Chief Executive. Pro-democracy campaigners emphasized that the promised universal suffrage should guarantee voters a genuine election. Currently, the Chief Executive of Hong Kong is selected by an Election Committee that is composed of 1,200 members – including individuals and special interest groups selected from the 28 functional constituencies, as prescribed in Annex I of the Basic Law.[39] Early on, a campaign called the Occupy Central for Love and Peace (hereinafter Occupy Central), which had been organized since March 2013, hoped that by means of a civil disobedience campaign, it would be possible to push Beijing to face the fact that there is a high demand for Hong Kong people to carry out a genuine election for their chief leader through a fair and impartial one-person-one-vote electoral system, as promised by Beijing in 2007.[40] Campaigners criticize that Beijing's political reform proposal is far from universal suffrage, considering it rules out civil nominations and only permits pre-approved candidates who are regarded as "patriotic" to run for the Chief Executive.

In September 2014, in order to demonstrate the discontent with the political reform proposal set by Beijing, two student organizations – the Hong Kong Federation of Students (HKFS, comprised of university students) and Scholarism (comprising secondary school students) – proposed a week-long class boycott. They asserted that the Hong Kong Government should renegotiate with Beijing and suggested a new framework proposal for political reform. The class boycott kicked off on 22 September 2014 with approximately 13,000 students participating in the Tamar Park sit-in, located in Admiralty, outside the Legislative Council complex. On the evening of 26 September,

36 "Full text: NPC Standing Committee decision on Hong Kong 2017 election" *South China Morning Post* (31 August 2014), at http://www.scmp.com/news/hong-kong/article/1582245/full-text-npc-standing-committee-decision-hong-kong-2017-election.

37 According to Article 45 of the Basic Law, the ultimate aim of the method for selecting the Chief Executive is "by universal suffrage upon nomination by a broadly representative nominating committee in accordance with democratic procedures".

38 Michael Davis, "The Basic Law, Universal Suffrage and the Rule of Law in Hong Kong" (2015) 38 *Hastings International and Comparative Law Review* 275.

39 Hong Kong Basic Law, Annex I (Rev. 2010); see also Albert Chen, Chapter 6.

40 Albert Chen, Chapter 6.

toward the end of the class boycott, secondary students (and many citizens) started to join the campaign, and student leaders initiated an action to reclaim Civic Square, which was surrounded by fences to prevent assemblies from being held in front of government headquarters. That was followed by clashes when a large number of police were sent to intercept protesters and used pepper spray and batons to disperse crowds without giving proper warning. On 28 September, the Occupy Central organizers declared the official launch of their campaign, which was initially planned to begin on the PRC's National Day of 1 October. Soon after, hundreds of thousands of people flocked to Admiralty to demonstrate their support of the movement. Multiple violent clashes took place when police adopted heavy-handed responses to clear ground and expel crowds with tear gas and other forceful measures. To block the tear gas thrown by police, protesters used open umbrellas as shields, which is how the "Umbrella Movement" received its name. That evening sparked a 79-day occupation movement that spread throughout multiple areas within Hong Kong.

On 20 October 2014, the High Court of Hong Kong granted injunctions to two transport groups (a taxi drivers' association and a minibus operators' group) against Mong Kok protesters, and to the owner of a commercial building (Goldon Investment, Ltd) next to the government headquarters in Admiralty, requesting that protesters leave the occupied sites.[41] According to these three injunctions, the plaintiffs were entitled to seek arrest warrants and request bailiffs to enforce them if the occupiers failed to comply with the court order. The Federation of Students released a statement showing respect for the court's decision, although it ultimately decided not to retreat from Mong Kok, but rather to shoulder any legal liabilities until significant debates with the government took place.[42] It also asked occupiers to decide for themselves if they would be willing to stay at the sit-ins after carefully considering the possible legal consequences (i.e. contempt of court), which might lead to custodial sentences.

On 10 November 2014, the Court of First Instance renewed an injunction[43] to clear the movement's Mong Kok site, and around the same time the police were authorized to assist the bailiffs for carrying out the injunction after receiving detailed court instructions.[44] However, the validity of the injunction was challenged by some legal scholars.[45] The concerns raised involved the appropriateness of invoking a civil court process for a public order issue, in addition to why the Hong Kong Government (the Department of Justice, thereafter, DOJ) did not take over the injunction applied from the transport associations, which are private rather than public entities, given the widespread nature of such

41 "Protesters defiant after High Court orders them to leave Mong Kok and Admiralty sites" *South China Morning Post* (20 October 2014), at http://www.scmp.com/news/hong-kong/article/1620708/hong-kongs-high-court-orders-occupy-protesters-mong-kok-leave.

42 Ibid.

43 CHIU LUEN PUBLIC LIGHT BUS CO LTD v. PERSONS UNLAWFULLY OCCUPYING OR REMAINING ON THE PUBLIC HIGHWAY NAMELY, THE WESTBOUND CARRIAGEWAY OF ARGYLE STREET BETWEEN THE JUNCTION OF TUNG CHOI STREET AND PORTLAND STREET AND/OR OTHER PERSONS HINDERING OR PREVENTING THE PASSING OR REPASSING OF ARGYLE STREET AND OTHERS [2014] HKCFI 2021; [2014] 6 HKC 298; HCA 2086/2014 (10 November 2014), http://www.hklii.hk/cgi-bin/sinodisp/eng/hk/cases/hkcfi/2014/2021.html.

44 Larry Ong, "Hong Kong's Top Legal Minds Challenge Court Injunctions against Occupy Movement" *Epoch Times* (17 November 2014).

45 For example, Johannes Chan, former Dean of the Faculty of Law, the University of Hong Kong, and Mr Justice Henry Litton, non-permanent judge of the Court of Final Appeal, both raised concerns about the injunctions.

injunctions and the finances required to pay the personnel, i.e. around 7,000 police officers, for its implementation.[46] In addition, public lawyers challenged the legal capacity of the injunctions which were originally granted by the High Court on 20 October 2014 on an *ex parte* basis, which in the common law is justified only in urgent cases, as the party affected was not present in court to defend their actions.[47] They claimed that the nature of the urgency was not justified, considering the occupation had already lasted for quite a while but no injunctions had been applied earlier. In terms of the effectiveness of the order, since the injunctions did not specify the ways for the plaintiffs to clear the site, how they would be executed in reality (e.g. following the ordinary process to first identifying individual protesters and then applying in court for the warrant before making arrests) also elevated further concerns.[48]

In March 2016, according to information released by the Security Bureau at the Legislative Council, during the 79 days of occupation, 955 persons were arrested by the police for various alleged offences, followed by another 48 persons arrested after the end of the occupation.[49] Among them, 182 persons had gone through the judicial process, including 74 persons who were convicted and 42 who were bound over for trial upon conclusion of court proceedings. As a result, the statistics offered from the Secretary for Security demonstrated that up to 31 January 2016, a total of 116 persons bore legal consequences related to their participation in the Occupy Movement.[50] The charges by which occupants were convicted included but were not limited to the following: unlawful assembly, assaulting police officer, possession of offensive weapon, common assault, indecent assault, criminal intimidation, theft, and possession of dangerous drugs.[51]

The statistics illustrate that about one-fifth of those who were arrested related to the Occupy Movement have so far been prosecuted. This raises the suspicion that such prosecutions may contain political symbolism, as some cases have taken an unusually long time for the Department of Justice to make prosecutorial decisions. That has led many to assert that the prosecutions function as a warning, aimed at deterring like-minded protesters; further, protesters should be aware that they can be arrested even a long time after the incident took place. According to the DOJ, however, the reason for such prosecutorial delays was due to the time required to collect evidence related to the alleged crimes. One example of such prosecutorial delay was demonstrated by the charges against student leaders of the Occupy Movement, which were announced in the end of August 2015, roughly about 11 months after the incident.[52] Joshua Wong, the 18-year-old student leader of Scholarism, was charged with unlawful assembly and inciting others to take part in an unlawful assembly for his activities in Civic Square, and the charges could

46 Ong (n. 44 above).

47 Ibid.

48 *South China Morning Post*, (n. 41 above).

49 Legislative Council HKSAR Press Release (2 March 2016), at http://www.info.gov.hk/gia/general/201603/02/P201603020641.htm.

50 Ibid.

51 Ibid.

52 Tony Cheung, "Trio of Occupy Central student leaders charged over protest that sparked 79-day movement" *South China Morning Post* (28 August 2015), http://www.scmp.com/news/hong-kong/law-crime/article/1852958/trio-occupy-central-student-leaders-arrive-hong-kong-police.

result in a sentence of up to five years.[53] According to Wong's lawyer, Michael Vidler, the prosecution comes nearly a year after the incident and is an abuse of due process because it was purposefully delayed.[54]

At issue here is what considerations and approaches the DOJ ought to adopt in reacting to the potential legal consequences derived from the Occupy Movement. According to the Basic Law, the role of the DOJ should be independent; its control of criminal prosecution needs to be operated in a way that is "free from any interference".[55] In addition, it has been argued that although there is prosecutorial discretion to decide whether or not to impose charges on public order cases, an appropriate prosecutorial response in accordance with the law is essential for consolidating the people's confidence towards the rule of law and the whole legal system.[56] To decide when to proceed and continue with a prosecution, the so-called two-component test has been established. Based on the Prosecution Code, a set of guidelines was released by the DOJ in September 2013. The decision to prosecute requires the satisfaction of the following two components: (1) the admissible evidence needs to be legally sufficient to justify instituting proceedings, i.e. likely to prove the offence, and (2) the general public interest must require that the prosecution be conducted.[57] The Code provides a non-exhaustive list with regard to the assessment of the public interest. Several considerations are listed for prosecutors to take into account. For example, the nature, circumstances, and seriousness of the offence, any deterrent effect of a prosecution, and the availability of alternatives to prosecution, such as a caution, warning, or other acceptable form of diversion.[58]

Before the Occupy Movement, taking an approach of restraint and diversion with the public order cases was not uncommon within the DOJ.[59] An important rationale behind this prosecutorial restraint is to find a graceful balance between the need of maintaining public order and the recognition of the exercise of the fundamental right to freedom of speech and assembly. In an assessment of what the best judicial response to civil disobedience could be, especially to those who held strong moral convictions and joined sit-ins in a non-violent manner, it has been recognized that the use of criminal sanctions may be fruitless and not necessarily in accordance with public interest.[60] As civil disobedients' action is motivated by promoting what they perceive as a public good to improve the society as a whole, the possible diversion adopted by the DOJ may also include community service as a way to reconcile the conflict brought to the community by the disobedients' choice of action.

53 Before this, Wong had also faced charges stemming from a protest in June 2014 that preceded the Occupy Movement for burning a white paper (Tony Cheung and Joyce Ng, "Student activist Joshua Wong faces charges over Hong Kong 'white paper' protest last year" *South China Morning Post* (6 July 2015), http://www.scmp.com/news/hong-kong/politics/article/1833331/student-activist-joshua-wong-faces-charges-over-hong-kong.

54 Wen Yuqing, "Young Leader of Hong Kong's Occupy Central Movement Hits Back After Arrest and Charges" *Radio Free Asia* (2 September 2015).

55 Article 63, Basic Law.

56 Simon Young, "Prosecution Response to Occupy Central" *HKU Legal Scholarship Blog* (11 November 2014), http://researchblog.law.hku.hk/2014/11/prosecution-response-to-occupy-central.html.

57 [5.3] of the Prosecution Code.

58 [5.9] of the Prosecution Code.

59 Young (n. 56 above).

60 Ibid.

The role of the court and the image of the rule of law

By scrutinizing the reasons provided by the three injunctions issued by the High Court of Hong Kong, it is possible to see that the image of the rule of law and its interaction with civil disobedience has been widely accentuated by Hong Kong's judiciary. In considering whether the injunctions should be continued, and by asking for directions to facilitate their enforcement, the Hong Kong court re-emphasized its position as an independent institution and claimed that its decisions would be made only by strictly applying the law, without considering any other political views behind the Occupy Movement.[61] In long and detailed reasoning, especially regarding the controversial issues surrounding whether a private individual may bring an action in public nuisance, the court looked into instances where an interlocutory injunction was granted, and went through a comprehensive factual assessment of the degree and extent of the damage or loss claimed to be suffered by the plaintiff.[62]

In addition, the court justified its overall evaluation by citing the matters that need to be taken into account in deciding whether an injunction shall be continually granted:

> Will the law best be served by preventive action? Will the grant of an injunction exacerbate the situation? Is the injunction likely to be effective or may it be futile? Will it be better to make it clear that the law will be enforced by prosecution and to appeal to the law-abiding instinct, negotiations, and moderate leadership, rather than provoke people along the road to martyrdom?[63]

Through recognizing that the injunction was unavoidably entangled with a decision of policy, which is open to conflicting considerations, sticking with the notion of the rule of law had become the court's persistent standpoint and also the way it chose to communicate with the wider Hong Kong society. In further explaining its order to effect an arrest in civil claims, the court demonstrated that its perception of the rule of law was something not to be negotiated:

> Under the rule of law, even if the defendants are of the view that a court order (including an ex parte order) is wrongly granted, instead of simply disobeying it, they should first comply with it but seek to challenge and argue against that order in court under due process and in accordance with the law.[64]

61 CHIU LUEN PUBLIC LIGHT BUS CO LTD v. PERSONS UNLAWFULLY OCCUPYING OR REMAINING ON THE PUBLIC HIGHWAY NAMELY, THE WESTBOUND CARRIAGEWAY OF ARGYLE STREET BETWEEN THE JUNCTION OF TUNG CHOI STREET AND PORTLAND STREET AND/OR OTHER PERSONS HINDERING OR PREVENTING THE PASSING OR REPASSING OF ARGYLE STREET AND OTHERS [2014] HKCFI 2021; [2014] 6 HKC 298; HCA 2086/2014 (issued on 10 November 2014); p. 6. See also Fu Hualing, Chapter 8.

62 In its reasoning, the court looked into whether the legal principles supporting the grant of an interim injunction were well established. Though recognizing that it is generally the authority of the Secretary of Justice (SJ) to bring a claim in public nuisance, the court made a further evaluation that the private individual – the transport groups – had indeed suffered a "particular, direct and substantial" injury beyond the rest of the public at large and therefore was eligible to bring a private claim.

63 Ibid., p. 15.

64 Ibid., p. 31.

It further cited Lord Hoffmann's words in *Department of Transport v. Lush*: "the law cannot allow obedience of its orders to be a matter of individual choice even on grounds of conscience".[65] Under this view, the rule of law cannot operate in a way that allows people's discretion for its compliance even if that disobedience is outside the grounds of conscience, such as with civil disobedience. According to the Hong Kong court, one's intentionally disobeying the law puts the rule of law under challenge, even if the disobedients would later be willing to accept the consequences of their deliberative action of breaking the law.[66] This narrow interpretation of the rule of law, from the court's perspective, is built upon the independence of the judiciary and the respect for the authority of the court, both of which contribute to the core foundation that has led to Hong Kong being "a civilized and orderly society".[67]

In the view of the High Court, civil disobedience was not deemed to be a legal method of action for those seeking to change law or policy. Rather, the court pinpointed its disagreement from the open suggestion that there is no challenge to the rule of law from disobedience of civil court orders, though such a challenge might put rule of law under threat.[68] Viewing its own function as a guardian of the rule of law, the court used injunctions as its primary method of communicating to the Hong Kong society, by claiming that it has the responsibility to protect the rule of law in order to provide "for the best interest[s] and benefit of the general public".[69] In addition, in order to make it clear to the occupiers that the civil orders should be obeyed, the court included a police authorization direction that provides the police the power to arrest and remove those who took part in the Occupy Movement sit-ins.[70]

Rhetoric emphasizing the safeguarding of the rule of law is easy to find throughout the court's rulings. In their view, those who engage in civil disobedience should follow the injunction, otherwise they deserve to be punished given that they have breached the law. This position echoes Mabbott's defence of the retributive stance in punishment theory, by treating civil disobedience akin to other types of unjustifiable disobedience. Thus any moral justification for civil disobedience had been excluded from the court's overall considerations in the injunctions, and neither had the weighting of harms and beneficial consequences, such as the promotion of democracy, been seriously taken into account in the court's reasoning. This attitude demonstrates the Hong Kong court's unrelenting mentality to civil disobedience, the latter of which is expected to function as a dialogue with the authority in order to create possible room for negotiation outside the existing legal order.

65 Ibid.

66 Ibid. The related adjudication wording is quoted as follows:

> "It is therefore wrong for any suggestions that the rule of law is not undermined or under challenged if people can freely or intentionally disobey the law first and then accept the consequences of breaking the law. The rule of law cannot realistically and effectively operate in a civilized and orderly society on this basis."

67 Ibid.

68 Ibid.

69 Ibid., p. 32.

70 Ibid., p. 33 ("Any police officer be authorized to arrest and remove any person who the police officer reasonably believes or suspects to be obstructing or interfering any bailiff in carrying out his or her duties in enforcing the terms of the injunction order herein, provided that the person to be arrested has been informed of the gist of the terms of this court order and that his action is likely to constitute a breach of the order and obstruction of the administration of justice, and that he may be arrested if he does not desist.")

Following the same reasoning, Hong Kong law enforcement agents have no discretion to decide cases based on standards of moral appropriateness. Rather, they must administer the arrests and punishments prescribed by law. On 21 July 2016, the Eastern court of Hong Kong convicted three student leaders of the Occupy Movement, including Scholarism leader Joshua Wong.[71] They were found guilty of unlawful assembly for illegally crashing into Civic Square at Tamar in September 2014. The three were released on bail, but sentencing was expected to be adjourned in mid-August. According to the court's ruling, the actions of the three "lead others to reasonably fear that such assembly might either damage the peace in society or that their behaviour could incite others to damage social peace".[72] Though the student leaders expressed their respect for the rule of law, they also demonstrated their disagreement of the verdict by claiming that freedom of assembly is a basic human right. For that reason, they did not support the requirement for advanced police approval, as such a requirement puts undue limits on the freedom of assembly in Hong Kong. According to one student leader, the verdict demonstrates that the courts were being used to deal with political issues that have not yet reached a consensus among the society itself.[73]

In March 2016 the High Court of Hong Kong released an adjudication supporting an appeal by the DOJ, which argued that the original sentence of 150 hours of community service to the protesters of the Occupy Movement was not heavy enough.[74] The four defendants, who smashed a door at the Hong Kong Legislative Council, were charged with the offences of both criminal damage and taking part in unlawful assembly. Three of them were later given jail time and released on bail, and the fourth defendant was placed on Community Service Order (CSO) in view of his age (aged 19).[75] The Principal Magistrate referred to *Secretary for Justice v. Cheung Chun Chin and Others* [2002] 2HKLRD 233, and claimed that for the offence of riot, "the court must pay regard to the level of violence used, the scale of the riot or affray, and the number of people engaged in execution".[76] As a result, the court argued that severe sentences "were needed to provide an adequate element of deterrence as well as a penalty which properly reflected the gravity of such offences".[77]

The court further justified its reasoning by arguing that it needs to send a clear message to the public: "while one has the constitutional right of freedom of expression and freedom to take part in an assembly, one must respect the law and order and cannot behave in such a destructive way, causing damage to properties".[78] It further claims that the defendants' actions were certainly "riotous" in nature, considering the violence used, the number of persons involved, and the intimidating nature and duration of the assembly. Further an immediate custodial sentence, to be used as a deterrence, needs to be imposed even for

71 "Joshua Wong found guilty of unlawful assembly in Hong Kong" *BBC News* (21 July 2016), http://www.bbc.com/news/world-asia-china-36852731.

72 Ibid.

73 Hudson Lockett and Gloria Cheung, "Hong Kong Court Convicts 3 Occupy Central Student Activists" *Financial Times* (21 July 2016), https://www.ft.com/content/7738f002-4f1c-11e6-8172-e39ecd3b86fc.

74 HCMA579/2015 HKSAR v. TAI CHI SHING AND OTHERS.

75 Ibid.

76 Ibid., p. 5.

77 Ibid.

78 Ibid., p. 10.

first-time offenders, as the court "will not condone such irresponsible and unlawful behaviour".[79]

The Hong Kong court's repeated requests to maintain law and order has constituted the core principle of the judiciary's response to the Occupy Movement in Hong Kong. The image of the rule of law was constructed by Hong Kong courts as complying with existing legal order and the well-functioning of Hong Kong society. The role of the courts in the Occupy Movement demonstrates a restrained attitude to civil disobedience that draws a clear-cut boundary between freedom and order, but refuses to further touch upon democratic values and the legitimacy of the current rules which underlie the composition of the existing legal order. Considering Daniel Farrell's defence under necessity in punishment theory, the extent to which civil disobedients could make an analogous defence in the Occupy Movement would ultimately depend on the courts' willingness and acceptance of the requirement of *urgency*, and whether the interpretation of this notion could accurately respond to the civil disobedients' claim for the prevention of unjust laws in Hong Kong.

In this sense, the notion of urgency, as discussed earlier in this chapter, may also be extended to confront a serious injustice, which includes but is not limited to the violation of principles against which fundamental rights are defined in a just society. The Hong Kong courts' response to the Occupy Movement excludes the possibility of the judiciary to further examine three independent but interrelated Hong Kong valuest – he rule of law, liberty, and democracy. On the other hand, justifications for civil disobedience often rely on its counter-nature to the tyranny of the majority. As Thoreau argued, individuals need to rely on their own conscience in order to act justly, as a minority cannot always confront the majority by voting when considering the use of political process in legal change. In Hong Kong, the context of civil disobedience is ironically contradictory, as the voices of the majority have been excluded from the voting system based on the territory's existing election rules. Under this circumstance, the legitimacy of the rules deserves stricter scrutiny as their very production is in essence counter-majoritarian.

Following the same logic, under the political restrictions as regards democratic voting in Hong Kong, one could further argue that civil disobedience can be deemed to be a moral right of conduct. The current political reality of Hong Kong echoes what Raz sets for the argument of a right to civil disobedience, by recognizing a moral right to political participation, which is nevertheless not recognized by law.[80] Raz's work points to a right to civil disobedience in Hong Kong, which should be included into a broader right of political participation. However, this does not mean that such a moral right is without any limitations. As Lefkowitz argues, treating civil disobedience as a moral right allows a means for citizens to contribute to other possible resolutions over collective decisions. The right to civil disobedience also needs to be constrained as a suitable compromise between the existing voting system and the need to accommodate continued debates throughout Hong Kong society.

What the courts would need to further consider, perhaps, is how to prevent a punishment from bringing an inevitable loss to the entire society, by solidifying the alienation of protesters and like-minded citizens who may be deterred by such a threat. Additionally, the courts could also take the initiative to continue such an important dialogue with the society, by allowing citizens to test the degree to which the principles of justice and liberty would

79 Ibid.
80 Raz (n. 25 above), p. 272.

be offended by engaging in civil disobedience. In so doing, the courts would not only lead to a more fair and just mind-set as regards adjudication, but also to a much more open and tolerant society.

Conclusion

The true meaning of adjudication, as noted above, lies in helping alleviate tensions in the society and also decreasing further dissent. Choosing tolerance rather than punishment as a response to civil disobedience creates an invitation by law enforcement agents to open a dialogue with the society, especially when a consensus has not yet been reached regarding the legitimacy of a particular law or policy, or in reaction to significant events. Under these circumstances, the delay of punishment until the effect of the law or policy becomes clearer creates room for debate to be continued.

The Hong Kong courts' injunctions and adjudications related to the Occupy Movement were mainly based on the restrictive notion of the rule of law, which focuses only on the rationale of law and order. These judicial responses have sent a strong message to Hong Kong society that, from the viewpoint of the court, the values inherent in the rule of law are not open for negotiation. However, given that civil disobedients are less likely to be deterred by punishment – given their strong motivations – the restrictive attitude of the court to withdraw itself from democratic debate may not be beneficial for the operation of rule of law in Hong Kong in the long run.

9 Dancing with the dragon

Closer economic integration with China and deteriorating democracy and rule of law in Taiwan and Hong Kong?

Chien-Huei Wu[*]

Introduction

The emergence of the Sunflower Movement and Umbrella Movement in Taiwan and Hong Kong in March and September 2014, respectively, reflect a resentment of the people in Taiwan and Hong Kong against closer economic integration with China, and their worries about deteriorating rule of law and democracy arising from a process of economic integration.

The Sunflower Movement was an immediate response to the questionable process for approving the Cross-Strait Trade in Services Agreement (Services Trade Agreement) between Taiwan and China, a follow-up agreement under the auspices of the Economic Cooperation Framework Agreement (ECFA).[1] Yet, weak legislative oversight and rubber-stamp approval of the Services Trade Agreement was not just a one-off, but rather conventional practice in dealing with negotiations over the agreements concluded between Taiwan and China, thus seriously undermining Taiwan's young democracy. Similarly, the Umbrella Movement is reflective of the anger of the Hong Kong people in their desperate pursuit of universal suffrage for the election of the Chief Executive, the prospects of which were dampened by the White Paper on the Practice of the "One Country, Two Systems" policy in the Hong Kong Special Administrative Region (HKSAR), issued by the State Council in June 2014.[2]

The deterioration of rule of law in Taiwan and Hong Kong is omnipresent and can be evidenced in a wide range of elements. In Taiwan, press freedom,[3] due process of law in

* Associate Research Professor, Institute of European and American Studies, Academia Sinica, Taipei, Taiwan. PhD in Laws, European University Institute, Florence, Italy. Email: wch@sinica.edu.tw. An earlier draft was presented in the Sunflower Discussion forum held in Institutum Iurisprudentiae, Academia Sinica, 15–16 December, and subsequently published in *Hong Kong Law Journal*. The author wishes to express his gratitude to the constructive comments of participants, in particular the organiser Brian Christopher Jones and his discussant Tun Jen Cheng, as well as Jimmy Chia Shin Hsu and Wen Tsong Chiou. The author also wishes to express his gratitude to Kuei Hong Lin and Chen Chi Su for their helpful research assistance.

1 The legal text of ECFA is available at http://www.ecfa.org.tw/EcfaAttachment/ECFADoc/ECFA.pdf.

2 The full text is available at http://news.xinhuanet.com/english/china/2014-06/10/c_133396891.htm.

3 In 2008, the *China Times* Group in Taiwan was purchased by Want Want Holdings, a food-manufacturing giant in Asia with extensive business interests in China, making Want Want Holdings a key player in Taiwan's mass media. Subsequently, the emerging potential for China to interfere in Taiwan's mass media gave rise to the anti-media monopoly movement. In 2009, Want Want Holdings proposed purchasing Next TV, *Next Magazine*, and *Apple Daily*, thus worsening the fears that Taiwan's mass media would be dominated by a single enterprise.

criminal proceedings[4] and excessive police violence are most critical.[5] As regards Hong Kong, the erosion of the rule of law is even more comprehensive, extending from judicial independence[6] to freedom of speech[7] and freedom of thought and conscience.[8]

In view of these developments, this chapter aims to provide an empirical analysis as to whether economic integration impedes the democratisation processes of Taiwan and Hong Kong and whether closer economic integration with China endangers rule of law in the latter entities. Given that rule of law and democracy are distinct but nonetheless interrelated concepts, this chapter, with a view to covering some core elements of these two concepts, chooses to use the World Bank Good Governance Indicators (the Good Governance Indicators) as a parameter to analyse the impact of Taiwan's and Hong Kong's economic integration with China. Also with a view to supplement the Good Governance Indicators, a neoliberal-oriented concept based on expert perception, this chapter also includes press freedom, a central element for democracy, by Freedom House and Reporters without Borders in order to reflect "public perception". The hope is that an empirical analysis of the impact of closer economic integration with China upon the performance of Taiwan and Hong Kong in the Good Governance Indicators and press freedom will shed some light on the "China Factor" debates.[9]

This chapter is organised as follows. First it discusses the complex relationship between trade, economic integration, democracy, and the rule of law, with a view to identifying "learning effects" and "undermining effects" in trading activities. It then presents various mechanisms through which China may exert its influence into Taiwan and Hong Kong. Next it describes the research design of this study: hypothesis, independent variables, dependent variables, and analytical tools. Finally, it presents the research results, and then discusses the chapter's results and conclusions.

4 For example, a controversial case relates to the execution of three Taiwanese charged with murder in China who fled to Taiwan. The men were sentenced to death based on the testimony of witnesses interrogated in China and evidence collected in China, and the case raises questions regarding due process protections guaranteed by Taiwanese criminal procedures and whether these might be undermined by the Cross-Strait Judicial Assistance and Joint Crime-Fighting Agreement signed between Taiwan and China.

5 Closer economic ties between Taiwan and China have also resulted in frequent visits to Taiwan by Chinese officials. During these visits, opposition parties and civil groups have staged demonstrations and protests, arguing that Taiwan is at risk of becoming overly dependent on China. In response, Taiwan's police have frequently exercised disproportionate violence, thereby posing a significant threat to the rule of law in Taiwan.

6 The independence of the judiciary in Hong Kong is meant to be protected by Hong Kong Basic Law (HKBL), Hong Kong's mini constitution. However, such assurances have not been as powerful as expected. Most importantly, the finality of the decisions of the Court of Final Appeal is subject to the challenges of the National People's Congress Standing Committee (NPCSC) through interpretations of the HKBL. Continuous reinterpretations of the HKBL by the NPCSC have not only substantially altered the constitutional framework set forth in the HKBL and eroded Hong Kong's autonomy, but have also had a chilling effect on the judiciary in Hong Kong, and especially with regard to human rights cases.

7 For example, in 1999, the Court of Final Appeal ruled that freedom of expression does not protect individuals from criminal punishment for desecrations of the national or regional flag. *HKSAR v. Ng Kung Siu* (FACC 4/1999), judgment dated 15 December 1999.

8 In 2012, the Bureau of Education in Hong Kong planned to add moral and national education to the curriculum in primary and secondary schools with particular emphasis on the Chinese identity of Hong Kong people.

9 Wu Jie-Min, "China Factors and Taiwan's Democracy [Zhongguo Yinsu yu Taiwan Minzhu]" (2009) 11 *Thoughts* [Sixiang] 141 (in traditional Chinese).

Trade, economic integration, democracy, and rule of law: Learning effects and undermining effects

Literature on the relationship between trade openness, economic integration, economic growth, the rule of law, and democracy abounds but diverges greatly. A couple of the main strands of such works relate to economic liberalisation and the rule of law or democratisation and how economic liberalisation impacts domestic rule of law and democracy.[10] In this vein, Alvarez, Buera, and Lucas find that economic integration can favour cultural transmission and intellectual exchanges through which countries can learn from their partners.[11] Building on this finding, Magistretti and Tabellini further elaborate on the themes of cultural exchange and the transmission of ideas, finding that less-developed countries would emulate democratic partners with better rule of law and thereby gradually democratise and improve their own rule of law. Further, they find stronger learning effects among similar countries.[12]

The second strand of academic work on economic integration and democracy relates to European integration, focusing on how such integration transforms new member states, neighbouring countries, or partner countries into democratic states. This work asks the same questions as this piece, but in a different (i.e. reverse) manner: whether economic integration will contribute to democratisation and rule of law in those relevant economies. Nonetheless, it is acknowledged that there is a significant difference between European integration and economic integration between Taiwan, China, and Hong Kong. In broad strokes, European integration is driven by a number of major European democratic countries and has established the "Copenhagen criteria" for new member states, one of which is a requirement that the state be democratic.[13] In the context of economic integration between Taiwan, China, and Hong Kong, China is far more powerful than the other two entities and is in no way democratic.[14] Thus, great care should be taken in transferring the

10 Remonda Bensabat Kleinberg and Janine A. Clark (eds), *Economic Liberalization, Democratization and Civil Society in the Developing World* (London: Palgrave Macmillan, 2000); Stephan Haggard and Steven Benjamin Webb (eds), *Voting for Reform: Democracy, Political Liberalization, and Economic Adjustment* (Oxford: World Bank/Oxford University Press, 1994); *cf.* Adrian Leftwicha, "Governance, Democracy and Development in the Third World" (1993) 14(3) *Third World Quarterly* 605; Thomas G. Weiss, "Governance, Good Governance and Global Governance: Conceptual and Actual Challenges" (2000) 21(5) *Third World Quarterly* 795.

11 Fernando E. Alvarez, Francisco J. Buera, and Lucas, Jr., Robert E., "Idea Flows, Economic Growth and Trade" (2013) NBER Working Paper Series No 19667, http://www.nber.org/papers/w19667.

12 Giacomo Magistretti and Marco Tabellini, "Economic Integration and Democracy: An Empirical Investigation" http://economics.mit.edu/files/11196, pp. 2–3.

13 To join the EU, a new member state must meet three criteria: politically, the new member state must be equipped with stable institutions guaranteeing democracy, rule of law and protection of human rights; economically, there must be a well-functioning market economy, which is able to compete with the EU market; finally, the new member state has to accept all the EU *acquis*. These criteria were set out for in the 1993 Copenhagen European Council and thus referred to as the "Copenhagen criteria".

14 An alternative question may be asked: whether China trade with Taiwan, a democratic country with better rule of law, will contribute to the democratisation and rule of law in China. This issue has been frequently raised in the debates relating to whether and how Taiwan can serve as a model for the greater China area. See, e.g. Taiwan, China, and Hong Kong Bruce J. Dickson, "China's Democratization and the Taiwan Experience" (1998) 38(4) *Asian Survey* 349. Nonetheless, this chapter focuses on the impact of closer economic integration between China, Taiwan, and Hong Kong upon the rule of law and press freedom of the latter entities and chooses not to investigate the potential impact upon China.

European experience to the context of economic integration between Taiwan, China, and Hong Kong.

Third, the dominant development discourse maintains that economic liberalisation will lead to the rule of law and democratisation, which is reinforced by good governance disciplines prescribed by the Washington institutions.[15] This development discourse has attracted numerous critiques,[16] not least because the discourse to date has failed to answer whether closer economic integration with an undemocratic country that lacks the rule of law will threaten domestic democracy and the rule of law in the democratic country. Besides, in a globalised economy, the danger of a "race to the bottom" in environmental and labour standards has been well documented and heatedly debated.[17] However, the threat of a "race to the bottom" in terms of the rule of law and domestic democratic governance remains unexplored.

This chapter aims to explore whether learning effects may turn out to be the undermining effects, namely, whether trading with an undemocratic country that only possesses a rudimentary rule of law structure such as China would undermine a country's political development. I also attempt to investigate possible mechanisms by which these undermining effects might be channelled into Taiwan and Hong Kong. Below, I will identify those different mechanisms, which may or may not be shared by both Taiwan and Hong Kong. After that, I will use existing datasets to test whether Taiwan's and Hong Kong's democracy and rule of law are actually undermined through these mechanisms.

Various mechanisms for China to transmit the undermining effects to Taiwan and Hong Kong

Institutional legal framework

During economic integration processes, the most important channels through which China may exert influence upon Taiwan and Hong Kong are the legal frameworks laid down by ECFA and the Closer Economic Partnership Arrangement (CEPA),[18] its subsequent agreements, and their implementation and supervision cooperation councils/committees. On the one hand, ECFA and CEPA are the most powerful instruments fostering economic integration between Taiwan, China, and Hong Kong. On the other hand, the regular negotiation mechanisms in Taiwan, China, and Hong Kong – especially the "two associations mechanism" established by the Straits Exchange Foundation (the SEF) and the

15 John Williamson, "What Should the World Bank Think about the Washington Consensus?" (2000) 15(2) *World Bank Research Observer* 251; Charles Gore, "The Rise and Fall of the Washington Consensus as a Paradigm for Developing Countries" (2000) 28(5) *World Development* 789.

16 See, e.g. Narcís Serra and Joseph E Stiglitz (eds), *The Washington Consensus Reconsidered: Towards a New Global Governance* (Oxford: Oxford University Press, 2008).

17 See, e.g. Ernst Ulrich Petersmann, "Time for United Nations 'Global Compact' for Integrating Human Rights into the Law of Worldwide Organizations: Lessons from European Integration" (2002) 13 *European Journal of International Law* 621; Philip Alston, "Resisting the Merger and Acquisition of Human Rights by Trade Law: A Reply to Petersmann" (2002) 13 *European Journal of International Law* 815; Robert Howse, "Human Rights in the WTO: Whose Rights, What Humanity? Comment on Petersmann" (2002) 13 *European Journal of International Law* 651; James Harrison, *The Human Rights Impact of the World Trade Organisation* (Oxford: Hart, 2007); Jochem Wiers, *Trade and Environment in the EC and the WTO: A Legal Analysis* (Groningen: Europa Law Publishing, 2003).

18 The legal text of CEPA is available at http://www.tid.gov.hk/english/cepa/.

Association for Relations across the Taiwan Straits (the ARATS)—also serve as a forum through which China may exert influence on Taiwan and Hong Kong. In addition, ECFA and CEPA have also established an ECFA committee or steering committee,[19] with a view to overseeing the implementation of ECFA and CEPA, resolving disputes arising therefrom and engaging in regulatory cooperation. The ECFA committee and steering committee thus serve as good fora for officials from Taiwan, China, and Hong Kong to meet regularly. Given the lack of transparency in the decision-making processes of these committees, the legitimacy of them adopting binding decisions has been severely questioned. Further, as the memberships of these committees are composed wholly of individuals appointed by executive branches, it is doubtful whether the ECFA committee or the steering committee could be considered democratically accountable. In the absence of democratic accountability, it is possible that Taiwan's and Hong Kong's democracies could be undermined in due time.

Inter-agency regulatory cooperation

In addition to the ECFA/CEPA framework, closer economic integration between Taiwan, China, and Hong Kong has given rise to frequent visits and contacts among similar regulatory agencies and between these three entities. For example, the heads of financial supervision, which includes banking, securities, and insurance, concluded a memorandum on financial supervision and cooperation on 16 November 2009.[20] Similarly, the heads of the Central Banks in Taiwan and China signed a memorandum of understanding (MoU) on currency clearing and cooperation on 31 August 2012.[21] These MoUs established the parameters for regulatory dialogues between Taiwan and China. The supervisory authorities of Taiwan and China meet periodically to engage in regulatory cooperation and information exchange. This inter-agency regulatory cooperation offers good opportunities for China to exert influence on Taiwan and Hong Kong, and may lead to a "race to the bottom" in regulatory standards. In fact, the institutionalised inter-agency regulatory cooperation between Taiwan, China, and Hong Kong has developed a system of international network governance as envisaged by Ann-Marie Slaughter.[22] Yet, this governance network is frequently in tension with democracy.[23] Further, it is debatable as to whether this inter-agency cooperation has developed a stronger sense of collegial partnership (in particular, the regulatory dialogues and meetings under the two associations mechanism between the SEF and ARATS), which may prevent the principals (the people and the legislature) from effectively controlling the agents.[24] Such fears have been supported in Taiwan by the congressional rubber-stamping of the Services Trade Agreement between Taiwan and China within a mere 30 seconds after its introduction, which sparked public outrage and ultimately led to the Sunflower Movement.

19 ECFA, Art 11; CEPA, Art 19.

20 Available at http://www.rootlaw.com.tw/LawArticle.aspx?LawID=A040310001010000-0981116.

21 The full text is available at http://www.cbc.gov.tw/public/Attachment/29712203571.pdf.

22 See Anne-Marie Slaughter, *A New World Order* (Princeton: Princeton University Press, 2005).

23 Peter Bogason and Juliet A. Musso, "The Democratic Prospects of Network Governance" (2006) 36(1) *The American Review of Public Administration* 3, 5–6.

24 On the principal-agency theory and trade negotiations, see, e.g. Andreas Dür and Manfred Elsig, "Principals, Agents, and the European Union's Foreign Economic Policies" (2011) 18(3) *Journal of European Public Policy* 323.

Taiwanese merchants associations

Moving beyond the public domain, China's influence over Taiwan and Hong Kong may also be channelled through private fora. These private fora may engage in activities under the auspices of enterprise associations and the commercial practices of individual enterprises. It is notable that a vast number of Taiwanese merchant associations are located in China. The original objectives of these Taiwanese merchant associations were to safeguard the rights and interests of Taiwanese enterprises in China and to serve as a bridge between those enterprises and central or local governments in China. However, Taiwanese merchants associations have turned out to be perfect instruments for China to exert influence in Taiwan.[25] Such merchant associations are registered in China and subject to Chinese government supervision. Additionally, they tend to maintain close relations with Chinese authorities, and particularly their regional or local Taiwan offices. The nominations or elections for the heads of those Taiwanese merchant associations usually have significant political implications, as seen below.

Examples of China exercising influence through Taiwanese merchant associations can be seen through the following. First, in 2012, during the Lunar New Year holiday (when the presidential election was being held in Taiwan), airline ticket fares, predominantly for Chinese airlines, between China and Taiwan were sharply reduced. This move was seen as an attempt by China to bolster the vote for the pro-China candidate, Ma Ying Jeou (馬英九).[26] The same tactics were employed in the 2014 local elections. Moreover, the Association of Taiwan Investment Enterprises on the Mainland, a union of various Taiwanese merchant associations in China, along with other institutions, campaigned for the Kuomintang candidate. On that occasion, the former president of the SEF, Chiang Pin Kung, was also a participant.[27]

Mergers and acquisitions, joint economic activities, and illicit commercial practices

China's influence in Taiwan and Hong Kong through private fora may also be seen in various commercial activities. The most illustrative example of China's influence over Taiwan and Hong Kong in the private commercial area is the failed attempted acquisition and merger of Next TV, *Next Magazine*, and *Apple Daily* by Want Want Holdings. *Apple Daily* in Hong Kong was subject to a number of disturbances, including the hacking of its website and blockage of its distribution channels. *Apple Daily* even sought an injunction from Hong Kong courts to order that the blockage be dissolved.[28]

Private commercial practices also provide channels for China to extend its influence to other sectors, such as financing and clinical medical trials. In the context of the cross-strait CEO summit held in December 2014, five major Taiwanese banks and five major Chinese banks signed an MoU with a view to strengthening collaboration in major lending

25 On the role of Taiwanese businessmen as an instrument for China's unification policy, see, e.g. Shu Keng and Gunter Schubert, "Agents of Taiwan-China Unification? The Political Roles of Taiwanese Business People in the Process of Cross-Strait Integration" (201) 50(2) *Asian Survey* 287.

26 Jens Kastner, "Politics Seen in Cheap China-Taiwan Flights" *Asia Times*, Greater China (8 December 2011).

27 *Formosa Newsletter* (24 November 2014), http://www.my-formosa.com/DOC_70906.htm.

28 Thomas Chan, "Apple Daily Seeks Ban against Anti-Occupy Protesters outside Its Headquarters in Tseung Kwan O" *South China Morning Post*, City p. 2 (16 October 2016).

activities. At the same time, an MoU allowing mutual recognition of the results of clinical trials of new drugs by eight major medical institutions in Taiwan and China was also inked.[29] In fact, these two MoUs are nested in bilateral agreements concluded by Taiwan and China under the two associations mechanism between the SEF and ARAT. Thus, these commercial collaboration activities are indeed backed by various public authorities.

Highlighting how problematic such an arrangement can be, the commercial activities in question may not always be legal. Good examples are the widespread food scandals in Taiwan, which resulted in two Taiwanese food giants, Ting Hsin International Group and Uni-President Group, gaining notoriety due to their unsafe practices. Uni-President has also carved out a large part of the Chinese food market with the help of its distribution services via chain stores, and the Ting Hsin International Group had been praised as an example of the "returning salmon" model, given its large success in China. These two food giants have been at the centre of a series of food scandals in recent years,[30] raising questions as to whether illicit commercial practices common in China will be transmitted to Taiwan through companies which have subsidiaries in China or may be heavily invested there.

Embedded "One Country, Two Systems" constraint

Hong Kong faces strict external constraints in its pursuit of democracy and the safeguarding of rule of law because of the embedded "One Country, Two Systems" approach. How much democracy and rule of law Hong Kong residents may enjoy is largely dependent on China's interpretation of this constitutional principle. Indeed, since the handover to Chinese rule in 1997, China has continuously redefined and narrowed Hong Kong's autonomy. The interpretation of the HKBL by the NPCSC is thus a powerful instrument for China to exert its influence in Hong Kong. Hong Kong's pursuit of democracy and the rule of law are akin to a bird in a cage trying to learn to fly, while the available space is gradually compressed.

China's influence in Hong Kong is now omnipresent. The prime example of this is the Liaison Office of the Central People's Government in the HKSAR (the Liaison Office), which is reported to have intervened in Legislative Council elections,[31] and which repeatedly condemned the Occupy Central Movement, maintaining that the legality of the decision of the NPCSC is not subject to question.[32] Another example can be found in the state immunity case heard by the judiciary of Hong Kong, in which the Office of the Commissioner of the Ministry of Foreign Affairs of the People's Republic of China in the HKSAR (OCMFA) submitted three letters stating that the consistent and principled position of China on state immunity is "absolute immunity", and that such competence falls outside the jurisdiction of Hong Kong courts.[33] Overall, Hong Kong's democracy and rule of law are seriously vulnerable, and indeed subject to significant Chinese influence.

29 *New Talk* (16 December 2014), http://newtalk.tw/news/2014/12/16/54837.html.

30 Stacy Hsu, "Uni-President Joins Casualty List" *Taipei Times* (25 October 2014), p. 1.

31 *Liberty News* (8 September 2012), http://news.ltn.com.tw/news/politics/paper/613470/print.

32 *BBC News* (14 December 2014), http://www.bbc.co.uk/zhongwen/trad/china/2014/12/141214_occupy_central_cahkms_conference.

33 For more on this case and the OCMFA's intervention in the proceedings, see Chien-Huei Wu, "'One Country, Two State Immunity Doctrines': A Pluralistic Depiction of the *Congo* Case" (2014) 9(2) *National Taiwan University Law Review* 197.

Research design

Hypothesis

Through this research I attempt to turn on its head the conventional study of "learning effects", which suggests that when less-developed countries trade with developed countries, more democratic countries and those with a more enhanced rule of law, the less-developed countries will gradually democratise, adopt, and improve their domestic rule of law. I aim to explore whether closer economic integration with China, an undemocratic country with poor rule of law, would undermine democracy and the rule of law in Taiwan and Hong Kong. Specifically, I test whether such "undermining effects" are present in trading with China, and might penetrate into Taiwan and Hong Kong via the aforementioned mechanisms. I thus propose the following hypothesis:

> Closer economic integration with China will result in the deterioration of democracy and the rule of law in Taiwan and Hong Kong, because "undermining effects" may be transmitted to Taiwan and Hong Kong through a number of mechanisms, public or private.

Independent variables: Taiwan's and Hong Kong's economic integration with China, and how to evaluate it

Economic integration may be closely related to trade liberalisation, such as the elimination of tariffs and non-tariff barriers. This task has been carried out mainly by the General Agreement on Tariffs and Trade (GATT) and its successor, the World Trade Organization (WTO). However, economic integration goes beyond trade liberalisation. Whether economic integration necessitates a minimum degree of harmonisation or even a transfer of regulatory (or sovereign) power is subject to debate.[34] However, as the European experiences suggest, the four fundamental freedoms – namely, free movement of goods, free provision of services, free movement of capital, and free movement of persons – are the driving forces for the formation of economic integration.

In the context of economic integration between Taiwan, China, and Hong Kong, such freedoms have developed at difference rates. While the free movement of goods has been largely liberalised, the free provision of services and movement of capital are works in progress, and the free movement of persons remains largely prohibited (except for tourism purposes). Therefore, I choose four subsets of data to indicate the degree of economic integration between China, Taiwan, and Hong Kong: trade in goods, trade in services, foreign direct investment (FDI), and visits by Chinese citizens (legal and illegal immigrants, service providers, and tourists). I further construct the trade dependence of Taiwan and Hong Kong (as regards both imports and exports) on China in terms of trade in merchandise and in services by looking at the ratio of total volume of imports from/exports to China against their total volumes of imports and exports. Therefore, I have the following four subsets of data: (1) free movement of goods: dependence of Taiwan and Hong Kong

34 On this subject, see, e.g. William Wallace, "The Sharing of Sovereignty: the European Paradox" (1999) 47(3) Political Studies 503; Walter Mattli, "Sovereignty Bargains in Regional Integration" 2(2) International Studies Review 149.

merchandise imports/exports on trade with China; (2) free provision of services: dependence of Hong Kong imports/exports on China in the trade in services (Taiwan's services trade statistics are unavailable); (3) free movement of capital: FDI inflows and outflows between Taiwan and Hong Kong, and China; and (4) free movement of natural persons: Chinese tourists to Taiwan and Hong Kong, legal and illegal Chinese immigration to Taiwan and Hong Kong, including Chinese service professionals in Taiwan. These four subsets of data are illustrated below in Figures 9.1 to 9.4.

Dependent variables: Good Governance Indicators and press freedom

In appreciating the changes in the rule of law and democracy in Taiwan and Hong Kong, I use the Good Governance Indicators to capture some of the characteristics that these two concepts possess. From the outset, the Good Governance Indicators define governance as follows:

> the traditions and institutions by which authority in a country is exercised. This includes (a) the process by which governments are selected, monitored, and replaced; (b) the capacity of the government to effectively formulate and implement sound policies; and (c) the respect of citizens and the state for the institutions that govern economic and social interactions among them.[35]

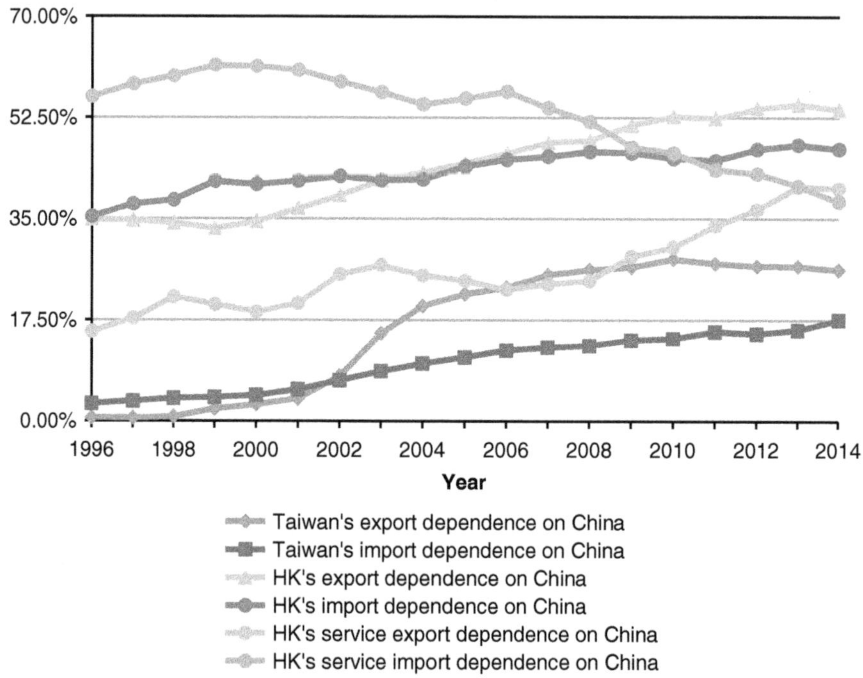

Figure 9.1: Independent variables (Trade dependence on China)

Source: twbusiness.nat.gov.tw/ and Census and Statistics Department, Hong Kong

35 Daniel Kaufmann, Aart Kraay and Massimo Mastruzzi, "The Worldwide Governance Indicators: Methodology and Analytical Issues" (2011) 3(2) *Hague Journal on the Rule of Law* 220, 222.

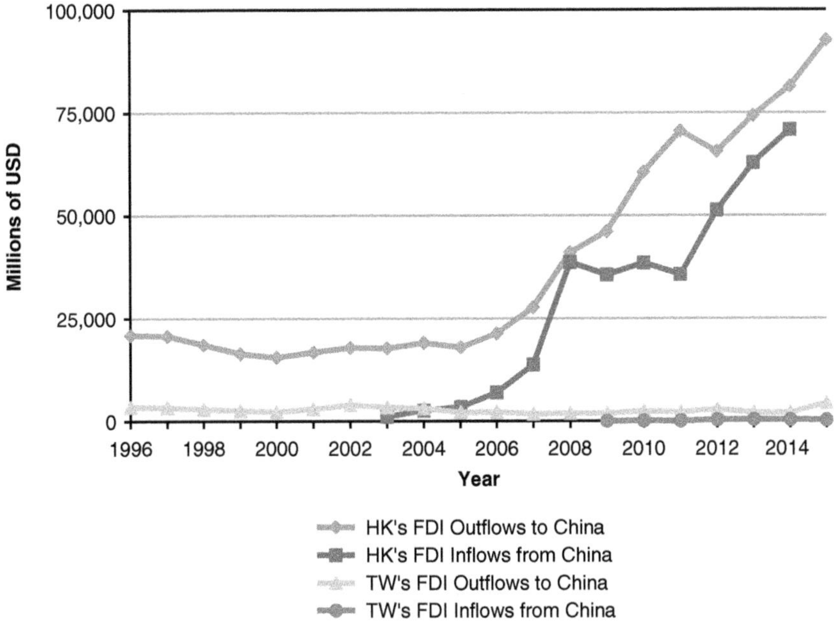

Figure 9.2: Independent variables (FDI inflows from and outflows to China)

Source: Combined from UNCTAD and Investment Commission, MOEA, Taiwan and National Bureau of statistics of China

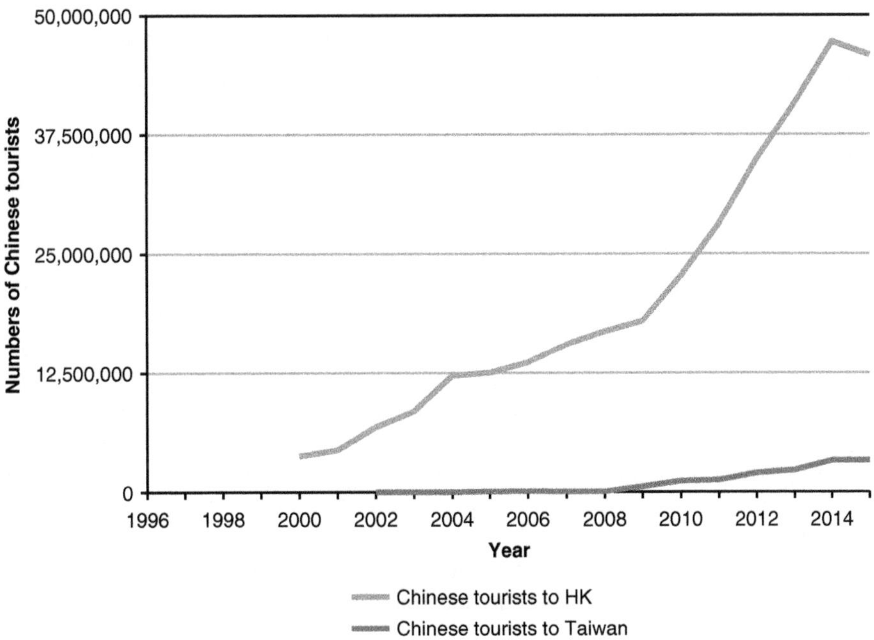

Figure 9.3: Independent variables (Chinese tourists to Taiwan and Hong Kong)

Source: Census and Statistics Department, Hong Kong. Tourism Board, Hong Kong. National Immigration Agency, Taiwan

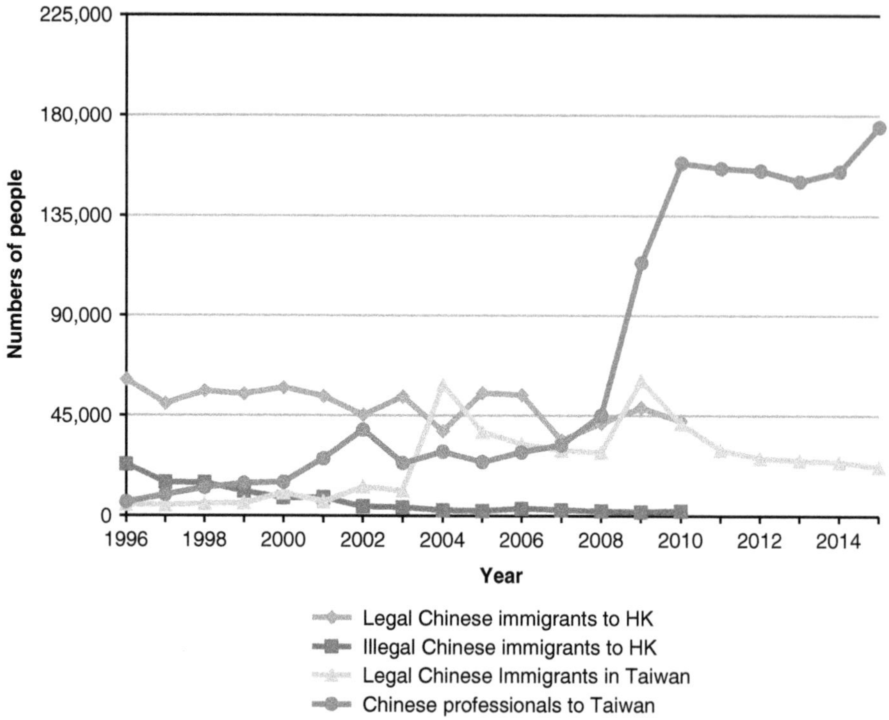

Figure 9.4: Independent variables (Chinese immigrants and professionals to Taiwan and Hong Kong)

Source: Census and Statistics Department, Hong Kong and National Immigration Agency, Taiwan

Based on this definition, two dimensions are constructed and the Good Governance Indicators thus cover six elements: voice and accountability; political stability and the absence of violence; government effectiveness; regulatory quality; control of corruption; and rule of law. These six elements touch upon some of the key issues regarding the rule of law and democracy. Of particular interest to this chapter is control of corruption, rule of law, and voice and accountability, which reflect the key elements of a democratic society with rule of law. The Good Governance Indicators have been widely and extensively used in political and legal studies to measure the legal and political environment of a given country.[36] Since this chapter aims to evaluate the improvement or deterioration of rule of law and democracy in Taiwan and Hong Kong after being closely integrated with China's economy, the Good Governance Indicators provide a good measurement tool. In addition, given that press freedom is an essential element of democracy and a hotly debated issue in Taiwan and Hong Kong, I also include the press freedom indexes from Freedom House and Reporters without Borders in my study.

The performances of Taiwan and Hong Kong in terms of the six Good Governance Indicators and press freedom reports are illustrated below in Figures 9.5 to 9.7.

36 As of 2 August 2016, according to Google Scholar, Daniel Kaufmann, Aart Kraay, and Massimo Mastruzzi's paper on "Governance Matters VIII: Aggregate and Individual Governance Indicators, 1996–2008" has been cited 6,402 times.

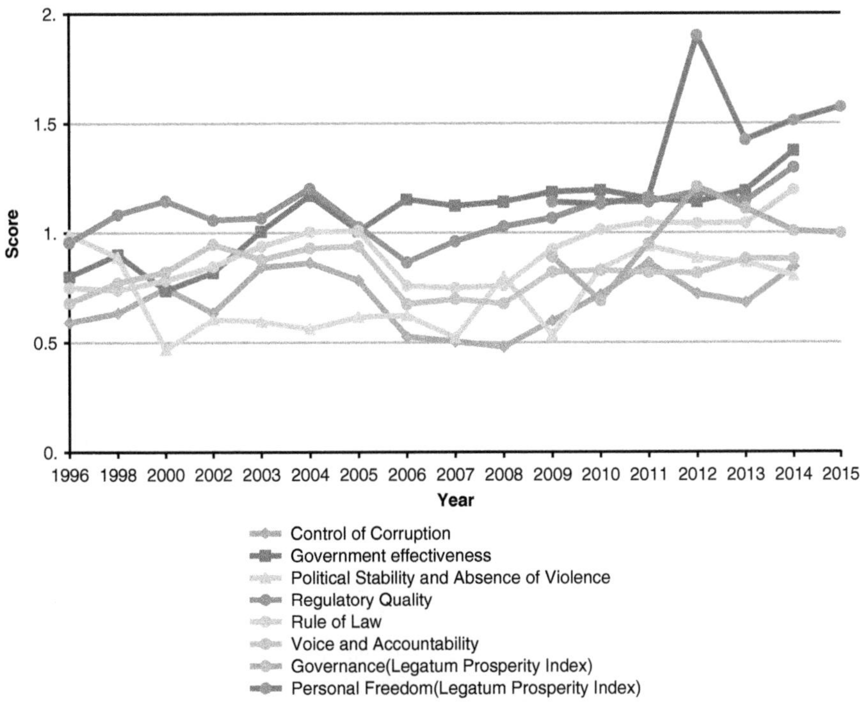

Figure 9.5: Dependent variables (Governance Index and Legatum Property Index of Taiwan)

Source: Combined from World Bank and Legatum Prosperity Index

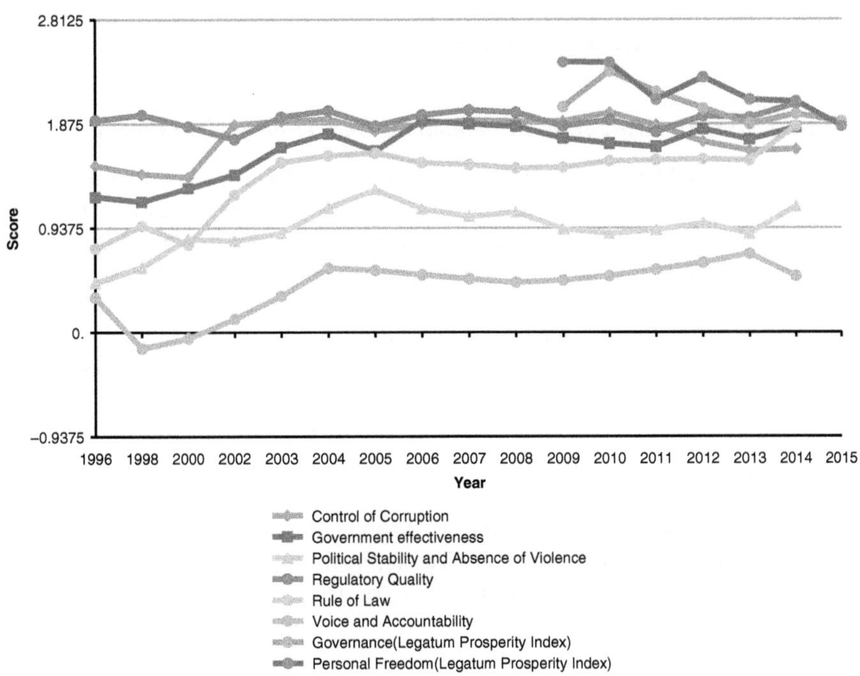

Figure 9.6: Dependent variables (Governance Index and Legatum Property Index of Hong Kong)

Source: Combined from World Bank and Legatum Prosperity Index

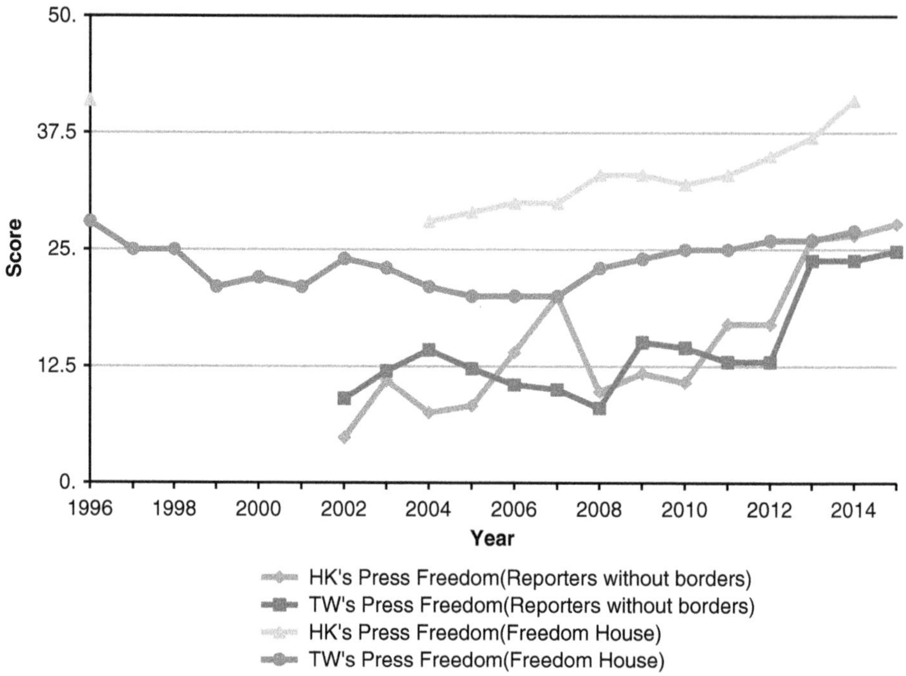

Figure 9.7: Dependent variables (Press freedom from Freedom House and Reporters without Borders)

Source: Combined from Reporters without borders and Freedom House

Analytical tool: Gnu Regression, Econometrics, and Time-Series Library

For my analysis, I used Gnu Regression, Econometrics, and Time-Series Library, an econometrics package created by Allin Cottrell of Wake Forest University and further improved by Riccardo Lucchetti of the Università Politecnica delle Marche.[37] I tested the correlation between the economic integration of Taiwan and Hong Kong with China against their performances in terms of the World Bank Good Governance Indicators and the press freedom reports. Based on the *p*-value, the threshold for weak, strong, and very strong relations between independent variables and dependent variables are 0.10, 0.05, and 0.01, respectively.

Research results

This research yields some consistent results, as documented in the appendix. In the context of the World Bank Good Governance Indicators, in those indictors where correlation is found (governance effectiveness and the rule of law), the dependence of Taiwan's

37 For a brief review of this software, see J. Wilson Mixon Jr. and Andy Ryan Smith, "Software Reviews: Teaching Undergradate Econometrics with GRETL" (2006) 21(7) *Journal of Applied Econometrics* 1103.

merchandise trade on China is positively related to the performance of Taiwan as measured by those two indicators. More precisely, irrespective of whether imports or exports are measured, the dependence of Taiwan's trade in goods with China is positively related to government effectiveness and the rule of law. Similar findings are applicable to Hong Kong. I find a consistent positive correlation between the dependence of Hong Kong's merchandise imports and exports on China, and its performance in all the Good Governance Indicators, except for regulatory quality. However, when it comes to trade in services, the results are quite different. Both in Hong Kong's services export and import dependence, I find no significant correlation between them, control of corruption, political stability, and regulatory quality. In the remaining three indicators, Hong Kong's service export dependence on China is positively related to its performance on the Good Governance Indicators, whereas its service import dependence is negatively related.

Regarding the free movement of capital, the relationship between FDI inflows from China and outflows to China appears non-existent, except on two indicators. Taiwan's FDI outflows into China are negatively related to government effectiveness; Hong Kong's FDI inflows from China and outflows into China are negatively related to the control of corruption in Hong Kong.

Regarding the free movement of persons, I find some consistency in the movement of Chinese immigrants, legal or illegal, to Hong Kong in relation to its performance in the Good Governance Indicators. In those indicators where correlations are found to exist, they are all negatively related to the movement of Chinese immigrants to Hong Kong, regardless of their legality. By contrast, the movement of legal Chinese immigrants to Taiwan is, perhaps surprisingly, positively related to Taiwan's government effectiveness. With respect to Chinese tourists, the relationship between their visits to Taiwan and Hong Kong and the latter entities' performances in the Good Governance Indictors results in a positive correlation. A similar finding applies to the visits of Chinese professionals to Taiwan.

Finally, regarding press freedom, I find a consistent negative relationship between Taiwan's and Hong Kong's economic integration and their press freedom in every category of this research, except for Hong Kong service import dependence on China. Specifically, there is a negative relationship between Reporters without Borders' Freedom Index and Hong Kong's export/import merchandise and service export trade dependence on China, FDI inflows from China to Hong Kong, visits of Chinese tourists to Hong Kong, Taiwan's export merchandise trade dependence on China, and visits of Chinese professionals to Taiwan. Similarly, in Freedom House's measure of press freedom, a negative relationship is also found in relation to Hong Kong's export/import merchandise and service export trade dependence on China, FDI inflows from China to Taiwan and Hong Kong, Chinese tourists to Taiwan and Hong Kong, illegal immigrants from China to Hong Kong, and the visits of Chinese professionals to Taiwan.

Discussion and conclusion

According to the research results, I find that merchandise trade, regardless of whether examining imports or exports; trade openness; and subsequent closer economic integration, even with an undemocratic country with a poor rule of law record, will enhance the performance of the pertinent trading nation with regard to Good Governance Indicators. This finding may be viewed as confirming the conventional wisdom that trade openness improves a trading nation's rule of law. According to my research, the positive effect is more sweeping in Hong Kong than in Taiwan. The reason for this may be that Hong Kong is more closely integrated with China, as can be seen in its merchandise trade dependence with China.

When economic integration moves from merchandise trade to services, the picture becomes more muddled. Whereas Hong Kong's dependence on the export of services to China is still positively correlated with most Good Governance Indicators, service import dependence on China is negatively related. This may lend some support to the position of the Sunflower Movement: that the service trade agreement being a "Trojan horse" threat is not entirely fictional. If Taiwan's closer economic integration with China regarding trade in services leads Taiwan to become overly dependent on China, this could eventually impede good governance in Taiwan. At the same time, such a finding is also in line with the economic development patterns observed in Taiwan and Hong Kong, which are heavily reliant on exports in order to realise trade surpluses. The penetration of China's services into Taiwan and Hong Kong has been detrimental not only in economic respects but also in legal and political respects. Economically, the over-reliance on China for the services sectors may lead to a trade deficit in the service sectors of Taiwan and Hong Kong against China, which could eventually threaten the health of these two entities' economies. Legally and politically, services export from China, in particular through the mode of commercial presence, may jeopardise good governance and press freedom in Taiwan and Hong Kong.

While person-to-person exchanges through free movement of persons constitute an important element of cultural transmission and exchange of ideas in trading activities, it need not necessarily have a positive impact on the performances of Taiwan and Hong Kong in terms of Good Governance Indicators. As my research demonstrates, Chinese immigrants to Hong Kong, legal or illegal, are negatively related to Hong Kong's Good Governance Indicators. This may help to explain why the free movement of persons remains the most sensitive uncharted field in the liberalisation of international trade or in the processes of economic integration.

Finally, the press freedom indexes of Freedom House and Reporters without Borders speak almost unequivocally, except for Hong Kong's service dependence on China, about the negative impact of closer economic integration with China. These figures also provide some support for the anti-media monopoly movement in Taiwan, as worries about closer economic integration with China undermining press freedom appear to have some basis in fact.

Ultimately, despite the neoliberalism bias of the Good Governance Indicators, closer economic integration with China – an undemocratic country with a poor record of rule of law – may result in worse governance in Taiwan and Hong Kong. Freedom House and Reporters without Borders measures indicate that closer economic integration with China will result in undermining effects regarding the freedom of the press in Taiwan and Hong Kong, leading to the conclusion that, ultimately, to "dance with the dragon" takes great skill and care.

Dependent variables		*Worldwide Governance Indicators (World Bank) 1996–2012*						*Reporters without Borders 2002–2012*	*Freedom House 1996–2012 (HK lacks 1997–2003)*
Independent variables		*Control of corruption*	*Government effectiveness*	*Political stability and absence of violence*	*Regulatory quality*	*Rule of law*	*Voice and accountability*	*Press freedom*	*Press freedom*
Merchandise export dependence on China	TW	IN	***(1.52142; 2.94e-06)	IN	IN	**(0.804352; 0.0208)	IN	IN	IN
	HK	**(1.28313; 0.0491)	***(2.66640; 0.0001)	**(1.53063; 0.0314)	IN	***(3.52062; 7.78e-05)	***(2.74168; 6.82e-05)	***(**97.5128; 0.0039)**	***(77.7585; 0.0015)
Merchandise import dependence on China	TW	IN	***(3.51092; 5.72e-07)	IN	IN	***(2.14278; 0.0040)	IN	**(102.765; 0.0208)	IN
	HK	***(177.859; 0.0045)	***(0.0045; 3.40e-05)	***(4.17605; 0.0023)	IN	***(7.16937; 0.0002)	***(4.69776; 0.0036)	***(**236.445: 0.0066)**	***(177.859; 0.0045)
Service export dependence on China	TW	N/A	N/A	N/A	N/A	N/A	N/A	N/A	N/A
	HK	IN	**(1.79187; 0.0290)	IN	IN	***(3.07092; 0.0018)	**(1.99712; 0.0141)	***(81.6672; 0.0026)	***(49.1507; 0.0004)
Service import dependence on China	TW	N/A	N/A	N/A	N/A	N/A	N/A	N/A	N/A
	HK	IN	**(**–1.75962; 0.0290)**	IN	IN	***(**–2.68969; 0.0078)**	***(**–2.26390; 0.0030)**	***(–73.1371; 0.0030)	***(–51.5021; 0.0001)
FDI outflows to China	TW	IN	**(**–0.000150138; 0.0215)**	IN	IN	IN	IN	IN	IN
	HK	IN	IN	IN	IN	IN	IN	IN	IN
FDI inflows from China	TW	IN	IN	IN	IN	IN	IN	IN	**(0.00607781; 0.0179)
	HK	**(–3.12066e-06; 0.0160)	IN	IN	IN	IN	IN	***(0.000190073; 0.0097)	***(**0.000153934; 3.03e-06)**

(*Continued*)

Dependent variables		*Worldwide Governance Indicators (World Bank) 1996–2012*						*Reporters without Borders 2002–2012*	*Freedom House 1996–2012 (HK lacks 1997–2003)*
Independent variables		*Control of corruption*	*Government effectiveness*	*Political stability and absence of violence*	*Regulatory quality*	*Rule of law*	*Voice and accountability*	*Press freedom*	*Press freedom*
Visits of Chinese tourists	TW	IN	**(7.85605e-08; 0.0125)	***(9.48976e-08; 0.0081)	***(7.33806e-08; 0.0052)	***(9.45053e-08; 0.0023)	IN	*****(3.76120e-06; 0.0003)**	*****(1.84996e-06; 0.0005)**
	HK	***(-6.78908E-09; 0.0010)	IN	IN	IN	**(6.57089e-09; 0.0197)	**(6.74012e-09; 0.0317)	****(4.58667e-07; 0.0002)**	*****(2.92235e-07; 1.35e-05)**
Legal Chinese immigrants	TW	IN	***(6.56052e-06; 0.0090)	IN	IN	IN	IN	**IN**	IN
	HK	****(−1.70712e-05; 0.01105)**	****(−1.99696e-05; 0.02033)**	IN	IN	****(−2.25137e-05; 0.03676)**	IN	IN	IN
Illegal Chinese immigrants	TW	N/A	N/A	N/A	N/A	N/A	N/A	N/A	N/A
	HK	*****(−2.55263e-05; 0.00185)**	*****(−3.20844e-05; 0.00165)**	*****(−3.06418e-05; 0.00036)**	IN	*****(−4.15726e-05; 0.00044)**	***(−1.96932e-05; 0.07666)**	IN	*****(0.000489241; 0.00415)**
Visits of Chinese professionals	TW	IN	***(1.90322e-06; 0.0034)	*(1.19993e-06; 0.0872)	**(1.01533e-06; 0.0143)	***(1.74457e-06; 0.0006)	IN	****(5.14140e-05; 0.0177)**	**(2.12374e-05; 0.0233)
	HK	N/A	N/A	N/A	N/A	N/A	N/A	N/A	N/A

Note:

1. Only negative correlations are in bold type.
2. Our null hypothesis:
   H0: There is no relationship between the independent variable and the dependent variable.H1: There is a relationship between the independent variable and the dependent variable. Where: H0 = the null hypothesis; H1 = the alternative hypothesis.
3. N/A stands for Not Applicable. IN stands for Insignificant, in which the p-value is not significant enough to reject the null hypothesis; therefore, the independent variable and the dependent variable are unrelated.
4. Based on the p-value, *** stands for very strong relations; ** stands for strong relations, * stands for weak relations.
5. A positive or a negative relationship is expressed as *, **, or *** (coefficient; p-value)
6. As for the press freedom of Reporters without borders and Freedom House, a higher score indicates a lower degree of freedom. Therefore, if there is a positive relationship between any independent variable and the score of press freedom, it represents that there is a negative relationship between the independent variable and the degree of the press freedom.

10 A divided society

Chinese public opinion on resistance movements, democracy, and rule of law

*Han Zhu**

Background

In 2014, the Occupy Central (OC) Movement in Hong Kong and the Sunflower Movement in Taiwan were heated topics worldwide, and within China this was no exception. Between the two high-profile movements, the former has attracted more attention in Chinese media and society since it was directly related to the "One Country, Two Systems" policy. In fact, the OC Movement is the first widely reported and discussed democratic movement that has occurred within PRC territory since the 1989 Tiananmen Square movement. It thus provides a rare opportunity to observe Chinese public opinion, especially as regards democracy and civil disobedience in the post-1989 era. Although there have been empirical studies on the participants in the OC Movement,[1] as well as on the influence of the China factor on the Sunflower Movement,[2] no systematic research has been conducted with regard to public opinion towards the two movements and the relevant issues involved in each. As more and more activists, scholars, and politicians realize that the development of democracy in Mainland China is vital for that in Hong Kong – and perhaps even in Taiwan – the consciousness of democracy and the rule of law for Mainland Chinese is certainly one of the key factors worth observing in the discussion on the development of democracy and political movements throughout the three regions.

However, there are some important questions that we must first consider: what impact have the OC and Sunflower Movements had on Mainland China? Besides the official cliché criticism of these two movements, how do common Chinese citizens view the civil disobedience movements in these two regions? Further, how much do Chinese citizens know about these two movements? To date only a handful of media reports based on sporadic interviews have revealed the attitudes of Mainland Chinese towards the OC Movement,

* Assistant research officer, Centre for Chinese Law, Faculty of Law of The University of Hong Kong. Email: hanzhu@connect.hku.hk. The author would like to thank several friends and colleges for assisting with data collection and analysis. Without their help, this research would not have been possible. Their names are not disclosed for security reasons. The author would also like to extend gratitude to all the respondents who took the time and "risks" to participate in the survey.

1 E.g. Samson Yuen and Edmund Cheng, "Hong Kong's Umbrella Protests Were More than Just a Student Movement" *ChinaFile* (1 July 2015), https://www.chinafile.com/reporting-opinion/features/hong-kongs-umbrella-protests-were-more-just-student-movement; also *see* five public opinion polls conducted by the Public Opinion Programme of the University of Hong Kong, https://www.hkupop.hku.hk/english/report/mpCEnOCC/index.html.

2 E.g. Jieh-min Wu, "Citizen Resistance Movements in Hong Kong and Taiwan under the Influence of 'China Factor'" in Xie Zhenglun (ed.), *Dongya diqu de hezuo yu heping* (*Coordination and Peace in East Asia*) (Taipei: Qianwei, 2014), pp. 130–144.

which have been mostly negative.[3] In contrast, some Mainland Chinese activists have expressed support for the OC Movement, and their public activism has resulted in serious crackdowns.[4] Their courage to openly support the OC Movement is in sharp contrast with the mainstream views held throughout Chinese society.

This chapter aims to examine public opinion on the two civil disobedience movements in Hong Kong and Taiwan, with a focus on the former. Questionnaire surveys were conducted with Mainland Chinese citizens to evaluate the consciousness of democracy and the rule of law, and also to explore the gap between ordinary citizens and the *weiquan* (rights defence) sector.[5] The article attempts to provide answers to some bewildering developments of democracy and liberalism under China's authoritarianism, such as the passivity of a wider civil society towards democracy and the emergence of young elites who have been educated overseas, but who remain critical of the "Western-style" democracy and liberalism. It also provides some perspective for the *weiquan* sector in Mainland China and the civil societies in Hong Kong and Taiwan, regarding the opportunities and obstacles they face in mobilizing wider public support for rights campaigns and democratic movements.

As some academics have justifiably pointed out, political consciousness is an abstract concept that is difficult to directly observe, often requiring multi-dimensional measurements.[6] The OC Movement provides a valuable opportunity to probe the political consciousness of the public in contemporary China. The survey solicited the respondents of three types of Mainlanders as a means to differentiate and compare the attitudes among ordinary Chinese citizens: individuals who live in Mainland China, overseas Mainland Chinese (mostly students residing in Hong Kong), and the *weiquan* activists (who are either located in Mainland China or overseas). The survey was designed to answer the following questions:

(1) How do Chinese citizens view the OC and Sunflower Movements? What is the gap between the consciousness of common citizens and the *weiquan* sector, and what is the difference between citizens in Mainland China and their counterparts overseas (particularly in Hong Kong)?
(2) In the opinion of Chinese citizens, is there any difference between democracy and the rule of law? Does nationalism influence their opinions on the OC Movement, democracy, and the rule of law?

3 The most influential one might be a *NYT* report: Andrew Jacob, "In Beijing, Young Chinese See Little to Cheer in Hong Kong Protests" *New York Times* (11 October 2014), http://cn.nytimes.com/china/20141011/c11beijing/en-us/; another *NYT* article mentioned the ignorance of most Chinese citizens of the OC Movement in Hong Kong: Edward Wong and Didi Kirsten Tatlow, "Beijing Blocks Reports on Hong Kong Democracy Movement" *New York Times* (30 September 2014), http://cn.nytimes.com/china/20140930/c30block/en-us/.

4 See "Chinese Authorities Make Arrests in Attempt to Prevent Pro-Democracy Campaigns on Mainland" *New York Times* (10 October 2014), http://cn.nytimes.com/china/20141010/c10detentions/en-us/; "Four mainlanders jailed for supporting Occupy Central" *EJ Insight* (8 April 2016), http://www.ejinsight.com/20160408-four-mainlanders-jailed-supporting-occupy-central/.

5 The *weiquan* sector refers to a small but influential group of lawyers, rights NGOs, citizen activists, legal experts, and liberal intellectuals who seek to defend civil rights through legal mobilization or other activism. For a detailed introduction on the term "*weiquan*", see Jonathan Benney, *Defending Rights in Contemporary China* (Oxford: Routledge, 2012), pp. 12–34.

6 Jianhua Zhu *et al.*, "Public Political Consciousness in China: An Empirical Profile" (1990) 10 *Asian Survey* 992, 994.

(3) Does free access to information and media influence the opinions of Mainland Chinese towards social movements, democracy, and the rule of law?

Data and methods

Quantitative data collection methods

Quantitative data was collected through a questionnaire survey, which was mainly conducted from January to April 2016. Collection began after the incidents surrounding the forced disappearance of five booksellers in Hong Kong, which were publicly reported both in Hong Kong and throughout Mainland China in January 2016.[7] The survey questionnaire included asking about respondents' views on this incident along with the OC Movement, with the aim of evaluating the possible differences between the opinions of Chinese citizens towards democracy and the rule of law.

As stated above, the respondents were categorized as: (1) ordinary Chinese citizens who reside in Mainland China (hereinafter "Mainland Chinese" or "Category 1"), (2) Overseas Mainlanders, who were mostly university students residing in Hong Kong (hereinafter "Overseas Mainlanders" or "Category 2"), and (3) Mainlanders involved with *weiquan* activism, primarily rights advocacy lawyers and NGO activists (hereinafter the "*Weiquan* sector"). The sample was selected by convenience and strongly relied on snowball sampling. Table 10.1 shows the number of respondents in the three categories. Among the 478 completed questionnaires, 441 were web-based[8] while 37 were performed by hand (mainly collected in Hong Kong).

The process of distributing and collecting questionnaires was in itself an interesting field study, which to some extent reflected the political atmosphere in China and the diversity of Chinese Mainlanders' attitudes towards the survey's "sensitive" issues. During the direct distribution of 62 questionnaires, only one respondent openly rejected the questionnaire due to disinterest and lack of knowledge in political issues, and three potential participants did not respond. Many of the respondents joked that they were risking their life to complete the questionnaire and might be invited "to drink tea" (i.e. be questioned by the authorities).[9] A government official at the county level claimed to have little knowledge about the incidents, consulted party-state opinions on the issues, and filled in the questionnaire accordingly. An unexpected response from many respondents indicated that the questionnaire was too difficult, while a few said that throughout the survey, they realized their ignorance of the events, and expressed interest in learning more about the relevant issues. These responses partly explain why conducting surveys like these is such a sensitive

7 E.g. "Missing, Presumed Detained: Hong Kong Publishers of Books Critical of China Go Missing" *South China Morning Post* (4 January 2016), http://www.scmp.com/news/hong-kong/law-crime/article/1877932/missing-presumed-detained-hong-kong-publishers-books; "A Few Hongkongers should not Cast Cloud over 'One Country, Two Systems'" ***Huanqiu Shibao*** (***Global Times***) (4 January 2016), p. 15; "The Hong Kong Bookseller Incident was Media Hype" ***Huanqiu Shibao*** (***Global Times***) (6 January 2016), p. 14.

8 The author first tried a widely used survey website in Mainland China to distribute the questionnaire, but it was deleted by the administrator immediately after it was sent to the first respondent. Then, the author used SurveyMonkey, an electronic platform for collecting data, but it was too slow for those in Mainland China who could not open the survey webpage, so the author had to use another survey website based in Mainland China (jinshuju.net) to collect the data in private.

9 Online chatting records on file with the author.

Table 10.1 Number of respondents

	Category		*Number of respondents*
1	Mainland Chinese		**323**
2	Overseas Mainlanders		**135**
2.1	*Mainlanders in Hong Kong (mainly college students)*		*112*
2.2	*Mainlanders in Taiwan*		*4*
2.3	*Mainlanders in Foreign Countries*		*19*
3	*Weiquan* sector		**20**
		Total	**478**

issue and largely forbidden in Mainland China, as the survey itself increases access to information and might potentially change the understanding and opinion of the respondents. The process of conducting the survey itself clearly demonstrated the following: sensitivity when discussing political issues; fear of disclosure and resultant self-censorship; apolitical and apathetic mentalities; the blocking of information; and also, the enthusiasm of a few Chinese individuals towards the issues surveyed. Each of these factors provided a glimpse into the political atmosphere and public consciousness within contemporary Chinese society.

Limitations of data collection

Due to issue sensitivity, the survey had to be privately conducted in a low-profile manner, and thus the questionnaires were first distributed among acquaintances based on personal relations through snowballing, which inevitably limited the number and type of respondents. Due to the lack of a public channel when conducting the survey, some localities – such as Xinjiang and Tibet – are not covered. A large number of respondents have similar backgrounds to that of the author, particularly in terms of social status and age, which resulted in several major limitations.

a. A large number of respondents came from middle-class urban areas, while only a few peasants and workers from rural areas participated. Although the data might not be sufficient enough to demonstrate the difference in the opinions regarding the different classes, the opinions of the middle class may serve as an important indicator since they have long been expected to be an important force for democratization and legal development in transitional countries.[10] The survey results on the attitudes of Overseas Mainlander Chinese towards the OC Movement were mainly sampled from college students in Hong Kong, as many Hong Kong universities have been significantly involved in the movement. Since most Mainland students in Hong Kong are postgraduates, this strongly influenced the demographic distribution in terms of respondent education level (see Figure 10.1).

Similarly, 91.6% of the respondents were aged 20–39 years old (Figure 10.2), which means a vast segment of the population (those 40+) is underrepresented in this survey.

10 Another survey on political ideologies of Chinese also primarily concentrated on middle-class male elites; see Jennifer Pan and Yiqing Xu, "China's Ideological Spectrum" *MIT Political Science Department Research Paper 2015-6*, http://papers.ssrn.com/sol3/papers.cfm?abstract_id=2593377, p. 5.

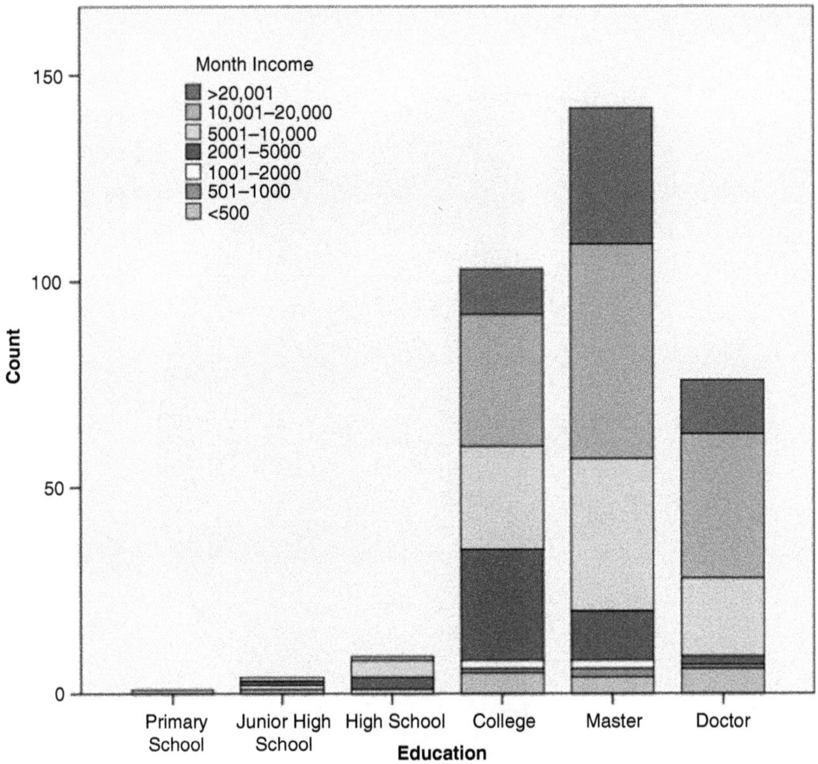

Figure 10.1 Education and income level of respondents

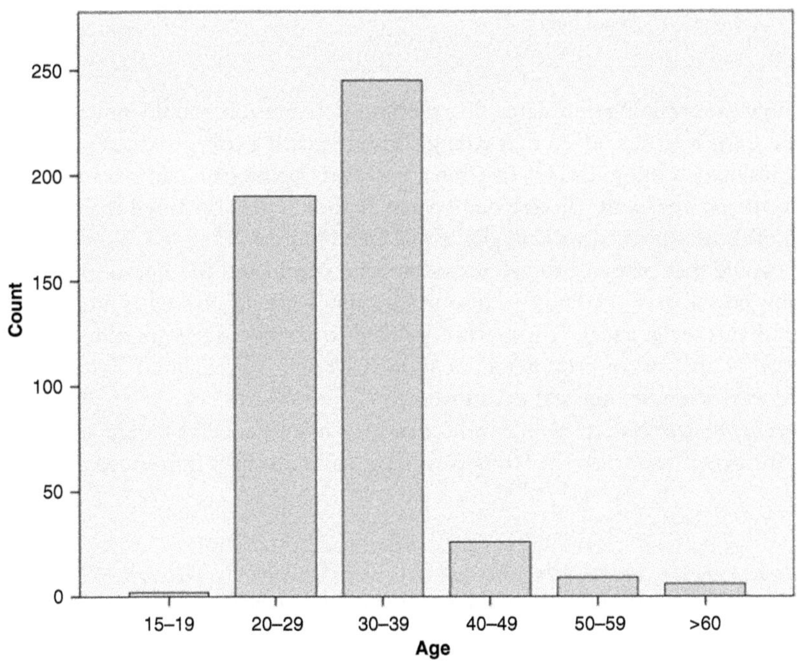

Figure 10.2 Age of respondents

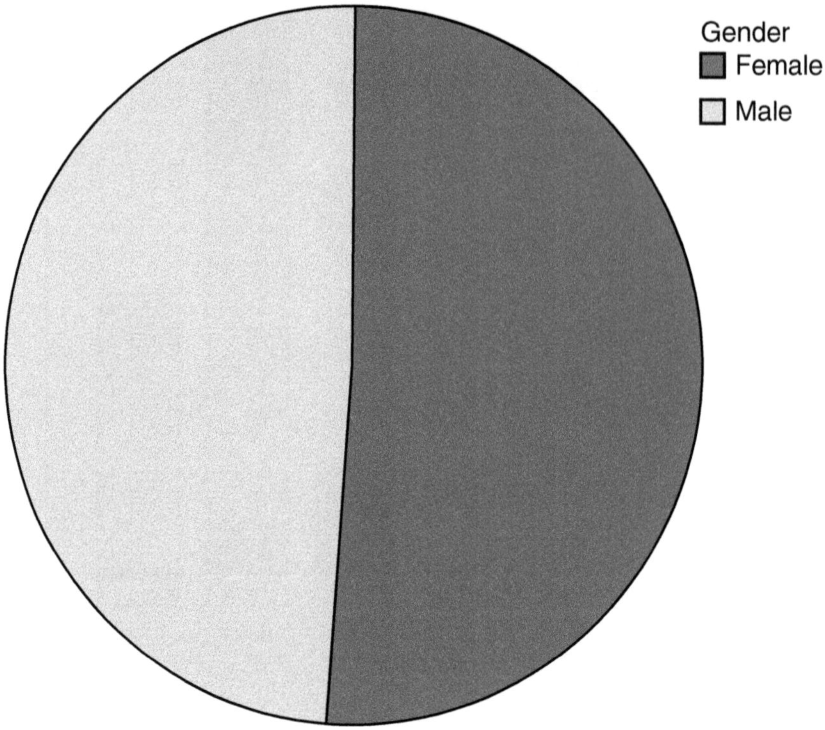

Figure 10.3 Gender of respondents

While certainly constraining the data, this significant limitation should not lead one to disregard the study's results, given that younger citizens with a college education or higher are the political and economic elites in China, and their opinions could have far-reaching influence on the prospects of Chinese democracy. It should also be noted that the gender distribution of those surveyed was roughly equal (see Figure 10.3).

b. It is possible that many of the respondents who completed the questionnaire might be more knowledgeable of the two civil disobedience movements, as well as more informed about political and social issues. Those who declined to complete the questionnaire might comprise part of the larger proportion of individuals who were afraid to do so, were apathetic, or who strongly opposed the movements.

c. Another factor worth keeping in mind is that the survey was being conducted when the "Fish Ball" Incident[11] took place in Hong Kong, which might have influenced the attitudes

11 The civil unrest of the so-called "Fish Ball" Incident occurred on the night of 8 February 2016 until the next morning. The incident escalated from the government's crackdown on unlicensed hawkers selling delicacies including fish balls (a popular Hong Kong street food) during the Lunar New Year holidays. Violent clashes broke out between police and protesters. See "Protesters and Police Clash at Chinese New Year Festivities in Hong Kong" *New York Times* (8 February 2016), http://www.nytimes.com/2016/02/09/world/asia/protesters-and-police-clash-at-lunar-new-year-festivities-in-hong-kong.html?_r=1.

of Mainland Chinese towards social movements and rule of law in Hong Kong. Due to time limitations, the questionnaire did not solicit opinions on the "Fish Ball" Incident.

Official media reports on the OC and Sunflower Movements

Prior to discussing the survey's findings, it is necessary to first briefly review the media coverage of the OC Movements in Mainland China for a general idea of how the state depicted this movement and the relevant issues.

The OC Movement, as well as the Sunflower Movement, occurred when the new central leadership led by President Xi Jinping (習近平) came forward and attempted to consolidate political power. Under the new central leadership, mass and social media have been subject to intensified monitoring,[12] and the mainstream media has been more actively mobilized to propagate party ideology. Discussions over high-profile events are increasingly strictly prohibited compared to previous periods.[13] On the other hand, the state-controlled media now plays a far more active role in response to high-profile issues, and constantly takes the moral high ground to denounce opinions unfavorable to the state.[14]

It was under this media environment in which the OC and Sunflower Movements were framed and reported in Mainland China.[15] The China Media Project of Hong Kong University tracked daily reports on the OC Movement in the Chinese media. According to their publicized databases and the media reports I collected, most mainstream media and online news websites, such as Sohu, Sina, and Tencent, only cited the news releases from the Xinhua News Agency or *The People's Daily*, sources which serve as the most authoritative "mouthpiece" of the state. The Chinese-language Global Times (环球时报) is almost the only mainstream media outlet that published original reports or commentary articles on the OC and Sunflower Movements.

Based on the content analysis of the media reports, the media in Mainland China, generally speaking, formed an overarching anti-OC Movement frame. In sum, four distinct subframes were put forward, namely, the "hostile foreign forces" (境外敌对势力) frame, the disorder/instability frame, the illegal nature frame, and the pro-independence/nationalism frame; all were constructed by the mainstream media in China to extensively criticize the OC Movement.

(1) "*Hostile foreign forces*": This frame was used by the state to stigmatize the 1989 Tiananmen Square movement.[16] By using the same tactic, the official media also accused the OC Movement of being manipulated by "hostile foreign forces". The

12 See Freedom House, "China: Freedom of the Press 2015", https://freedomhouse.org/report/freedom-press/2015/china.

13 Jacques deLisle *et al.*, "Introduction: The Internet, Social Media, and a Changing China" in Jacques deLisle *et al.* (eds), *The Internet, Social Media, and a Changing China* (Philadelphia: University of Pennsylvania Press, 2016), pp. 14–15.

14 E.g. see China Human Rights Lawyers Concern Group, *Report on the 709 Crackdown* (Hong Kong: China Human Rights Lawyers Concern Group, 2016).

15 The China Media Project of HKU has done excellent work in tracing the trends of media report on the OC Movement in Mainland China, http://cmp.hku.hk (visited 12 April 2016); also see Natalie Choi, "Perspective on the Occupy Central Demonstrations in Hong Kong: A Critical Discourse Analysis on English-Language Press in Hong Kong SAR, Taiwan and China", Master's dissertation in Language Sciences, Stockholm University (2015), http://www.diva-portal.org/smash/get/diva2:907318/FULLTEXT01.pdf.

16 Qian Gang, "'Foreign Forces' in 1989" (21 August 2014), http://www.storm.mg/article/23465.

"hostile foreign forces" were constantly labeled as the "black hand" when official media reported on the OC Movement.[17]

(2) *Disorder/instability*: This frame includes several sub-themes about the OC Movement, including a negative impact on the Hong Kong economy[18] (as well as how the Hong Kong economy has lagged behind other Mainland Chinese cities and suffered as a result of the movement),[19] the call by Hong Kong citizens to restore order, and the (supposed) chaos caused by the OC Movement.[20]

(3) *Illegal nature frame*: The media reports accentuated how the OC Movement violated the law, and some reports focused on the legal measures taken by the Hong Kong Government as to how they handled the event and targeted OC participants. The media also covered commentary articles written by legal professionals who strongly denounced the movement, while articles written by liberal intellectuals or others inclined to support the OC Movement were blocked in the official mass media and could only be accessed through social media, some of which disappeared soon afterwards.[21]

(4) *Pro-independence/nationalism frame*: This depiction of the OC Movement is mainly constructed of two sub-themes: the emergence of a pro–Hong Kong independence movement, and the comparison of the current situation with colonial Hong Kong. News reports and commentaries indicated that Hong Kong locals never asked for democracy during the colonial period under British rule and now, after the 1997 handover, enjoy more democracy.[22] The official media also highlighted how the central government and Mainland China have supported economic development in Hong Kong,[23] and emphasized the importance of tourists from Mainland China in contributing to the Hong Kong economy.[24]

17 E.g. "Hong Kong Media Discloses Student Informers Supported by UK and US" *Huanqiu Shibao* (*Global Times*) (21 September 2014), p. 10; "Western Media Define Hong Kong's 'Occupy Central' as A Color Revolution" *Zhongguo Xinwen* She (*China News Service*) (5 October 2014); Mo Jihong, "We Must Resolutely Chop Off the Black Hands Behind 'Occupy Central'" *Zhongguo Wang* (*China.org.cn*) (8 October 2016), http://opinion.china.com.cn/opinion_45_111045.html.

18 E.g. "'Occupy Central' Has a Serious Adverse Effect on the Economic Livelihood of Hong Kong" *Shenzhen Dushibao* (*Shenzhen Metropolis Daily*) (30 September 2014), A02.

19 E.g. "What's Wrong with Hong Kong's Economy?" *Caixin* (5 October 2014), available at http://international.caixin.com/2014-10-05/100735335.html.

20 E.g. "Occupy Central Severely Disturbs Social Orders in Hong Kong" *Shenzhen Dushibao* (*Shenzhen Metropolis Daily*) (8 October 2014), A02.

21 E.g. "'Occupy Central' is not A Normal Way for Expression Freedom" *Renmin Ribao* (*People's Daily*) (2 October 2014), p. 4; Zou Pingxue, "'Occupy Central' Severely Impairs the Rule of Law Tradition of Hong Kong in Three Aspects" *Xinhuawang* (*Xinhuanet*) (3 October 2014), http://news.xinhuanet.com/talking/2014-10/03/c_1112710063.htm; also see Mo (n. 17 above).

22 E.g. "Former British Senior Officer: It's Hypocritical for UK and US to Criticize China Hong Kong Pro-Democratic Not Pursuing Democracy" *Renminwang* (*People.cn*) (4 September 2014), http://hm.people.com.cn/n/2014/0904/c42272-25601482.html.

23 E.g. "10 Questions About Hong Kong 'Occupy Central'"(香港"占中"十问), *Zhongguo Xinwen She* (*China News Service*) (3 October 2014), http://www.chinanews.com/gn/2014/10-03/6649570.shtml.

24 Xie Xiyu *et al.*, "Occupy Central Impact Hong Kong Tourism and Hong Kong Tourism Sectors are Worried" *Xinhuawang* (*Xinhuanet*) (14 October 2014), http://news.xinhuanet.com/gangao/2014-10/14/c_1112824706.htm.

On social media, such as the two most widely used – Sina Weibo (Chinese version of Twitter) and the "Wechat Moments" (微信朋友圈) – postings that documented what was happening at the sites of the OC Movement disappeared almost as quickly as they appeared (this also applied to any pro-OC Movement postings). The authorities even applied a technical measure to block postings by overseas Wechat users in the later stages of the OC Movement: Wechat users in the Mainland were blocked from getting access to the postings on "Wechat Moments" of their overseas friends, but this did not deter overseas users from uploading or reading postings on any other Wechat account.[25] According to the China Media Project, a search of "Hong Kong" on Weibo during the protests returned "mostly entertainment, finance and tourism related results, with odd scattered results including mention of the protests".[26]

Major findings of the survey

General attitudes: Large gap between Weiquan sector and ordinary Mainlanders

The statistical results echo the impression that Chinese Mainlanders, in general, are inclined to hold negative attitudes towards the OC Movement, in which an average of 53.7% (n=246) of Mainland Chinese and Overseas Mainlander respondents are opposed or strongly opposed to the OC Movement. Unsurprisingly, this is in sharp contrast with the attitude of the *Weiquan* sector, as only two respondents were opposed to the OC Movement and 85% (n=17) supported the cause (including 50% with strong support). In contrast, only 11.8% (n=38) of Mainland Chinese and 19.3% (n=46) of the Overseas Mainlanders have a positive attitude towards the OC Movement (see Table 10.2 and Figure 10.4).

As for the Sunflower Movement, all of the respondents in the three categories demonstrated even less knowledge or concern of that movement, compared to the OC Movement. As many as 77.1% (n=249) of the Mainland Chinese and nearly 66.7% (n=90) of the Overseas Mainlanders displayed indifference or had no idea about the Sunflower Movement, while only 25% (n=5) of the respondents from the *Weiquan* sector displayed indifference about the movement. Nevertheless, the pattern as regards support/opposition is largely similar to that of the OC Movement. In terms of the Mainland Chinese and Overseas Mainlanders, those with a negative attitude (15.8% (n=51) and 18.5% (n=25), respectively) still somewhat outnumbered the supporters. Only one respondent from the *Weiquan* sector was opposed to the Sunflower Movement. A majority (70%) of the respondents from the *Weiquan* Sector tended to support the Sunflower Movement, but this is true for only 7.1% (n=23) of Mainland Chinese and 14.9% (n=20) of Overseas Mainlanders (See Figure 10.5 and Table 10.3).

25 Based on my personal experience and confirmation with other mainlanders living in Hong Kong. This measure is also mentioned in an online article that details how posts on Weixin are censored, see Qing Zijin, "Test: How Weixin Contents are Censored" (4 February 2015), https://pao-pao.net/article/357.

26 David Bandurski, "China's Selective Silence on Hong Kong" *China Media Project* (29 September 2014), http://cmp.hku.hk/2014/09/29/36250/.

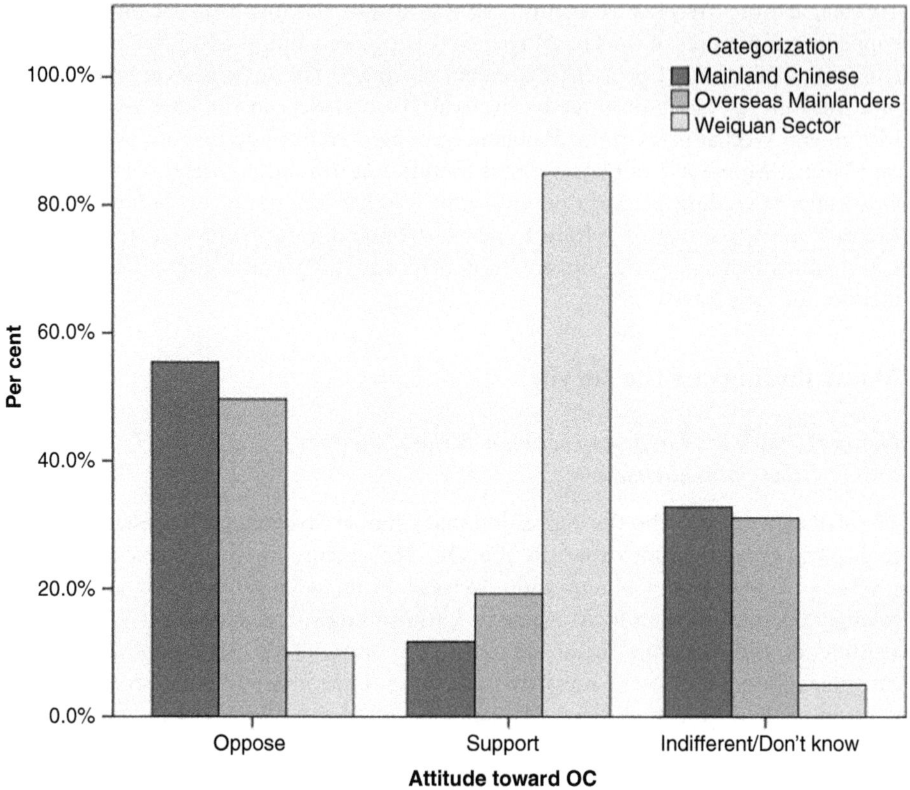

Figure 10.4 Respondents' general opinion of OC Movement (n=478)

Table 10.2 Mainlanders' general attitudes towards the OC Movement

Category	*Strongly support*	*Somewhat support*	*Indifferent/ Don't know*	*Somewhat oppose*	*Strongly oppose*
1. Mainland Chinese	**11.8%**		**32.8%**	**55.4%**	
	1.5%	10.3%		34.7%	20.7%
2. Overseas Mainlanders	**19.3%**		**31%**	**49.7%**	
	3.0%	16.3%		37.8%	11.9%
3. *Weiquan* Sector	**85%**		**5%**	**10%**	
	50%	35%		10%	0

No significant correlation between "overseas locality" and attitude towards the OC Movement

The survey showed that there was no significant difference between the attitudes of Mainland Chinese and Overseas Mainlanders ($P > 0.05$). However, there was a mild correlation between "overseas locality" and attitude towards the Sunflower Movement ($P < 0.05$). A possible reason for the difference might be that most of the Overseas Mainland Chinese living in Hong Kong directly felt the negative effects of the OC

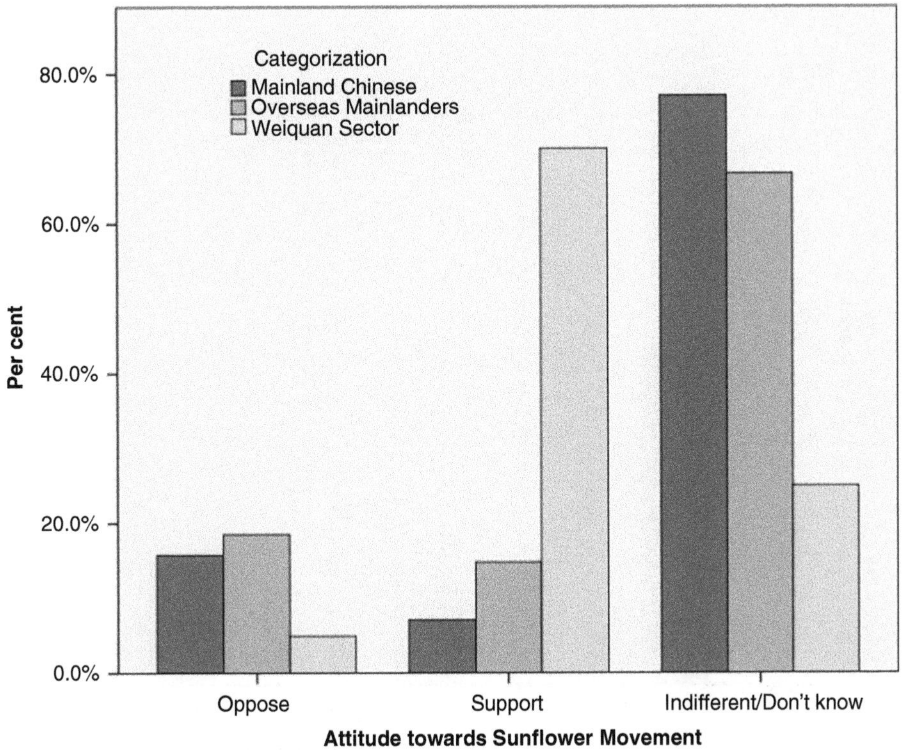

Figure 10.5 General opinion of respondents about Sunflower Movement (n= 478)

Table 10.3 Mainlanders' general attitudes towards the Sunflower Movement

<table>
<tr><th>Category</th><th>Strongly support</th><th>Support</th><th>Indifferent/ Don't know</th><th>Oppose</th><th>Strongly oppose</th></tr>
<tr><td>1. Mainland Chinese</td><td colspan="2">7.1%</td><td>77.1%</td><td colspan="2">15.8%</td></tr>
<tr><td></td><td>0</td><td>7.1%</td><td></td><td>12.4%</td><td>3.4%</td></tr>
<tr><td>2. Overseas Mainlanders</td><td colspan="2">14.9%</td><td>66.6 %</td><td colspan="2">18.5%</td></tr>
<tr><td></td><td>3.0%</td><td>11.9%</td><td></td><td>14.8%</td><td>3.7%</td></tr>
<tr><td>3. Weiquan Sector</td><td colspan="2">70%</td><td>25%</td><td colspan="2">5%</td></tr>
<tr><td></td><td>30%</td><td>40%</td><td></td><td>5%</td><td>0</td></tr>
</table>

Movement, and were thus more inclined to oppose it, all the while supporting the Sunflower Movement of which they did not feel any direct effects.

In addition to the insignificant difference between the attitudes of Mainland Chinese and Overseas Mainlanders towards the OC Movement, another indicator of the influence of locality is the significant correlation between the localities and whether the respondents thought that the OC Movement was influenced by "foreign forces" ($p=0.001$). Significantly fewer Overseas Mainlanders (39.3%, $n=53$) accepted that there were "foreign forces" behind the OC Movement, compared to the beliefs of Mainland Chinese (55.1%, $n=178$) (see Figure 10.6).

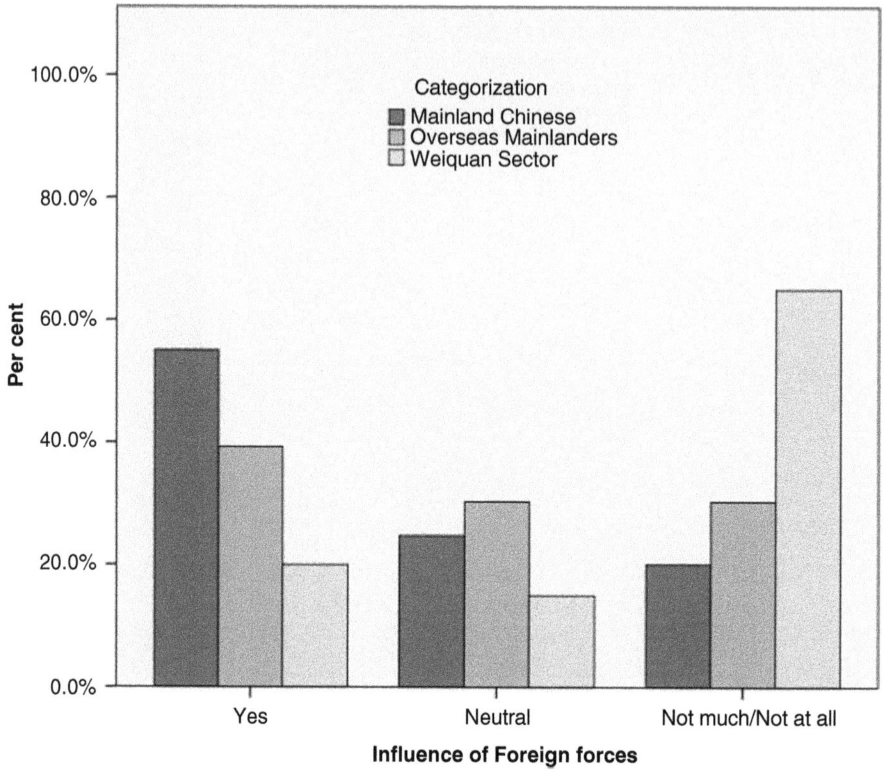

Figure 10.6 (Q10) Do you think that OC was influenced by "foreign forces"?

To some extent this contrast indicates that the depiction of the influence of foreign forces on the OC Movement by state media had an effective impact in shaping the views of Mainland Chinese. The survey data also demonstrates that the Hong Kong media was the primary source of information for Overseas Mainlanders, who relied much less on the official mass media of Mainland China (only 14.8%, n=20). In contrast, official news reports were the primary source for Mainland Chinese respondents when accessing Hong Kong news. The media sources of the *Weiquan* sector also presented a striking contrast with Mainland Chinese, as their primary media source for overseas information was obtained by "climbing over the wall", i.e. using private virtual networks/proxy servers to access the Internet (see Table 10.4).

Significant correlation between media sources and attitudes towards the OC Movement

Compared to the localities, there was a significant correlation between media sources and respondents' attitudes towards the OC Movement (see Tables 10.5 and 10.6).

1. *Different media sources of Mainland Chinese respondents (Category 1)*
   If media sources are categorized into three different groups, such as: 1) official news, 2) overseas information sources, and 3) social media, then supporters and

Table 10.4 Top three media or information sources for respondents

Category 1: Mainland Chinese (n=323)		
1. Social media	53.6%	
2. News websites*	50.8%	(Official news*** 85.5%)
3. Official mass media**	34.7%	
Category 2: Overseas Mainlanders (n=135)		
1. Hong Kong media	64.4%	
2. Social media	54.1%	
3. News websites	28.1%	
Category 3: Weiquan *Sector (n=20)*		
1. "Climb over the wall" for overseas news	65%	
2. Social media	55%	
3. Hong Kong media	40%	

* "News websites" refers to major Internet and commercial media, such as Sohu.com, Sina.com, and Tencent.com (see Question 19, Appendix Questionnaire), which are strictly monitored by the state.

** "Official mass media" refers to state-controlled mainstream media, such as *The People's Daily*, China Central Television (CCTV), *Global Times*, and local newspapers (see Question 19, Appendix Questionnaire).

*** As mentioned, regarding the matter of Occupy Central, China's news websites almost exclusively cited news releases from official sources; therefore, both news websites and the official mass media are classified as "official news" here.

opponents of the OC Movement in Mainland China relied on different resources for obtaining Hong Kong news (see Table 10.6). Overseas information sources were the primary media source of Mainland Chinese respondents who held a more sympathetic view towards the OC Movement. In contrast, "official news", which consists of news from the official PRC mass media and news websites, constituted the most important information source, along with social media, for Mainland Chinese respondents opposed to the OC Movement (see Table 10.5).

There was also a large gap between the use of "climbing over the wall" software to gain overseas information between supporters and opponents of the OC Movement in Mainland China, as only 7.7% (n=19) of those opposed to the OC Movement did this for information, in contrast to the 50% (n=32) who supported the OC Movement (see Table 10.5).

2. *Media sources of Overseas Mainlanders (Category 2)*
   Table 10.7 shows that the major sources of obtaining HK information for Mainland Chinese and Overseas Mainlanders are significantly different, as over half of the latter relied on the Hong Kong media as their primary source, while most of former relied on news sources from within Mainland China.

Table 10.5 Primary sources of HK information: Supporters vs. Opponents in Mainland China

(Q19: Please choose the three major media sources that you use to obtain Hong Kong news.)

Respondents	*Official news*		*Overseas information sources*			*Social media*
	Official mass media	*News websites*	*Circumvent firewall*	*Friends in HK*	*HK media*	
Supporters (n = 38)	15.8%	21.1%	55.3%	21.1%	26.3%	68.4%
Opponents (n = 179)	39.1%	62.6%	6.1%	16.8%	14.5%	56.4%

Table 10.6 Chi-square correlations between media source and attitude towards the OC Movement (excluding *Weiquan* Sector) (n=458)

	Attitude towards the OC movement					
	Strongly oppose	*Oppose*	*Indiffer-ent*	*Support*	*Strongly support*	*Don't know*
Official mass media	48.2%	27%	27.9%	12.7%	0	27%
News websites	50.6%	57.7%	36.9%	18.2%	0	40.5%
Social media	45.8%	61.3%	53.2%	58.2%	77.8%	27%
Hong Kong media	28.9%	27.6%	30.6%	47.3%	44.4%	5.4%
"Climb over the wall"	8.4%	7.4%	12.6%	52.7%	33.3%	2.7%
Pearson chi-square tests						

		Attitude towards the OC Movement
Media	**Chi-square**	166.452
	df	25
	Sig.	0.000

Table 10.7 Different media sources of Mainland Chinese and Overseas Mainlanders

Media	*Locality*	
	Overseas Mainlanders	*Mainland Chinese*
Official media	14.8%	34.7%
News websites	28.1%	50.8%
Social media	54.1%	53.6%
HK media	64.4%	14.9%
"Climb over the wall"	17.8%	13.0%
Information from friends in HK	25.2%	17.3%

Pearson chi-square tests

		Locality
Media	**Chi-square**	148.021
	df	5
	Sig.	0.000

Among Overseas Mainlanders, there was also a significant correlation between media sources and attitude, as the 76.9% (n=20) who supported the OC Movement used the Hong Kong media as their primary source of information, in contrast to the 64.2% (n=43) who were opposed to the OC Movement. In terms of the latter, the official news sources in Mainland China remained one of their primary sources even if they were residing outside of China, while only 3.8% (n=1) of the Overseas Mainlanders who supported the OC Movement used the official mass media for information. In general, including other resources such as "climbing over the wall"[27] and news from Hong Kong friends, overseas news was the dominant information source for Overseas Mainlanders who supported the OC Movement, along with social media (50.0%, n=13). In contrast, their reliance on official news from Mainland China was almost negligible. However, Overseas Mainlanders who

27 Overseas mainlanders might also use a VPN to climb over the firewall when they return to Mainland China.

opposed the OC Movement relied almost the same on the three major sources for news on Hong Kong: official news from Mainland China (56.7%, n=38), Hong Kong media sources (64.2%, n=43), and social media (55.2%, n=37).

Further analysing the spectrum of Hong Kong media that Mainlanders accessed demonstrated no salient correlation between Hong Kong media and attitudes towards the OC Movement (p=>0.05). Nevertheless, few Mainlanders, even those opposed to the OC Movement, read the pro-establishment newspapers, such as the Takungpao (大公报) and Wenweipo (文汇报). In the neutral or liberal zone, such as the *South China Morning Post* (SCMP) and *Apple Daily* newspapers, the number of supporters was slightly higher than those who were opposed to the OC Movement (see Figure 10.7).

It is worth noting that both Mainland Chinese and Overseas Mainlanders who either supported or opposed the OC Movement strongly relied on social media for information, which explains why the Chinese government has further increased their control over these

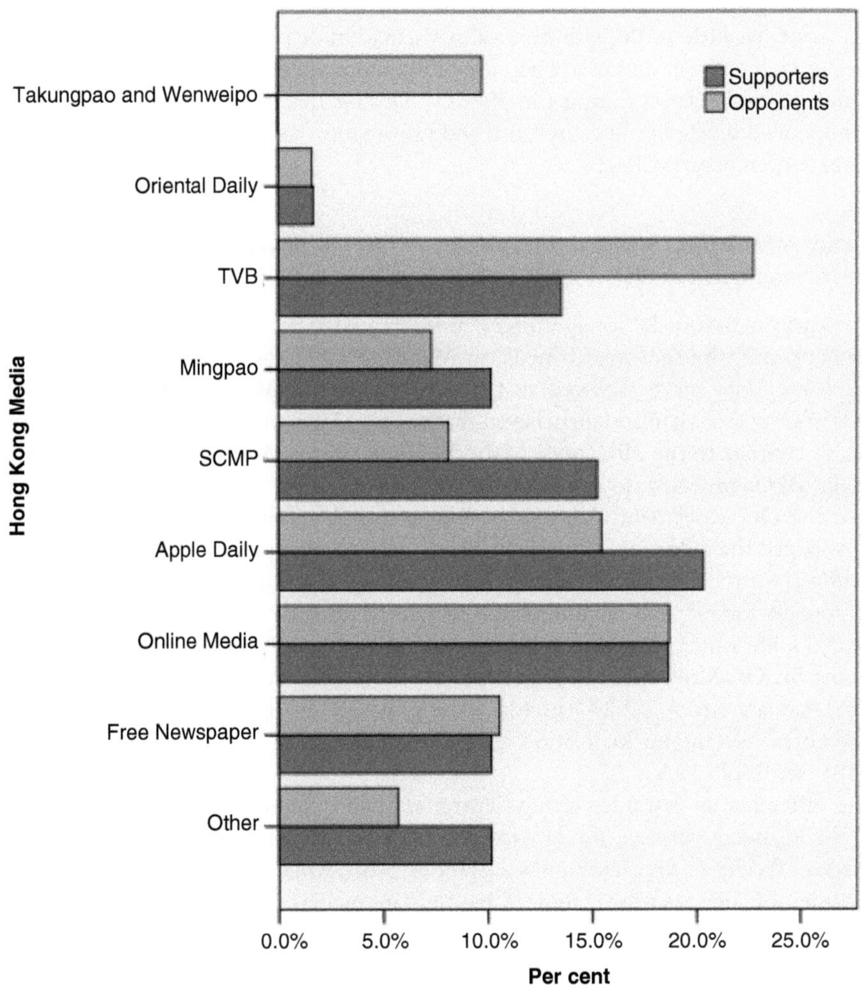

Figure 10.7 Hong Kong media sources frequently accessed by Mainlanders (Q20: Which Hong Kong media source do you most frequently access?)

Table 10.8 Influence by foreign forces (n=478)

(Q10: Do you think that Occupy Central was influenced by "foreign forces"?)					
	Very much	*Somewhat*	*Neutral*	*Not much*	*Not at all*
1. Mainland Chinese	**55.1%**		**24.7%**	**20.2%**	
	22.9%	32.2%		14.6%	5.6%
2. Overseas Mainlanders	**39.3%**		**30.4%**	**30.3%**	
	8.9%	30.4%		20.7%	9.6%
3. *Weiquan* Sector	**20%**		**15%**	**65%**	
	10%	10%		30%	35%

channels in recent years, particularly when high-profile events, such as the OC Movement, take place.

The findings contrast with a statement made by Andrew Nathan in the mid-1980s that media usage has little to do with political participation or political competence. It may be partly due to his sample and partly because of the more open public discussion over democracy and political reform during the 1980s.[28] During that period, even the official print media openly discussed political reform, and information sources were not as diversified as those of contemporary China.

Negative correlations between perceptions of "foreign forces" and attitudes towards OC

As previously mentioned, "foreign forces" were framed as the villain in interpreting the OC Movement, both by the official media in Mainland China as well as the leftist media in Hong Kong. The survey showed that 55.1% (n=178) of Mainland Chinese and 39.3% (n=53) of Overseas Mainlanders believed that the OC Movement was influenced by foreign forces, in contrast to the 20% (n=4) of the *Weiquan* sector. More importantly, respondents from the *Weiquan* sector do not necessarily consider foreign forces as a negative reason to oppose the OC Movement. Among the four respondents from the *Weiquan* sector who acknowledged the influence of "foreign forces", none were opposed to the OC Movement. In contrast, for the other respondents there was a significant correlation between agreeing that "foreign forces" had an influence and overall attitude towards the OC Movement ($p = 0.001$). For other participants, however, "foreign forces" were an important reason for opposing the OC Movement. Among the Overseas Mainlanders who believed that "foreign forces" had an effect, 79.2% (n=42) were opposed or strongly opposed to the OC Movement, while among Mainland Chinese, the percentage was almost the same (78.6%, n = 140) (see Table 10.9).

The difference in attitudes vividly illustrates how differently the *Weiquan* sector and other Mainlanders perceive foreign factors. "Foreign forces" to the former might be a comrade or facilitator for causes and social movements, while for the latter, "foreign forces" are hostile to China (as propagandized by the state media).

28 Andrew J. Nathan, *Chinese Democracy* (Berkeley: University of California Press, 1985), pp. 251–253.

Table 10.9 Attitude of respondents who acknowledged influence of "foreign forces" towards OC Movement (n=478)

<table>
<tr><th></th><th>Strongly support</th><th>Support</th><th>Indifferent/ Don't know</th><th>Oppose</th><th>Strongly oppose</th></tr>
<tr><td rowspan="2">1. Mainland Chinese</td><td colspan="2">1.7%</td><td rowspan="2">19.7%</td><td colspan="2">78.6%</td></tr>
<tr><td>0</td><td>1.7%</td><td>44.9%</td><td>33.7%</td></tr>
<tr><td rowspan="2">2. Overseas Mainlanders</td><td colspan="2">1.9%</td><td rowspan="2">18.9%</td><td colspan="2">79.2%</td></tr>
<tr><td>0</td><td>1.9%</td><td>50.9%</td><td>28.3%</td></tr>
<tr><td rowspan="2">3. Weiquan Sector</td><td colspan="2">75%</td><td rowspan="2">25%</td><td colspan="2">0</td></tr>
<tr><td>25%</td><td>50%</td><td>0</td><td>0</td></tr>
</table>

A complicated picture: Consciousness of democracy versus rule of law

This survey demonstrated an interesting but complicated phenomenon: the consciousness of democracy and the rule of law of Chinese in Mainland China.

(1) Most Mainlanders in general do not reject but are instead pragmatic about democracy, and in particular they are practical about the pro-democracy movements, which is consistent with previous findings.[29] Rather than viewing democracy as an independent and desirable political ideal, most are more concerned with the ineffectiveness or impact that might be brought about by democracy and democratic movements.

First, for most ordinary Mainlanders, democracy itself can hardly stand alone as a desirable ideology which deserves to be pursued. These citizens also project their own thoughts onto Hong Kong locals: only a small proportion of Mainlanders (most of whom support the OC Movement) believe that the OC Movement was caused by the desire of Hong Kong citizens for democracy, while most of them believe that current social and economic problems in Hong Kong were the primary reasons. This contrasts with findings on the motivations of Hong Kong locals who participated in the OC Movement. Empirical studies show that the demand for democracy was the primary reason for 87% of Hong Kong participants who took part in the OC Movement, while the other two major reasons were government apathy towards the demands of the protesters and the way that the police handled the event.[30] Economic improvement is not given as an important reason for participating in the OC Movement.[31]

Second, the survey found that few Mainland Chinese and Overseas Mainlanders are opposed to the OC Movement because they think that Hong Kong should not adopt a "Western-style democracy" (10.1% (n=18) Mainland Chinese, and 9.5% (n=4) Overseas Mainlanders). The three highest-ranked reasons for opposing the OC Movement were mainly concerned with practical social and economic issues, including: the negative effect on social-economic development in Hong Kong (68.3%, n=168), deepening divisions

29 E.g. Che-po Chan, "The Political Pragmatism of Chinese University Students" in Suisheng Zhao (ed.) *China and Democracy: Reconsidering the Prospects for a Democratic China* (Routledge, 2014), p. 223; Andrew J. Nathan, "The Puzzle of the Chinese Middle Class" (2016) 2 *Journal of Democracy* 15; Pan and Xu (n. 10 above).

30 Yuen and Cheng (n. 1 above).

31 Ibid.

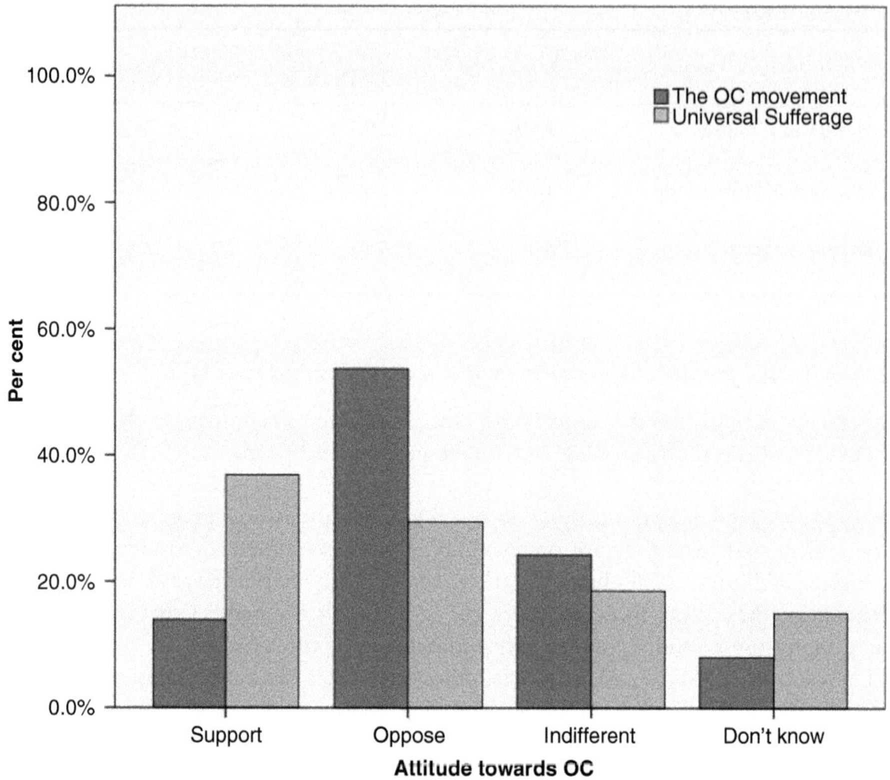

Figure 10.8 Comparison between attitudes towards the OC Movement and the agenda of universal suffrage (excluding *Weiquan* sector)

within society (62.6%, n=154), and the overly radical strategy of Occupying Central (58.5%, n=144).

Third, individuals who were opposed to the OC Movement did not necessarily oppose its agenda of universal suffrage. While 53.7% (n=246) of Mainland Chinese and Overseas Mainlanders were opposed to the OC Movement, only 29.5% (n=135) were opposed to its agenda of universal suffrage (see Figure 10.8). To some extent, this finding echoes a survey by Lianjiang Li, which showed that over 85% of the respondents agreed that, in principle,

Table 10.10 Attitudes towards the OC Movement and the agenda of universal suffrage (excluding *Weiquan* sector)

	The OC Movement	*The agenda of the OC: Universal suffrage*
Support (incl. strongly support)	14%	36.9%
Oppose (incl. strongly oppose)	53.7%	29.5%
Indifferent	24.2%	18.6%
Don't know	8.1%	15%

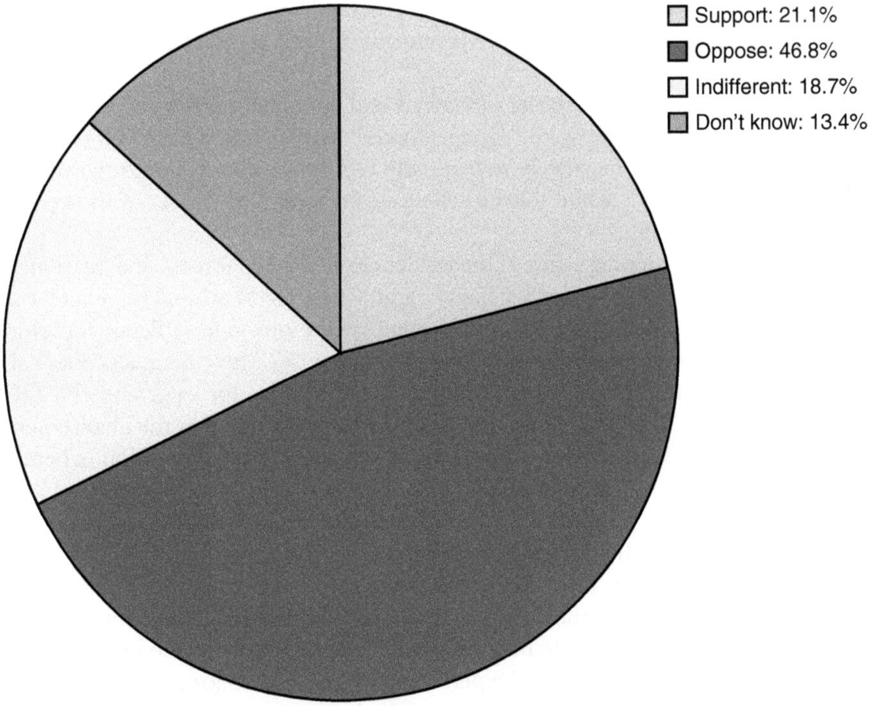

Figure 10.9 Attitude of OC opponents towards universal suffrage (Mainland Chinese and Overseas Mainlanders)

the township head should be popularly elected, and over 65% of the respondents agreed that the state chairman should be elected through ordinary democratic voting.[32]

A large proportion of the respondents were opposed to the OC Movement because they disagreed with its radical actions, as opposed to its agenda. As Figure 10.9 shows, among the opponents of the OC Movement, less than half were opposed to universal suffrage, and 21.1% (n=52) even gave their approval. If respondents who were indifferent to universal suffrage or did not know what universal suffrage meant are excluded, the percentage who gave their approval is as high as 55.6%. Among those who were opposed to the OC Movement but agreed with universal suffrage, the highest-ranking reason for their opposition was the radical actions of the OC Movement (67.3%, n=35). Only seven of them were opposed to the OC Movement for the reasons that Hong Kong should not implement a Western-style democracy (n=2) or that Hong Kong has enjoyed more democracy compared to its colonial period (n=5).

(2) There was a significant negative correlation between nationalism and attitude towards democracy and pro-democratic movements.

32 Lianjiang Li, "Right Consciousness and Rules Consciousness in contemporary China" (2010) 64 *The China Journal* 47, 59.

As the analysis above indicated, there was a negative correlation between whether a respondent accepted "foreign forces" as the culprit behind the OC Movement and the attitude of a respondent towards the OC Movement, as well as his/her perception of democracy.

There was a significant gap between the supporters and opponents of the OC Movement on whether they agreed that there were "foreign forces" involved, in which 74% (n=182) of those Mainlanders who felt negatively towards the OC Movement believed that it was influenced by "foreign forces", while this was the case for only 6.3% (n=4) of those who supported the OC Movement.

There was also a gap in the acceptance of the influence of "foreign forces" and "nationalism sentiment" between the Mainland Chinese and Overseas Mainlanders. While the majority of the former indicated that the involvement of the pro-independence forces in Hong Kong and foreign forces were reasons for opposing the OC Movement, less than half of the latter indicated these two factors as the primary reasons for opposing the OC Movement; and only 35.8% (n=24) of Overseas Mainlanders indicated that the involvement of the pro-independence forces in Hong Kong was a reason for their opposition, whereas this was a factor for 50.3% (n=90) of Mainland Chinese respondents (see Table 10.11).

(3) The rule of law is more valued than democracy, and while the ideal of democracy might be valued, pro-democratic movements are not.

Compared to the democratic movement, the respondents in general demonstrated a more supportive attitude towards the rule of law, as indicated by their different attitudes towards the OC Movement and the Lee Bo incident.[33] If the respondents who did not know about the Lee Bo incident are excluded, the percentage who were opposed to the arrest of Lee Bo is as high as 58.6% (n=143). Violation of the law and the "One Country, Two Systems" policy were the highest-ranking reasons for opposing the arrest of the five booksellers, although the official media has also portrayed the Lee Bo incident to involve "foreign forces".[34] Even among those who were opposed to the OC Movement, 41.2% (n=49) were still opposed to the arrest of Lee Bo (not including those who were indifferent or did not know about the Lee Bo incident). Among the respondents who supported the arrest of Lee Bo, only 8.1% (n=5) believed that there was involvement of foreign forces, and 40.3% (n=25) felt that Mainland Chinese authorities handled the case according to the law.

As discussed above, the survey demonstrated that even those opposed to the OC Movement did not necessarily reject the idea of true democratic elections. Forty-six of the respondents were opposed to the OC Movement but agreed on its agenda of universal suffrage, and their primary reasons for opposing the movement were social and economic concerns, rather than anti-democratic concerns. This demonstrates that, like many Hong

33 Five staff of a Causeway bookstore in Hong Kong were reportedly "forced to disappear" in early 2016 for planning to publish a book on President Xi Jinping's private life. They were later found to be detained in Mainland China since October 2015. One bookseller named Lee Bo was last seen in Hong Kong and later found to have crossed the Chinese border without travel documents. Lee's disappearance and the detention of the five booksellers caused widespread concern that the Chinese authorities had violated the Basic Law and infringed upon the basic rights of Hong Kong citizens. See "Timeline: Hong Kong's Missing Bookseller and What We Know So Far" *South China Morning Post* (1 March 2016), http://www.scmp.com/news/hong-kong/law-crime/article/1903405/timeline-hong-kongs-missing-booksellers-and-what-we-know-so.

34 *Global Times*, "A Few Hongkongers should not Cast Cloud over 'One Country, Two Systems'" (n. 7 above).

Table 10.11 Primary reasons for opposing the OC Movement

Mainland Chinese rank	*Reason*	*Overseas Chinese rank*
1st **65.9%**	Impairs economic and social development in HK	2nd **74.6%**
2nd **59.8%**	The strategy of Occupy Central is too radical	3rd **55.2%**
3rd **57.5%**	Deepens social division	1st **76.1%**
4th **52.0%**	Intervention of "foreign forces"	4th **55.2%**
5th **50.3%**	Involvement of pro-independence forces in HK	5th **35.8%**
6th **16.8%**	HK already enjoys enough democracy and freedom compared to its colonial period	6th **9%**
7th **10.1%**	No need to implement Western democratic election	7th **7.5%**
8th **2.2%**	Other	8th **3%**

Kong locals, a substantial proportion of Mainland Chinese were opposed to the strategies utilized by the OC Movement, instead of its agenda for democracy.[35]

Conclusion: Generalization of findings and implications

Gap between Mainland Chinese and Overseas Mainlanders

There are often discussions about the phenomenon in which overseas young Chinese elites return to China only to hold nationalistic and negative attitudes towards liberal democracies.[36] This survey demonstrates that overseas experience has a certain degree of correlation with attitudes towards democracy and democratic movements, although the impact did not reach statistical significance. Nevertheless, Overseas Mainland Chinese in this study were less influenced by the framing of "foreign forces" by Chinese state propaganda outlets, a finding which was largely attributed to the local media and information overseas that they were able to access. However, there was almost no difference between the Overseas Mainlanders who still strongly relied on official news sources from the Mainland, with their counterparts living in Mainland China. This finding indirectly demonstrates the effect of state propaganda controlled by Chinese authorities.

35 According to a public opinion poll conducted by the Public Opinion Programme of the University of Hong Kong in April 2013, 35% Hong Kong respondents opposed the electoral reform proposal backed by Beijing, while only 25% supported the OC Movement. The result of the poll is available at https://www.hkupop.hku.hk/english/report/mpCEnOCC/index.html.

36 See Rowena Xiaoqing He, "Identifying with a 'Rising China'? Overseas Chinese Student Nationalism" in Edward Vickers and Krishna Kumar (eds), *Constructing Modern Asian Citizenship* (New York: Routledge, 2014), pp. 314–340.

Effectiveness of state propaganda on shaping public consciousness in Mainland China

State propaganda has been effective in shaping the opinions of Chinese citizens towards high-profile events, including public consciousness as regards social movements and democracy. The use of "foreign forces" and "nationalism sentiments" to frame these events as constructed by the official media has been successful, particularly within Mainland China. The state-led nationalism frame in the case of the OC Movement, as well as the Sunflower Movement, fits with what Comaroff and Stern described as the "outward-directed sentiments that heap hostility upon others",[37] and such outward-directed nationalism has had an obvious negative correlation with Chinese people's opinions on pro-democracy campaigning in Hong Kong.

Nevertheless, the survey also demonstrates good possibilities that access to different information sources may change individual opinions and help counteract state propaganda. However, the slight difference in the attitudes between Mainland Chinese and Overseas Mainlanders, and the salient differences between the respondents who have access to different information sources, demonstrate that it is not the locality that is crucial, but whether initiative is taken to obtain information on those matters. As a Chinese intellectual Zhou Lian pointed out,

> Except for the two different kinds of futures predicted by Orwell and Huxley, there might be a third possibility that: on the one hand people are forbidden to read while on the other hand they automatically stop reading anymore; on the one hand they are deprived of obtaining information, on the other hand they are flooded by the sea of garbage information; on the one hand the truth is concealed while on the other hand the truth is being submerged ...[38]

Positive and negative sides of Chinese consciousness towards democracy and the rule of law

The survey accentuates the dichotomy between the consciousness of democracy and the rule of law. On the positive side, few Chinese are opposed to the idea of democracy. Many respondents opposed to the OC Movement did not oppose universal suffrage, and few believed that Hong Kong should not implement a "Western-style democracy". Most of the respondents were opposed to the OC Movement because they felt that it had negative social and economic repercussions.

Moreover, a relatively high rate of opposition to the Lee Bo incident demonstrates that Chinese citizens place high value on the rule of law. It appears here that nationalism is much less effective in impacting views regarding the rule of law. Nevertheless, the negative correlation between attitudes towards the rule of law and democracy casts doubt over what Pei Minxin states: that rights consciousness has become a crucial driver of "democratic resistance".[39] It seems that for most ordinary Chinese citizens, there is no connection between democracy and a guarantee of the rule of law and individual rights.

37 John L. Comaroff and Paul Stern, "New Perspectives on Nationalism and War" in John L. Comaroff and Paul C. Stern (eds) *Perspectives on Nationalism and War* (Amsterdam: Gordon and Breach, 1995), p. 4.

38 Zhou Lian, *Zhengyi de Keneng* (*Possibility of Justice*) (Beijing: Zhongguo Wenshi chubanshe, 2015), p. 22.

39 Pei Minxin, "Rights and Resistance: the Changing Context of the Dissident Movement" in Elizabeth Perry and Mark Selden (eds), *Chinese Society: Change, Conflict and Resistance* (New York: Routledge, 2010), pp. 32–56.

For those who are keen to see a democratic transition for China, the findings of this research also provide a gloomy side to the public consciousness of democracy and political movements. The survey demonstrates that the views of democracy for Chinese people remain quite pragmatic and utilitarian. For the large number of Mainlander respondents in this study, the value of democracy is weighed against other values and elements, such as social welfare and economic development.

This study accentuates that besides nationalism, pragmatism is another important factor that negatively correlates with Chinese citizens' opinions of democratic movements and democracy. Social and economic stability and development are the principal standards for ordinary Chinese citizens in evaluating democratic movements and democracy, even though some of them approve of democratic arrangements, such as universal suffrage. To a certain extent, the findings echo Havel's argument that the post-totalitarian system is built on "foundations laid by the historical encounter between dictatorship and the consumer society".[40] The willingness of ordinary Chinese citizens to surrender higher values when faced with material certainties also probably contributed to the adaptability of the authoritarian system in China.[41]

Implications for the Weiquan sector and civil societies in Hong Kong and Taiwan

With regard to the consciousness of democracy and the rule of law, the gap between the consciousness of the *Weiquan* sector and ordinary Chinese citizens was, unsurprisingly, strikingly large. The ordinary Chinese middle-class people might be called "realists",[42] while the members of *Weiquan* sector are probably the rare but active idealists in Chinese society. Under nationalism sentiments, the tension between Mainland Chinese and Hong Kong societies has intensified during and after the OC Movement.[43] In contrast, the *Weiquan* sector, along with a small proportion of ordinary citizens, share the same pro-democracy stance as the participants in the OC Movement. The crackdown on China's *Weiquan* sector before and after the OC Movement has further driven *Weiquan* activists to the social movement sector (SMS) in Hong Kong and Taiwan. Since they are facing the same "common authoritarian enemy", the SMS and rights activism groups in the three regions have increasingly interacted with each other.[44]

In the face of increasing aggressiveness from the Chinese party-state, the coalitions among civil societies in the three regions are important forces for resisting the influence and infiltration of authoritarianism in the three regions. As Andrew Nathan pointed out, there has been an increasingly negative impact of China's authoritarianism on global

40 See Vaclav Havel, "The Power of the Powerless" in Vaclav Havel *et al.* (eds), *The Power of the Powerless: Citizens against the State in Central-Eastern Europe* (New York: Sharpe, 1985), p. 38.

41 Generally see Nathan (n. 29 above).

42 Ibid., p. 15.

43 See Lily Kuo, "The Uglier Side of Hong Kong's Umbrella Movement Pits Chinese against Chinese" *Quartz* (3 November 2014), http://qz.com/290228/the-uglier-side-of-hong-kongs-umbrella-movement-pits-chinese-against-chinese/; also see Public Opinion Programme of the University of Hong Kong, "HKU POP Release Latest Survey on Hong Kong People's Ethnic Identity" (22 December 2014), https://www.hkupop.hku.hk/english/release/release1211.html.

44 See Hung Ho-fung and Iam-chong Ip, "Hong Kong's Democratic Movement and the Making of China's Offshore Civil Society" (2012) 3 *Asian Survey* 504.

democratization,[45] so it is unsurprising that Hong Kong and Taiwan, two neighbours of Mainland China, feel the most direct influence of its power. The rights advocacy sector of the civil society, regardless whether it is in Mainland China or Hong Kong or Taiwan, comprises the crucial players for resisting the expansion of authoritarian power.[46]

However, the mobilization of a wider sector of civil society in Mainland China has long been a vital but difficult issue for activists. This is now also a problem for the civil societies in Hong Kong and Taiwan which needs to be taken into consideration when discussing the promotion of democracy in the two regions, and which is inevitably associated with the development of law and democracy in Mainland China. Improving democratic consciousness and counteracting state propaganda are still challenging tasks for the *Weiquan* sector in contemporary China. In fact, this study shows that the prospect of mobilizing support for legal development seems to be more promising in current Chinese society.

It is hoped that this study helps to enrich current understanding regarding the public consciousness of democracy and the rule of law in contemporary China. More importantly, this study may also evoke discussions on the development of democracy in Hong Kong and Taiwan into a larger context that incorporates ordinary Chinese citizens and the *Weiquan* sector in Chinese civil society. Ultimately, the public consciousness of democracy and law is vital to the trajectory of democracy and rule of law in Mainland China, which inevitably influences events in Hong Kong and Taiwan. After all, "nothing is stronger than an idea whose time has come".[47]

45 Andrew J. Nathan, "China's Challenge" (2015) 1 *Journal of Democracy* 156–70.

46 As Jiunn-rong Yeh also pointed out, the primary underlying issue of the Sunflower Movement was the increased engagement across the Taiwan Strait, and that "the transformation to civic constitutionalism in the light of Taiwan's Sunflower Movement bears tremendous significance ... to China and Hong Kong". See "Marching towards Civic Constitutionalism with Sunflowers" (2015) 45 *Hong Kong Law Journal* 315, 329.

47 An oft-quoted saying paraphrased from "[a]n invasion of armies can be resisted; an invasion of ideas cannot be resisted". Victor Hugo, *History of a Crime: The Testimony of an Eye-Witness* (translated by T. H. Joyce and Arthur Locker, New York: Mondial, 2005), pp. 408–409.

Appendix Questionnaire (Originally supplied in Chinese to all participants)

1. Do you know about the OC movement?

❑ Very well ❑ Somewhat ❑ Not much ❑ Not at all

2. Do you know about the universal suffrage and political reform in Hong Kong?

❑ Very well ❑ Somewhat ❑ Not much ❑ Not at all

3. Please choose the members of the "Occupy Central Trio" (choose 1 to 3 individuals):

❑ Jasper Tsang Yok-sing (曾鈺成)
❑ Leung Chun-ying (梁振英)
❑ Chan Kin Man (陈健民)
❑ Chu Yiu-ming (朱耀明)
❑ Leung Kwok-hung(梁国雄)
❑ Don't know
❑ Benny Tai Yiu-ting (戴耀廷)
❑ Eric Tat Ming Cheung (张达明)
❑ Joshua Wong (黄之锋)
❑ Raymond Wong Yuk-man (黄毓民)
❑ Jimmy Lai Chee-ying(黎智英)

4. Do you know about the white paper on Hong Kong issues released by the State Council in 2014?

❑ Very well ❑ Somewhat ❑ Not much ❑ Not at all

5. How do you feel about the OC movement?

❑ Strongly support (*please go to Q7*)
❑ Support (*please go to Q7*)
❑ Neutral (*please go to Q7*)
❑ Oppose (*please go to Q6*)
❑ Strongly oppose (*please go to Q6*)
❑ Don't know (*please go to Q7*)

6. Main reasons for opposing the Occupy Central movement:

❑ No need to implement Western-style democratic election
❑ Hong Kong already enjoys enough democracy and freedom compared to its colonial period
❑ Involvement of pro-independence forces in Hong Kong
❑ Impairs economic and social development in Hong Kong

- ❑ Deepens social division
- ❑ The strategy of Occupy Central is too radical
- ❑ Involvement of overseas forces
- ❑ Other

7. Do you agree with the demands of the Occupy Central movement, i.e. to implement genuine universal suffrage so that candidates from the establishment or the pan-democratic campaigns can run for elections?

❑ Strongly agree ❑ Agree ❑ Indifferent ❑ Oppose ❑ Strongly oppose
❑ Don't know

8. Do you agree that the Hong Kong police should have fired tear gas to disperse the Occupy Central participants?

❑ Strongly agree ❑ Agree ❑ Neutral ❑ Oppose ❑ Strongly oppose
❑ Don't know about the event

9. Do you agree that Occupy Central impairs the rule of law in Hong Kong?

❑ Strongly agree ❑ Agree ❑ Neutral ❑ Oppose ❑ Don't know

10. Do you think that Occupy Central was influenced by "foreign forces"?

❑ Very much ❑ Somewhat influenced ❑ Neutral ❑ Not much
❑ Not at all

11. What do you think are the reasons for the occurrence of the Occupy Central movement?

- ❑ Political ideals of Hong Kong locals in their pursuit for democracy and freedom
- ❑ Dysfunction of Hong Kong political system and governance
- ❑ Dissatisfaction of Hong Kong locals with economic and social development
- ❑ Dissatisfaction of Hong Kong locals about the increasingly reduced cultural/social/economic gap between Hong Kong and Mainland
- ❑ Influence by foreign forces
- ❑ Influence by pro-independence force in Hong Kong
- ❑ Influence by colonial culture
- ❑ Don't know
- ❑ Other

12. How many times have you been to the site of the Occupy Central movement?

❑ 0 ❑ 1–2 ❑ > 2 ❑ Refuse to answer

13. Do you know about the Sunflower Movement in Taiwan?

❑ Very much ❑ Somewhat ❑ Not much ❑ Not at all

14. Do you agree with the Sunflower Movement?

- ❑ Strongly agree (*please to to Q16*)
- ❑ Agree (*please go to Q16*)
- ❑ Indifferent (*please go to Q16*)
- ❑ Oppose (*please to to Q15*)
- ❑ Strongly oppose (*please go to Q15*)
- ❑ Don't know (*please go to Q16*)

15. Reasons for opposing the Sunflower Movement:

- ❑ Violates the Constitution and rule of law
- ❑ Influenced by pro-independence ideologies in Taiwan
- ❑ Unwise to oppose trade treaty
- ❑ Shouldn't occupy the Legislation Yuan and the Executive Yuan
- ❑ Don't know
- ❑ Other

16. Do you know about the "disappearance" of Hong Kong bookseller Lee Bo and others?

❑ Very well ❑ Somewhat ❑ Not much ❑ Not at all

17. Do you agree with the coercive measures that the authorities took towards Lee Bo and others?

❑ Strongly agree ❑ Agree ❑ Indifferent ❑ Oppose ❑ Strongly oppose
❑ Don't know

18. What is your opinion on the disappearance of Lee Bo and four other booksellers?

- ❑ Violates the rule of law principle
- ❑ Violates "One Country, Two Systems" principle
- ❑ Mainland authorities handled the case according to the law
- ❑ Lee Bo and others were punished for their own wrongdoings
- ❑ Involvement of foreign forces
- ❑ Don't know
- ❑ Other

19. Please choose the three major media sources that you used to obtain Hong Kong news:

- ❑ Official mass media in Mainland China (e.g. CCTV, Global Times, and local newspapers) (*please go to Q21*)
- ❑ News websites (e.g. Sina.com and Tecent.com) (*please go to Q21*)
- ❑ Social media (e.g. Weibo and Weixin) (*please go to Q21*)
- ❑ Hong Kong media (*please to to Q20*)
- ❑ Climb over the wall to gain access to overseas media (*please go to Q21*)
- ❑ Information from friends in Hong Kong (*please go to Q21*)
- ❑ Other (*please go to Q21*)

20. Which Hong Kong media source do you most frequently access? (Please select 1 to 3 responses):

- ❑ Mingpao
- ❑ Takungpao
- ❑ Apple Daily
- ❑ Wenweipo
- ❑ Oriental Daily
- ❑ TVB
- ❑ South China Morning Post
- ❑ Online media
- ❑ Free newspapers
- ❑ Other

21. Your gender:
22. Your age:
23. Your education:
24. Your monthly income:
25. Your place of residence:
26. Number of times that you have visited Hong Kong/length of period of stay in Hong Kong:
27. Your occupation in Hong Kong/Mainland China:

Part IV

Wider perspectives on the movements

11 Democratic political obligation with Chinese characteristics

Civic defiance in Taiwan and Hong Kong

Brad R. Roth[*]

Introduction

The above chapters illuminate a pair of signal moments in the history of Asian political development: the recourse, in Taiwan and Hong Kong, to distinctively liberal-democratic forms of civic defiance. Although operating in very different contexts, the Sunflower and Umbrella (or "Occupy Central") Movements, respectively, sought in similar fashion to reconcile disobedience to constituted authority with loyalty to the polity's constitutional premises. These efforts posed normative questions with which liberal-democratic theorists have long grappled. Although the subject matter of both controversies was specifically Chinese – in the sense of addressing the power and influence of the People's Republic of China (PRC) over the development of polities in its shadow – the protests posed normative questions common to liberal-democratic constitutional orders the world over. The chapters herein thus speak far less to traditional Chinese (or "Asian") values than to universal dilemmas of political obligation in the era of the modern state.

At the same time, both movements represent components of struggles for self-determination, not directly against "alien subjugation", but against policies perceived to undermine the capacity of the respective political communities to exercise their inalienable "right to determine their political status and to pursue their economic, social and cultural development".[1] This aspect is distinctive, in that while the protests were internal to local polities to which the demonstrators manifested ultimate loyalty, their civic defiance was directed against those very polities' perceived failures of resistance to the encroachment of an external power that claims sovereignty. The Sunflower Movement both anticipated and furthered the victory of political forces committed to Taiwan's self-assertion vis-à-vis the PRC. In contrast, the Umbrella Movement, situated in a polity more vulnerable to PRC retaliation, was a more perilous undertaking, both for its participants, and more tellingly, for the polity itself; perhaps inevitably, the movement's militancy outran the short-term political will of its constituents, necessitating retreat.

* Professor of Political Science and Law, Wayne State University. JD, Harvard University, 1987; LLM, Columbia University, 1992; University of California, Berkeley, 1996.

1 See, e.g. Common Article 1 of the 1966 Human Rights Covenants. *International Covenant on Civil and Political Rights* (opened for signature 19 December 1966), art. 1, 999 U.N.T.S. 171, 171[hereinafter ICCPR]; *International Covenant on Economic, Social and Cultural Rights*, (opened for signature 19 December 19, 1966), art. 1, 993 U.N.T.S. 3, 3 [hereinafter ICESCR]; Declaration on Principles of International Law Concerning Friendly Relations and Co-operation Among States in Accordance with the Charter of the United Nations (hereafter "Friendly Relations Declaration"), G.A. Res. 2625 (XXV) (1970).

The discussion below will set forth a normative-theoretical framework for assessing questions of political obligation and principled disobedience. It will then apply that framework to the issues raised in the various contributions to this volume.

Political obligation and civil disobedience

Governmental decisions provisionally resolve conflicts of moral judgement within political communities.[2] As Immanuel Kant noted:

> Even if we imagine men to be ever so good natured and righteous before a public lawful state of society is established, individual men, nations, and states can never be certain that they are secure against violence from one another, because each will have his own right to do what *seems just and good to him*, entirely independent of the opinion of the others.[3]

Thus, as John Rawls noted, "Up to a certain point it is better that the law and its interpretation be settled than that it be settled rightly."[4] A territorially-based political community solves this problem through the centralization of legislative, adjudicative, and executive authority, a centralization predicated on a notional commonality – however often illusory or imposed – of core interests and values within the political unit.

Contrary to what is often imagined, civil disobedience – unlike other forms of principled disobedience[5] – actually presupposes political obligation: a presumptive content-independent obligation to comply with a positive enactment bearing the status of valid law for one's own community.[6] It is for that reason that the Rev. Dr Martin Luther King posited such strict limitations on what counts as civil disobedience:

2 See generally Jeremy Waldron, *The Dignity of Legislation* (Cambridge University Press, 1999), at pp. 36–62; Jeremy Waldron, *Law and Disagreement* (Oxford: Clarendon Press, 1999), pp. 232–254, 282–312.

3 Immanuel Kant, *The Metaphysical Elements of Justice*, trans. John Ladd (Indianapolis: Bobbs-Merrill, 1965), sec. 44, p. 76, quoted in Jeremy Waldron, "Special Ties and Natural Duties" *Philosophy and Public Affairs* 22 (1993), 3, 4–5, 14–15. Waldron's work has built substantially on the observation that Kant attributed the perils of the state of nature not to selfishness, but to moral vehemence.

4 John Rawls, *A Theory of Justice* (Cambridge, MA.: Harvard University Press, 1971), p. 389.

5 Rawls's examination of political obligation draws distinctions among several forms of principled disobedience. John Rawls, *A Theory of Justice* (Cambridge, MA.: Harvard University Press, 1971), pp. 350–391. For Rawls, "[t]he problem of civil disobedience … arises only within a more or less just democratic state for those citizens who recognize and accept the legitimacy of the constitution". Ibid., p. 363. Although he may have exaggerated in characterizing "a more or less just democratic state" as the only occasion for civil disobedience (Gandhi and King may well have disagreed), he was surely correct to highlight this device's distinctiveness. In contrast, militant resistance rejects the legitimacy of the prevailing order, whereas conscientious refusal or conscientious evasion – which prioritizes a perceived moral duty over the state's demands, however grounded, and may intend no political statement as such – has no necessary connection to the issue of legitimacy.

6 "Certainly in a state of near justice there is a presumption in favor of compliance in the absence of strong reasons to the contrary." Rawls (n. 4 above), p. 389; but see Allen Buchanan, "Democracy and Commitment to International Law" (2006) 34 *Georgia Journal of International and Comparative Law* 305, 309 (asserting that rejection of the principle of political obligation – what R. P. Wolff and others have championed as "philosophical anarchism", see Robert Paul Wolff, *In Defense of Anarchism* (New York: Harper and Row, 1970), pp. 18–19 – might nowadays "not unreasonably" be presented as "the dominant philosophical view"); A. John Simmons, *Moral Principles and Political Obligations* (Princeton, NJ: Princeton University Press, 1979), p. 200 (obedience to even the most plausibly legitimate political authorities "remains as much in need of justification as disobedience").

> In no sense do I advocate evading or defying the law as the rabid segregationist would do. This would lead to anarchy. One who breaks an unjust law must do it openly, lovingly, (not hatefully as the white mothers did in New Orleans ...) and with a willingness to accept the penalty.[7]

Indeed, King sought disciplined demonstrations that would model the just society sought to be built, with the demonstrators manifesting genuine rule of law values while exposing the essential lawlessness of their adversaries.

Such restraint in the face of injustice makes sense because, notwithstanding the imagined "right to rule" that appears as a foil in some anti-authoritarian literature, political obligation in the liberal tradition is owed primarily to the political community of which the individual is a member. The obligation is owed only derivatively to the established constitutional order (let alone to those persons exercising governmental authority in its name), contingent on the authenticity of that existing order's standing to represent the political community.[8] And even where such standing is clouded, decisions about disobedience must take into account the impact on the political community's capacity to fulfil its essential tasks, mindful of the fact that even illegitimate governments frequently perform indispensable functions.

The idea of legitimate authority is fundamentally ambiguous, referring simultaneously to the moral evaluation of governmental actors' exercise of coercive power and to the moral evaluation of individuals' decisions to obey or disobey governmental decisions to which they are subject. These may appear to be two sides of the same coin, as reflected in R. P. Wolff's premise that "Authority is the right to command, and correlatively, the right to be obeyed."[9] But the two "rights" (even if that be a proper characterization) are not "correlative": as they pertain to the duties of distinct sets of actors, they implicate different sets of considerations. There is no necessary contradiction between the legitimate exercise of governmental coercion and justified resistance to that very exercise.[10] Even dissidents who acknowledge the overall legitimacy of the political order may reasonably find specific terms of that order sufficiently wrongful on the merits as to justify one or another form of civic defiance – including "indirect" civil disobedience, involving breaches of laws, such as those against trespassing, that are not themselves being challenged. But it would not follow that government officials could be impugned for enforcing the breached laws. This is a defining paradox of civil disobedience.

7 Martin Luther King, "Letter from a Birmingham Jail" (16 April 1963), http://www.historicaltextarchive.com/sections.php?op=viewarticle&artid=40.

8 Instructive in this regard is the distinction drawn in international law between the "state" – the territorially-based political community that abstractly bears rights, obligations, powers, and immunities in the international order – and the "government" – the ruling apparatus that concretely asserts rights, incurs obligations, exercises powers, and confers immunities on behalf of the state. This is a relationship of principal and agent. See Brad R. Roth, *Sovereign Equality and Moral Disagreement* (Oxford: Oxford University Press, 2011), pp. 81–82, 169–220. This understanding of the relationship reflects the essence of social contract theory, which emphasizes the (notional) consent of each individual to become bound to the political society, followed by the society's appointment of a government to implement the terms of that initial consent – a government that can be resisted where it acts *ultra vires* of that role. See John Locke, *Second Treatise of Government* (1690), chs. 7–11, 18, 19.

9 Wolff (n. 6 above), p. 4.

10 Nor, for that matter, would it necessarily follow from a valid obligation that any other actor is licensed to employ coercion or force to compel compliance. See Roth, *Sovereign Equality and Moral Disagreement* (n. 8 above), p. 80, 91. Obligatoriness and compulsoriness are independent, if often overlapping, phenomena.

The foundations of political legitimacy rest first on what Ronald Dworkin refers to as "structural conditions" of moral membership – namely, a shared political history within relatively stable boundaries and (optimistically) other commonalities conducive to at least a potential for mutual trust.[11] Dworkin further speaks of "relational conditions" of moral membership – that each member have "a *part* in any collective decision, a *stake* in it, and *independence* from it", and that its benefits and burdens be distributed "with equal concern for all"[12] – that pertain to the mode of governance rather than to the configuration of the political community, and that track his own conception of fundamental justice.

Civil disobedience is an attempt, not to exercise power directly, but to challenge authority in such a way as to arouse the conscience of the community, either to reform the constitutional order to reflect the community's authentic political morality, or to prevail upon officials to conform their exercises of power to standards already embodied in the constitutional order's principles, correctly understood. Whereas other forms of civic defiance represent a break either with a political community or with its espoused principles of public order, civil disobedience is an act of loyalty. Practitioners must adjust their tactics to a careful reading of their target audience, which may be more averse to chaos than to the injustices being protested.

It is against this conceptual backdrop that one can assess the Sunflower and Umbrella Movements. Both movements, operating in the name of their respective political communities and those communities' espoused constitutional principles, sought to appropriate the mantel of genuine lawfulness, in contrast to their adversaries' extemporary exercises of power.

The Sunflower and Umbrella Movements as struggles for self-determination

"All peoples have the right to self-determination; by virtue of that right they freely determine their political status and freely pursue their economic, social and cultural development."[13] There has always been less to this statement than meets the eye. Although the formulation confers a right of sovereign independence on communities authoritatively certified as discrete "peoples" for these purposes, the international legal order has never developed a stand-alone definition of a "people".[14] The United Nations General Assembly in 1960 ascribed such peoplehood to the permanent populations of Charter-specified Non-Self-Governing Territories, which were deemed to include any "territory which is geographically separate and is distinct ethnically and/or culturally from the country administering it" and which is subject to "administrative, political, juridical, economic, or

11 Ronald Dworkin, "The Moral Reading and the Majoritarian Premise" in Harold Hongju Koh and Ronald Slye (eds) *Deliberative Democracy and Human Rights* (New Haven: Yale University Press, 1999), pp. 81, 103.

12 Ibid.

13 This formulation initially came to prominence in the United Nations Declaration on the Granting of Independence to Colonial Countries and Peoples, G.A. Res. 1514 (XV) (1960) (89–0–9), ¶ 2, and was reaffirmed by the Security Council in S.C. Res. 183 (1963), ¶ 4. It was repeated in 1966 in Common Article 1 of the 1966 Human Rights Covenants. ICCPR, art. 1; ICESCR, art. 1.

14 The Charter itself speaks in the name of "We the Peoples of the United Nations". UN Charter, preamble. Since the foundational principle of "sovereign equality" of member states, *ibid.*, art. 2(1), is predicated on the Organization's enumerated purpose to "develop friendly relations based on respect for the principle of equal rights and self-determination of peoples", ibid., art. 1(2), the implication is that states are the presumed manifestations of the self-determination of the peoples that they encompass.

historical" factors that "arbitrarily place it in a position or status of subordination".[15] These criteria were overtly designed to encompass "territories which were then known to be of the colonial type",[16] without any consideration of how they might apply elsewhere.

A decade later, the General Assembly sought to clarify as follows:

> Nothing in the foregoing paragraphs shall be construed as authorizing or encouraging any action which would dismember or impair, totally or in part, the territorial integrity or political unity of sovereign and independent States ***conducting themselves in compliance with the principle of equal rights and self-determination of peoples as described above and thus possessed of a government representing the whole people belonging to the territory without distinction as to race, creed or colour.***[17]

Subsequent iterations have broadened the last clause of the qualifier to speak of "a government representing the whole people ... without distinction of any kind",[18] without, however, giving any authoritative elaboration of the implications for subordinated groups within integral territories of existing states.

The threat to territorial integrity has chilled the international community from applying the self-determination right outside the colonial context,[19] and the international legal order has been reluctant to ascribe legal personality to sub-national groups.[20] Nonetheless, in its

15 G.A. Res. 1541 (XV) (1960) (69–2–21), Annex, Principles I, IV, V. The "territory and its peoples" realize self-determination in one of three ways: "(a) Emergence as a sovereign independent State; (b) Free association with an independent State; (c) Integration with an independent State." The first option is framed not only as an absolute right, but as the presumptive outcome, whereas the latter two choices are laden with requisites calculated to assure that they result from a genuine exercise of popular will. See *ibid.*, Principles II, VI. VII, VIII, IX.

16 Ibid., Principle I.

17 G.A. Res. 2625 (n. 15 above) (emphasis added). This was a test that Rhodesia and South Africa were intended to fail, but that garden-variety "scientific socialist" and "Bandung nationalist" one-party regimes, "representing" their populations within the terms established by their prevailing ideologies, were intended to pass. See, e.g. Antonio Cassese, *Self-Determination of Peoples: A Legal Reappraisal* (Cambridge: Cambridge University Press, 1995), 115–18 (discussing the preparatory work to the safeguard clause, which reveals concessions to non-liberal-democratic states).

18 See G.A. Res. 50/6 (1995); United Nations World Conference on Human Rights, Vienna Declaration and Programme of Action, 25 June 1993, 32 I.L.M. 1661, 1665 (1993).

19 See., e.g. International Court of Justice, *Accordance with International Law of the Unilateral Declaration of Independence in Respect of Kosovo*, Advisory Opinion of of 22 July 2010 (hereinafter, Kosovo Advisory Opinion), http://www.icj-cij.org/docket/index.php?p1=3&p2=4&k=21&case=141&code=kos&p3=5, holding, 10–14, that the declaration, as such, "did not violate international law", but declining to address the declaration's legal consequences. The Court there noted that states have expressed "radically different views" on "[w]hether, outside the context of non-self-governing territories and peoples subject to alien subjugation, domination, and exploitation, the international law of self-determination of peoples confers upon part of the population of an existing State a right to separate from that state" and on "whether international law provides for a right of 'remedial secession' and, if so, in what circumstances". Ibid., ¶ 82.

20 The dominant approach has been to ascribe international rights solely to individual "persons belonging to such minorities". See ICCPR (n. 13 above) art. 27; Declaration on the Rights of Persons Belonging to National or Ethnic, Religious and Linguistic Minorities, G.A. Res. 47/135 (18 December 1992). That approach has the advantage of averting an ensuing rivalry between "national" minorities accorded group rights and "non-autochthonous" minorities denied them, as well as avoiding any endorsement of cultural restrictions that an autonomous group might impose on individuals in its midst. Nonetheless, various efforts have been undertaken to confer international status on minority groups as such. See Malcolm N. Shaw, "Peoples, Territorialism, and Boundaries" (1997) 8 *European Journal of International Law* 478, 486 (citing European documents, such as the Council of Europe's 1995 Framework Convention for Protection of National Minorities, that, "while extremely cautiously formulated and accompanied by significant provisos", introduce "a territorial dimension into minority rights within the territorial framework of independent states").

2007 Declaration on the Rights of Indigenous Peoples,[21] the UN General Assembly sought to underscore indigenous people's participatory rights (principally, "the right to autonomy or self-government in matters relating to their internal and local affairs") by attributing to them the right to self-determination, including the right to "freely determine their political status",[22] while at the same time paradoxically excluding any impairment of existing states' "territorial integrity or political unity".[23]

Whether or not fully or consistently acknowledged in the international order, the essential principle may be articulated as follows: all human beings have a right to be "possessed of a government representing the whole people belonging to the territory without distinction"; the sovereign entity must be a plausible manifestation of the self-determination of all of the society's historically distinct components on effectively equal terms.[24] This requisite pertains to the structural and relational terms of membership that Dworkin invokes, as discussed above. Where inhabitants of a historically discrete sub-national territory – discrete on whatever bases might be politically salient, whether or not ethnic or cultural – are confronted with impositions that "arbitrarily place them in a position or status of subordination", these differently-situated nationals come to constitute a distinct political community, bearing a collective right to pursue their economic, social, and cultural development in their territories through separate decision-making processes.

On this theory, Taiwan's historical distinctness establishes it as a discrete entity entitled to resist the efforts of China to coerce it into yielding its de facto independence. Although the Taipei Government originally predicated its sovereignty claims on its representation of "One China", it has since the early 1990s effectively withdrawn that assertion, and governs itself as a discrete sovereign entity seeking (albeit largely through indirect means) its own international legal personality.[25] Even former President Ma Ying-jeou, for all of his efforts to enhance Cross-Strait relations, never ceased to affirm "the sovereignty and dignity of the Republic of China on Taiwan" and to insist that the "future of Taiwan shall be decided commonly by the 23 million people on Taiwan".[26]

Yet in seeking to ram through the Cross-Strait Service Trade Agreement (CSSTA) in 2014, President Ma flouted constitutionally mandated processes of legislative deliberation for the sake of an agreement that augured economic dependency on a politically aggressive external power. Even former US Secretary of State Hillary Clinton cautioned that this

21 G.A. Res. 61/295 (12 September 2007) (143–4–11) (the dissenting votes were the United States, Canada, Australia, and New Zealand).

22 Ibid., art. 3.

23 Ibid., art. 46. This qualification – which entails a seeming literal contradiction – apparently assuaged African states that had theretofore insisted that the "principle of self-determination applies only to peoples under colonial and/or foreign occupation". African Group, *Draft Aide Memoire on United Nations Declaration on the Rights of Indigenous Peoples* (9 November 2006).

24 Indeed, the UN Charter effectively predicates states' very sovereignty on their embodiment their territorial populations' self-determination. See UN Charter, preamble ("We the Peoples ..."), arts. 1(2), 2(1) ("sovereign equality" following from the "equal rights and self-determination of peoples").

25 See Brad R. Roth, "The Entity that Dare Not Speak Its Name: Unrecognized Taiwan as a Right-Bearer in the International Legal Order" (2009) 4 *East Asia Law Review* 91.

26 President Ma Ying-jeou, Remarks at the 2011 ILA Asia-Pacific Regional Conference, (30 May 2011), pp. 6–7, http://www.cils.nccu.edu.tw/Opening%20Address%20of%20President%20Ma%20Ying-jeou.pdf. See Brad R. Roth, "Parsing 'Mutual Non-Recognition and Mutual Non-Denial': An International Law Perspective on Taipei's Current Framework for Cross-Strait Relations" (2012) 30 *Chinese (Taiwan) Yearbook of International Law and Affairs* 15.

deepening of Cross-Strait economic relations could render Taiwan "vulnerable" and urged "sharp eyes and a calm mind" in examining such a proposal.[27]

The Sunflower Movement represented precisely such vigilance. In an effort to forestall the loss of effective self-determination, students took direct action against the effort of then-ruling Kuomintang (KMT) to circumvent legislative examination of the CSSTA's details. In so doing, the movement stood up both for existing constitutional processes and for the underlying capacity of the political community to maintain control of its destiny.

Whereas Taiwan enjoys de facto statehood (albeit under menace), Hong Kong is subject to Chinese sovereignty, yet under terms designed to preserve the former British colony's historically distinct patterns of development. Under the "One Country, Two Systems" legal formula, the Hong Kong Special Administrative Region (HKSAR) is supposedly guaranteed "a high degree of autonomy" and the continued enhancement of popular participation in governmental affairs, including in the election of the Chief Executive.[28]

In betraying this latter promise though new qualifications imposed in 2014, PRC authorities cast a cloud over the future of Hong Kong's autonomy. As in the case of the Sunflower Movement, it fell to grassroots activists to undertake civic defiance both to insist on respect for the existing constitutional norms being flouted and to awaken the political community to the threat of creeping encroachments on its capacity for self-government. The Umbrella Movement, like the Sunflower Movement, undertook lawbreaking in service of both the community's laws and the community's very capacity to make its own laws.

Taiwan: Breaking the law to resist the undermining of sovereignty's foundations

Brian Christopher Jones and Yen-Tu Su portray the Sunflower Movement as an exercise in "confrontational contestation". From their perspective, the protracted physical occupation of the Legislative Yuan and other associated acts of civic defiance "exemplify what Daniel Markovits terms as democratic disobedience, the goal of which is to ensure that a well-functioning democratic process corrects the perceived democratic deficits in the law and politics of the day".[29] Jones and Su point to polls showing majority popular support for the protesters. But they also, indispensably, offer a theoretical framework within which to justify confronting a duly elected government with civic defiance that, while not seeking overthrow, went well beyond the meek, symbolic appeals to conscience that King and Rawls associated with civil disobedience. The Sunflower Movement exercised power from below, substantially disrupting legislative processes. At moments, Jones and Su appear to

27 "Hillary Clinton Warns Against Over-Dependence on China" *Associated Press* (24 June 2014), http://www.etaiwannews.com/etn/news_content.php?id=2513205.

28 According to Article 45 of the Basic Law:

> The method for selecting the Chief Executive shall be specified in the light of the actual situation in the Hong Kong Special Administrative Region and in accordance with the principle of gradual and orderly progress. The ultimate aim is the selection of the Chief Executive by universal suffrage upon nomination by a broadly representative nominating committee in accordance with democratic procedures.

Basic Law of the Hong Kong Special Administrative Region of the People's Republic of China [Basic Law], http://www.basiclaw.gov.hk/en/basiclawtext/images/basiclaw_full_text_en.pdf.

29 Brian Christopher Jones and Yen-Tu Su, "Confrontational Contestation and Democratic Compromise: The Sunflower Movement and Its Aftermath", chapter 1.

celebrate this phenomenon for its own sake, as a contribution *per se* to democratic vibrancy.[30] But sensibly, they go beyond this to invoke the procedurally and substantively undemocratic nature of the act being protested.

As Jones and Su note, President Ma and the legislative allies sought a peremptory ratification of the trade pact, in violation both of existing parliamentary procedures and of democratic principles of deliberation. This act reflected both an aggrandizement of executive power and the exploitation of a legislative majority to wipe out the oversight role of the legislative minority. Moreover, a fast-track approval of a trade deal would have denied adversely affected sectors any influence over a decision with consequences for their lives and livelihoods.

Most significantly of all, perhaps – though not especially emphasized by Jones and Su – the CSSTA augured an undermining of the ultimate democratic value: sovereignty, after all, is what there is to be democratic ***about***. The obstruction of the CSSTA's ratification served democracy by helping to preserve the polity's long-term capacity for democratic decision-making, in the face of an overbearing authoritarian power that openly declares a prerogative to absorb the Taiwanese irrespective of their consent.

Jiunn-rong Yeh adds further arguments for the constitutional and democratic quality of the Sunflower Movement.[31] He references the contributions of civic defiance at various stages of the Taiwanese process of democratic reform over the last generation, and suggests that Taiwan's democratic development compares favourably with that of east central Europe, where an emphasis on formal institution-building has coincided with a withering of civic engagement.[32] He further notes the democratic qualities embodied in the Sunflower Movement's conduct:

> It turned out that the student groups exercised a high degree of discipline and, not long after their occupation, won social support through impressive dialogue with both the general public and government authorities. The student groups argued in constitutional terms about rights infringement, due process and the boundaries of congressional oversight and public monitoring in concluding the trade pact with China. Passionate lectures about contemporary constitutional law topics were offered in the occupied legislature and even in the surrounding streets. With general concern regarding the accountability of the President and the legislature, the student/civic groups continued to discuss and propose issues for constitutional reform.[33]

Rather than regarding elected officials and unelected judges as the sole guardians of constitutionality, Yeh suggests a civic constitutionalism that assigns this task to the active citizenry.[34]

30 Ibid., citing Philip Petit, *On the People's Terms: A Republican Theory and Model of Democracy* (Cambridge: Cambridge University Press, 2012), at p. 226 (democratic life must have an "antagonistic" character). Of course, "two can play at that game": unless one is indifferent to the very political outcomes about which contestants evince such seriousness, one might be given pause by the thought of such tactics being undertaken in service of less wholesome causes.

31 Jiunn-rong Yeh, "Marching towards Civic Constitutionalism with Sunflowers", chapter 3.

32 Ibid.

33 Ibid.

34 Yeh specifically invokes Bruce Ackerman, *We the People: Foundations* (Cambridge, MA: Harvard University Press, 1991). Even more fitting might be the provocative Richard D. Parker, "Here, The People Rule: A Constitutional Populist Manifesto" (1993) 27 *Valparaiso U.L. Rev.* 531, assailing the elitist presumptions that permeate the American academic discourse that celebrates judicial review of legislation.

Yeh points out that the Sunflower Movement's actions furthered democracy by subjecting the executive's unbalanced view of the separation of powers to critical popular scrutiny, by educating the public on constitutional and policy issues, and even by drawing a police overreaction that invigorated debate about human rights and official uses of force. Moreover, the negotiated conclusion of the occupation of the Legislative Yuan was not the end of the Movement's efforts to engage citizens in constitutional vigilance, but a step in the building of organizations dedicated to this mission. And of course, the resounding electoral defeats suffered by the ruling party in the wake of these events speak to the public's verdict on the worthiness of the Movement's objectives.

Whereas the Jones–Su and Yeh chapters accept that civic action on behalf of constitutionalism and democracy may collide with valid legal restrictions, Wen-Chen Chang critically scrutinizes the legal framework governing civic protests.[35] While cataloguing the progress made after the Martial Law period to establish constitutional rights to peaceful assembly, she laments the persistence of legal restrictions in Taiwan under the Assembly and Parade Act. Although the Constitutional Court has established a principle of content-neutrality in speech regulation, it has confirmed the constitutionality of permit requirements and criminal sanctions, both of which involve substantial discretion and are prone to partisan selectivity (including with respect to non-prosecution of politically favoured demonstrators). Chang criticizes the 2014 Constitutional Court decision that reaffirmed the permit requirement, preferring the dissenting opinion that would have substituted a notification requirement, thereby establishing a presumption in favour of permission for the demonstration.[36]

In 2009, Taiwan undertook to observe the International Covenant on Civil and Political Rights (ICCPR),[37] and passed implementing legislation to give the ICCPR's provisions direct effect in domestic courts.[38] Chang notes that ICCPR Article 21, on the right of assembly, is significantly more protective than current Taiwanese law. Although the ICCPR does not disallow a permit requirement, restrictions on peaceful assembly not only must be specified by a pre-existing law, but must be "necessary in a democratic society in the interests of national security or public safety, public order (*ordre public*), the protection of public health or morals or the protection of the rights and freedoms of others".[39] The government thus bears a burden of justification in limiting peaceful demonstrations (even if some of the permissible justifications – especially "public order" and "public morals" – are unhelpfully vague).

Of potentially even greater significance, Chang observes, the ICCPR has been interpreted to bar criminal sanctions against peaceful demonstrators who are not attempting to overthrow the government or to participate in violence.[40] That interpretation prompts questions about what disobedient acts, beyond demonstrating without a permit, might be thereby immunized, but even a starting presumption against criminalization of non-violent demonstrator offences would bolster the protection of dissidents, rather than leaving them

35 Wen-Chen Chang, "The Right to Free Assembly and the Sunflower Movement", chapter 2.

36 Ibid., citing JY Interpretation No. 718 (2014).

37 ICCPR (n. 13 above).

38 Chang, (n. 35 above).

39 ICCPR (n. 13 above), art. 21.

40 Chang (n. 35 above), citing Alexandre Charles Kiss, "Permissible Limitations on Rights" in Louis Henkin (ed.), *International Bill of Rights: International Covenant on Civil and Political Rights* (Columbia: Columbia University Press, 1981) p. 297.

in need of the prosecutorial leniency that Jones and Su urge in such cases in the name of democratic compromise.[41]

Whereas Chang is concerned with legal reform to bolster the rights of Sunflower-style demonstrators, Cheng-Yi Huang looks to the broader need for reform of the outmoded Republic of China (ROC) Constitution and of legislation enacted pursuant to that constitution's delegations of authority. Of particular concern is the Act Governing Relations between the People of the Taiwan Area and the Mainland Area (1992), which confers inordinate control over Cross-Strait relations to the Executive Yuan – a source of the 2014 CSSTA controversy. At an even deeper level, Huang objects to the constitution's rhetorical insistence on a national identity tied to China, in disregard of the current generation's ever more dominant sense of Taiwanese identity. Like many other independence-minded Taiwanese constitutional scholars, Huang favours a constitutional re-founding. That suggestion, of course, risks a crisis of Cross-Strait relations, as the PRC has repeatedly indicated that it would regard such a move as a provocation.[42]

On the whole, this volume's chapters on the Sunflower Movement establish that, despite its recourse to a more confrontational approach than liberals sometimes associate with civil disobedience,[43] the Movement falls squarely within that category's essential parameters. The Movement's conduct, by its limited objectives and restrained tactics, evinced loyalty to the political community and even to the constitutional order. Far from defying democracy, the Movement acted to frustrate a Cross-Strait policy that lacked both the procedural and substantive requisites of democratic legitimacy, and that threatened to undermine the political community's capacity for future democratic decisions. That this is not a parochial conclusion is evident from the subsequent election results, which delivered crushing blows to the ruling party and changed the direction of Cross-Strait policy.

Hong Kong: The struggle for meaningful electoral competition under "One Country, Two Systems"

As Albert H. Y. Chen explains, the Umbrella (Occupy Central) Movement's campaign of civic defiance came in response to the 31 August 2014 decision of the PRC's National People's Congress Standing Committee (NPCSC) to impose restrictive conditions on the nominating process that was to lead to the election by universal suffrage of a new Chief Executive in 2017.[44] By requiring that all candidates receive majority approval from a nominating body consisting overwhelmingly of PRC-friendly representatives of organized

41 Jones and Su (n. 29 above).

42 It should be noted that, contrary to what is often imagined in independence-minded circles, a new constitution unambiguously renouncing the antiquated ROC claim to the Mainland would not appreciably bolster Taiwan's case for international recognition as a state. From an international law perspective, constitutions presuppose rather than establish statehood. See Roth, "The Entity that Dare Not Speak Its Name" (n. 25 above).

43 See Jones and Su (n. 29 above). It should be recalled that the more conservative Rawls was not only expressly concerned with the criteria of appropriate disobedience in a "more or less just democratic state", without prejudice to bolder methods in other circumstances, but was incorporating – more magnanimously than any conventional constitutional framer – a role for civic defiance within a governmental scheme of his own creation. Rawls (n. 4 above) pp. 350–391. It thus stands to reason that, in this narrow context, symbolic defiance aimed purely at consciousness-raising would be the limit of what he wished to license.

44 Albert H. Y. Chen, "The Law and Politics of Constitutional Reform and Democratization in Hong Kong", chapter 4.

"sectors" of society,[45] the PRC sought to guarantee that the Chief Executive be someone who "loves the country" and will serve its "sovereignty, security and development interests" as well as "the long-term prosperity and stability of Hong Kong".[46]

From the standpoint of the dissidents, such vetting of the candidates fails to comply with the Basic Law's promise of "selection of the Chief Executive by universal suffrage upon nomination by a broadly representative nominating committee in accordance with democratic procedures".[47] If interpreted in light of international standards for political participation,[48] this provision can be construed to preclude the kind of pre-selection on which the PRC insists, whereas interpretation in light of previous patterns of HKSAR practice would allow for the screening out of candidates who would be confrontational toward the PRC. At a deeper level, the conflict pertains to the ambiguity of Hong Kong's relationship to PRC sovereignty in the context of "One Country, Two Systems", and at a deeper level still, reflects the paradox that the Basic Law's envisioned electoral process would, in Chen's words, "mov[e] the political systems of Hong Kong and of mainland China further apart in the course of time (unless the latter also democratizes)".[49] Chen concludes that the contradictions are unresolvable, and that the inevitably resulting tensions raise serious questions about whether Hong Kong's social stability and prosperity can be maintained.

Fu Hualing details the manifestations of these contradictions in Hong Kong's institutional life, as the Hong Kong Court of Final Appeal has attempted to assert jurisdiction over constitutional questions, only to face the reality that the NPCSC ultimately "makes, interprets and implements the Basic Law according to its legal theories and political interest, in the process forcing Hong Kong into a constitutional confrontation that it is bound to lose".[50] This dynamic has led many Hong Kong residents to sense that not only will the promise of universal suffrage prove hollow, but the HKSAR's officially guaranteed "high degree of autonomy" will gradually slip away. Press freedom has declined, corruption is on the rise, economic prosperity is eroding, and the political order systematically subordinates Hong Kong's interests to those of the Mainland.

In response, Umbrella Movement activists, in occupying streets in major business districts of the city, sought to take the constitution into their own hands. As Fu describes:

45 As Chen explains, the nominating committee, like the committee that presently elects the Chief Executive, would consist of persons elected:

> from four sectors, with equal numbers of members from each sector. The sectors are (a) business (comprising mainly corporate voters in various commercial, financial and industrial fields), (b) professional bodies, (c) labour and other social sectors, and (d) the political sector (including legislators, Hong Kong deputies to the NPC and Hong Kong members of the Chinese People's Political Consultative Conference, etc.).

Chen (n. 44 above). Chen reports that, "the majority of the committee's members were indeed 'pro-China', 'pro-Establishment' or 'patriots', and those who were pan-democrats or sympathetic to them only constituted a minority (slightly more than one-eighth) in the Election Committee". Ibid., pp. 18–19.

46 Chen (n. 44 above), quoting the 31 August 2014 Decision of the NPCSC.

47 Basic Law (n. 28 above), art. 45.

48 See, e.g. ICCPR, arts. 2, 25 (guaranteeing full participation without distinctions such as "political or other opinion").

49 Chen (n. 44 above).

50 Fu Hualing, "Political Protest in High-Income Societies: The Case of the Occupy Central Movement in Hong Kong", chapter 5.

> During the days in OCM, streets are the court rooms, and occupiers and their supporters become lawyers, judges, and lawmakers. For a brief moment, they appeared to be in charge of their constitutional destiny. For the young generation of people in Hong Kong who have grown in the shadow of the Basic Law controversies, the bargains that were struck by generations before them were simply not acceptable. They demanded to exercise the power to decide what constitutional law is for them.[51]

In the course of this undertaking, the demonstrators were met with an uncharacteristically excessive use of force by the police, likely attributable to political direction. They also faced violence from thugs associated with business owners whose operations were being disrupted by the street occupations. But more importantly, after enjoying strong popular support in the early going, the Movement began to encounter a backlash as the occupations dragged on and much of the populace began to fear a descent into chaos.[52]

Even more dauntingly perhaps, the Umbrella Movement was confronted with injunctions, solicited by adversely affected constituencies, issued by a judiciary with a strong reputation among Hong Kong residents as a politically neutral guardian of one of the city's most highly regarded values: the rule of law. In a polity where most of the levers of power are in the hands of an unaccountable establishment, the availability of recourse to independent courts has been a rare asset for the aggrieved.[53] However, where courts in authoritarian systems maintain their ability to prevail upon authorities, they typically accomplish this by strict adherence to a positivistic methodology that eschews extra-legal considerations,[54] and this adherence worked against the demonstrators here. Unimpressed by the protesters' moral arguments, the courts applied the letter of the law, citing the rights of those on whose activities the disruptions impinged. Confrontation with a well-reputed judiciary was not an option for a movement predicated on a constitutionalist ethos. Fu observes: "It was the authority of the court and the willingness of the people in the city to obey the rule of law that effectively suppressed the democratic impulse."[55]

Given the limitations of the courts' capacity to vindicate Hong Kong interests vis-à-vis the PRC authorities and of the courts' capacity to address the street occupations as anything other than breaches of a legal civil order, it seems evident that a civic constitutionalism "from below" in this context needed to transcend existing positive legal frameworks, to rally the political community to a new constitutional vision. As Daniel Matthews reports, "a shift took place that took the movement away from arguing for change within the existing constitutional framework of Hong Kong towards a more radical, performative *living out* of a democratic alternative in the occupation camps themselves".[56] This radicalization was nonetheless consistent with the ethos of civil disobedience, as it evinced a loyalty to the political community's essential norms that manifested itself in a peaceful and orderly re-appropriation and reorganization of public space (and ultimately, in a negotiated withdrawal in the face of court injunctions). Matthews emphasizes the "performative" rather than "purely cognitive" nature of the Umbrella Movement's occupation activities. "The

51 Ibid.

52 Ibid.

53 Ibid.

54 For an examination of courts' tactical uses of positivism in authoritarian systems, see Mark J. Osiel, "Dialogue with Dictators: Judicial Resistance in Argentina and Brazil" (1995) 20 *Law and Social Inquiry* 481, 491–95.

55 Fu (n. 50 above).

56 Daniel Matthews, "The *Nomos* of the Umbrella Movement", chapter 6.

sharing of food, collective and consensual decision making, the maintenance of and aesthetic engagement with the streetscape" represented "experiments in living, rather than in legal interpretation".[57] Yet ultimately, for Matthews, whether this exercise had any lasting educative impact on the political community remains very much an open question.

In the aftermath of these events, Chih-hsing Ho considers whether civil disobedience must necessarily give rise to punishment[58] – a theme also explored by Jones and Su in the Sunflower Movement context.[59] Although civil disobedience is characteristically marked by a willingness to accept punishment – the braving of that risk is indeed typically part of the theatrics that give civil disobedience its tactical punch – it does not follow that prosecution is an unproblematic response. Punishments of non-violent lawbreakers (including those responsible for minor property damage) that are disproportionate to the seriousness of the offences and the resultant harms should properly be classified as a form of political repression. Even moderate punishments, though plausibly needed even in democratic societies to prevent disruption from being cost-free, may be out of keeping with the goal of restoring social peace. It may also be criticized as failing to manifest appropriate respect for loyal and committed fellow citizens whose disobedience was motivated by a genuine and reasonable moral outrage, and who conducted themselves in a disciplined and responsible, if not lawful, manner.

As Ho notes, the Hong Kong courts have taken a fairly unyielding line on punishments for the demonstrators who violated injunctions, and especially those who caused property damage.[60] The apolitical, positivistic stance discussed above – combined, perhaps, with doubts about the PRC's continued tolerance for their independence should the unrest in the city be perceived in Beijing as getting out of hand – has inhibited the Hong Kong courts from treating the demonstrators' political commitments as a mitigating factor.

This volume's chapters on the Umbrella Movement tell a much more sombre story than do the chapters on Taiwan's Sunflower Movement. With no real opportunity to address the external behemoth that imposes the last word on the interpretation of the Basic Law, the Umbrella Movement found itself in a confrontation with local actors who were either pro-establishment or concerned above all to maintain peace and order. The street occupations represented a call for a new constitutional project that would allow genuine self-government, but their practitioners also exercised tactical restraint, and ultimately retreated to avoid alienating the community whose self-assertion they were seeking to mobilize.

Conclusion

The Sunflower and Umbrella Movements both combined civic defiance with a democratic constitutionalist ethos, breaking laws of their respective political communities in a peaceful and restrained manner for the sake of bolstering those communities' very capacity to make

57 Ibid.

58 Chih-hsing Ho, "To Punish or Not to Punish: The Question of Civil Disobedience and the Umbrella Movement", chapter 8.

59 Jones and Su (n. 29 above). Those authors are principally concerned to lament the Ma Ying-jeou Administration's failure to recognize that a decision to forgo prosecution "would have been a grand democratic compromise that … is the optimal result for a stable and healthy democracy"(*ibid.*). After Sunflower Movement allies swept the 2016 Presidential and legislative elections, some, but not all, of the charges against the demonstrators were dropped.

60 Ho (n. 58 above).

their own laws. They evinced loyalty both to their political communities and to those communities' espoused constitutional premises, and in their conduct (by and large) observed what might be called a "rule of law from below". Although their defiance exceeded the marking the archetypical cases implicitly invoked by John Rawls in formulating his criteria of civil disobedience, these Movements are properly classified within that liberal-democratic tradition of loyal opposition.

The above chapters explicate both the shared characteristics of the two Movements and the disparities in the challenges that they faced. The Sunflower Movement acted to call out official circumvention of established democratic decision-making procedures and the threat it posed to the political community's existing independence, whereas the Umbrella Movement struggled to expand democratic space within a quasi-autonomous political community subordinated to the will of an external authoritarian power. The latter project was far more fraught than the former. As Jones and Su note, "To the extent that the Umbrella Movement in Hong Kong has achieved less than the Sunflower Movement in Taiwan in terms of public policy is only because winning an endgame for democracy is far more difficult than winning a mid-game within democracy."[61] Both projects, however, attest to the vibrancy of the liberal-democratic spirit within societies on the PRC's periphery – perhaps the greatest threat to the authoritarian regime's pretensions to speak for "One China".

61 Jones and Su (n. 29 above).

12 Democracy and constitutionalism in China's shadow

Sunflowers in Taiwan and Umbrellas in Hong Kong

*Jacques deLisle**

Taiwan and Hong Kong are polities that show the potential, and challenges, of democratic politics and constitutional governance in Chinese-speaking and culturally Chinese areas. Taiwan is an increasingly consolidated success, if still in some respects a troubled one. In Hong Kong, democracy and constitutionalism are still only promised, aspirational, or, at most, very incompletely achieved. Both Taiwan and Hong Kong live in the shadow of an authoritarian People's Republic of China that claims sovereignty over them (and that, in the case of Hong Kong, has formally and effectively reclaimed sovereignty, subject to what Beijing regards as only self-imposed limits).

In 2014, Taiwan's Sunflower Movement and Hong Kong's Umbrella Movement (which grew out of the Occupy Central Movement) illustrated in particularly dramatic form the impact that real and perceived challenges from China have on constitutional development and democratic or pro-democracy politics. These "China effects", and other less Beijing-driven features of the two movements, have been complex and ambivalent in the pair of politically lively places at the PRC's periphery. They can be grouped into a few categories, many of which are well illustrated, or intriguingly suggested, by chapters in this volume. Several of these categories show similarities – albeit sometimes only at a relatively high level of generality – between Taiwan and Hong Kong. Differences between the two cases are striking and significant as well. The Sunflower Movement and the Umbrella Movement also offer some troubling insights about the prospects for legal-political aspects of Cross-Strait and Hong Kong–Mainland relations.

China as the source of challenges/crisis

In both Taiwan and Hong Kong, the challenge to local democracy and trigger for constitutional crisis came in large part from China and China's conceptions of sovereignty and politics for the two areas. At a macro level, this has been obviously true for many years and has characterized Beijing's approach. Throughout the PRC's existence (and before), Chinese leaders have regarded Taiwan and Hong Kong (as well as Macao) as inalienable territory of China and the people living there as Chinese. In this view, the two areas' separation from Chinese sovereignty was not only illegitimate but a nullity – the product of "unequal treaties" from the nineteenth century that were invalid and void *ab initio*. Under this analysis, there could be no question of "recovering" sovereignty because sovereignty never was – nor could have been – lost. As the principal PRC provision in the Joint Declaration that returned Hong Kong

* Stephen A. Cozen Professor of Law & Professor of Political Science; Director, Center for East Asian Studies, University of Pennsylvania Law School.

to China put it, China had (merely) "decided to *resume the exercise* of sovereignty", effective on 1 July, 1997, the date of Hong Kong's reversion.[1]

This position has underpinned long-standing views from Beijing that have had significant implications for constitutionalism and democracy in Taiwan and Hong Kong. Because, in Beijing's conceptual framework, China's sovereignty over Chinese territory cannot be derogated and is inalterably unitary, any "local" exercise of sovereignty over the territories and people of Taiwan and Hong Kong can be undertaken only on the basis of powers delegated by the Chinese sovereign – and, moreover, delegated only as an exercise of discretion that is, in principle, reversible. That is the basic logic of the "One Country, Two Systems" model that PRC leaders developed early in the Reform Era – initially with an eye to Taiwan but first applied to Hong Kong.[2]

Constitutional development and democracy in Hong Kong have, quite obviously, felt the impact of this PRC premise, which consigns the Hong Kong Basic Law to a jurisprudential limbo: for Hong Kong, the Basic Law is a super-constitution, in the sense that the people and government institutions of Hong Kong cannot themselves alter it and have only limited and less-than-final authority to interpret it; for the central government, the Basic Law ultimately can be no more than a mere statute – perhaps an especially solemn and entrenched one, but in principle subject to amendment by the national legislature and subject to central government interpretation based on limited consultation with Hong Kong representatives. This feature of Hong Kong's Basic Law has been at the heart, and at the root, of many of the major controversies in Hong Kong in the run-up to reversion and in the nearly two decades since Hong Kong returned to Chinese rule. Occupy Central and the Umbrella Movement are among the most dramatic and recent concrete instances of a broader pattern that also has included earlier controversies in central government–Hong Kong legal-political relations, including ones concerning democratic elections, the authority of the Hong Kong courts, and legislation or proposed legislation affecting civil and political rights.[3]

Beijing's position on democracy in the Hong Kong Special Administrative Region (SAR), its interpretation of provisions in the Basic Law on democratic elections, and the Chinese leadership's worries about threats to political control and order in Hong Kong did much to drive the emergence and development of Occupy Central and the Umbrella Movement. Following on a similar April 2004 decision that had rejected calls for universal

1 See, e.g. Wang Tieya, "International Law in China: Historical and Contemporary Perspectives" (1990) 221 *Recueil des cours* 237–262; Xue Hanqin, *Chinese and Contemporary Perspectives on International Law: History, Culture and International Law* (The Hague: Martinus Nijhoff, 2012), pp. 26–34; Jacques deLisle, "Sovereignty Resumed: China's Concept of Sovereignty for Hong Kong and its Implications for the SAR and US–PRC Relations" (Summer 1998) *Harvard Asia Quarterly* 21–23; Joint Declaration of the Government of the United Kingdom of Great Britain and Northern Ireland and the Government of the People's Republic of China on the Question of Hong Kong (1984), art. 1 (italics added).

2 See generally Jacques deLisle and Kevin P. Lane, "Hong Kong's Endgame and the Rule of Law (I): The Struggle over Institutions and Values in the Transition to Chinese Rule" (1997) 18 *University of Pennsylvania Journal of International Economic Law* 195–254; Jacques deLisle, "The Chinese Puzzle of Taiwan's Status"(2000) 44(1) *Orbis* 35–62.

3 On the pre-reversion period, see ibid., Jacques deLisle and Kevin P. Lane, "Hong Kong's Endgame and the Rule of Law (II): The Battle over 'the People' and the Business Community in the Transition to Chinese Rule" (1997) 18 *University of Pennsylvania Journal of International Economic Law* 811–1047. Several of the post-reversion instances are discussed later in this chapter and in chapters in this volume, most notably the ones by Albert Chen and Fu Hualing.

suffrage elections for the 2007–2008 cycle, China's National People's Congress Standing Committee (NPC-SC) in December 2007 rejected proposals from democrats in Hong Kong to move more quickly (specifically, by 2012) to much more fully democratic elections for the Chief Executive and Legislative Council.[4] This decision formed the key backdrop to the Occupy Central Movement. The need to adopt rules to govern the 2017 selection of a Chief Executive – a choice that the NPC-SC decision said could be made by universal suffrage – was Occupy Central's initial focus. Beijing's rejection, in an August 2014 NPC-SC decision, of more thoroughgoing democratic rules for that election (ones that might have allowed widely participatory "civic nomination" of candidates for Chief Executive, rather than nomination by a majority of the members of an elite, 1,200-member, generally pro-Beijing committee modelled on the ones that had previously selected Chief Executives) precipitated the protests that became the Umbrella Movement. The pattern continued after the Umbrella Movement, with yet another NPC-SC interpretation of the Basic Law, this time declaring that the law's "oath-taking" requirement precluded the seating of two young, newly elected, pro-independence members of LegCo (with roots in the Umbrella Movement) who had deviated from the text of the oath, partly in a vulgar manner, to express their disdain for the central government.[5]

Not for the first, or last, time, Beijing's decisions had driven pro-democracy elements in Hong Kong to challenge China's agenda and expectations concerning politics and governance in Hong Kong. In demanding greater democracy in the near term and more rapid realization of the Basic Law's "constitutional" commitment to universal suffrage, Occupy Central and the Umbrella Movement challenged Beijing's schedule for – and limits to – political change in Hong Kong. More broadly, the movement reacted to – and rejected – Beijing's view of the degree of control that the central government had, or should have, over the pace and trajectory of political change and constitutional development in Hong Kong. At a still more fundamental level, the movement threatened to move the locus of politics in Hong Kong outside the cosy confines of a Beijing-controlled and only gradually or incompletely democratizing framework of institutions instantiated by the SAR's "mini-constitution" and into the streets (or, less dramatically, into the hands of the Hong Kong public).

In this volume, Albert Chen and Fu Hualing provide notably parallel accounts of the origins of the Umbrella Movement and Occupy Central that indicate how much these "China side" factors – especially, but not limited to, the NPC-SC's decisions concerning

4 Decision of the Standing Committee of the National People's Congress on Issues Relating to the Methods for Selecting the Chief Executive of the Hong Kong Special Administrative Region in the Year 2007 and for Forming the Legislative Council of the Hong Kong Special Administrative Region in the Year 2008 (adopted at the Ninth Session of the Standing Committee of the Tenth National People's Congress on 26 April 2004); Decision of the Standing Committee of the National People's Congress on Issues Relating to the Methods for Selecting the Chief Executive of the Hong Kong Special Administrative Region and for Forming the Legislative Council of the Hong Kong Special Administrative Region in the Year 2012 and on Issues Relating to Universal Suffrage (adopted at the Thirty-First Session of the Standing Committee of the Tenth National People's Congress on 29 December 2007).

5 Decision of the Standing Committee of the National People's Congress on Issues Relating to the Selection of the Chief Executive of the Hong Kong Special Administrative Region by Universal Suffrage and on the Method for Forming the Legislative Council of the Hong Kong Special Administrative Region in the Year 2016 (adopted at the Tenth Session of the Standing Committee of the Twelfth National People's Congress on 31 August 2014). Standing Committee of the Twelfth National People's Congress, Interpretation of Article 104 of the Basic Law of the Special Administrative Region of the People's Republic of China (7 November 2016).

election rules in Hong Kong – contributed to the movement's emergence. Chen, quite rightly, adds that the ultimate roots of the Umbrella Movement can be traced still further back, including to the long transitional period that ran from the negotiation of the 1984 Joint Declaration that provided for Hong Kong's return to China, through the drafting of the Basic Law, to Hong Kong's formal reversion in 1997 and post-reversion controversies that predate the NPC-SC decisions of the 2000s and 2010s. Fu persuasively assesses how profound the difficulties are for China in trying to govern a region that is, in constitutional principle and social practice, committed to some degree of democracy – a situation that makes Umbrella Movement–style conflicts relatively likely.

As in Hong Kong's Umbrella Movement, so, too, in Taiwan's Sunflower Movement, China and its positions concerning sovereignty and politics were key factors in triggering the movement's emergence. Despite obvious differences between the two cases that are, in part, a reflection of Beijing's thorough inability to exercise the sovereignty that it claims to hold over Taiwan, a locally perceived, PRC-originating threat to democratic and constitutional governance was a common feature of Taiwan's Sunflower Movement and Hong Kong's Umbrella Movement. To be sure, the connections to China were more attenuated and complicated in Taiwan's case.

The Sunflower Movement occurred in the context of a proposed economic pact with China and the threats it was seen to pose, at least indirectly, to Taiwan's democracy and constitutional order. The key catalyst for the Sunflower Movement was the belief among the protesters and their supporters among Taiwanese politicians – mostly in the Democratic Progressive Party (DPP) – that the Kuomintang (KMT) leadership of the Legislative Yuan (LY) was running roughshod over democratic processes and disregarding ordinary, minority-interest-protecting legislative procedures to rush through the Cross-Strait Services Trade Agreement (CSSTA) that was backed by China and supported by Ma Ying-jeou's (馬英九) government. The precipitous cutting off of parliamentary debate on the CSSTA (after a mere thirty seconds), the absence of article-by-article legislative scrutiny, the Ma administration's arguments that submission of Cross-Strait agreements to the legislature for review was a mere political courtesy and not a constitutional requirement – these were behaviours and attitudes that participants in the movement and their supporters saw as undemocratic and inconsistent with established ways of doing things in a key constitutional institution (the LY) that was, in their view, acting in the service of a policy agenda emanating from Beijing and pressed by a Taiwanese Government that was, as they saw it, excessively accommodating towards China.

Notably, the Sunflower Movement's most immediate progenitor – the Wild Strawberry Movement of 2008 – also had responded to a perceived China-originating threat to democracy-related, constitutionally grounded liberties in Taiwan. A visit by a senior Chinese Taiwan affairs official (the fruit of Ma's policy of rapprochement towards the mainland) prompted measures to limit popular protests against the visit, which in turn led to a mass movement against such restrictions.

The Sunflower Movement focused on shoring up democratic norms and constitutionally empowered institutions to address the China-related perils that the movement's participants and supporters discerned in the failed effort to push the CSSTA through the LY. Tellingly, the movement and its allies sought, and secured commitments to adopt, a comprehensive supervisory law for Cross-Strait agreements that will provide for more thorough and probing review of proposed accords by the democratically elected representatives who comprise Taiwan's legislature, and that also will provide for more institutionalized public input.[6]

More basic, even existential, questions about relations with China and implications for democracy and constitutionalism in Taiwan framed and underlay the issues immediately at stake in the Sunflower Movement. In the eyes of some of the harsher critics of the Ma Government in the Sunflower Movement and beyond, the administration's approach to the handling of the CSSTA and other issues in Cross-Strait relations reflected a penchant for opacity and a troublingly authoritarian temperament that grated against more popular (or populist) notions of democracy, and that had helped to prompt a reinvigoration of politically engaged civil society organizations in Taiwan during Ma's presidency.[7]

Those who joined or supported the Sunflower Movement and other generally like-minded Taiwanese saw the CSSTA – nested, as it was, among more than twenty accords related to the 2010 Economic Cooperation Framework Agreement – as one of many steps that increased Taiwan's economic dependence on China and, in turn, its vulnerability to the political uses of economic leverage by Beijing. The CSSTA flap thus fit into the long-running, wider-ranging critical narrative that Beijing's approach to the "Taiwan question" is to increase Cross-Strait economic integration as a preliminary step to addressing political issues and as a means to achieving Taiwan's acquiescence in China's claims to sovereignty over the island under a framework with a family resemblance to the "One Country, Two Systems" model – a potential outcome that would have profound and potentially transformative implications for Taiwan's constitutional order.

In this volume, Jiunn-rong Yeh traces the origins of the "civic constitutionalism" manifested in the Sunflower Movement partly to a China-related source: the "ambiguous" Cross-Strait policies that had subjected Taiwan's "political institutions" and "civic structure" to "serious tests". Yeh also notes that prominent among the Sunflower Movement's concerns was the possibility that the CSSTA would give China more political control over Taiwan. Brian Christopher Jones and Yen-Tu Su discern four goals of "democratic justice" pressed by the Sunflower Movement, three of which are among the China-sourced or China-related threats noted above to Taiwan's democratic constitutional order. These include "defending" against a "Trojan horse" Chinese attack on Taiwan's democracy and sovereignty through the CSSTA and related measures; an undermining of

6 Several draft versions of the supervisory law have been in play. See, for example, Office of Information Services, Executive Yuan, Republic of China, "Executive Yuan Approves Draft Bill on Cross-Strait Agreement Supervision" 3 April 2014, http://www.ey.gov.tw/en/News_Content2.aspx?n=1C6028CA080A27B3&s=38451DE4C3084458; Katherine Wei, "DPP Lawmakers Agree to Support Cross-Strait Pact Supervisory Law" *China Post* (27 March 2014); Mainland Affairs Council, Executive Yuan, Republic of China (Taiwan), "MAC: Executive Yuan Draft Version of Cross-Strait Agreement Supervisory Act Allows Legislative Yuan Full Advance Participation and Full Post Supervision and Meets Cross-Strait Exchange Demands" (9 June 2014) http://www.mac.gov.tw/ct.asp?xItem=109798&ctNode=6337&mp=3.

7 See, for example, James Wang, "The Only Loser in this Mess is Ma Ying-jeou" *Taipei Times* (25 April 2014); "Editorial: 'Pro-democracy' is not 'Anti-China'" *Taipei Times* (10 December 2014); J. Michael Cole, "Taipei Flirts with 'Authoritarianism Lite' amid Political Crisis" *China Policy Institute: Analysis* (1 May 2014), https://cpianalysis.org/2014/05/01/taipei-flirts-with-authoritarianism-lite-amid-political-crisis/; Ming-sho Ho, "The Resurgence of Social Movements under the Ma Ying-jeou Government: A Political Opportunity Structure Perspective" in Jean-Pierre Cabestan and Jacques deLisle (eds) *Political Changes in Taiwan under Ma Ying-jeou* (London: Routledge, 2014), pp. 100–119.

democracy by an "imperial executive" suffering from a democratic deficit and bent on pushing through a pact desired by China; and the "winner take all" approach to politics of a KMT administration and LY that combined "pro-China" attitudes with support for "concentration of powers" in Taiwan's Government. Chien-Huei Wu offers quantitative evidence to support the Sunflower Movement's concern that closer economic integration with China – of the sort that the CSSTA would promote – does indeed pose a threat to at least one key pillar of democratic constitutionalism in Taiwan (as well as Hong Kong): a free press.

The intertwining of politics and law

Related to the nature of the China-based challenges described above, the Sunflower Movement and the Occupy Central/Umbrella Movement illustrated and extended a peculiar characteristic of politics in Taiwan and Hong Kong. In both places, politics (and, specifically, democratic politics) is disproportionately about law, and such law is primarily about political matters (and, specifically, constitutional questions).

The type of issues on which Occupy Central and the Umbrella Movement focused have been the defining features of politics – and, certainly, of highly controversial, mass-public-engaging politics – in Hong Kong in recent years. Those politics have been about legal and, specifically, constitutional questions: how democratic would the process be for the selection of the next Chief Executive and members of future Legislative Councils (LegCo)? How would the relevant constitutional document – the Basic Law – be interpreted in answering these questions?

The controversies that precipitated the movement in 2014 echoed ones that had defined politics since Hong Kong's return to Chinese rule had become imminent: would the democratizing election rules adopted by the last colonial government (primarily, expanding vastly the electorate for the functional constituencies that chose many of the members of LegCo) be accepted by Beijing and deemed consistent with the Basic Law such that the last pre-reversion legislature could "ride the through train" to become the first SAR legislature? Would the Bill of Rights Ordinance, adopted in the twilight of colonial rule and incorporating provisions of the major international human rights covenants into Hong Kong law, succeed in entrenching those norms as supra-legislative, quasi-constitutional constraints on existing laws and future legislation?[8] How much authority and autonomy would Hong Kong's Court of Final Appeal enjoy in a system where its powers were limited by the superior authority of a central government body in Beijing (the NPC-SC) to "interpret" the Basic Law, and where the court's temerity in purporting to review Hong Kong–affecting enactments of the National People's Congress was beaten back by an NPC-SC Interpretation in an early controversial case

8 Legislative Council of the Hong Kong Special Administrative Region, "Establishment of the Provisional Legislative Council", http://www.legco.gov.hk/yr97-98/english/est/estab.htm (describing decision at Second Plenary Session of the Preparatory Committee for the Hong Kong Special Administrative Region, 24 March 1996, to establish a "Provisional Legislative Council" and thereby to "derail" the "through train"); Cap. 383: Hong Kong Bill of Rights Ordinance (1991); see also deLisle and Lane, "Hong Kong's Endgame (I)" (note 2 above).

concerning mainland-born children's right of abode in Hong Kong?[9] Would the SAR legislature adopt a law against sedition, treason, subversion, and secession that the Basic Law contemplated but that threatened to impose restrictions at odds with liberal-democratic values that many in Hong Kong held dear?[10] How would the Basic Law's principle of "gradual and orderly progress" towards democratic elections for the Chief Executive and legislature be interpreted and applied?[11] In which electoral cycle would universal suffrage finally be allowed for such positions and how would candidates be nominated to stand for the crucial post of Chief Executive in the SAR's executive-dominated government?[12]

This last question, which was at the centre of Occupy Central and the Umbrella Movement, is, thus, the lineal descendant of earlier kindred controversies. And it has, in turn, spawned new conflicts over follow-on questions, for example: Would those who were not willing to swear a robust form of allegiance to the Basic Law and SAR structure, and to eschew calls for independence, be allowed to stand for office in future elections? Would newly elected LegCo members who expressed opposition to the Beijing government by misstating the words of the required oath be barred from taking office?[13] These are just some of the examples of politics about laws about political/constitutional issues that have characterized Hong Kong politics from before 1997 to the present.

Several of the contributions to this volume engage this aspect of the Umbrella Movement and its antecedents. Fu's and Chen's accounts of the historical background to the movement and the specific issues over which Occupy Central, the Umbrella Movement, the Beijing and SAR governments and their Hong Kong allies struggled are, fundamentally, studies of the remarkably law-centred (and, specifically, constitutional and "political" law-centred) politics of Hong Kong from pre-reversion days through the 2014 protests. For both scholars, the Umbrella Movement is the latest step along a long road that can be traced back through the series of NPC-SC decisions and interpretations concerning elections in Hong Kong, the struggle over anti-secession and anti-sedition legislation, the conflicts over the powers of the Court of Final Appeal, and, in Chen's account, all the way back to early colonial-era decisions to implant British common law rule of law but not Westminster-style parliamentary democracy.

9 See Basic Law of the Hong Kong Special Administrative Region, article 158 (1990); *Ng Ka Ling v. Director of Immigration*, 1 HKC 291 (HKSAR Court of Final Appeal 1999); Standing Committee of the Ninth National People's Congress, Interpretation by the Standing Committee of the National People's Congress of Articles 22(4) and 24(2)(3) of the Basic Law of the Hong Kong Special Administrative Region of the People's Republic of China (26 June 1999); Lin Feng, "The Constitutional Crisis in Hong Kong – Is it Over?" *Pacific Rim Law & Policy Journal*, Vol. 9 No. 2 (2000): 281–315; Albert H. Y. Chen, "Constitutional Crisis in Hong Kong: Congressional Supremacy and Judicial Review" (1999) 33(4) *International Lawyer* 1025–1040.

10 Basic Law, article 23; Ngok Ma, "Civil Society in Self-Defense: The Struggle against National Security Legislation in Hong Kong" (2006) 14(44) *Journal of Contemporary China* 465–482.

11 Basic Law, articles 45, 68; see also, Explanations on "The Basic Law of the Hong Kong Special Administrative Region of the People's Republic of China (Draft)" and Its Related Documents (Third Session of the Seventh National People's Congress on 28 March 1990).

12 See the NPC-SC decisions of 2004, 2007, and 2014 noted earlier in this chapter.

13 Statement by HKSAR Government Regarding 2016 Legislative Council Election (14 July 2016), http://www.info.gov.hk/gia/general/201607/14/P2016071400753.htm.

Chen characterizes the Occupy Central/Umbrella Movement as a "social movement that drew on legal norms", and he undertakes to address the apparent paradox of the protesters and the NPC-SC both arguing that their irreconcilable positions were based on a proper interpretation of the Basic Law. Fu argues that constitutional and legal instruments have been the means of choice for Beijing to limit Hong Kong's political autonomy and democratization. Although noting that Hong Kong's pan-democrats often have faced criticism for "judicialising" politics and thereby "politicizing" courts, Fu finds that the law-centredness of Hong Kong politics often has worked to the disadvantage of pro-democracy groups, in part because Hong Kong courts typically confine themselves to narrowly legal analyses that leave little room for the larger political-constitutional questions (as in the case of the injunctions that pro-government complainants obtained against the Umbrella Movement's activities), or sometimes that the courts venture into more political-constitutional questions but do so on a battlefield tilted in favour of the PRC's non-judicial political institutions (as in the case of the NPC-SC's action rejecting the Court of Final Appeal's decision in the *Ng Ka Ling* right of abode case or the NPC-SC's interpretation of the LegCo oath-taking provision, which truncated still-pending court proceedings). Chih-hsing Ho largely shares the first part of Fu's assessment of Hong Kong's courts, offering a detailed critique of their reluctance to consider issues beyond the law on the books and considerations of law and order when issuing injunctions, and adjudicating criminal charges, against Umbrella Movement participants. In a different vein, Daniel Matthews acknowledges that Hong Kong's peculiar constitutional structure contributed to the "perspicuously legalistic tone and orientation" of the Umbrella Movement's pro-democracy politics, and the central place of "interpretive battles" over the rule of law, civil disobedience, and proposals for constitutional change in the movement. He laments, however, that the obvious importance of such legal issues risks obscuring the larger political features of the movement.

Taiwan's Sunflower Movement was a broadly similar instance of a broadly similar pattern of law and politics. The protests, the occupation of the legislature, and the controversy over the CSSTA and the LY's handling of it did much to define the politics of the moment in Taiwan, with repercussions stretching at least to the end of the decade. It is generally accepted among analysts of Taiwan's electoral politics that the Sunflower Movement – the legal and constitutional issues that motivated it and that it spotlighted, and the political energy it generated, particularly among young voters – helped to explain the sweeping DPP victories in the 9-in-1 local elections in November 2014, the ensuing disarray in the KMT, and the DPP's capturing of the presidency and an unprecedented legislative majority in the January 2016 elections, in addition to the Sunflower Movement–spawned New Power Party's emergence as the third-largest party in the LY.[14] The CSSTA and the controversy surrounding it came to be emblematic of more general public concerns – to which DPP and NPP candidates explicitly and successfully appealed – that Cross-Strait rapprochement had been proceeding too rapidly under Ma, with too few benefits and too many risks for Taiwan, including direct and indirect risks to Taiwan's democratic constitutional order.

14 See, for example, Linda van der Horst, "The Rise of Taiwan's 'Third Force'" *The Diplomat* (6 January 2016), http://thediplomat.com/2016/01/the-rise-of-taiwans-third-force/; Ankit Panda, "The One Big Takeaway from Taiwan's Historic Election" *The Diplomat* (19 January 2016), http://thediplomat.com/2016/01/the-one-big-takeaway-from-taiwans-historic-2016-election/.

As in Hong Kong, the politics of the popular movement in Taiwan was in large part about legal issues, including constitutional or quasi-constitutional ones. As noted above, a principal demand of the Sunflower Movement was the adoption of legislation on parliamentary supervision of Cross-Strait agreements. Such a law has evident implications for the constitutional balance of powers between the legislature and the president. So, too, did the political pressure on the Ma administration to foreswear acting on its separation-of-powers-related argument that Cross-Strait accords generally need not be submitted for legislative approval.[15] The outrage at the way the LY handled the CSSTA bill that spawned the Sunflower Movement also fed into broader calls to reform procedures in the legislature, to redress the majority party's resort to problematic measures to silence the minority, and to consider reforms to a caucus system that allowed a handful of legislators to block parliamentary action (a problematic feature that has made the shortcuts the KMT leadership in the LY employed for the CSSTA tempting and, by some lights, justifiable).

The Sunflower Movement, in focusing on legal questions involving democratic and constitutional issues, reprised a familiar dynamic in Taiwan's recent political history. Facing pressure from a growing pro-democracy movement (partly in exile and partly ensconced in the DPP's informal predecessor, the *dangwai*) in the 1980s, President Chiang Ching-kuo (蔣經國) undertook a major legal change – ending martial law decrees rooted in the Nationalists' conflict with the communists on the Chinese mainland – that removed a key barrier to democratization and the implementation of the Republic of China's (ROC) formally democratic and liberal constitution. Earlier, a key moment in the genesis of Taiwan's pro-democracy movement had been the politically controversial criminal prosecution of participants in the 1979 Kaohsiung/*Meilidao* Incident who pressed publicly for democratic political change. In Taiwan's move to full democracy during the 1990s under President Lee Teng-hui (李登輝), constitutional law and democratizing political change were deeply intertwined as Taiwan's Council of Grand Justices issued constitutional interpretations, and Lee's Government secured the adoption of Additional Articles to the Constitution that led to fully democratic elections for Taiwan's legislature and president and revised the powers of the major governmental institutions. A major factor in pushing forward these changes was the Sunflower Movement's closest precedent: the student-led Wild Lily Movement, which also had a strikingly legal focus, demanding the end of the National Assembly and the Temporary Provisions (the law that had suspended the operation of much of the constitution during Taiwan's long martial law era), and a government commitment to progress towards political reforms, including democratization.

Under Lee's successor, Chen Shui-bian (陳水扁), Taiwan's contentious politics often focused on international law–implicating questions of Taiwan's status as a sovereign state and possible moves towards stronger formal assertions of independence. Those issues were framed partly in constitutional terms, and, specifically, possible constitutional amendments invoking or addressing democracy. Chen pushed for constitutional replacement – a move that arguably suggested (although it did not necessarily imply) a declaration of a new,

15 This administration's argument was based primarily on a controversial reading of the Articles Governing Relations between the People of the Taiwan Area and the Mainland Area and the Standards for Handling Treaties and Agreements, which arguably required only reporting to the LY "for reference" in the case of Cross-Strait accords. See also Shih Hsiu-chuan, "Caucus Whips Agree on Detailed Review of Cross-Strait Service Trade Agreement" *Taipei Times* (26 June 2013); Yen-Tu Su, "Translating Protest into Law Test for Sunflowers" *Taipei Times* (4 May 2014).

separate state. His rhetoric and reform agenda raised concerns – which he sought to assuage on various occasions, including in his first inaugural address – that he would seek to amend the constitution's provisions on the national name and territory (which, in the existing constitution, arguably imply that the territory of Taiwan is part of a larger China). Chen also won passage of constitutional amendments that revised provisions governing the legislature (most notably by reducing its size and bringing its election cycle into line with that of the president), eliminated the National Assembly (a body that pro-democratic constitutional reforms largely rendered irrelevant), and adopted the referendum as an essential mechanism for constitutional amendment. Chen and his allies presented their constitutional reforms as a means to strengthen democracy in Taiwan by giving voters a more direct and effective voice, and by bringing the formal reach and basis of ROC Government institutions into alignment with the people of Taiwan whom they governed and served.[16] The general pattern seems likely to continue in the post-Sunflower Movement period: the new government that came to power in 2016 launched a "truth and reconciliation" or "transitional justice" process to investigate the era of KMT authoritarian rule – a purportedly democracy-vindicating and (through "healing") democracy-strengthening move that critics in Taiwan and the Chinese mainland saw as threatening to undermine further the connection between contemporary Taiwan and the one-China-compatible "Republic of China" regime embedded in the mainland-born and KMT-created ROC constitution.

In this volume, several of the authors – including Yeh, Jones and Su, Wen-Chen Chang, and Cheng-Yi Huang – analyse the Sunflower Movement from the perspective of the deep and complex connections between (constitutional) law and (democratic) politics in Taiwan. Yeh, for example, frames his assessment of the Sunflower Movement as a moment of "civic constitutionalism" in which the protesters, and the wider public responding to them, focused to a remarkable degree on constitutional and near-constitutional legal issues, including separation of powers (rejecting the Ma government's claim that legislative oversight of Cross-Strait negotiation would encroach upon executive prerogatives and demanding legislation to provide for legislative and public supervision of such agreements); holding public *salons* on constitutional law (with lectures from leading scholars); enhancing the role of the public vis-à-vis government institutions (by achieving disclosure of CSSTA-related information that the government had withheld); and raising the salience of core human rights norms thatare embedded in Taiwan's constitution and laws (particularly in the context of the police use of force against the protesters who sought to expand the occupation from the LY to the Executive Yuan). As Yeh rightly points out, civil society efforts to effect legal changes related to political issues, and with constitutional underpinnings, have become perennial phenomena in Taiwan, not limited to dramatic movements such as the Sunflowers or Wild Lilies.

Chang offers an intriguing Sunflower-focused parallel to Fu's assessment of how legal actions against the protesters played out in Hong Kong. Chang describes more positive and hopeful outcomes for Taiwan's movement participants, with a new democratically elected government headed by a party that was generally sympathetic to the movement, and with

16 See generally Jacques deLisle, "Reforming/Replacing the ROC Constitution: Implications for Taiwan's State(-like) Status and US policy" *Woodrow Wilson International Center Asia Program Special Report* (November 2004), 12–18; Jacques deLisle, "International Contexts and Domestic Pushback" in Bruce Gilley and Larry Diamond (eds) *Political Change in China* (Boulder, CO: Lynne Reiner, 2008), pp. 198–201.

courts that have looked favourably on state compensation suits brought by injured protesters, and seem likely to look critically at prosecutions of the protesters.

Part of Yeh's analysis and much of Huang's account see the law-and-politics connection operating at more fundamental levels. For Yeh, the Sunflower Movement may be something of an Ackermanian "constitutional moment" in which citizen political action fundamentally alters the constitutional order, in this case by making it more "civic" or citizen-controlled. Somewhat similarly, Huang sees the Sunflower Movement as reflecting the aspirations of a citizenry empowered by its experience of democracy to create a new constitutional identity different from the still-too-China-linked one intractably embedded in the ROC's written constitution.

Direct democracy, "illegal" protests, and the appeal to transcendent principles

The Sunflower Movement and the Umbrella Movement took direct, popular democracy to new heights in Taiwan and Hong Kong. They also posed in acute forms the question of the constitutional or democratic legitimacy of illegal protest actions undertaken in the name of democratic or democratic-constitutionalist norms. For the protesters and for many analysts, possible justifications for such concededly "illegal" actions lay in appeals to transcendent principles of democracy, constitutionalism, and other related norms.

To be sure, large-scale public protests on political matters, including questions of democracy and constitutional issues, are hardly unprecedented in Taiwan since it began its democratic transition or in Hong Kong since its reversion to China. Taiwan has seen the 1990 Wild Lily Movement (calling for direct democratic elections) and the 2008 Wild Strawberries Movement (which began as a protest over the Ma Government's actions to suppress protests targeting the visit to Taiwan by the chair of the PRC's Association for Relations Across the Taiwan Straits, and which evolved into demands for revisions to a public order law that protesters saw as unduly burdening constitutional rights to free speech and assembly), the 2007 Red Shirt Army protests (led by former DPP chief Shih Ming-teh (施明德), denouncing corruption in the Chen administration and demanding Chen's removal from office – a possibility provided for in the ROC constitution), and many other lesser examples. In responding to the handling of the CSSTA and the issues of democracy and constitutional government that it raised, the Sunflower Movement extended this tradition, especially that of the student-led Wild Lily and Wild Strawberry protests.

In the Hong Kong SAR, issues of democracy and constitutionalism often have drawn large groups of protesters to the streets, sometimes in demonstrations marking the anniversaries of the territory's 1 July 1997 reversion to China. Major foci of such protests include: the 1999 NPC-SC interpretation of the Basic Law, sought by the Hong Kong SAR government, to overturn the controversial decision by Hong Kong's Court of Final Appeal (concerning the right of abode in Hong Kong of mainland-born children of lawful Hong Kong residents), which protesters regarded as a threat to the judicial autonomy promised to Hong Kong under the Basic Law; the 2003 proposed legislation to implement the Basic Law's anti-sedition and anti-secession provision, which critics saw as threatening civil liberties and inconsistent with democratic norms; the 2005 SAR Government-proposed electoral reform package (itself proffered in the aftermath of the 2004 NPC-SC decision rejecting universal suffrage for the 2007 Chief Executive and 2008 LegCo elections) that failed to offer universal suffrage for future selections of the SAR Chief Executive and for all seats in LegCo (eliminating the functional constituency seats filled by votes of narrow electorates); the 2007 NPC-SC decision that set 2017 as the earliest possible date for universal suffrage and left terms for future electoral laws so vague that Hong Kong democrats worried about limits to democracy in 2017 and beyond. Occupy Central and the Umbrella Movement are squarely within this lineage, arising in response to the most recent NPC-SC decisions concerning Hong Kong's democratization and implementation of the electoral provisions in the SAR's mini-constitution (including the fateful 2014 decision that prompted the protests that became the Umbrella Movement).

But none of the prior popular movements in Taiwan in the democratizing/democratic era reached the level of the Sunflower Movement, with its 24-day occupation of the Legislative Yuan and attempted occupation of the Executive Yuan, or its apparent impact on party politics and election outcomes, or (if some of the contributors to this volume are correct) its potential to alter conceptions of democratic constitutionalism in Taiwan. So, too, none of the prior post-reversion movements in Hong Kong equalled the Umbrella Movement, with its 79-day occupation of major public spaces near government offices and in commercial centres, its provocation of harsh responses from the SAR Government and strident denunciation by Beijing, and its impetus to proposals (some also pressed by Occupy Central) for ambitious near-term changes of constitutional magnitude – including robustly democratic "civic nomination" for Chief Executive candidates, and even some calls for Hong Kong independence.

The two movements also broke new ground in so squarely raising the question of whether illegal protest actions are legitimate (and, if so, on what basis). Participants, their defenders, and their critics all acknowledge that some of the protesters' actions violated existing laws that were at least facially constitutional laws adopted through constitutionally proper means. Yet, protesters and their supporters and many analysts claimed, such concededly unlawful actions were, nonetheless, legitimated by more fundamental principles of democracy and constitutionalism.

This set of issues, perhaps more than any other, is the focus of this volume. Several contributors offer analyses that lead to the conclusion that the protesters' illegal actions should not be subject to prosecution, largely because they are justified in light of some higher norms. Thus, Jones and Su characterize the Sunflower Movement as a case of "confrontational contestation" in which citizens undertook illegal acts of "democratic disobedience" to advance a vision of democracy that was at least defensible (and perhaps much more than that), not revolutionary, and at odds with the problematically narrow one embraced by those in control of the institutions of government. For Jones and Su, this appeal to more fundamental values of democracy and democratic governance arguably trumps ordinary strictures of the "rule of law" or "law and order", and, at minimum, it argues for the state's foregoing prosecution of the protesters in a "democratic compromise" to achieve a "democratic peace" and to find the best way forward for Taiwan's democracy. Yeh offers a broadly similar, if less explicit, argument. He sees the protests and occupation of the LY as an exercise of "civic constitutionalism" that invoked international human rights and comparative constitutional norms, and did so through direct citizen action outside law-prescribed channels – a method that is arguably legitimate as a general matter and that is more clearly supportable where the ordinary mechanisms of representative democracy fall short (as they had in the context of the CSSTA review process).

Chang looks to universal human rights norms, particularly the International Covenant on Civil and Political Rights' (ICCPR) provisions on free speech and freedom of assembly and the ICCPR's broader support for democracy, as the proper metrics for evaluating the actions of the Sunflower Movement's participants. She argues for using such norms to establish the relevant standards for what the law should be, to interpret Taiwan's constitution, to strike down more restrictive laws, or, at least, to provide a basis for eschewing conviction of participants in the movement for violating overly restrictive ROC laws (and for holding government to account for its excessive restrictions upon, and use of force against, the protesters). Huang, too, links a sympathetic assessment of the Sunflower Movement's law-violating methods to the younger generation's embrace of norms of self-government and a democratic constitutional identity that are at odds with the crabbed law-on-the-books order framed by the ROC constitution and legislation (particularly laws addressing Taiwan's status vis-à-vis China).

In a broadly similar – but bleaker – vein, Ho criticizes the Hong Kong courts' narrowly legalistic and law-and-order-focused approach to cases arising from the Umbrella Movement. Using the lens of a rich political theory literature on civil disobedience and law-breaking resistance to unjust laws, Ho sees the protesters' actions as advancing values – liberty and democracy – that are as valid and compelling as the rule-of-law values that were invoked by the courts. She sees the occupiers' unlawful actions as possibly justified, or at least warranting the state's foregoing prosecution, because Hong Kong's political and constitutional order excluded the voice of the majority of its citizens – an easier situation in which to defend disobedience to unjust laws than would be the case in the context of the more well-functioning democratic politics that generated much of the legal-political theory that Ho draws upon.

Like Yeh's and Huang's accounts of Taiwan's Sunflower Movement, Fu's and Chen's descriptions of Hong Kong's Occupy Central/Umbrella Movement point to the protesters' invocations of explicitly extra-legal, fundamental political principles, such as democracy, or "genuine" universal suffrage and free elections meeting "international standards", or "civic constitutionalism". Somewhat similarly, Matthews emphasizes the importance to the Umbrella Movement of appeals to norms and narratives of "rights" and "oughts" that go far beyond the constraining positive law of the SAR. For Fu, as for Ho, the existing order's effective blockage of society's aspirations for the implementation of such principles can justify resorting to means that violate existing laws.

While these normatively rich analyses in this book take the Sunflower Movement and the Umbrella Movement as their primary or exclusive focus, the general problems and patterns they assess are far from new to Taiwan and Hong Kong politics. Arguments for the democratic and constitutional legitimacy of the illegal political protests of 2014 resonate with broader and longer-term features of legal-political discourse in Hong Kong and Taiwan. That discourse is, in its broadest sense, a conflict between positivism and something akin to "naturalism" (meaning, here, taking as the relevant standard some form of transcendent and fixed normative principles that are not subject to change, even by procedurally/constitutionally proper means of legislation or constitutional interpretation or amendment).

In Hong Kong, those who have pressed for democracy – and, more modestly, for democratic interpretations of the Basic Law, and, collaterally, for stronger protections of human rights – have had to cope with an adverse environment of positive law since well before Hong Kong's reversion to Chinese rule. The late colonial system of governance that defined the political-legal system that was to remain largely in place under the promise of "continuity" made in the Joint Declaration was far from democratic. This was true notwithstanding the limited democratizing reforms introduced during the twilight of British rule and the more ambitious but still limited changes (including vast expansion of the electorates for the functional constituency seats in the legislature) introduced at the eleventh hour by Governor Chris Patten and later overridden by China.

A document with an impeccable positivist pedigree as an act of the National People's Congress exercising its sovereign powers to define the terms of governance over Chinese territory and citizens (and, moreover, adopted to implement in domestic law an international agreement), the Basic Law was vague and loose in its commitments to democratization. Controversial and offensive to democratic values as they were, the NPC-SC interpretations and decisions rejecting calls from Hong Kong for more rapid progress to full democratic elections were not indisputably indefensible in terms of the Basic Law's text or the NPC-SC's authority to interpret it. Much the same can be said about the Basic Law's text, the NPC-SC's interpretive powers, and its use of those powers to limit the authority of Hong Kong's Court of Final Appeal and reject notions of judicial autonomy embraced by liberals and democrats in Hong Kong. So, too, the pre-reversion Hong Kong Bill of Rights Ordinance boldly sought to entrench core international human rights norms in Hong Kong law, but the attempt to give such norms near-constitutional or quasi-constitutional status above ordinary Hong Kong legislation faced the positivist difficulty that Hong Kong's constitutional order provided no ready basis for creating laws with that status.

Advocates for democracy and greater protection for civil-political rights have been able to make credible, often persuasive, positivist arguments about proper or permissible interpretations of the Basic Law and the Joint Declaration, and they have done so in the context of numerous constitutional and lesser legal controversies in Hong Kong, including ones centring on various provisions in the Basic Law, such as article 24 on the right of abode, article 23 on sedition, treason, subversion, and secession, articles 25, 45, 68, 104 and annexes on democratic elections for the Chief Executive and LegCo, and so on. But given the counterarguments they have had to face and the institutional allocation of authority to amend and interpret the Basic Law, those who press for democracy and democratic constitutionalism have had to rely heavily on less positivist, more "naturalist" arguments. From battles over legal-political change during the pre-reversion period up through the Umbrella Movement and subsequent controversies over rules governing qualifications to stand for LegCo elections in 2020 or, in the case of the oath-taking controversy, to assume office after elections in 2016, they have embraced and asserted more diffuse and more fundamental arguments about broad principles of democratic governance (which are in a general way ensconced in the Basic Law and Joint Declaration), the rights of Hong Kong people to democratic self-governance, and the civil and political rights that are part of the customary international law of universal human rights, the obligation of good or legitimate government to respect its citizens' civil and political liberties and their democratic preferences, and so on. On this view, the fact that government actions falling short of these norms might be claimed, plausibly, not to violate the Basic Law or Joint Declaration is not an adequate answer, and can leave such measures still illegitimate and a proper target of public protests and movement politics.[17]

In Taiwan, the positivist constraints on democratic constitutionalism have been less intractable because the ROC constitution can be, and has been, altered by constitutionally valid democratic means. Thus, the Additional Articles to the constitution adopted under Lee Teng-hui and Chen Shui-bian effectuated many of the unquestionably

17 For a more extended version of this argument, with examples from the pre-reversion period, see deLisle and Lane, "Hong Kong's Endgame" (notes 2 and 3 above).

democratic and purportedly democracy-promoting changes discussed above. They provided for universal suffrage democratic elections, created the referendum as a tool of governance and constitutional amendment, and revised provisions defining and empowering government institutions – including the LY, the National Assembly, the premier, the Control Yuan, and so on – that were seen as flawed in terms of overarching conceptions of democracy and democratic constitutional governance.[18] While major changes to the positive law of the constitution thus sometimes have been procedurally possible in Taiwan, they often have been politically difficult, and their advocates at times have pressed for them in terms that stress norms of democracy (or rights or even constitutionalism) that could be called extra-constitutional, supra-constitutional, or constitution-legitimating.

For those in Taiwan who link democratic constitutionalism to Taiwan's international autonomy, sovereignty, or, especially, formal independence, positive law (including the constitution) has been notably constraining – not least because of the reaction that certain formal changes would elicit from Beijing. The ROC constitution and Taiwan's laws more generally therefore have been subjected to criticism, and calls for change, on the basis of more fundamental democratic and constitutionalist principles that transcend the written documents. This pattern was most evident in grappling with questions of sovereignty and statehood, the national name, and the national territory during the Lee Teng-hui and Chen Shui-bian presidencies. Thus, for example, the formulation that Beijing derided as Lee's "two-state thesis" was in fact not so radical a departure from the positive law of a non-two-state constitution. What Lee offered was a tortured locution that avoided flat-out repudiation of constitutional provisions that retained some vestiges of a "one China" framework. Rather than defining Cross-Strait relations as between a state of Taiwan and a state of China, Lee spoke of "a special state-to-state relationship" that did not fit fully into either of the conventional categories of domestic or international relations. And he proclaimed that the "Republic of China" (not "Taiwan") was "a sovereign, independent state", had been so since 1912 – a time when the ROC clearly claimed all of China – and thus had "no need to declare independence" again.[19] The earlier Lee-era Articles Governing Relations between the People of the Taiwan Area and the Mainland Area reflected a similar position – assuming two "areas", not asserting two "states". Lee also had adopted the Guidelines for National Unification, and repeatedly reaffirmed their contents. The Guidelines accepted – however counterfactually and however much as a project for the indefinite future – the possibility of an eventual return to a single government and constitutional framework for the mainland and Taiwan.[20]

Chen went further than Lee, and began to speak of Taiwan as an independent sovereign state, without always identifying it with the ROC. But Chen, too, acquiesced at key points on key issues, bowing to the political constraints on changes to positive law, including the ROC constitution. The "four noes and one not" in his first inaugural speech pledged, in various ways, fidelity to elements of Lee's legacy and the non-two-state-like elements in the existing constitutional framework: no declaration of independence, no change of the

18 Additional Articles of the Constitution of the Republic of China (Taiwan) (various dates).

19 Responses to Questions Submitted by Deutsche Welle – Lee Teng-hui. President, Republic of China, 9 July 1999, http://fas.org/news/taiwan/1999/0709.htm; deLisle, "Chinese Puzzle" (note 2 above), pp. 49–52.

20 Articles Governing Relations between the People of the Taiwan Area and the Mainland Area (1992, amended through 2010); Guidelines for National Unification (4 March 1991).

national name (from "Republic of China"), no addition of "special state-to-state" relations to the constitution, no referendum on Taiwan independence, and not abolishing the Guidelines for National Unification or the related National Unification Council.[21] In his second term, Chen ultimately forwent his goal of constitutional replacement (which could have embodied a claim that a new, "second", and "non-China" state had been created – a possibility the PRC rejected with pointed legal formality in its 2005 Anti-Secession Law). Chen settled for constitutional revisions that steered clear of seeking changes to the national name and territory, and (in any explicit way) claims of Taiwan's status as a separate sovereign state. President Tsai Ing-wen (蔡英文), suspected by many in Beijing of being "another Chen", has reaffirmed acceptance of constraints embodied in the ROC constitution and other positive laws. In the singularly high-profile setting of her 20 May 2016 inaugural address, Tsai notably reaffirmed that Cross-Strait relations would be conducted "in accordance with the Republic of China Constitution, the Articles Governing Relations between the People of the Taiwan Area and the Mainland Area, and other relevant legislation".[22] This has notably not been enough to assuage Beijing's concerns about the troublesome link between constitutional law and possibly separate sovereignty: even before Tsai's precedent-breaking telephone conversation withe US President-elect Donald Trump raised new concerns about Taiwan's quest for more fully state-like status, the mainland's Cross-Strait policy circles were expressing concern that Tsai's government might tinker with constitutional positions on the national territory of the ROC as a means to pursue "soft" independence.

Faced with such constraints in positive law that are, to a significant extent, indirectly imposed by China, the Taiwanese have turned to invoking universal or transcendent principles to protect or enhance their autonomous, liberal-democratic constitutional order against threats posed by Beijing's agenda of eventual unification (and intractable opposition to formal independence). From the first steps towards democratization during the last days of Chiang Ching-kuo, through the full-fledged democratization and constitutional interpretations and revisions of the Lee Teng-hui era, the "pushing of the envelope" on independence and the incomplete constitutional revision of the Chen Shui-bian years, the otherwise-very-different Ma Ying-jeou presidency, and into the early days of the Tsai Ing-wen administration, Taiwan's leaders – along with many Taiwanese who support or criticize them (including participants in the Sunflower Movement and other mass movements that preceded it) – have repeatedly invoked several factors to bolster Taiwan's claims to a distinct liberal-democratic constitutionalist order (and the international stature that helps protect this autonomous order). These factors include: robust and stable self-governance over the island and the people who live there, the shared identity of the people who live in Taiwan, the government's democratic accountability to the people (especially on issues – most of constitutional magnitude – that would affect Taiwan's autonomy or independence and, in international legal terms, the right of the Taiwanese to self-determination as a people), well-consolidated democratic institutions and practices, and a strong record on human rights. The first several elements speak to the classic criteria for statehood – and the security that comes with it – under

21 Chen Shui-bian, "Taiwan Stands Up: Towards the Dawn of a Rising Era" (Inaugural Address, 20 May 2000). The last of these five pledges was the only one that would not have entailed a change to the constitution. Chen arguably violated it when he announced a "suspension" but not an "abolition".

22 Tsai Ing-wen, Inaugural Address (20 May 2016).

international law. The latter ones engage the international norms that matter for a state or state-like entity's international stature, especially in the post–Cold War era.[23] The Taiwanese invocation of these aspects of Taiwan's political and constitutional practice has been framed frequently in terms of principles – international, universal, or otherwise normatively binding – that go beyond, that are deeper than, and that, in some cases, once were at odds with, the text of the ROC constitution. While these types of arguments have been an important part of the repertoire of those who have wielded great political power in Taiwan, they have been even more central – and indispensable – for those who have challenged official positions, whether in calling for formal independence or participating in social movements seeking more fundamental change to the political system.

The revenge of political economy

The Sunflower Movement and the Occupy Central/Umbrella Movement marked what we might call the "revenge of political economy" in the democratic politics of Taiwan and Hong Kong. In a world where democratic politics often is about economic issues, Taiwan and Hong Kong have been relative outliers. The pro-democracy activists and movements in Hong Kong began during the pre-reversion era with – and have long retained – a heavy emphasis on such issues as the constitutional structure for Hong Kong, the pace of democratization, protection of civil liberties, preservation of the rule of law in politically sensitive cases, and so on. A common critique of Hong Kong's pan-democrat politicians – and an asserted source of electoral weakness – has been that they have lacked a fully articulated and earnestly advocated economic platform.[24]

From the 1990s on, electoral politics and popular democracy in Taiwan have focused overwhelmingly on political issues, narrowly defined – such as the pace of democratization, issues of national identity, sovereignty, independence, the high politics of Cross-Strait relations, and so on. Observers of Taiwan's domestic politics have long and repeatedly waited for the national election that would finally be about "normal" issues, such as economic and social policy.[25] Under presidential candidate Tsai Ing-wen in 2012, the DPP moved to

23 For a fuller version of this analysis, see deLisle, "Chinese Puzzle" (note 2 above), pp. 55–60; deLisle, "International Contexts and Domestic Pushback" (note 16 above), pp. 192–201.

24 See, for example, Joseph S. Y. Cheung, "The Pro-Democracy Movement: A Lost Decade?" (2007) 2007/2 *China Perspectives* 14–26; Center for Northeast Asian Policy Studies, Brookings Institution, "The 2004 Legislative Council Elections and Implications for US policy towards Hong Kong", 15 September 2004, pp. 2–9 (remarks of Sonny Lo Shiu-hing), https://www.brookings.edu/wp-content/uploads/2012/04/20040915.pdf; see also Alvin Y. H. Cheung, "Melancholy in Hong Kong" (Winter 2014) *World Policy Institute*, http://www.worldpolicy.org/journal/winter2014/melancholy-hong-kong. The point is also implicit in Fu's references in this volume to the criticism that Hong Kong's pan-democrats are the "party of barristers" and that the focus on democracy issues has made most Hong Kong political parties "single-issue machines".

25 See generally China Real Time Report, "A 'Normal' Election Shows Taiwan's Progress" *Wall Street Journal* (26 November 2010) (quoting Shelley Rigger), http://blogs.wsj.com/chinarealtime/2010/11/26/a-normal-election-shows-taiwans-progress/; Steve Tsang, "In Praise of a 'Normal' Election" (1 September 2012) http://nottspolitics.org/2012/01/09/in-praise-of-a-normal-election/; Jacques deLisle, "Taiwan's 2016 Elections and Cross-Strait Relations" FPRI E-Note (4 February 2016), http://www.fpri.org/article/2016/02/taiwans-2016-elections-and-cross-strait-relations/; Shelley Rigger, "It's Old Versus New In Taiwan's Presidential and Legislative Elections" FPRI E-Note (24 September 2015), http://www.fpri.org/article/2015/09/its-old-versus-new-in-taiwans-presidential-and-legislative-elections/.

increase attention to such issues (as reflected in the campaign slogan "fairness and justice" (*gongping zhengyi*)), and Ma Ying-jeou had promised economic progress as a pillar of his successful campaign in 2008. But Cross-Strait relations and the many political issues with which they are entangled have continued to occupy an outsized place in Taiwan's national elections, including in 2016. Tsai's campaign – and her inaugural address – emphasized economic revitalization, social and economic justice, strengthening the social safety net, and increasing opportunities for the young, yet much of Tsai's focus still remained on assuring Beijing and Washington that she would pursue stability in Cross-Strait relations.

Although still greatly focused on the partly China-driven, primarily political issues of democracy and constitutionalism, the Umbrella Movement and the Sunflower Movement may have heralded something of a partial shift. The two movements brought economic issues nearer the centre of politics, and specifically mass-movement democratic politics. Analyses of the two movements generally agree that the economic anxiety, especially of educated young people, was a secondary factor in the movements' emergence. The students who took the lead in the Umbrella Movement – and ran ahead of the more cautious tactics and clearly defined agenda of the middle-aged leaders of the initial Occupy Central Movement – added frustration about their own seemingly dim career prospects to the longer-standing movement politics focused on political democratization.[26] Here, still, China-related issues remained central, but new economic worries interacted with them. Political concerns about Beijing's recalcitrance towards Hong Kong's democratization and erosion of Hong Kong's autonomy resonated with simmering economic resentment towards the mainland in Hong Kong, which manifested itself in forms as diverse as complaints about mainlanders behaving rudely as shoppers in upscale Hong Kong stores, jamming Hong Kong hospitals' maternity wards to give birth to babies who would then have a right of abode in Hong Kong, and taking desirable professional jobs in the SAR.

In the Sunflower Movement, the place of partly China-linked economic concerns was prominent and straightforward. In Taiwan's relatively lacklustre economy, the university students who spearheaded the movement were unhappy about more than politics. They were greatly and openly concerned about their prospects for employment and advancement. Their attack on the CSSTA focused immediately on political procedural issues, but it unfolded in a context of shifting views in Taiwan – especially among the young – about the political economy of relations with China.[27] Simply, the relevant narrative in Taiwan was shifting from one in which the principal question was the familiar one of whether the benefits of economic integration with the mainland were worth the political risks (that Beijing will use its economic leverage to political ends) towards a more economics-focused

26 See, for example, Samson Yuen and Edmund Cheung, "Hong Kong's Umbrella Protests Were More than Just a Student Movement" *ChinaFile* (1 July 2015), https://www.chinafile.com/reporting-opinion/features/hong-kongs-umbrella-protests-were-more-just-student-movement; Lauren Hilgers, "Hong Kong's Umbrella Revolution Isn't Over Yet" *New York Times Magazine* (18 February 2015); Peter Cai, "Hong Kong Protests about Economics as Much as Democracy" *East Asia Forum* (10 October 2014), http://www.eastasiaforum.org/2014/10/10/hong-kong-protests-about-economics-as-much-as-democracy/.

27 Jenny W. Hsu, "Young Protesters Shaking Up Taiwan's China Policy" *Wall Street Journal* (1 April 2014); Lee Teng-hui, "Taiwan's Hopes and the Duty of its Youth under Globalization" *Thinking Taiwan* (27 February 2015), http://thinking-taiwan.com/taiwans-hopes-and-the-duty-of-its-youth-under-globalization/; Jeffrey Wasserstrom, "Taiwan's Sunflower Protests: Q&A with Shelley Rigger" *Dissent* (11 April 2014), https://www.dissentmagazine.org/online_articles/taiwans-sunflower-protests-a-qa-with-shelley-rigger; James H. Hughes, "Sunshine in Taiwan" (2014) 39(2) *The Journal of Social, Political, and Economic Studies*.

question of whether economic integration with the mainland was providing the promised economic benefits to Taiwan (or was benefiting more than a few at the very top). For educated young people in Taiwan (and for other Taiwanese as well), the prospect of liberalization of the Cross-Strait trade in services seemed directly threatening because it seemed likely to expose them to competition from lower-wage mainland peers (all the more so given the widespread if mistaken expectation that major liberalization of immigration rules would be part of the package of CSSTA-related changes). As noted earlier, the Sunflower Movement is generally thought to account for some of Tsai's and the DPP's increased focus on economic issues during the 2016 election cycle.

This turn to political economy issues in Taiwan and Hong Kong and the politics of their relationships with the mainland implies that Taiwan and Hong Kong are perhaps becoming less exceptional polities, and that the more ordinary tools of political science analysis can be applied to analyse their democratic and electoral politics. Several chapters in this volume point to the significant role of economic issues in the two movements, and some illustrate the fruitfulness of conventional political economy analyses. Jones and Su rank the Sunflower Movement's call for socioeconomic justice in an age of neoliberal free trade agreements among the movement's four principal proffered democratic justifications. Fu notes that rising concerns among the Hong Kong public about sputtering growth and economic well-being formed the backdrop to the Umbrella Movement.

Wu uses empirical techniques to argue that the Sunflower and Umbrella Movement protesters' economics-focused fears were basically right and that Hong Kong and Taiwan have become examples of a variation on a venerable international political economy theory: economic dependence on a more-powerful state can lead to vulnerability to political influence – in this case, anti-democratic influence – from that state.[28] Fu explicitly frames his analysis of the Umbrella Movement in terms of demands for democracy in a high-income society, implicitly invoking another long-standing political economy nostrum about the positive relationship between economic development and pressure for democratization.[29]

Sunflowers versus Umbrellas – Key contrasts between the Taiwan and Hong Kong cases

As the foregoing examination of similarities between Taiwan's Sunflower Movement and Hong Kong's Occupy Central/Umbrella Movement suggests and as the chapters in this volume illustrate, the two movements present a ripe topic for fruitful comparative inquiry. Yet, comparative analysis is as much about differences as it is about similarities. As the chapters in this book also show (and as earlier sections in this chapter and the chapters by Chang, Wu, and Jones and Su specifically note), there are important distinctions between the two cases. To a significant extent, the variances reflect more fundamental contrasts between Taiwan and Hong Kong that – although obvious – warrant mention here.

The names of the two movements offer inadvertent, yet strikingly apt, paired metaphors. "Sunflowers" still manage to bloom in Taiwan, despite the shadow cast by China and its agenda towards what it regards as the Chinese territory and people across the Strait. In

28 See, for example, Albert O. Hirschman, *National Power and the Structure of Foreign Trade* (Berkeley: University of California, 1981).

29 See, for example, Seymour Martin Lipset, "Some Social Requisites of Democracy: Economic Development and Political Legitimacy" (1959) 53 *American Political Science Review* 69–105.

Hong Kong, however, "Umbrellas" were needed to shield against the storm of criticism and rejection from Beijing and its allies in the government and society of a place that had been under Chinese rule (and, in the view of many Hong Kongers, increasingly constraining Chinese rule) for more than a decade and a half.

Participants in the Umbrella Movement – and the citizens of Hong Kong more generally – have had only very limited control over the trajectory of democratization and constitutional development in their polity. Participants in Occupy Central and the Umbrella Movement were reacting to the latest in a series of discouragingly democracy-limiting *faits accomplis* from the NPC-SC in its rulings on the Basic Law, and from a compliant, executive-dominated SAR Government with a non-democratically elected Chief Executive and a relatively weak legislature with half of its members selected by undemocratic functional constituencies and, as the oath-taking controversy in 2016 showed, even democratically elected legislators are at risk of Beijing-driven ouster..

Umbrella Movement activists – along with Occupy Central participants and other advocates for democracy and democratic constitutionalism in Hong Kong – were engaged in an uphill struggle, relying on a relatively meagre toolkit of rational persuasion, moral suasion, blocking legislation that would implement Beijing's and the SAR Government's favoured policies, exerting pressure through public protests, and perhaps imposing collateral political and economic costs on the local and central governments. They could, and did, offer cogent arguments about the proper interpretation of the Basic Law. But formal, authoritative powers of interpretation (as well as amendment) lay beyond their reach, and ultimately in Beijing.

In invoking broad, arguably universal, norms of democracy and rights, they could, and did, appeal to local and international public opinion. But public opinion in Hong Kong was never better than mixed or divided, and some of it turned distinctly negative towards the Umbrella Movement, as some Hong Kongers grew frustrated with the disruptions to traffic and business or found the protesters' demands too radical (including the call for the Chief Executive to step down) or too unrealistic (especially in the face of Beijing's reaction).[30] International public opinion, although generally sympathetic, was predictably evanescent and unlikely to move a resolutely resistant Beijing. The disruption caused by the movement, and the serious discontent and deep dissatisfaction revealed by the movement, signalled that Hong Kong's recipe for economic success – long enduring but always fragile and perpetually evolving – might be in jeopardy if Beijing and the SAR Government were not more accommodating towards demands for political change.[31] But to invoke the spectre of economic decline and to excite concerns among multinational enterprises about Hong Kong's desirability and feasibility as a place to do business was playing with fire. And it might still fail to persuade, or might turn public opinion against

30 Edward Wong, "Some Hong Kong Residents, Weary of Disruptions, Find Fault with Protesters' Methods" *New York Times* (2 October 2014); Niv Horesh, "How Hong Kong's Democracy Protesters Overplayed Their Hand" *China Policy Institute: Analysis* (27 November 2014), https://cpianalysis.org/2014/11/27/how-hong-kongs-democracy-protesters-overplayed-their-hand/.

31 See, for example, the concerns raised by the Hong Kong business community: Mark Hanrahan, "Is Democracy Bad for Business in Hong Kong?" *International Business Times* (9 September 2014), http://www.ibtimes.com/democracy-bad-business-hong-kong-1681116; "What Do the Protests in Hong Kong Mean for Global Firms" *Fortune* (6 October 2014), http://fortune.com/2014/10/06/what-do-the-protests-in-hong-kong-mean-for-global-firms/; but see also Sijia Jiang, "World Bank Says Occupy Protests Fail to Impact Hong Kong's Business Climate" *South China Morning Post* (29 October 2014).

democracy advocates, or might bring an economically pyrrhic victory in the political-legal battle.

None of this is to say that the long quest for democracy and constitutionalism in Hong Kong is doomed or that activist and protest movements will not play an important part in its progress. Although the Umbrella Movement activists famously adopted more radical in-the-streets tactics, their broader repertoire (including their appeals to legal and principled arguments, political opinion at home and abroad, and possible economic consequences) borrowed liberally from the playbook that advocates of democratization and liberal-democratic constitutional rule have developed and used since the 1980s. The arc of Hong Kong's political history is long, but it may still bend towards democracy and constitutionalism (although 2047 – the end of the 50-year minimum promise of autonomy and continuity – looms as a disconcerting, and not all that distant, milepost).

Participants in Taiwan's Sunflower Movement faced a more promising environment. Like the Occupy Central/Umbrella Movement activists, they were taking politics into their own hands to challenge what they saw as dysfunctional and inadequately democratic practices by the ordinary institutions of government and politics. Unlike their Hong Kong counterparts, however, they could hope to effectuate change – and have their grievances addressed – partly through existing democratic and constitutional channels. They were operating in a political system where constitutional interpretation and amendment were prerogatives of Taiwanese institutions and actors, including the constitutional court, the democratically elected political branches, and the people themselves (indirectly through elections and directly through referenda), and where the president and parliament were genuinely accountable to the people through democratic elections with universal suffrage.

Participants in the Sunflower Movement opposed, successfully, action in the legislature on a measure favoured by the government and the legislative majority party. Although pro-democracy forces in Hong Kong also have been able to block government-backed legislative action through pan-democrat members of LegCo and a variety of extraordinary parliamentary and political manoeuvers, the Sunflowers sought, and got, more. They received commitments to new legislation to address their concerns about legislative processes and democratic accountability – including through the supervision law that would subject Cross-Strait agreements to more thorough scrutiny by democratically elected representatives and by the public. The movement is generally, and quite plausibly, credited with affecting the outcome of the 2014 local and 2016 national elections and thereby changing the government's perspective on issues that motivated the movement.[32] One of the two major political parties adopted significant parts of the movement's agenda.

32 Tao Yi-feng, "The 'Sunflower Movement' and the 2016 Taiwan Presidential Elections" *Asia Times* (18 December 2015), http://atimes.com/2015/12/the-sunflower-movement-and-the-2016-taiwan-presidential-elections/; Linda van der Horst, "As Taiwan Prepares for Election, a Third Party Brings Sunflower Movement Activist Issues to the Fore" *National Post* (12 January 2016); Min-hua Huang, "Taiwan's Changing Political Landscape: The KMT's Landslide Defeat in the Nine-in-One Elections" *Brookings East Asia Commentary* (8 December 2014), https://www.brookings.edu/opinions/taiwans-changing-political-landscape-the-kmts-landslide-defeat-in-the-nine-in-one-elections/; Shim Jae Hoon, "Taiwan Post-Election Look: Youth Power Dumps KMT Rule" *Asia Times* (30 May 2016), http://atimes.com/2016/05/taiwan-post-election-look-youth-power-dumps-kmt-rule/.

And the movement led directly to the founding of the party that won five seats in the LY (more than any party other than the DPP or the KMT).

As its electoral impact in part reflects, the Sunflower Movement also was able to attract more robust and effective public support than was Hong Kong's Umbrella Movement. Some of the Sunflower Movement's methods – including the length and manner of the occupation of the LY and the attempted takeover of the Executive Yuan – drew significant criticism, and their goals were not universally shared in Taiwan's often-polarized politics.[33] But the multipronged message of criticizing LY procedures as undemocratic, the CSSTA's deepening of economic integration with China as ill-advised, and the government's aims and methods (both in handling the CSSTA and in manhandling the protesters) as insufficiently reflecting public opinion and democratic values, resonated broadly with a populace that thought, correctly, that it could (and believed that it rightly should) have a say over such matters. Taiwan's international status is sufficiently robust – and different from Hong Kong's – that the US and others in the global community would react strongly if Beijing were to attempt to interfere in Taiwan's democratic politics and constitutional development in a way that resembled its intervention in Hong Kong and against the Umbrella Movement.

The Sunflower Movement did not operate in a context where China was irrelevant to democratic and constitutional development, but the China-imposed constraints were qualitatively more marginal and less constraining in Taiwan than in Hong Kong. The redlines Beijing draws do matter for democratic politics and constitutional development in Taiwan, and they are a significant factor in the absence of mass political movements for formal independence in Taiwan, or any major Taiwanese party's full-throated endorsement of formal independence. More than one Taiwanese president has faced de facto Chinese-imposed limits on constitutional revisions that he or she otherwise would have pursued to further indigenize or normalize or, arguably, democratize Taiwan's constitutional order. China-driven constraints necessitated Lee's tortured characterization of Taiwan's status and sovereignty, compelled much of Chen's "four noes and one not" and severely limited his agenda for constitutional reform or replacement, formed the backdrop for Ma's "three noes" (no unification, no independence, no war) and the 1992 Consensus's "one China" principle, and dictated Tsai's profession of fealty to the ROC constitution and the Lee-era Articles on Relations between the People of the Taiwan Area and the Mainland Area as the basis for her conduct of Cross-Strait relations. Nonetheless, the contrast between Taiwan's somewhat China-shaded sunflowers and Hong Kong's China-drenched umbrellas is dramatic and significant.

What the Movements imply about China and Cross-Strait/ Mainland–Hong Kong relations

Finally, the Sunflower Movement and the Umbrella Movement – and, more so, Beijing's reactions to them – offer a few interrelated lessons about prospects for China and its relations with Taiwan and Hong Kong.

First, the two movements cast doubt on assumptions that appear to have underlain much of China's approach to politics in Hong Kong and Taiwan. Chinese sources' public

33 Brian Hioe, "Beyond the Sunflower Movement: Present Issues for Future Taiwanese Activism" *Thinking Taiwan* (16 May 2014), http://thinking-taiwan.com/beyond-the-sunflower-movement/.

assessments of the Umbrella Movement returned to a familiar refrain that outside forces were surely to blame for political troubles in Hong Kong. They insistently pointed to foreign "black hands" behind the movement and complained of outside "interference" in Hong Kong politics.[34] This reprised an old tactic of attacking attempts to "internationalize" issues of Hong Kong's domestic politics and governance.[35] China's behaviour towards the Umbrella Movement suggested an expectation that the old adage – long pressed by some of the Hong Kong business elites with whom Beijing often deals – would hold true that Hong Kong is an "economic city" and not a "political city", such that the central government need not take terribly seriously apparent popular demands for democratic political change. Although it is too soon to reach definitive conclusions, the youthful participants in the Umbrella Movement may have shown that Beijing erred if it anticipated that simply "waiting out" the now-middle-aged-or-older firebrands who began to push for democracy and a democratic constitution during the pre-reversion period would be a successful strategy to secure a politically compliant Hong Kong.[36]

The Sunflower Movement and the DPP electoral revival that it helped to bring about appear to teach a parallel lesson, calling into question the PRC's apparent or express beliefs concerning Taiwan's politics. These include an assumption that, despite strong evidence of rising Taiwanese identity, there was no unbridgeable divide between the people on the two sides of the Strait (whom Xi Jinping (習近平) reaffirmed, in his high-profile November 2015 Singapore meeting with Ma Ying-jeou, were "one family").[37] They also include an expectation that a policy of relatively open-ended tolerance for the Cross-Strait status quo, "peaceful development" of Cross-Strait relations, and long-term deepening of economic integration between the mainland and Taiwan, ultimately would lead to the peaceful realization of Beijing's ultimate goal of formal unification. And they included the related assumption that there was widespread support in Taiwanese society for closer Cross-Strait relations along the lines pursued by the twice-victorious Ma Ying-jeou (whose campaigns had emphasized a Cross-Strait policy of rapprochement) and the likely long-term-dominant KMT-led "blue" bloc, notwithstanding the setbacks suffered under "green" politicians such as the now-disgraced Chen Shui-bian and the now-superannuated Lee Teng-hui.[38] The Sunflower Movement and its electoral and broader political aftermath also had two

34 See, for example, Hua Yiwen, "Why Is the US So Keen on 'Color Revolution'?" *People's Daily Online* (11 October 2014), http://en.people.cn/n/2014/1011/c98649-8793283.html; "How China Frames the News on Occupy", China Media Project, University of Hong Kong (8 October 2014), http://cmp.hku.hk/2014/10/08/36344/.

35 See, for example, "Internationalizing of HK Affairs Violates Basic Law" *China Daily* (Hong Kong edition) (21 December 2003); "Hong Kong Public Firmly against Internationalizing Hong Kong Issues" *Xinhua Net* (17 March 2004), http://news.xinhuanet.com/newscenter/2004-03/17/content_1370945.htm.

36 See, for example, "Democracy in Hong Kong: Political City" *Economist* (6 September 2014); Louise do Rosario, "Future Shock" *Far Eastern Economic Review* (19 May 1994), p. 24 (quoting Lu Ping, director of the State Council's Hong Kong and Macau Affairs Office, "Hong Kong has always been an economic city, never a political city"); Mark P. Lagon, "Beijing's Ruler versus Hong Kong's Heroes" Freedom House, *Freedom at Issue* (23 September 2015), https://freedomhouse.org/blog/beijing-s-ruler-versus-hong-kong-s-heroes (stressing connections across three generations of democracy activists, including the Umbrella Movement leader).

37 "Xi Tells Ma: No Force Can Pull Us Apart" *Xinhua* (7 November 2015), http://news.xinhuanet.com/english/2015-11/07/c_134793106.htm.

38 See Gang Lin, "Beijing's New Strategies towards a Changing Taiwan" (2016) 25(99) *Journal of Contemporary China* 321–355.

more immediate – if, for now, still tentative – adverse implications for Beijing's Taiwan policy: wariness towards closer economic ties with the mainland increasingly extended from concern that the political risk was not worth the economic gains to a view that those economic ties were not beneficial for Taiwan in the first place; and the future orientation of Taiwan's voters may be more green, if the heavily pro-DPP youth vote persists (whether because of a distinctive political orientation of a new generation, the habit-instilling effect of a first voting experience, or the partisan implications of the strongly Taiwanese-rather-than-Chinese identity of Taiwan's young people).[39]

Assessments of the Sunflower Movement and the Umbrella Movement in this book reveal the extent to which the movements laid bare the profoundly conflicting visions of democracy and constitutionalism held by movement participants and their sympathizers, on one side, and Beijing and those whom Beijing saw as allies or co-operators, on the other. That is the message of the examinations by Chen, Fu, Matthews, and Ho of the stark differences between the conceptions of democracy that were embraced by the Umbrella Movement and those that were insisted upon by the SAR Government, the authorities in Beijing, pro-government/pro-Beijing parties and activists in Hong Kong, and, in some respects, Hong Kong's courts. It is also the somewhat more complex and subtle message of Chang, Yeh, Jones and Su, and others who analyse the differences between the Sunflower Movement's views of democracy and constitutionalism and the notions supported by the Ma Ying-jeou government (which Beijing regarded as an acceptable and reasonably accommodating interlocutor).

Second, as this suggests, the Sunflower Movement and the Umbrella Movement, and Beijing's reactions to them, struck another blow to long-standing but increasingly strained expectations that democracy and constitutional government, and the quest for them, in Taiwan and Hong Kong would help foster kindred changes in the PRC. As early as the 1980s, a common trope was a hope that the mainland – or at least (or as a first step) relatively liberal Guangdong – might become more "Hong Kongized". Many in Hong Kong's legal and legal-academic community plunged into projects and programmes that have sought (whether or not explicitly) to instil and propagate rule-of-law values and practices in the PRC.[40] The Umbrella Movement and Occupy Central either made clearer or increased – depending on how one assesses the movement – the gap between the legal and political norms that activists in Hong Kong advocated and what authorities in the mainland would tolerate. Moreover, the events surrounding the Umbrella Movement indicated, to the movement's official and orthodox critics in China (and their allies and advisers in Hong Kong), a close association between democratic and constitutional reform, on one hand, and disorder and even sedition or secession (something some of the more radical participants in the movement went on to urge), on the other.

A similar pattern occurred in Taiwan. Lee Teng-hui's Guidelines for National Unification embraced the possibility (albeit perhaps disingenuously) that China's political order might

39 See generally Alan D. Romberg, "Sunshine Heats Up Taiwan Politics, Affects PRC Tactics" (Summer 2014) 44 *China Leadership Monitor*; Shihao Han, "The Radicalized Generation and the Populist Party – Where will the Cross-Strait Relationship Go?" *China Focus* (2 June 2016), http://chinafocus.us/2016/06/02/the-radicalized-generation-and-the-populist-party-where-will-the-cross-strait-relationship-go/.

40 See, for example, Willem van Kenemade, *China, Hong Kong, Taiwan, Inc.: The Dynamics of a New Empire* (New York: Knopf, 2010), ch. 13; Lynn White and Li Cheng, "China Coast Identities: Regional, National and Global" in Lowell Dittmer and Samuel S. Kim (eds) *China's Quest for National Identity* (Ithaca, NY: Cornell University Press, 1993), pp. 181–187.

someday come to resemble Taiwan's democratic, rule-of-law, human rights–protecting, constitutionalist system, and thereby create the preconditions for unification on terms acceptable to the people of Taiwan.[41] Ma Ying-jeou explicitly put forward the idea that Taiwan's system of democratic constitutional government would be a model for all of China to follow.[42] But these read as rhetorical posturing or distant (or hollow) hopes – all the more so after the Sunflower Movement. Beijing's position consistently has been no more accommodating than a "One Country, Two Systems" framework that pledges a long-term, potentially open-ended tolerance for enclaves of more democratic-constitutionalist systems in Taiwan and Hong Kong. That model is, of course, far from a China-wide convergence towards Hong Kong or Taiwan models. "Outside" efforts to foster such an outcome smack of the "peaceful evolution" that Beijing has long derided as an impermissible, offensive, and threatening goal of US policy.[43] Chen Shui-bian famously suspended Lee's "unification" framework. Tsai Ing-wen has dropped Ma's political evangelism towards China in favour of an approach – shared to varying degrees by her predecessors – of stressing Taiwan's democratic and related accomplishments simply on their own merits, without much regard for their potential impact on China. And Beijing's disappointment at the DPP's return to power, and wariness towards Tsai and what Beijing perceives as her possibly too-Chen-like agenda, have, at least for the time being, taken some of the lustre off the recently improving image of Taiwan's political order in official and orthodox PRC assessments.

In this volume, Wu argues that any view that democracy and constitutionalism in Taiwan and Hong Kong could change China is too optimistic a picture: far from creating a channel to effect liberalizing or democratizing or rule-of-law-promoting change in China, deepened ties with the mainland threaten to erode the necessary foundations for democratic constitutional governance in Taiwan and Hong Kong. Han Zhu's contribution, focusing on public opinion in the mainland, points to an almost equally bleak conclusion. Perhaps reflecting the persisting power of official media and the propaganda apparatus in China, the mainland public appears largely to share the official view of the evils of the Umbrella Movement. The partial exception is the members of the small and beleaguered "rights protection" (*weiquan*) sector in mainland society. As Zhu argues, this pattern augurs ill not

41 Guidelines for National Unification ("the two sides of the Taiwan Straits should foster a consensus of democracy, freedom and equal prosperity"; aims of unification include "safeguarding human dignity, guaranteeing fundamental human rights, and practising democracy and the rule of law"; "in the mainland area economic reform should be carried out forthrightly, the expression of public opinion there should gradually be allowed, and both democracy and the rule of law should be implemented"; Cross-Strait consultations on unification should "map out a constitutional system to establish a democratic, free, and equitably prosperous China").

42 See, for example, Ma Ying-jeou, "Taiwan's Renaissance" (Inaugural Address, 20 May 2008) §§ I, III ("Taiwan is the sole ethnic Chinese society to complete a second democratic turnover of power. Ethnic Chinese communities around the world have laid their hopes on this crucial political experiment. By succeeding, we can make unparalleled contributions to the democratic development of all ethnic Chinese communities. This responsibility is ours to fulfill. … During these last six decades, the destinies of the Republic of China and Taiwan have been closely intertwined. Together, the two have experienced times good and bad. On the jagged path towards democracy, the ROC has made great strides. Dr Sun Yat-sen's dream for a constitutional democracy was not realized on the Chinese mainland, but today it has taken root, blossomed and borne fruit in Taiwan.")

43 See, for example, Russell Ong, "'Peaceful Evolution', 'Regime Change' and China's Political Security" (2007) 16(53) *Journal of Contemporary China* 717–727; Yan Kunlun, "To Avoid Color Revolution, First Go against Peaceful Evolution" *Global Times* (16 December 2014), http://opinion.people.com.cn/n/2014/1216/c1003-26215322.html.

only for China's transformation towards a more Hong Kong – or Taiwan – style political order; it also indicates potential trouble for Taiwan and Hong Kong, where the trajectories of democracy and the rule of law will be affected by what happens in those fields in the mainland.

Third, in light of these relatively dim prospects for Taiwan or Hong Kong "changing China", the road ahead for those who seek to protect and promote democracy and constitutional governance in Taiwan or Hong Kong may well lie in a direction that is at least broadly consistent with the Sunflower Movement and the Umbrella Movement. This entails developing and entrenching more deeply elements of democracy and constitutional governance at home, and winning international support for such values and accomplishments, as shields against possibly mounting pressure from China. In Taiwan, this mind-set has been present since the Lee Teng-hui years, as Taiwanese leaders, officials, activists, and ordinary citizens have: achieved and consolidated a democratic, human rights–protecting, increasingly well-institutionalized constitutional regime; played the "values card" hard and well with international audiences, in touting Taiwan's accomplishments in these areas and its conformity to related international norms (often in pointed contrast to the situation in the PRC); and asserted Taiwan's claim to the status of a self-determining sovereign state or something close to it.[44]

In Hong Kong, the potential is more modest and the efforts have been more desperate, but the orientation is similar. For many years, pro-democracy advocates and movements have pressed for interpretation and implementation of the Basic Law in ways that are relatively protective of democracy-related political rights and broader human rights, and that make constitutionally defined institutions as democratically accountable as possible. They have fought defensive battles against erosion of political autonomy and the rule of law. They have sought to engage sympathetic international audiences by engaging substantive norms of democracy and human rights, invoking formal legal commitments (including the treaty-like Joint Declaration) and (at the most extreme edge of post–Umbrella Movement politics) contemplating the chimera of Hong Kong independence.

As many of the chapters in this volume vividly show, Taiwan's Sunflower Movement and Hong Kong's Umbrella Movement have been at the ardent forefront – or, as their adversaries might put it, radical fringe – of such efforts. They have not only been part of the broad and long-running drive in both polities to deepen and secure democracy and constitutionalism at home. They also went further and pressed for more radically democratic change, asserting that state institutions, conventional political parties, and more moderate civil society groups did not go far enough in embracing true democracy or the right kind of constitutionalism.

44 See Jacques deLisle, "Soft Power in a Hard Place: China, Taiwan, Cross-Strait Competition and US Policy" (2010) 54(4) *Orbis* 493–524.

Index

For Product Safety Concerns and Information please contact our EU
representative GPSR@taylorandfrancis.com
Taylor & Francis Verlag GmbH, Kaufingerstraße 24, 80331 München, Germany

www.ingramcontent.com/pod-product-compliance
Ingram Content Group UK Ltd.
Pitfield, Milton Keynes, MK11 3LW, UK
UKHW050754180926
475701UK00007B/1046

* 9 7 8 0 3 6 7 1 9 1 8 6 3 *